The State and Democracy
in Africa

Edited by

Georges Nzongola-Ntalaja
&
Margaret C. Lee

Africa World Press, Inc.

P.O. Box 1892
Trenton, NJ 08607

P.O. Box 48
Asmara, ERITREA

Africa World Press, Inc.

P.O. Box 1892
Trenton, NJ 08607

P.O. Box 48
Asmara, ERITREA

Copyright © 1997, 1998 African Association of Political Science (AAPS)
First Africa World Press, Inc. Edition, 1998

First published in 1997
by the African Association of Political Science (AAPS)

Cover Design: Jonathan Gullery

Library of Congress Cataloging-in-Publication Data

The state and democracy in Africa / edited by Georges Nzongola-Ntalaja
& Margaret C. Lee -- 1st Africa World Press ed.
    p.   cm.
  Originally published: African Association of Political Science,
c1997.
  Includes bibliographical references.
  ISBN 0-86543-637-1 (hb). -- ISBN 0-86543-638-X (pbk.)
  1. Democracy--Africa. 2. Civil society--Africa. 3. Africa-
-Politics and government--1960- I. Nzongola-Ntalaja, Georges,
1944- II. Lee, Margaret C. (Margaret Carol), 1955-
III. African Association of Political Science.
JQ1879.A15S83 1998
320.96'09'049--dc21
                            98-10466
                              CIP

This book is dedicated to the memory of Claude Ake,
Emmanuel Hansen, and Anthony Rweyemamu.

Contents

Preface and Acknowledgments

This book is a product of the research agenda approved by the General Assembly of the African Association of Political Science (AAPS) in January 1993, at its 20th Anniversary Congress in Dar es Salaam, Tanzania. Its title corresponds to the theme adopted for the 1993-1995 biennium, namely, "The State and Democracy in Africa." With so much attention being given to the issue of democracy on the continent, why should AAPS publish yet another collection of academic papers on this theme?

We believe that there is a need to bring some order to the debate on democracy and the democratic transition in Africa. The dominant or external discourse on the subject has placed so much emphasis on elections that even dictators can now claim to be democrats because they are willing to hold multiparty elections. The ease with which the international community seems to confer a seal of approval on any semblance of liberal democracy in Africa increases the danger of a caricatural identification of democracy with elections and multipartyism.

AAPS is particularly well placed to bring some sense of theoretical and methodological rigor to the discourse on democracy. The Association was among the few professional organizations to dare raise the issues of democracy and democratization in Africa during the early 1980s, when it was not yet fashionable to do so. As part of the network of African researchers associated with the Third World Forum (TWF), AAPS participated actively in the TWF program on "Alternative Futures for Africa," which was funded by the United Nations University (UNU) and the Swedish Agency for Research Cooperation with Developing Countries (SAREC), among others. Nearly all the studies on democracy contributed to the TWF-UNU research project on the state and the problem of development, were by AAPS scholars. These papers were published in 1987 and 1988 as *Popular Struggles for Democracy in Africa*, and *Afrique: la longue marche vers la démocratie*, respectively. This book is a forerunner to much of the current discourse on democracy in Africa.

The intellectual leadership of AAPS has manifested itself not only on the issue of democracy, but also with respect to scholarly analysis on ethnicity and the national question, and peace and security. This is part and parcel of the AAPS tradition of politically committed or socially relevant scholarship. The major source of this tradition is the founding of the Association in December 1973 in Dar es Salaam, at the height of both the national liberation struggle in Southern Africa and the Tanzanian experiment with radical social transformation under the ideology of *Ujamaa*. Dar es Salaam was then the seat of the Liberation Committee of the Organization of African Unity (OAU) and the nerve center of the armed struggle in Southern Africa, serving as headquarters for numerous liberation movements. The city was also the leading center of African intellectual life, then dominated by the Dar es Salaam school of African historiography, with Walter Rodney as its anchor, and by progressive thinking in other academic disciplines such as law, economics and political science.

In this context, AAPS founders were for the most part scholars and intellectuals engaged either in the armed liberation struggle or in social movements committed to the radical transformation of postcolonial Africa. They were not ivory tower professors. Then, as today, the major aim of AAPS is to stimulate an open debate on issues of major concern to the people of Africa, foster critical thinking in order to create new knowledge, and encourage problem-solving research.

At the same time, the Association has no party line, either theoretically or politically. The position that all viewpoints are welcome was underlined at the January 1987 Nairobi Workshop on "Constitutionalism and Political Change in East Africa," whose rich and stimulating debates on Uganda and Sudan underscored the need for tolerance and respect for diversity. Today, this position is being promoted and reinforced through most of the Association's research, educational, and service activities, notably our continent-wide public forum program; the Viewpoint feature of the *AAPS Newsletter*; scholarly articles in the *African Journal of Political Science;* and edited volumes such as this book.

More than four years have passed since the book was conceived as part of a research, conference, and publication project by the AAPS Executive Committee. The project itself could not have been undertaken and completed without the generous contribution of ideas, talent, time, and money by many individuals and groups, too numerous to be mentioned here. However, some individuals and groups do deserve special mention.

We are especially grateful to the Ford Foundation and SAREC, now a department of the Swedish International Development Cooperation Agency (SIDA), whose initial support and encouragement were critical for the success of the project. The Ford grant for the AAPS research program covered expenses related to the various phases of the project, including the 10th Biennial Congress, held between August 20 and 24, 1995, in Ibadan, Nigeria, and the publication of the conference papers. SAREC, for its part, provided core support for research and the administrative infrastructure, without which the project could not be implemented successfully. Jonathan Moyo of the Ford Foundation's Nairobi office, and Stefan Molund at SAREC, were extremely helpful with their suggestions and comments.

The support of other organizations for this and other AAPS activities also contributed to the success of the project. In 1994, AAPS moved its headquarters from Nairobi to Harare, where a fulltime secretariat was eventually established. We are very grateful to the Harare-based Southern African Political Economy Series (SAPES) Trust for giving AAPS the support and assistance needed to effect a successful transition.

As this transition process began to unfold, the Carnegie Corporation of New York provided a generous and timely grant toward the institutional strengthening of the Association. Other grants followed in 1995 and 1996, and included funds for our public forum program. It was while attending a two-day forum of the Zaire AAPS National Chapter, the *Association Zaïroise des Sciences Politiques* (ASPO), held on August 3-4, 1995, in Kinshasa, that one of the editors of this volume heard a lively presentation on a new kind of civil society actor in Zaire, the "street parliamentarians." The speaker, Professor Kalele-ka-Bila, was immediately invited to present his paper at the Ibadan Congress later that month.

In addition to Carnegie, whose support helped activate AAPS chapters and launch the public forum program continentally, the Washington-based National Endowment for Democracy (NED) and the Konrad Adenauer Foundation have found sufficient merit in the program to help it develop further. We are very grateful to these organizations, and wish to acknowledge the personal interest that Patricia Rosenfield and Andrea Johnson at Carnegie, Learned Dees at NED, and Michael Schlicht of the Adenauer Foundation's Harare office, have shown in AAPS.

Two other organizations provided funds for the 1995 biennial congress in Ibadan. The Rockefeller Foundation awarded AAPS a grant to cover the travel and living expenses of scholars from Francophone Africa. The International Development and Research Centre (IDRC), a Canadian agency, did the same for scholars from Eastern and Southern Africa. These generous contributions are greatly appreciated, and they are acknowledged here for helping AAPS maintain its Pan-African character.

None of the donors bears responsibility for the views expressed in this book, which are soley those of the authors. Needless to say, these views do not represent an official position by AAPS.

All but the first chapter in this volume were selected from papers prepared for the Ibadan Congress. While it includes the general assembly of the Association, the AAPS biennial congress consists mainly of an academic symposium or conference, whose theme, as previously mentioned, is chosen two years in advance. In spite of their evident strengths, the papers published here cannot convey the full measure of the success of the conference. Academically, it was one of the best conferences ever held by AAPS. The quality of the oral presentations was very high, and nearly all panels went over at least one hour beyond their allotted time. We would like to extend our sincere thanks to Professor Adele Jinadu, his Local Organizing Committee, and the Nigerian Political Science Association (NPSA), for their help in making the conference a great success.

We wish to thank the AAPS Administrative Secretary, Professor Kwame Ninsin, and his entire staff at AAPS House in Harare (Dieneba N'diaye, Elizabeth Remba, and Thompson Mpemba), for their contribution to the successful management of the project. A special word of appreciation is due to Dieneba N'diaye for her mastery of computer skills, which helped enormously in the preparation of the manuscript and the designing of the book cover.

Finally, this book is dedicated to Claude Ake, Emmanuel Hansen, and Anthony Rweyemamu. They were, respectively, the first editor of the *African Journal of Political Economy* (AJOPE), the AAPS professional journal, now renamed the *African Journal of Political Science* (AJPS); the onetime AAPS research and publications director; and AAPS first president (1973-75). While their untimely deaths shocked and saddened us, as AAPS members we are compelled to reflect on the lessons of their exemplary life and work. Ake remained one of the few eminent political scientists to resist the temptation of serving the military dictatorship of General Ibrahim Babangida as a praise-singing technician of change from above in Nigeria. Hansen did work as Cabinet Secretary in the second Rawlings regime in Ghana, but he resigned from his high state position once he realized that the so-called Rawlings revolution was not moving into the direction of empowering the people. As for Rweyemamu, he exemplified the qualities of intellectual leadership that are badly needed in Africa today, including moral integrity, a passion for the truth, and a critical perspective on all things political.

The lesson that emerges the best from their legacy is to heed Amilcar Cabral's call on African intellectuals to identify with the deepest aspirations of the people for freedom and material prosperity. This implies active involvement in the democratization process against entrenched rulers, who are determined to undermine, or even block, the democratic transition. For Ake, Hansen, and Rweyemamu, the development of AAPS into a strong professional association should go hand in hand with greater involvement in the promotion of basic human rights in Africa. This is the new challenge.

Georges Nzongola-Ntalaja and Margaret C. Lee
Harare
May 1997

Introduction

Georges Nzongola-Ntalaja and Margaret C. Lee

This book is a modest attempt to understand the quest for democracy in Africa today, to assess the strengths and weaknesses of the social forces struggling to realize it, and to examine the role of the state in either promoting or blocking the democratic transition. The studies which follow present some of the current interdisciplinary research related to ongoing democratization processes throughout the African continent. The 16 chapters in the volume are organized around four main themes: general considerations on the question of democracy and the democratic transition, Chapter 1; an analysis of some of the key actors in the struggle for democracy and political space, Chapters 2 to 5; a critical assessment of the role of the state in the democratic transition, Chapters 6 to 14; and an examination of the relationship between democracy and human rights, with particular emphasis on the rights of women, Chapters 15 and 16.

Democracy and the Democratic Transition in Africa

The first theme is dealt with in Chapter 1, by Georges Nzongola-Ntalaja, in which he presents a detailed analysis of the meaning of democracy, universally as well as in the African context, and examines the major problems facing the democratic transition in Africa today. Looking at democracy from a philosophical, historical, and comparative perspective as a universal principle of governance, the author sees it as a moral imperative, a social process, and a particular type of political practice applicable to all human societies. He thus rejects the notion that democracy is something being imported into Africa from the outside. The critical question today is not that of Africanizing democracy, but rather the necessity of democratizing Africa.

In the second part of the chapter, Nzongola-Ntalaja examines the internal and external environments of the democratic transition in Africa, and concludes with an assessment of the prospects for democracy today. With few exceptions, he maintains, the neopatrimonial states of postcolonial Africa are basically hostile to democracy and the democratic transition. Their democratic rhetoric notwithstanding, state leaders have used all the means at their disposal to block, undermine, or slow down the democratic transition. They have often succeeded in this regard, thanks to the weakness of the democracy movement and the accommodating attitude of the international community. For a variety of reasons, many international actors seem eager to take African leaders' professed commitment to democracy at face value. Having so abusively identified democracy with elections, they are at times prepared to certify even openly rigged elections as satisfactory, "by African standards."

However important these external influences, distractions, or obstacles might be, Nzongola-Ntalaja sees the internal environment as the primary arena and determinant of the democratization process. If the momentous changes in Eastern Europe and South

Africa did play a part in influencing ongoing changes on the African continent, the current struggle for democracy resulted mainly from the crisis of legitimacy of the postcolonial state, which has failed to meet the people's aspirations for freedom and material well-being. To correct this situation, a new and vibrant political movement arose to end authoritarianism and to restructure the state for purposes of building democracy and achieving social progress. Unfortunately, the contradictory and uneven process of transformation has adversely affected the social and economic fabric, exacerbating political tensions and conflicts. Consequently, the democratic transition is proving to be a more complex and long-drawn-out process than expected.

Actors in the Democratization Process

The second theme dealt with in the book concerns the relevant social forces in the struggle for democracy and the expansion of the political space. Democracy can neither be imported from abroad, nor be handed down to the people on a silver platter by Africa's rulers. The people of Africa must democratize the continent on their own. As stakeholders of the democratic transition, civil society organizations are key actors in this transformation process. Major civil society actors and organizations which have played, and continue to play, a critical role in the democratic transition are women, students, trade unions, lawyers, professional associations, human rights groups, religious institutions, and the urban masses. The contributions by Onalenna Selolwane, Akiiki Mujaju, Mulambu Mvuluya, and Kalele-ka-Bila, in Chapters 2, 3, 4, and 5, respectively, present four case studies on this role.

The women's struggle for equality in Botswana is the subject matter of Selolwane's analysis in Chapter 2. She points out that this struggle has taken a more overtly political character in the 1990s as a demand for increased representation and political space for women in the decision-making structures of the state and political parties. Since its independence in 1966, Botswana has retained all the trappings of liberal democracy, including regularly held multiparty elections. It is therefore significant that the establishment should put up such a resistance to granting women equality with men in political, economic, and social rights. The Botswana case is of definite relevance to "other African countries seeking a return to liberal democratic rule and multiparty competition for government power."

In Chapter 3, Mujaju assesses state-civil society relations in Uganda since independence. His study focuses on women, university students, the youth in general, trade unions, and peasant cooperatives. Based on a comparative analysis of the Milton Obote and Idi Amin regimes with the current regime of Yoweri Museveni's National Resistance Movement (NRM), the chapter shows that there is no significant difference in the way the state deals with civil society. Rather than accepting independent civil society organizations as responsible partners in governance, the Ugandan state has sought to undermine their autonomy and force them to toe the government line. Moreover, the best way to achieve this objective and to prevent civil society organizations from becoming countervailing forces against the state, is for the latter to set up its own, government-oriented organizations. All the major Ugandan regimes — Obote, Amin, Museveni — were tempted by the anti-democratic urge of maintaining authoritarian control over society.

The next two chapters are studies in the role of the popular masses in the democracy movement in Zaire, a country which reclaimed its pre-1971 name of "Democratic

Republic of the Congo," on May 17, 1997. In Chapter 4, Mulambu examines the crucial or determining role that the popular masses, particularly those of Kinshasa, the nation's capital, played in the democratization process between 1990 and 1992. It was their total rejection of the Mobutu regime that forced the Zairian dictator to concede to the holding of the national conference in 1991-92, and their radicalism which compelled an overwhelming majority of the conference to elect opposition leader Etienne Tshisekedi, their idol, as prime minister of the transitional government. Although Mobutu illegally dismissed Tshisekedi three months after he assumed power, none of the prime ministers who succeeded him was able to govern effectively, since each one of them was seen as illegitimate by the people.

Mulambu's analysis is complemented by Kalele's presentation in Chapter 5 of a major grassroots organization created in early 1993 to advance the radical change agenda of the popular struggle for democracy. Known as *parlementaires-debout,* or street parliamentarians, the group comprised men and women, young and old, educated and non-literate, whose main activity consisted of assembling each day around the corner from major newspaper stands to discuss politics and decide on what actions to take in order to advance the cause of democracy. Unable to purchase newspapers because of the economic crisis, the group met near newspaper stands to read the headlines and, if necessary, rent a paper to have an entire article read to the gathering. The information from newspapers was supplemented by reports from individuals in close touch with members of the political class: drivers, domestics, and relatives of some big men's mistresses. After the debate over the reported news and rumors, the group would decide on the course of action to take.

The participants called themselves "parliamentarians" by analogy, because what they did was similar to the work of a parliament. The main difference was that they did their work standing (*debout*) on street corners. Until the arrival of Laurent Kabila and his *Alliance des Forces Démocratiques pour la Libération du* Congo-Zaïre (AFDL) on the political scene, the major task of the street parliamentarians, as the self-appointed people's legislature for the democratic transition, was to support the radical opposition and its leader, Tshisekedi, while at the same time taking corrective action against opposition politicians who either wavered from the radical mass line, or were bought by the Mobutu camp. The actions taken consisted mainly of public denunciations, although acts of physical violence against "traitors" did take place on rare occasions.

The State and the Democratic Transition

The third theme examined in the book, and the one that gives it its title, is the relationship between the state and democracy. Does the state facilitate or impede democracy? Under what conditions does the state promote or block the democratic transition? What do people expect from the new democracies that have replaced the authoritarian state in Africa? Answers to these and related questions are provided in Chapters 6 to 14, which present case studies in democratic transition in a few countries: South Africa, Nigeria, Ghana, and the Portuguese-speaking African countries.

South Africa
South Africa, the last country to undergo political change from a colonial-settler state to majority rule, is the subject of Chapters 6 to 8, by Margaret Lee, Geoffrey Wood, and Cheryl Hendricks, respectively. In Chapter 6, Lee examines the challenges facing the

Mandela government, from the conflict between the African National Congress (ANC) and the Inkatha Freedom Party (IFP), to meeting the expectations of the majority population with respect to the economic and social dividends of liberation. Her analysis is based on the first fifteen months of ANC rule. While emphasizing the need for a resolution to the ANC-IFP conflict on the form of state, authority over traditional rulers and other issues as being essential to peace and security in South Africa, she sees the Mandela government as also facing tremendous challenges with respect to enhancing the living standards of the black majority, maintaining political stability, and enhancing democracy in a country long polarized on ethnic and racial lines.

That the future of South Africa's fledgling democracy hinges on the Mandela government's performance in these critical areas, particularly that of social progress and improvements in day-to-day living, is also the conclusion that Wood draws from his analysis in Chapter 7. Based on a survey of 220 voters in the Eastern Cape Province, the study assesses public attitudes toward the new political order in South Africa, including views on democracy, political participation, and the government's economic and social policies. While political party support remains essentially a function of racial divisions, even ANC supporters are determined to hold the new government to its election promises. In a situation where there is a vacuum of political alternatives, Wood fears that dissatisfied voters may turn to extra-constitutional methods to express their grievances.

Economic and social grievances may also exacerbate ethnic tensions. This is particularly the case when politically marginalized elites, such as National Party (NP) and IFP leaders, would use ethnicity to gain power, and remain in office only if they can offer material rewards to their followers. This is one of the salient characteristics of the relationship between ethnicity, the national question, and the state, which is examined in Chapter 8 by Hendricks. She points out that the debate over the form of state between federalists and unitarists is inextricably linked to ethnicity, for the simple reason that provincial boundaries largely correspond to ethnic settlements. Her conclusion is that, if properly handled, ethnic diversity need not become a destabilizing factor in South African politics.

Nigeria

The next four chapters deal with Nigeria, where two experiments in multiparty democracy (1960-66 and 1979-83) were terminated by military coups d'état. In fact, during 27 of Nigeria's 37 years as an independent nation, the military have ruled the country. Three of the chapters examine the aborted attempt to return the country to civilian rule in the early 1990s, including the annulment of the presidential election of 1993, while the fourth chapter looks at the question of decentralization or democratic governance at the local level.

The contributions by Jibrin Ibrahim and Said Adejumobi in Chapters 9 and 10, respectively, focus on the theory and practice of engineering change from above. Between January 1986 and June 1993, the military administration of General Ibrahim Babangida — who was reverently referred to as "IBB" by his admirers and sycophants — pretended to be seriously engaged in democratizing Nigeria through a carefully managed program of transition to civilian rule. Ibrahim's contribution is a strong indictment against the role of intellectuals, and in this particular case, that of professional political scientists, as the architects and managers of the transition charade. It is the *cri de coeur* of a younger political scientist concerning the evident lack of deontology by eminent scholars, who obviously put their political ambitions and material interests above intellectual integrity and social responsibility. He accordingly calls them "IBB professors" for their attempt to cover up, through hero worship and apologetic writings, Babangida's resistance against the popular struggle for democracy.

Adejumobi, for his part, examines two aspects of political engineering by the Babangida regime: state created political parties and a politically manipulated electoral process. For a country that has never known a one-party system under civilian rule, Nigeria came close to resembling the typical African party-state, in which the state and the party are indistinguishable. On October 7, 1989, the Babangida regime set up two political parties, together with their statutes, manifestoes, and government programs. Both the National Republican Convention (NRC) and the Social Democratic Party (SDP) were centrist parties, the first a "little to the right" of the center and the second, a "little to the left," but all committed to pursuing the economic policies of the Babangida regime. These were consistent with the structural adjustment programs of the International Monetary Fund (IMF) and the World Bank.

As for the electoral process, Adejumobi's analysis of its fraudulent character is reinforced by the contribution of Abubakar Momoh in Chapter 11 on the annulment of the presidential election of June 12, 1993. The first part of the chapter looks at the politics leading up to the election, with Momoh's description of the political transition program being somewhat a recapitulation of issues and events already mentioned by both Ibrahim and Adejumobi. On the other hand, the remainder of the chapter focuses on post-election politics, with emphasis on the controversy over the electoral results and the annulment. This controversy raises the following four questions. Firstly, why were the two presidential candidates acceptable to Babangida, Moshood Abiola of the SDP and Bashir Tofa of the NRC, wealthy business people? Secondly, why did Abiola wait a full year before claiming his victory, when the political momentum was already lost? Thirdly, why did Abiola's prominent supporters within the political class, including his vice presidential running mate Babagana Kingibe, abandon him? And fourthly, why did the conflict over June 12 assume an ethnic coloration, with Abiola's strongest support coming from his Yoruba homeland of western Nigeria? Momoh provides answers to these critical questions, in addition to elucidating the role of General Sani Abacha, the new military strongman, in this whole affair.

The last chapter on Nigeria looks at a very different, but essential, aspect of the democratic transition in Africa. In Chapter 12, Dele Olowu examines the attempts since 1976 to decentralize the state and establish institutions of democratic governance at the local level, with increased capacity for economic and social development. After two decades of these attempts at revitalizing and strengthening local governments, Nigeria has produced the opposite results, namely, a more centralized state, politically and economically. This is hardly surprising, given the fraudulent character of the democratization from above described in the first three chapters on Nigeria. However, Olowu goes beyond this general political context to an examination of the policy instruments without which decentralization can become effective. Needless to say, such instruments cannot be fully effective in the absence of an enabling environment for democracy and basic human rights.

Two Other Cases: Ghana and Portuguese-speaking Africa

The examination of the third theme ends with a discussion of two other cases of democratic transition in Africa. The first case is in Chapter 13, in which Amos Anyimadu looks at the structural aspects of Ghanaian constitutions and their implications for the national question. He argues that since independence, Ghana has been marked by a constitutional culture in which the concept of the integral state informs the manner in which the nation is defined in unitarist terms to overcome, rather than accommodate, ethnic diversity. Such a culture not only leaves little room for the protection of ethnic minorities, it also accentuates the centralizing features of the state to the detriment of institutional autonomy and democratic governance at the regional and local levels. Anyimadu points out that even the 1992 Constitution, in which there is an effort to devolve administrative responsibilities to regions, does not considerably enhance state decentralization in Ghana. The country's president retains too much authority with respect to the creation of new districts and the appointment of district political heads.

The second case is that of the democratic transition in the five Portuguese-speaking countries of Angola, Cape Verde, Guinea-Bissau, Mozambique, and Sao Tome and Principe. It is examined by Carlos Lopes in Chapter 14. Cape Verde and Sao Tome and Principe were among the first African countries to move from the one-party system to multiparty democracy, in 1991. There, as in Guinea-Bissau, political liberalization has not gone hand in hand with economic recovery. Likewise, the economies of Angola and Mozambique were greatly disrupted, if not entirely destroyed in some sectors, by destabilization from apartheid South Africa and by civil wars, with the liberation regimes losing their base of support because of growing polarization in income distribution. Rather than easing economic hardship, the externally imposed policies of structural adjustment in the four poorer countries have helped, just as Angola's debt burden has done, to further erode the state's capacity for development as well as its legitimacy.

It is in this context that Lopes wonders whether the democratic transition is possible under political and economic models imposed from the outside, in countries that are heavily dependent on promises of support from the international community. Even the holding of multiparty elections often requires external financial assistance. For him, resolving the current crisis of governability and enhancing the prospects for democracy in the Portuguese-speaking countries will require alternative models of participation and wealth distribution based on the concrete historical and empirical conditions of these countries.

Human Rights and Democracy

The fourth and last theme examined in this book is that of the relationship between democracy and human rights in general, and the rights of women, in particular. As defined by one of the editors in Chapter 1, democracy is a "continuos process of promoting equal access to fundamental human rights and civil liberties for all." This includes the right to peace and security, and fair and humane treatment of citizens, residents, and visitors, by the state. The contributions by Horace Campbell and Victor Ayeni in Chapters 15 and 16, respectively, address this important subject, from different but interrelated perspectives.

Campbell approaches the subject from a Pan-African perspective historically and internationally. For him, the problems of democracy, human rights, and peace in Africa cannot be fully understood without reference to the decisions and actions of key actors in the international community since World War II, namely, the major world powers and United Nations agencies. The pursuit of their own agendas, in collaboration with local rulers dependent on external support for political survival, has often resulted in gross violations of human rights. The chapter gives numerous examples of these violations, and calls for a progressive agenda for ending all forms of dehumanizing violence, including violence against women in domestic, reproductive, and war situations. Campbell reaffirms the strong and dialectical linkage between democracy and basic human rights, and sees a people-oriented, emancipative, politics as the most promising way of achieving democracy, peace and security. He defines the latter in an all-inclusive manner as incorporating physical, economic, and social security, together with the right to reconstruction and development for people emerging from war and destabilizing conflict situations.

Whereas Campbell looks at reproductive and other basic rights of women, Ayeni focuses on women as civic persons with rights to equal access to the protection and opportunities that the state provides for citizens. The rights of women are analyzed here in connection with the lack of gender sensitivity in "ombudsman," or public advocacy and protection, institutions in Africa. Originating in Sweden, such institutions have been created all over the world to help protect citizens against negligence, arbitrariness, or wrongful actions by the state, and to help correct situations of discrimination and unequal access to public services. It is ironic, Ayeni points out, that institutions with such a mandate should reproduce the indifference with which women are treated in the larger administrative system in Africa. From the data available to him, it appears that women are greatly underrepresented as officers in "ombudsman" institutions, and complaints by women constitute a negligible fraction of all cases brought to such institutions in Africa.

Conclusion

This book is a study of the issues of democracy and democratization in Africa, with emphasis on the roles of civil society and the state in the democratic transition. After clarifying the meaning of democracy as a universal principle of governance and the applicability of the concept to Africa, the book examines the major problems facing the democratic transition on the continent as a whole. This is followed by four studies on the role of civil society organizations in the struggle for democracy and the expansion of the political space: one each on Botswana and Uganda, and two on Zaire. More than half of the contributions to the volume are devoted to a critical assessment of the role that the state plays in promoting, undermining, or blocking the democratic transition. There are three case studies on South Africa, four on Nigeria, and one each on Ghana and the Portuguese-speaking countries. The book concludes with two studies on democracy and human rights, the rights of women in particular, with the first looking at the issue in a broader historical and international context, while the second focuses on the democratic rights of women as citizens deserving equal access to state protection and services.

The quest for democracy in Africa today is a genuine demand of the people, and not an externally-driven initiative. While preaching democracy and human rights, the international community has taken a very accommodating attitude toward authoritarian rulers, who are objectively opposed to genuine democracy and do their best to slow down, undermine, or even block the democratic transition. In the face of this often violent resistance to democratic change, the UN and the major world powers seek to prevail upon the popular forces to reach compromises with the forces of the status quo. A major question for the democratic forces is how to overcome the resistance of the entrenched rulers and the ambivalent attitude of the international community to bring about meaningful change with as low a cost in human and material resources as possible. The ultimate goal is to transform the state in such a way that it becomes an ally rather than an obstacle in the democratization process. When this is realized, state and democracy will no longer be incompatible in Africa.

1

The State and Democracy in Africa

Georges Nzongola-Ntalaja

Since 1988, the people of Africa have risen to replace one-party and military dictatorships with multiparty democracy. From its violent outbreak in October 1988 in the streets of Algiers, this new social movement for democracy has manifested itself all over the continent, changing the rules of the political game and bringing about meaningful reforms in the institutions of the postcolonial state.

This momentous development is above all a function of the declining capacity of the African state for development. In fighting colonialism, people expected that independence would usher in a new era of freedom and material prosperity.[1] What they inherited, however, was a state that was deficient in managing the economy and the natural environment on the one hand, and whose nature and performance often gave rise to divisions and conflicts, on the other. Hence the rise of the "second independence" movement in Congo-Kinshasa (Zaire), popular insurrections with a similar theme in Chad and Uganda, and numerous social movements elsewhere.[2]

These instances of revolt against the neocolonial state constitute the antecedents of the new social movement for democracy, which is basically concerned with fulfilling the failed expectations of independence. Also significant as contributing factors to the strength of the democracy movement were the sustained liberation drive by the African National Congress (ANC) and the Mass Democratic Movement between 1984 and 1990 in South Africa, and the rapid collapse of the Stalinist system in Eastern Europe and the former Soviet Union between 1989 and 1991.

The fact that Nelson Mandela could resume normal political activity after 27 years in prison was a welcome development for freedom loving people all over the world. On the other hand, it did astonish a lot of people in independent Africa, who by then were accustomed to expect most of their famous political prisoners not to get out of jail alive. That the hated white supremacy state could be seen as having some humanity resulted in laying bare the great inhumanity of the African state against its own people.[3]

As for the changes in the East, they had an immediate and more concrete demonstration effect in Africa. For if the monopoly of the single party could break down so swiftly in countries whose security apparatus had considerable resources for repression, it was inevitable that the fragile state of postcolonial Africa would give in to any determined challenge to its authority, particularly once its neocolonial cover had lost its raison d'être, the fear of communism.

It is against this background that this book seeks to examine the relationship between the state and democracy in Africa today. Is the quest for democracy an externally driven initiative or a genuine demand of the African people? Why have so many promising transitions failed to bring about democratic change? What are the prospects for fulfilling the people's aspiration for democracy and social progress? Answers to these and related questions require a clearer understanding of the concept of democracy as well as its applicability to Africa; and an analysis of the democratic transitions now taking place with a view to identifying the factors likely to enhance or impede the chances of sustaining the democratization process.

The Concept of Democracy and its Applicability to Africa

Controversies abound concerning the feasibility of democracy and democratic governance in contemporary Africa. There are those who see cultural and economic obstacles to democratization in Africa. For some, democracy is an alien phenomenon that is being imported into a society whose culture places more emphasis on the community than on the individual, and is therefore incapable of internalizing liberal democratic values.[4] For others, the economic preconditions of democracy, which include a solid middle class, are still absent in much of Africa.[5]

I start from the thesis that Africa is a repository of human values that are fully compatible with the very foundations of democracy as a political concept. Unfortunately, these values were undermined, and thus stunted, in their development, by both colonial oppression and postcolonial misrule. There is no question of *Africanizing democracy*. The key demand of the moment is rather to *democratize Africa*. This is to say that we cannot import or Africanize democracy because the latter is something that is *universal*.

Universality of Principles, Specificity of Institutions and Practices
Democracy is not an exclusive property of Western societies. Democratic norms and principles are universal, but the institutions which inform democracy and the concrete forms of its political practice may vary in time and space (i.e., through historical epochs and from country to country). The noted British historian C. Northcote Parkinson (author of *Parkinson's Law*) has this to say about the universality of democracy:

> In commenting upon the course of history, St. Augustine is shrewd enough to suggest (as did Sallust before him) that the Athenians exceeded other people more in their publicity than in their deeds. Most subsequent scholars have been more credulous, one result being a surprisingly widespread belief that the Athenians were the inventors of democracy. That they were nothing of the kind is tolerably clear. What we owe to the Athenians is not the thing itself or even its name but the earliest detailed account of how a democracy came into being, flourished and collapsed. Of the Indian democracies, which were probably older, we have all too little precise information. There is, however, a sense in which many people have had a measure of democracy in their village life.[6]

That many of the people of precolonial Africa experienced a measure of democracy at the village level and, indeed, beyond in larger political communities has been well established by historians. As elsewhere, there was democracy in Africa, in addition to tyranny and other forms of rule. The sociological reality of ancient Africa is too complex to be simplified through the lenses of Afrocentric romantics as a golden age of freedom, or those of Eurocentric Afro-pessimists as an epoch of despotism. Those who accept the cultural obstacle thesis seem to fall into this second group. Francis Akindés for example, takes the Bight of Benin state of ancient Dahomey as typical of the authoritarianism of precolonial Africa and sees a continuity between this and political practice in post-colonial Africa.[7] Such an approach not only glosses over the impact of the Atlantic slave trade on political institutions and practices in West and Central Africa, but also minimizes the role of colonial despotism as a school for postcolonial rulers. The diversity of political institutions in an area as culturally homogenous as Bantu Africa attests to the influence of ecological, historical, and other factors in shaping different forms of rule in precolonial Africa.[8]

As a universal form of rule with specific manifestations in time and space, democracy is a political concept founded on three underlying ideas, namely, democracy as a *value*, a *process* and a *practice*. I shall attempt to develop each of these ideas as basic foundations of democracy as a universal concept, and indicate its relevance in the African context.

Democracy as a Moral Imperative

Democracy is above all a moral value or *imperative*, that is, a basic human need, a necessity, and therefore a political demand of all freedom loving human beings. What, then, is this imperative? It is basically a *permanent aspiration of human beings for freedom, for a better social and political order, one that is more human and more or less egalitarian*. This is a sociological fact. In all human societies, people always feel the need to improve their material conditions of life as well as to feel freer — whatever the real situation might be. This *need* becomes *a necessity,* or even *a political demand for a new social project,* when their situation deteriorates, or when they are in a period of crisis.

This demand for a better life seems to be common to all great world philosophies and religions: it is the search for the *Kingdom of God on Earth.* In his excellent essay *The Heavenly City of Eighteenth Century Philosophers,* the historian Carl Becker argues that the *philosophes* of the Enlightenment — Diderot, Montesquieu, Rousseau, Voltaire — were mostly interested in building on earth St. Augustine's heavenly city, but this time with up-to-date materials like natural science, humanism, the idea of progress, etc. Closer to us in time, Karl Marx, too, attempted to create the Augustinian city with even better, stronger, and more useful materials in order to attain his utopia of egalitarian and non-conflictual society, a society without social classes but with material abundance for all.

The democratic values of individual human worth and solidarity that are evident in the writings of the *philosophes* and Karl Marx, respectively, are values around which the concept of democracy is best articulated within the African context. They define the traditional African concept of a person both as an individual and as a social being.

In African societies, the individual is conceptualized as a *vital force*, whose existence transcends the temporal body in which a person is objectified in his or her earthly life. This is the essential or more fundamental difference between humans and other living species, including animals. Hence the necessity of respecting the originality and the particularity of each person, respect of the latter's *individuality* or individual human worth. This is the foundation on which Africans, like peoples elsewhere, base the idea of the *inviolability* of the human person as well as his or her *inalienable right* to life and security. The security of people and their goods is one of the basic democratic principles recognized all over the world.

Although the intrinsic worth of the individual is recognized the world over, in Africa, the individual is considered as fully human only through his or her dialectical relationship to *sociability* or the ability to live in society. Not only are we Africans the first humans in world history, we are also the humans with the greatest attachment to our ancestral lands. For us, human existence is meaningless unless it is lived in society, and this from the family to larger social units. And it is out of this experience that the values of *solidarity* (family ties, ethnic identity, patriotism) are born. Needless to say, these values can also be exploited by demagogues to produce anti-democratic effects like ethnic and racial particularism, ethnic cleansing or purification, and genocide. Hence it should be emphasized that as a moral imperative, democracy implies *tolerance* for all sorts of *diversity,* including physical differences among people.

The ideal of a more democratic and socially rewarding society is likely to emerge among peoples whose group rights, and individual worth as human beings, have been systematically undermined. The search for a new social order often leads to a dualistic vision of reality akin to the *Manicheism* of the world of St. Augustine, in which there is an irreconcilable dichotomy between the forces of evil and the forces of good, between the earthly city under the control of the devil and the heavenly city of God.

Much closer to us, the Manichean world of colonialism so well described by Frantz Fanon in *The Wretched of the Earth* did, with its triple configuration of economic exploitation, political repression, and cultural oppression, incite the pioneers of the African independence struggle to raise people's consciousness in a collective mobilization for total emancipation from colonial servitude. Today, moral decay, together with the destruction of the economic and social fabric of our countries by postcolonial dictators, has compelled all freedom loving people to rise up in a new social movement for political change. The struggle for democracy in Africa today is thus a moral imperative.

Democracy as a Social Process

Like any human construction, democracy is never perfect. It is a *continuous process of promoting equal access to fundamental human rights and civil liberties for all.* By this we mean (1) the fundamental rights of the human person to life and security; (2) freedom of religion, assembly, expression, press, association, etc.; (3) economic, social, and cultural rights — the idea here being that democracy is meaningless when the basic needs of the population are not satisfied; and (4) the rights of peoples, including the inalienable right to self-determination.

Given its association with the quest for freedom and a better social order, the concept of democracy is incomplete without reference to the notion of fundamental human rights. Democracy is that social process through which people strive to expand these rights, together with the political space necessary for promoting and defending them effectively. Central to this process is the idea that a good political order is one in which the state is capable of satisfying the material and spiritual needs of its citizens. This idea, which was dear to ancient and medieval philosophers like Aristotle and St. Thomas Aquinas, was revived by Jean-Jacques Rousseau during the Enlightenment. In a major epistemological break with the dominant paradigm of *liberal democracy,* with its emphasis on the social contract limiting the powers of the state over individual citizens so as to protect the latter's property and civil rights, Rousseau posed the question of *social democracy* and proposed the following empirical test for good governance:

> What is the object of political association? It is the preservation and prosperity of its members. And what is the surest sign that they are preserved and prosperous? It is their number and population. Do not, then, go and seek elsewhere for this sign so much discussed. All other things being equal, the government under which, without external aids, without naturalization and

without colonies, the citizens increase and multiply most, is infallibly the best. That under which a people diminishes and decays is the worst. Statisticians, it is now your business; reckon, measure, compare.[9]

It is evident that in this age of birth control, such a test will have to focus more on the quality of life than on the size of the population. For the best measure of social decay today is not so much the decline in population figures as the evils of malnutrition, disease, unsanitary living conditions, lack of economic opportunity, internal wars, and the state's violation of the political, economic, social, and cultural rights of citizens. In ancient Africa, individuals and groups felt free to vote with their feet whenever these rights were no longer guaranteed. They moved away and established new political communities elsewhere. Our oral traditions are rich in testimonies of how Africans experienced democracy as a process of expanding political space in this manner.

Under colonialism, the anticolonial struggle was aimed precisely at promoting these basic rights and liberties. It was by identifying the colonial system itself as the major obstacle to the total emancipation (political, economic, social, and cultural) of the colonized that the different social classes of African society formed a political alliance against colonialism. Led by petty bourgeois intellectuals, peasants, workers, the urban unemployed, and other fractions of colonized society formed a common front in the struggle for independence. This resulted in the birth of the modern democracy movement in Africa, whose objectives included not only an end to white rule but also better jobs, better pay and working conditions, more schools and health clinics, affordable modern amenities and, above all, a better future for children.

The democratization process currently under way is a logical consequence of the non-fulfillment of these expectations of independence. It is a reaction to the failure of the postcolonial state to realize the national project, namely, genuine independence, national integration, economic development, and social justice. Instead of making progress towards these goals, Africa is still afflicted with the woes of tribalism and the negative effects of misguided economic policies such as costly white elephants, a deteriorating social infrastructure, a declining standard of living, growing inequality, the reappearance of epidemics that had apparently disappeared (e.g., sleeping sickness, bubonic plague), together with the emergence of deadly new ones (HIV, Ebola), and general misery among ordinary people. The declining capacity of the African state to ensure personal and economic security is the major reason why Africa has the highest number of refugees in the world today. Enhancing democratic rights is the only way of averting this human tragedy. The struggle for democracy is a social process aimed at radically changing this deteriorating situation to bring improvements in the material life of the people.

Democracy as Political Practice

Having looked at democracy as a moral imperative and as a social process, we can now examine its third defining characteristic, namely, democracy as *political practice* or a *form of rule,* which is also its best known feature. Democracy, in this instance, refers to a specific manner of organizing and exercising power in accordance with certain universal norms and principles. There are two levels at which this can be examined: the level of the principles themselves, and that of the institutions and procedures of government which are compatible with democratic principles.

Following are the most frequently mentioned universal principles of democratic governance:

1. *The idea that legitimate power or authority emanates from the people,* who exercise it either *directly* through popular assemblies (e.g., the African *Palaver*), or *by delegation* through elected assemblies, elected executives, or some other mode of representation (e.g., dignitaries like lineage heads or elders in some African societies).

2. *The concept of rule of law ("Etat de droit"* in French), which means that power should not be arbitrary, and that its exercise must be circumscribed by a set of rules with respect to its limits and mode of operation. According to this principle, the parameters of state power and the sphere of governmental authority are well defined and limited, so as to allow space for other societal actors. By limiting the realm of governmental regulation, democracy recognizes that there are human activities which are best dealt with by other institutions such as the family or voluntary associations. Moreover, the concept of rule of law implies that within the public sphere, everything is done in conformity with the law, and that there exists a judicial system capable of ensuring the impartiality of the law as well as the protection of the rights and liberties of individuals and groups.

3. *The principle that rulers are chosen by and are accountable to the people.* The element of choice implies that democracy is *government by the consent of the governed,* who must approve not only the rules by which they are administered, but also the rulers themselves, as well as the policies the latter will implement. Here is where the notion of *accountability* comes in: that rulers are accountable to the people for their acts. In the precolonial Bantu kingdoms of Central, East, and Southern Africa, where the rulers were supposed to have command over everything, including natural elements like rain, wind, storms, lightning, etc.,[10] the test of accountability was so severe that they often paid with their life for failing it. Kings could be held responsible for prolonged droughts, calamitous storms, and the infertility of both soils and women.

4. *The right of citizens to participate in the management of public affairs* through free, transparent and democratic elections; through decentralized governmental structures; and through nongovernmental organizations (NGOs). This implies the right to organize freely, political and trade union pluralism, and the independence of the organizations of civil society from the state.

5. *Finally, the right of people to change a government that no longer serves their interests, or the right to revolution.* The 19th century US President Abraham Lincoln is best known for his definition of democracy as "government of the people, by the people, and for the people." Little is known of his equally eloquent defense of the right to revolution. In 1848, while a member of the US Congress, Lincoln made a passionate speech on January 12 against the US invasion of Mexico in which he stated that

> any people anywhere, being inclined and having the power, have the right to rise
> up, and shake off the existing government and form a new one that suits them
> better. This is a most valuable — a most sacred right — a right, which we hope
> and believe, is to liberate the world.[11]

By coincidence, 1848 was also the year of bourgeois revolutions in Europe and the year in which Karl Marx and Friedrich Engels set out on their political journey to liberate the world by publishing the *Communist Manifesto.* Now, some 150 years later and less than ten years after the collapse of Stalinist regimes in Eastern Europe and the former

Soviet Union, the right of people to overthrow an undemocratic regime is widely recognized as a *democratic right.*

The second notion associated with the concept of democracy as political practice has to do with the existence of institutions and procedures of government which are compatible with democratic principles. As a form of rule based on the consent of the governed, democracy requires those institutions likely to help the people fulfill their deepest aspirations, while maximizing their presence in the political space. Accordingly, democracy is inconceivable without free and fair elections, representative government, and an independent judiciary. Moreover, these institutions are unlikely to perform in a satisfactory way in the absence of a vibrant civil society and a free press.

Beginning with E.E. Evans-Pritchard's work on the Nuer of Sudan, a long tradition of functionalist anthropology has shown that the essential governmental functions of rule making, rule application, and rule adjudication are found in all societies, including stateless ones. According to this logic, if a modern court of law is a more appropriate medium than the Nuer leopard-skin arbitrator for adjudicating complex economic disputes, political participation through regular elections and constituency organizations today may be the functional equivalent of participatory or direct democracy in less complex societies. But while political institutions and procedures may vary in time and space, the test of their democratic worth remains the same, to wit, whether or not they are consistent with democratic principles. Thus, if multipartyism is not necessarily synonymous with democracy, it is difficult, if not impossible, to show that a one-party system can be democratic.

With the exception of a few countries — Botswana, Mauritius, and some of the emerging democracies like Benin, Madagascar, and South Africa — contemporary Africa has greatly deviated from democratic norms and principles. Instead of having a truly representative government and the rule of law, arbitrary rule by military and civilian dictators continues to hold sway in much of the continent. The logic of neopatrimonialism, according to which the ruler is indistinguishable from the office he/ she occupies, pervades the entire system and erodes the formal institutions of government of any democratic content. Thus, even in countries where democratic institutions and procedures are supposedly respected, the result is democratic *formalism,* or democracy in form rather than content.

This kind of political practice is best exemplified by multipartyism *without democracy,* an aberration that manifests itself in a single party dominating the entire political space, lack of alternation in governing elites over a long period of time, electoral fraud, etc. In Africa, this pattern of rule has already worked for years in countries like Egypt, Senegal, and Tunisia. It is now rearing its ugly head in many countries in transition, where incumbents have learned how to play the new democracy game with surprising astuteness. With democracy itself being abusively identified with multipartyism and elections, the old dictators have turned their attention to weakening the democratic opposition by funding numerous political parties, and to electoral fraud, in order to stay in power. This has contributed to both prolonging and undermining democratic transitions in Africa.

Democratic Transitions In Africa

The democracy movement in Africa today is a social protest against the failure of the postcolonial state to live up to the people's expectations of independence, including the fulfillment of their basic human needs. A quarter of a century earlier, this protest had resulted in what peasants in the Bandundu region of Zaire called the struggle for a "second independence". Today, Africa is still one of the world's richest continents in natural resources, yet our people are among the poorest on earth. Our continent has some of the richest people in the world, with some individuals having a net worth in the billions of US dollars, while thousands of our people die regularly of easily preventable and curable diseases like diarrhea, malaria, or measles.

Given this background, what are the prospects for reasonably successful transitions to democracy in Africa today? Democratization is a continuous process as well as an ongoing struggle between the forces of change and those of the status quo. Now that most states have embarked on some kind of democratization, to what extent are the reformers within the state apparatus and those in the opposition committed to democratic principles? Are the new institutions being established a simple carbon copy of Western institutions, or do they have sufficient grounding in the African reality to uphold democratic values and sustain democracy? Is the new political environment any different from the old with respect to the promotion of fundamental rights associated with democracy? In the following three sections, I shall attempt to answer these questions by examining both the internal and external environments of the democratization process, and by assessing the prospects for the long march of postcolonial Africa to democracy.

The Internal Environment
As the primary stage of the struggle between the forces of the status quo and those of change, the internal environment is absolutely crucial as to its effects on the democratization process. Within the democracy movement itself, there is a glaring contradiction between the deepest aspirations of the masses, who constitute the rank and file, and the narrow class interests of its leadership. The latter is made up in most cases of deserters from the ruling circles of the *ancien régime,* who are more interested in settling accounts with their former boss and his entourage than in transforming the state radically by democratizing it and increasing its capacity to serve the people. Like most of the petty bourgeois leaders of the independence struggle, the new leaders are for the most part self-centered seekers of political power and material benefits. Their main preoccupation is to position themselves for political office in the new dispensation of the post-authoritarian era.

Evidence from both the aborted or failed transitions, and the countries where elected governments have replaced civilian or military dictatorships, suggests that there is little commitment to democratization as a process within the political class as a whole, including leaders of the democratic opposition.[12] Both powerholders and those seeking to replace them share a common political culture, one "that puts less emphasis on respect for the democratic process of open debate and transparent decision-making than on deal-making among politicians."[13]

This is a political culture in which opportunism takes precedence over principle, with most leaders failing to honor the agreements to which they subscribe in negotiations. Decisions taken at democratic gatherings like the national conference can easily be overturned behind closed doors by self-serving politicians, away from the vigilant eye of the masses. Interminable negotiations over the spoils of the political game, endless splits within political parties, and the shameless shifting from one political camp to another that is appropriately known as *"vagabondage politique"* (or political vagrancy) in Zaire, are typical behavioral patterns within the political class.

Even more devastating than the failure to respect the decisions of democratic assemblies and to honor signed agreements, are the lack of patriotism, the criminal fanning of ethnic hatred, and the willful destruction of the economic and social fabric of the country. Angola, Congo, Liberia, Somalia, and Zaire are but a few examples of countries where political leaders would rather destroy their homeland than accept the verdict of the ballot box or a position other than that of supreme chief. Africa is full of unpatriotic leaders who seem to believe that if they cannot run a country they might as well wreck it. Many seem to think that the shortest road to national leadership is a strategic retreat as a warlord to one's ethnic stronghold or military enclave, and the use of force and blackmail to obtain through negotiations or mediation what they had failed to gain democratically.

The fanning of ethnic conflict and the destruction of the economy by rulers who exploit crises to remain in office do constitute "violence against democracy."[14] The violent backlash by authoritarian rulers against the democratization process has resulted in genocide in Rwanda, large-scale massacres in Burundi, ethnic cleansing and economic chaos in Zaire, and communal violence in Congo and Kenya. A close examination of these and other conflicts which are tearing our continent apart reveals that it is among politicians and intellectuals, including prominent religious leaders, that one finds the people most responsible for these criminal and anti-democratic acts.

Thus, contrary to the elitist conceptions of democracy which are prevalent in the West, it is not among these social categories that one will find the strongest commitment to democracy. The forces which are crucial for the democratic transition in Africa are likely to be found among the working people (peasants, workers, and the lower petty bourgeoisie), and those intellectuals who would heed the call of Amilcar Cabral to abandon their class positions in order to identify fully with the deepest aspirations of their people.[15] It is from such intellectuals that capable leadership may be found for purposes of enhancing the role of civil society in the democratization process and democratizing the democracy movement itself.

The External Environment

Since the collapse of the Stalinist regimes in Eastern Europe and the former Soviet Union, the Western powers and the international financial institutions under their control have intensified their promotional campaign in favor of "democracy." Does the concept have the same meaning for them as it does for African people? Other than the support for the formal structures of multiparty and electoral politics, is there in the international community today a genuine commitment to democracy as defined in this chapter?

It is obvious that the objective conditions of the current globalization process do not favor democracy. The dogmatic assertion of the virtues of the market in the face of growing inequalities and social exclusion, even in the very centers of developed capitalism, is a sign of an anti-democratic tendency to discourage an open debate on alternative economic models. The gospel of economic liberalism has been elevated to the position of absolute truth, a sort of *"pensée unique"* (or single theory) against which there is no credible alternative.[16]

In reality, the need to subjugate Africa to the logic of global capitalist expansion is contrary to the requirements for democracy. It favors instead rule by a technocratic elite that can only be anti-labor, anti-people, and therefore anti-democracy. Thus, in spite of their declarations of good intention, the major forces in the world system prefer technocrats without a political base in the country to leaders who have a national constituency. While the latter are likely to listen to their constituencies, the former can be expected to be beholden to their foreign patrons. They will, accordingly, implement externally mandated policies likely to benefit their patrons to the detriment of their people.

Zaire offers an excellent example of this reality. Seven years have passed since President Mobutu Sese Seko succumbed to internal and external pressure to end the one-party system. A national conference of 2842 delegates from all walks of life met and adopted a comprehensive framework for the transition to democracy and elected the major opposition leader, Etienne Tshisekedi, as prime minister in August 1992. After three months of hesitation, President Mobutu decided to subvert the popular will by forcibly preventing the Tshisekedi government from running the country.

In the current phase of neocolonialism, in which the destiny of many a country in crisis is being determined by two or more foreign powers posing as "friends" of, or "the contact group" for, the country, a troika consisting of the United States, France, and Belgium somehow appointed itself to manage the democratic transition in Zaire. Unfortunately for the people of this country, the managers were more interested in promoting Western interests in general and French hegemony in Central Africa in particular, than in furthering the cause of democracy in Zaire.

Instead of punishing Mobutu for his violent backlash against democracy, the Western troika rewarded him by working with Catholic Archbishop Laurent Monsengwo, President of both the Sovereign National Conference and the Transitional Parliament elected by the conference, to revise the constitutional and institutional framework of the transition in a manner consistent with Mobutu's political survival. They did everything possible to keep from the general public damaging information on Western participation in political crimes, such as the assassination of Patrice Lumumba, and economic crimes, such as the construction of so many white elephants that have increased indebtedness without contributing to economic growth.

In the final analysis, the Western powers rejected the democratically elected prime minister because their interests would be better served by Mobutu, Monsengwo, and the technocrats associated with Leon Kengo wa Dondo, the longest serving prime minister of the Mobutu era. With Mobutu and Kengo, the very people who had driven the Zairian economy aground with their excessive corruption, Western powers and the Bretton Woods institutions could hope to recover the loans they had made to Zaire and help Western interests take over the public mining and other economic enterprises through privatization.

Incidentally, the national conference had decreed that the country was not obligated to repay those debts which did not benefit the economy in a tangible manner. All outstanding debts had to be renegotiated in view of where the money actually went. The conference also voted against a wholesale privatization of state enterprises, as this meant selling them on the cheap to foreign interests or to wealthy Zairians who had actually destroyed these formerly successful ventures through systematic pillage. To please his Western patrons, Kengo had no problem letting civil servants go unpaid for months, while he concentrated on repaying the external debt and making deals with French and other foreign interests to take over the parastatals.

The fact that major powers are primarily concerned with their own interests rather than in promoting democracy can be seen in their caricatural identification of the latter with elections. In themselves, elections do not ensure democracy. They can be manipulated through rules of the game that reduce the chances for fairness and by electoral fraud. Thus, it is too simplistic to identify democracy with the holding of elections. Some well-known Western political theorists have gone so far as to define democracy itself as the "competitive struggle for the people's vote."[17] The question of democracy goes beyond elections to the realization of democratic principles of governance and to the balance of social forces in the political community. For democracy is meaningless without economic and social rights. It means nothing to people who cannot eat properly, have a roof over their heads, find a job, send their children to school, and have access to a minimum of decent health care. These are the social gains of the post-independence period that external policies like structural adjustment are destroying in Africa today.

Sustaining democracy or a successful democratic transition requires that democratic regimes be capable of fulfilling the people's expectations. Failure to do so can derail the transition and bring about a serious questioning of the necessity of political change. Zambia is a case in point. It was one of the first countries in Africa to change government through free and fair elections, in 1991. President Kenneth Kaunda was defeated by trade unionist Frederick Chiluba. Once in power, the latter found it difficult to satisfy the people's aspirations. If the errors and weaknesses of the Chiluba regime have a lot to do with this failure, there is no doubt that part of the blame resides with the external environment. The democracy dividend of substantially reduced external debts and increased assistance from the world system did not materialize. Facing mounting social problems, the regime has progressively turned to authoritarianism.

Prospects for Democracy in Africa

I shall conclude this rapid survey of the democratization process in Africa with a summary of factors which seem to block a normal transition from authoritarianism to genuine democracy and those which are likely to promote and sustain it. At the present time, there are multiple blockages to the democratization process. Following is a description of four of them as major obstacles to the democratic transition.

The first obstacle is *the political immaturity of the democratic forces,* or those who designate themselves as such. As pointed out above, most of the leaders of the democratic opposition are deserters from the ruling circles of the *ancien régime* who are repositioning themselves for political office in the post-authoritarian era. This explains the high incidence of political opportunism, the endless divisions within opposition parties, the pronounced tendency towards political vagrancy, and the lack of respect for signed agreements and democratically adopted decisions that may not conform with their narrow personal interests. When this kind of behavior is combined with a lack of respect for the constitutional order and the democratic rules of the game, multipartyism turns into an anti-thesis of democracy and the democratic transition into a kind of political disorder (cases of Congo, Niger) or political "recreation" (case of Zaire).[18] Thus, the democratic transition cannot fare well when the leaders of the democratic opposition are so preoccupied with winning political office for their own material benefits and are consequently ready to prefer deal-making behind closed doors to transparent decision-making in open democratic processes. More often than not, they will end up betraying the deepest aspirations of ordinary people, whose own political immaturity manifests itself in an often uncritical support for such leaders.

The second obstacle is related to the first. It is *the weakness of the means of subsistence of the middle class and its exploitation by the ruling group* in order to paralyze the democratic forces. The leadership of the democratic opposition comes mostly from middle class or petty bourgeois social categories such as lawyers, university professors, medical doctors, and professional politicians. As professionals and intellectuals, these groups have for the most part experienced a steady deterioration in income during the last two decades of economic crisis in Africa. Economic hardships and a reduced standard of living have forced even those intellectuals who are least interested in a political career into jockeying for lucrative ministerial or other high government positions. Pressured both internally and externally to implement democratic reforms, the ruling groups have exploited this situation through the cooptation of intellectuals into the ruling circles and by funding nominal political parties with no social basis so as to divide and paralyze the real opposition. The contribution to this volume by Jibrin Ibrahim on Nigerian political scientists is an excellent example of such a situation. Other classic cases include Kenya and Zaire.

The third obstacle is the *monopoly of the public media by the incumbent regime*. Without access to national radio and television, the democratic opposition has an extremely difficult task in passing its message to its followers. Even when opposition newspapers do exist, they provide an inadequate medium of communication with the broad masses of the people, most of whom do not read newspapers.[19] In large cities, most of the politically conscious strata of ordinary people, which include informal sector operators and young school leavers, may learn about opposition calls for demonstrations, strikes, and other political actions from headlines in opposition newspapers, foreign radio broadcasts, and by word of mouth. This is not possible in the rural areas and small towns of the interior. On the other hand, the regime's monopoly of the public media can be used to disinform, create confusion, and paralyze the opposition.

The fourth and last major obstacle has already been referred to above as *violence against democracy*. This includes the intimidation of civil servants for purposes of preventing them from joining the democratic struggle, police repression of democracy and human rights activists, and systematically organized acts of violence against democracy. These do vary from country to country and include divide-and-rule strategies like the fanning of ethnic hatred, ethnic cleansing, wholesale massacres and genocide. Unlike the first three obstacles, which may slow down the democratic transition, violence against democracy has the effect of derailing it altogether.

In spite of these obstacles, and setbacks such as coups d'état (the case of Niger, 1996), and the restoration of the *ancien régime* (Zaire, 1994), the democratic transition in Africa is *irreversible*. Today, no state can succeed in wiping out the major gains of the democracy movement like freedom of expression, press, and assembly, as well as the penetration of the political space by NGOs. The people no longer fear Africa's dictators and their repressive machines, as they are determined to go forward until final victory.

Achieving this victory and sustaining the democratic gains made are a function of the environment within which the democratization process takes place. Important variables of an enabling environment include the development of a viable civil society, electoral politics and their outcomes, political arrangements made with respect to democratic governance, peace and security, and economic conditions.

The consolidation of one-party and military regimes entailed the demobilization of the social forces that had energized the independence struggle. It was accompanied by the banning of independent mass organizations and the paralyzing of civil society. Having enjoyed a monopoly over power and access to the resources under the control of the state, Africa's authoritarian rulers have and will continue to resist the renewed thrust of civil society organizations to expand the political space. Consequently, the democratic transition is likely to be a long one, indeed. We should not expect quick fixes, for what appears as victory at some point may turn out to be nothing of the kind, as attested by the Niger and Zaire examples mentioned above. What is important is the creation of a new political culture in which democracy may grow and be sustained, and political expression need not be confined to the state and political parties. Professional associations, NGOs, and independent mass organizations should flourish in order to challenge the status quo and help develop a viable civil society capable of limiting state power and of advancing the interests of the broad masses of the people.

Electoral politics and their outcomes constitute the second variable of the enabling environment for a successful democratic transition. Before the advent of one-party and military dictatorships during the second half of the 1960s and in the 1970s, free and fair elections did take place in independent Africa. The results were generally credible and widely accepted by both the contenders and the electorate. These elections, it should be noted, were organized and administered by the postcolonial state itself, with no external supervision and no international observers.

The corruption of political life since then is such that no election is credible today unless it is certified as such by foreign observers. Unfortunately, international surveillance is likely to be so superficial or to come so late in the electoral process — usually at the time of voting — that it is not sufficient for ensuring free, fair, and transparent elections. There are cases where it simply has been used to legitimize incumbent rulers. A consensus seems to be emerging continentally on the need for electoral administration to be entrusted to an independent electoral commission, one in which civil society organizations have a strong representation.

A very disturbing development is the tendency among losers, even those in elections that are widely seen as free and fair, to reject the verdict of the ballot box. Such a contempt for the popular will and democratic processes has been manifested as much by warlords and separatist leaders, as by rulers who were once part of the democratic opposition. It is a manifestation of a widely held conception of electoral outcomes as a zero sum game in which the winners get everything while the losers are denied not only access to state power and resources, but also their fundamental rights as human beings, including the rights to earn a decent livelihood and to personal security.[20]

Closely related to this is the third variable, namely, the post-electoral political arrangement for democratic governance. There seems to be an emerging consensus that the democratic transition in Africa must avoid the politics of exclusion. All the relevant political forces must have a share of executive power if the transition is to succeed. Power sharing, as this notion is called, is a position that makes a lot of sense in transitional situations. It may be argued that it should become an established feature of democratic governance in Africa for the foreseeable future. There is, firstly, a broad national consensus on economic and social policy in most African countries. Secondly, and most importantly, given the fact that the bone of contention in African political conflicts is control of the state and the resources to which the state has access, power sharing should reassure the losers and their followers that they will not be excluded from these resources. As a result, they may feel that their security is not threatened.

Power sharing is one of the contributing factors to peace and security, the fourth variable of the enabling environment. Internal conflicts and cross-border violence constitute the main threats to peace and security in Africa today. Cross-border violence is usually a function of refugee flows and disasters and/or of fighting between states and dissident movements using neighboring countries as rear bases. All of these phenomena are related to the search for a new social contract between the state and the society under its control. This involves the well-being and security of all citizens and residents. Refugees and dissident movements emerge in response to either the state's failure to meet these basic needs or its oppression of certain groups, particularly social and ethnic minorities. Just as it is likely to be sustained under conditions of peace and security, the democratic transition offers the best conditions for national reconciliation and social justice, which are the foundations of durable peace and comprehensive security.

The fifth and final variable of the enabling environment for a successful democratic transition is the economic situation. The question is whether or not democracy is sustainable under the current conditions of economic crisis in Africa. There is the notion that under poor economic conditions, it will be difficult for democracy to take root. The poor will make demands that the state cannot meet. Military elites, no longer receiving the privileges they had during easier times, will turn on elected leaders and remove them from office. Given the rising tide of regionalism and ethnic particularism, the various ethnic communities are likely to perceive political power in zero sum ways and thus engage in interethnic competition for state power.

Is this a realistic scenario? If so, what can be done to avoid a catastrophic breakdown of the democratization process? The democratic transition cannot be held hostage by the economic situation. For it is only by dealing effectively with the other four variables that economic conditions may improve and thus increase the chances for social democracy. Democracy as a moral imperative, a social process, and a political practice is not incompatible with low levels of economic development. However limited they might be with respect to fundamental human rights, the democratic experiences of Botswana, Mauritius, and the English-speaking Caribbean are there to bear witness to this.[21]

Democracy will not be handed down to the people of Africa on a silver platter. It can be realized only through sustained political struggle. Indeed democracy is the main result of this struggle. It is the ultimate prize won by a determined people who are committed to improving their lives economically and socially. Democracy is above all a moral imperative for any people who care about their dignity as human beings. It is a continuous social process of expanding political space in the interest of all, particularly the popular masses. And it is a political practice that empowers people to rise up against a decadent or oppressive political order to replace it with one likely to improve their material conditions of life and ensure a better future for their children.

Notes

[1] J. F. Ade Ajayi, " Expectations of Independence", *Daedalus,* Vol. 111, No. 2, 1982, pp. 1-6.

[2] See, among others, Nzongola-Ntalaja, *Revolution and Counter-Revolution in Africa* (London: Zed Books, 1987); Robert Buijtenhuijs, *Le Frolinat et les révoltes populaires du Tchad, 1965-1976* (The Hague: Mouton, 1978); Mahmood Mamdani and Ernest Wamba-dia-Wamba *(eds.), African Studies in Social Movements and Democracy* (Dakar: CODESRIA, 1995).

[3] See Henri Lopes, "My Grandmother and My Gallic Ancestors," *AAPS Newsletter,* June-September 1995, p. 17.

[4] Francis Akindés, *Les mirages de la démocratie en Afrique subsaharienne francophone* (Dakar: CODESRIA, 1996), pp. 162-175.

[5] The middle class thesis, which can be traced back to Aristotle's *Politics,* was

popularized by Seymour Martin Lipset, *Political Man: The Social Bases of Politics* (New York, Doubleday, 1960; new ed. Baltimore: Johns Hopkins University Press, 1981). On the relationship between democracy and wealth, see Henry S. Rowen, "The Tide Underneath the 'Third Wave'," *Journal of Democracy,* Vol. 6, No. 1, 1995, pp. 52-64.

[6] C. Northcote Parkinson, *The Evolution of Political Thought* (Boston: Houghton-Mifflin, 1958), p. 168.

[7] Akindés, pp. 178-179.

[8] For a brief summary of the political history of Bantu Africa, see Théophile Obenga, "Histoire du monde bantu," in Théophile Obenga and Simao Souindoula (sous la direction de) *Racines Bantu/Bantu Roots* (Libreville: CICIBA, 1991), pp. 121-150.

[9] Rousseau, *On the Social Contract* (1762), cited in Parkinson, pp. 205 and 311.

[10] Obenga, p. 149.

[11] *The New York Times,* October 31, 1990.

[12] Failed and aborted transitions include Algeria, Angola, Cameroon, Côte d'Ivoire, Gabon, Kenya, Niger, Nigeria, Sudan, Togo, and Zaire. Countries where elected governments have replaced dictatorships include Benin, Cape Verde, Central African Republic, Congo, Ghana, Guinea-Bissau, Madagascar, Malawi, Mali, Sao Tome and Principe, Tanzania, and Zambia. In this second category, there are cases in which the former rulers were retained (Ghana, Guinea-Bissau, Mozambique) or returned to power in a subsequent election (Benin, Madagascar).

[13] Georges Nzongola-Ntalaja, "The Democracy Movement in Zaire, 1956-1994," Paper presented at the Sixth Triennial Conference of the University of the Witwatersrand's History Workshop in Johannesburg, South Africa, July 13-15, 1994, and at the 16th World Congress of the International Political Science Association in Berlin, Germany, August 21 to 25, 1994.

[14] Amnesty International, *Zaire: Violence Against Democracy* (New York: Amnesty International USA, 1993).

[15] Amilcar Cabral, *Revolution in Guinea* (London: Stage 1, 1969).

[16] For a critique of this dogma, see Ignacio Ramonet, "La pensée unique", *Le Monde Diplomatique,* January 1995.

[17] Joseph Schumpeter, *Capitalism, Socialism, and Democracy* (New York: Harper & Brothers, 1942); Seymour Martin Lipset, "Reflections on Capitalism, Socialism, and Democracy," *Journal of Democracy,* Vol. 4, No. 2, 1993, pp. 43-55.

[18] President Mobutu of Zaire used to refer to the political scene in Kinshasa, where some 400 political party chiefs went around under the pompous title of *"Monsieur le Président"* in and outside Parliament, as "recreation." Rumor has it that he regretted "introducing democracy" so late, as this kind of political game was actually harmless, as it allowed politicians to vent their feelings and earn money doing so while leaving the real levers of state power to him.

[19] Kalele-ka-Bila's contribution to this volume shows how a grassroots political movement learned to deal with this handicap in Zaire.

[20] This conception was strengthened by events such as the aftermath of the 1985 elections in Liberia, where the losers, including Jackson Doe (the apparent, winner according to unofficial reports), were all eliminated from the political scene by the dictator, Samuel Doe. Jackson Doe was actually murdered. In a similar development, but one in which the military ruler did not contest the elections directly, the apparent winner of the 1993 presidential election in Nigeria, Chief M.K.O. Abiola, was

subsequently jailed on treason charges for having the audacity to proclaim himself president in 1994. Abubakar Momoh's contribution to this volume provides detailed information on this episode.

[21] The Botswana experience, and particularly its implication for women and their struggle for equality, is ably described in Onalenna Selolwane's contribution to this volume.

2

Gender and Democracy in Botswana: Women's Struggle for Equality and Political Participation

Onalenna Doo Selolwane

The women's struggle for equality in Botswana has, in the 1990s, taken on a more overtly political stance in demanding representation and political space in decision-making structures of government and political parties. This change was necessitated by the resistance to legal reform by Botswana's lawmakers and managers of the polity. Botswana's postcolonial history has served as the only African example where the state has steadfastly maintained the trappings of liberal democratic governance and the protection and guarantee of individual rights and freedoms that are consonant with this political system. So the resistance of the establishment to according women full, substantive equality with men, as guaranteed by the constitution, raises fundamental questions concerning the content and form of Botswana's democratic practice. It also highlights certain problems concerning the democratic process that may have significant lessons for other African countries seeking a return to liberal democratic rule and multiparty competition for government power.

This study is not a contribution to the debate on what does or does not constitute democracy, or whether or to what extent Botswana is a democracy. Rather, proceeding from the premise that political systems and democratic governance are historical processes whose form and content are defined through class and other social struggles, it focuses on the impact of the Botswana women's struggle on extending the boundaries of democracy and political practice. The history of democracy from ancient Greece to this century demonstrates that it evolved as a political process based on an exclusionary and hierarchical distribution of power. Only in recent times has democracy come to be associated in practice and theory with majoritarian principles and equality.[1] This processing of power has, for instance, normally excluded the majority of people on account of being women, servants/slaves, foreigners, and other non-propertied groups in a given polity.

The extension of participatory rights to such excluded social groups historically had to be won through struggles which were often violent and bloody. Examples include the women's suffragette movement, the civil rights struggles of black peoples in the Western world, national liberation struggles and, more recently, the struggle for majority rule in apartheid South Africa. Each of these struggles has extended the boundaries of democratic participation to include an ever widening circle of constituencies and issues which had previously been excluded from the processing of power. In analyzing the Botswana women's struggle for equality and political space, therefore, this chapter examines how this struggle extends the boundaries of democracy and raises questions about the problems of the democratic process. In particular, it focuses on the exclusionary nature of democratic practices as regards women in terms of the determination of who participates and to what extent, where democracy should take place, and what issues are legitimate concerns of democratic decision-making. The chapter also discusses the issue of territoriality as a factor in women's exclusion in political processes.

Gender and the Boundaries of Democracy in Botswana: The Problem of Women's Exclusion

When Botswana became an independent republic in 1966, this marked the ascendancy of a legal-rational constitution guaranteeing legitimation of government power through regular popular participation and multiparty competition. The people over whom this polity was extended were conferred equality of status and the right to participate, as well as various individual rights and freedoms. Ar ong those conferred this equality of status and the protection and guarantee of rights and freedoms were women. However, although they have consistently participated in the legitimation of government power as voters, Batswana women have not enjoyed their constitutionally guaranteed liberal rights and freedoms to the same extent as men. On the contrary, their participation in decision-making in both the public and private spheres of their lives is restricted by certain powerful conventions in the form of custom, traditions, laws, and political practices which make them subordinate to men and therefore limited in their capacity to make adult decisions concerning their lives and welfare.

During the past decade, and against the backdrop of the United Nations' decade for women and its theme of equality, peace, and development, Batswana women have become more sensitive to their rights to equality and greater political participation, and have articulated their demands more vocally. Until the mid-1980s, when Batswana women decided to test the substantiveness of Botswana's constitutional guarantee of their equality, the political practices and legal provisions of this country were not regarded as seriously problematic by women. However, when they challenged the 1982 Citizenship Amendment Act, which denied women married to foreign men the right to pass their citizenship on to their children, they were made aware, for the first time in Botswana's history, just how limited were the guarantees and protection of their individual liberties and freedoms as women. When the women lobbied against this act in the light of constitutional guarantees of equal rights and protection from discrimination, the activists were dismissed as a minority group which was totally out of touch with Tswana cultural values as well as being unrepresentative of the majority view of Batswana women.

This reaction on the part of the lawmakers and managers of the Botswana polity highlighted weaknesses and gaps in the character of political life and democratic practice in this country. It made women appreciate the fact that although they were a numerical majority in a political system supposedly based on popular legitimation of power, they did not in fact enjoy the substantive power to make decisions that could enhance their status and improve the quality of their lives. The quality of their political participation in the democratic processing of power was such that they conferred the power to rule on men, but did not share in this power in any way that could enhance and develop their economic, social, educational, employment, and political opportunities. Given that there was no law specifically restricting their participation in competing for the power to govern, it is necessary to establish just what it was that led to women being marginalized in the context of a political system that recognizes the power of the vote. It is also necessary to establish how far women can extend the boundaries of participation.

The Source and Historical Roots of Women's Exclusion

Part of the root of the problem is found in the traditional laws and cultural practices which had historically denied women legitimacy to claim a share in power and public forms of decision-making. Among the majority of the ethno-polities that inhabited the territory that became the Republic of Botswana in 1966, women had no legitimate claim to hereditary ascendancy to the power to rule. The traditional constitution guaranteed the right to succession to rule only to male heirs. Further, women were excluded from participating in the public assemblies where men debated tribal affairs and discussed other issues of public concern. Women could process their rights in these public assemblies only through their menfolk (fathers, uncles, husbands, brothers, sons).

Therefore, although the system valued consensual decision-making in many aspects of life, in the public arena such popular participation was extended only to men.[2] This traditional perception of men as legitimate leaders has not changed much with the transition from rule based on hereditary rights to rule based on popular legitimacy through electoral processes and universal adult suffrage. On the contrary, and in spite of constitutional guarantees of equality and protection from discrimination, there are several legal provisions and practices in postcolonial Botswana which have served to enhance mens' rights as rulers and to deny women legitimacy as stakeholders in the distribution of power, thus perpetuating traditional forms of arbitrary conferment of power.

The most powerful of these legal conventions is arguably the conferment of a minority status on the personhood of all women in terms of customary law, and women married in community of property according to common law. This legal convention does not recognize women as full adults who have the capacity to make decisions which have legal and social consequences for themselves as well as others. Having reduced them to minors, the convention provides for women's protection in the form of male relatives who are deemed capable of rational decision-making. Thus, in the private domain of the household or family, there is no full recognition of common interests that must be safeguarded for all individuals. The family, therefore, continues to be the place where democratic processing of decision-making is excluded. The integrity of women's personhood is therefore undermined, with the consequence that even their capacity to participate in the public domain of electoral processes, political office, and policy formulation is curtailed as their decision-making powers are subordinated to male guardianship and marital power.

Besides these legal limitations, women are faced with cultural practices that still do not recognize them as legitimate leaders. Neither the voting public nor the political party hierarchy which determines who should stand for political office, would normally support a female candidate to compete for office. Many potential female candidates react to this situation by simply not attempting to compete for public office, deeming themselves inadequate to the task, as well as in recognition of the fact that they are not likely to garner support. This has resulted in the anomaly where women, as majority voters, consistently use their acquired electoral powers to maintain the legitimacy of male rule and consistently validate it with their votes, while failing to recognize the legitimacy of other women's ambitions to compete for government power.

The extent to which this perception of illegitimacy is still embedded in post-independence Tswana culture was succinctly captured during a legal literacy workshop in 1990 when the women participants cautioned against taking an overtly political stance in seeking redress. The emphasis on women's voting power as an advantage which should be used to transform society was seen by some of the participants as too confrontational a stance to take.[3] Even as recently as 1996, when a workshop was held for women councilors and parliamentarians to consider ways of increasing the number of women in public office, some of the participants expressed concern that such discussions might encourage hostility toward men.[4] They also, however, conceded that culture and tradition imposed limitations which have not yet made it acceptable for women to be leaders of men.

Another factor limiting women's substantive political participation is their general lack of understanding of the relationship between their votes and the decisions made by those they have put into government. This lack of political sophistication has not just been confined to women, but is true of Botswana's voting public in general. Although they are party to the legitimating processes, most voters have insufficient understanding of the extent of the powers this system gives them. They therefore still regard their elected representatives in more or less the same light they did hereditary rulers.[5] Most voters lack sufficient appreciation of the fact that in a political system based on popular consent, they are entitled to question their elected representatives and demand accountability regarding all the policies, laws, and other decisions they make on their behalf. On the contrary, those who question the laws, policies, and practices of these elected representatives are viewed with some disquiet and suspicion, because they are perceived as wanting to usurp or undermine the natural authority of those meant to govern.

This lack of sophistication results from inadequate political education to prepare people for the transition from hereditary rule, to rule based on electoral processes. No single institution has been given the responsibility, or taken it upon itself, to provide this critical public service. The competitive and confrontational nature of party politics does not make political parties the best institutions for transmitting democratic culture through public education. With no formal institutionalization of this education by the government, liberal democracy in Botswana has been seriously underdeveloped. The voting public has been left to use the old value systems from traditional politics to interpret their role in the new liberal democratic process. Consequently, while the formal structures of liberal democratic governance have been put in place in terms of multiparty competition for government power; rule of law; protection and guarantee of individual rights and freedoms; and the separation of government power among the executive, the legislature and the judiciary, the majority of Batswana have not yet sufficiently learned how to function within these structures.

Consequently, civil society has remained underdeveloped while the state machinery and those who control it have developed a greater understanding of how to retain a monopoly over the system. Botswana has thus developed a unifocal power point centered on the state, which is not conducive to a healthy liberal democratic system. The predominance of the Botswana state has been enhanced by the fact that, unlike most other postcolonial African states, it has been able to deliver economic, educational, and general welfare development for the majority of the voters, and largely irrespective of ethnic background.[6] In the eyes of the general populace, therefore, the state (or specifically, the government of the day) knows exactly what has to be done by way of development, and has been so successful in doing it, that there is no questioning its methods or capacity to deliver. This had led to unsubstantial development of the multiparty system and pressure groups, as well as a compliant and ignorant voting public.

For women, this underdevelopment not only manifests itself in their unsubstantial participation in political processes and decision-making structures, but can also be seen in the extent to which issues concerning their interests and welfare are still regarded as matters that legitimately belong only in their private lives. Issues of marital violence, rape, and problems related to unequal control of resources within the family, are often treated as matters over which men have the final say. Consequently, women often endure serious violations of their human rights at the hands of their male relatives and close associates because these issues are deemed to belong to the private sphere and therefore not suited for public discourse and intervention. In Tswana law and custom, for instance, husbands have a right to chastise their wives, and marriage guarantees them access to conjugal rights which they sometimes feel at liberty to demand through coercion. Women who endure the violence that is so often associated with men's exercise of these rights are deemed virtuous if they do so in silence and within the privacy of their homes. This institutionalized license to violence and human rights violation has seen a growing incidence of violence against women by men who feel that their partners are demanding and exercising too much independence and must be 'chastised' to accept their subordinate position in the family. The breakdown in the institution of the family and marriage[7] is thus often perceived as the result of too much freedom for women.

Issues of unequal control of family property and productive resources are another area where law and practice favor men. Unless they are married to foreign men or have access to non community property, most married women in Botswana cannot independently own immovable property. In marriages where you have community property, the law treats joint estates of husbands and wives as the sole property of the man, who is fully entitled to dispose of such property without consulting his wife. In contrast, a wife who disposes of such property without the husband's consent is treated by law as a thief and can be prosecuted. As a result, wives have limited capacity to use such property as collateral to raise substantial loans. This, and the fact that wives cannot raise bank loans without the consent of husbands, limits their capacity to run for public office, which requires financial means. More importantly, the conferment of managerial power on the husband has serious consequences for the welfare of women and their children, particularly if the marriage breaks down, or the husband is irresponsible.

In the traditional Tswana system, there were checks and balances within the extended family system which provided safety nets against the absolute power of men. In the context of new liberal values which confer absolute rights of decision-making on the husband, the principle of the man as head of the household and sole manager of the family estate effectively erodes the checks and balances of the old system, without putting in new safety nets. Despite evidence that these men grossly abuse their "natural rights," with negative consequences for the livelihoods of women and their offspring,[8] there is still a strong cultural orientation toward maintaining the natural sovereignty of the husband within the family. There is therefore considerable resistance toward democratization of decision-making within the family and regarding the common property of husbands and wives.

While the principle of equality is now recognized as the cornerstone of democracy and fundamental to the enjoyment of human rights and freedoms, equality between the sexes, particularly in the context of the marriage institution and family life, is still deemed to be too dangerous to society by those in power. By 1996, Botswana was still among the nations that had not ratified the United Nations' Convention on the Elimination of all Forms of Discrimination Against Women. The law-making establishment still considers the notion of gender equality as too far reaching and too serious a challenge to the cultural and social practices that are based on the assumption that women are inferior to men and are incapable of rational and responsible decision-making. In the male hegemonic language of discourse, discrimination against women is actually perceived as protective action against a social group which is not naturally endowed with sufficient intelligence and strength to survive independently of male domination.

History shows that there is a strong link between the distribution of decision-making power, and access to, and control of, economic resources and other sources of power.[9] Early liberal democracy, for instance, was a preserve of men with landed property, and was therefore based on the assumption that only they had interests worth protecting. These men were thus accorded the sole right to be involved in decision-making with respect to property rights. The extension of political control through conquest, colonization, enslavement, and other forms of subjugation, has invariably gone hand in hand with limitations on control of material resources and related opportunities among the subjugated social groups. In postcolonial Africa, where the colonial period had eroded the indigenous resources of the poor, control of state power by the heirs of the colonial state has usually led to their amassing of wealth. This, in most instances, has also been accompanied by profound erosions of the legitimating powers of the electorate, and gross violations of human rights and freedoms.

In Botswana, where such extreme situations have been avoided, there is still evidence of a direct relationship between political power and the quality and extent of access to material resources. Women's limited political power, for instance, corresponds to their limited economic power. Women account for just 37 percent of Botswana's employed work force, and 25 percent of the managers of the economy, according to the 1991 Population Census. In the rural economy, their participation is limited by lack of adequate access to cattle and draught power, so they tend to perform relatively poorly in agricultural and food production. Hence, the greater likelihood of women falling into the poverty trap. In the context of the postcolonial state, where the state is the chief distributor of economic opportunities and development resources, women's capacity to influence distributional decision-making is critical to the enhancement of their development status.

The Territoriality of Democratic Exclusion

Territory also often limits the participation of individuals, particularly women, in the political processes and, therefore, determines the extent to which they may exercise freedoms and enjoy certain liberties. While global politics happens above the confines of political boundaries of modern nation-states, sovereignty is still recognized to be bounded by the political limits of the geographical space of nation-states. It is also within these boundaries that individual rights and freedoms are most protected, at least in theory. This means that while the actions of superpower nation-states like the United States of America may have direct consequences for the quality of life of the people of Botswana, these nationals have no right to determine who governs the US, as they have no voting power there. Conversely, corrupt and abusive governments can violate the human rights of their nationals with impunity, as the latter have limited recourse to protection outside the nation-state. As already noted, Botswana has enjoyed an enviable record as Africa's shining model of liberal democracy, so that the extreme forms of social marginalization and human rights abuses that have characterized the rest of postcolonial Africa have been absent from this country's political and economic development.

However, Batswana women have, until recently, suffered discrimination on account of the territorial boundaries of this Republic. The most pronounced source of their discrimination was, as previously noted, the 1982 Citizenship Amendment Act, which denied women the right to pass their citizenship to their children if they were married to foreign men. This law was seen by its male architects as an enrichment of Tswana cultural values, which recognized the husband as the natural head of the household and guardian of his children. In the context of the modern nation-state of liberal values, however, where rights and freedoms are conferred on the individual, and where nationality forms the basic legal contract between the individual and the state, the restriction of the passage of citizenship rights to the male line for married couples has had far reaching consequences for women.

It meant, for instance, that as long as they had minor children who could not travel by themselves, women's own freedom of movement between their countries of birth and the rest of the world was limited because their children were foreigners, whose movements were tied to those of the father. Many Batswana women suffered considerably on account of the restrictions imposed by this law. The act not only restricted women's freedom of movement, but also impinged on a variety of other freedoms, including the freedom to choose marriage partners, to establish families, or to make decisions concerning the welfare of their children. Batswana women therefore had to balance the consequences of marrying foreign men against the enjoyment of fundamental freedoms which the constitution purported to protect and guarantee.

Despite evidence of the enormous difficulties arising from this law, there was considerable resistance to changing it. Many Batswana saw the demand for change as a violation of deeply held value systems and therefore as an infringement on their culture. To that end the Botswana government fought long and hard to retain this enactment, even when the High Court ruled it unconstitutional. This resistance served to underline the extent to which the notion of equality between the sexes was unacceptable, even for a government founded on liberal democratic principles. The private domain is still deemed to be the natural site for individual men to exercise the right to be sovereigns over the women and children they live with. The conventional wisdom is that the state should preserve the internal organization and activities of the household in a way that guarantees the right of men to arbitrary power.[10]

But the arbitrary conferment of husbands' power to rule in the private domain of the family has consequences for women's capacity to participate in the public domain of electoral processes, political office, and policy formulation. Invariably, women become the objects of policy formulation, rather than participants in that decision-making. Further, even men are restricted from making individual choices, since the state assumes them to have a homogenous value system. As for women, they cannot fully enjoy the right to freedom and equality as long as they are regarded as minors who should process their interests through the men who are sovereigns in their private lives.

Gender Equality Through Political Education and Mobilization Campaigns

The Botswana women's struggle for equality took off formally in the 1980s as a single issue campaign to reform the 1982 Citizenship Amendment Act. This built up into a number of workshops, seminars, conferences, and research activities aimed at enlightening women and other members of society on the provisions of the law, the status it accorded women, and its social and economic consequences. Three seminars in particular marked the highlights of this campaign for reform. These were the 1987, 1989, and 1990 Legal Rights or Women-in-the-Law seminars organized by the recently established Emang Basadi Women's Association in collaboration with the Women's Affairs Division of the Ministry of Home Affairs. The seminars were intended for legal awareness raising and the mobilization of women to support the campaign for reform.

Targeted for intensive scrutiny and impact assessment were the Citizenship Act, the Married Person's Act, the Affiliations Proceedings Act, and related maintenance laws. Further, the seminars identified as a key area of concern the growing incidence of violence against women and the need to research the problem and identify concrete strategies for dealing with it

Largely meant to be action oriented, the seminars identified and recommended several remedial strategies in terms of reform and improvements in the way the police and the courts handled women's cases. To maximize the impact of these workshops, educational material explaining women's legal status and its consequences were produced[11] in both English and Setswana, and widely distributed to nongovernmental organizations (NGOs), government departments, libraries, educational institutions, and various other forums. This legal rights campaign was followed by the emergence of new NGOs taking up and expanding on various aspects of legal and human rights issues. Examples were the Metlhaetsile Women's Information Center and the Ditshwanelo Human Rights Center (among those with a local origin), and the Botswana chapters of the Women in the Law in Southern Africa (WILSA) and the Women in Law and Development in Africa (WILDAF). Largely research and/or counseling oriented, these NGOs added impetus to the human rights discourse in Botswana.

The issues they raised, and their interventionist approach, also influenced the older women's NGOs and other development agencies. The gender variable increasingly became recognized as one of the factors that should be taken into account in research, development planning and practice, policy formulation, the world of work and labor movement, and various other areas of life (including educational programs and curricula). A growing list of recommendations for policy change began to emerge from the activities of these various organizations. But the appeals for reform largely gathered dust in terms of policy shift and government intervention. Another part of the campaign took the form of court action against the government by a Motswana woman seeking relief from the detrimental effects of the Citizenship Act. This court case added to the growing pressure on the government for concrete reform.

By the early 1990s, however, it had become clear that despite the many calls for reform and the court ruling against the Citizenship Act, the government was very reluctant to change in favor of extending equal rights to women. There was even a suggestion that the government might be considering a referendum to solicit people's views on whether the state should amend the constitution to enshrine discrimination against women (and thereby uphold Tswana values of the superiority of men), or reform the offending laws in line with the constitutional guarantees of equality and freedom from discrimination. It was in this climate that the Emang Basadi Women's Association turned from its legal education campaign to political education and mobilization as a strategy for bringing about gender equality. Thus was born Botswana's first attempt at broad based political education aimed at sensitizing the voting public on the power potentially conferred on them by the liberal democratic political system.

Born of necessity in the context of an overwhelmingly powerful state and a correspondingly weak civil society, Emang Basadi's political education strategy is instructive as an instrument for consolidating democracy. Initially targeted for the short term impact on the course of events leading to the 1994 general elections, this program aimed at both pressurizing political parties to take greater cognizance of women's right to representation and equality of access to power; and mobilizing the voting public as well as potential female candidates to take greater responsibility for changing society and political practice in Botswana. Emang Basadi used consultative workshops and .eminars to facilitate the identification of the sources of women's poor representation in policy making.

As well as encouraging strong networks and collaborative effort across various agents of change, these workshops helped to identify the following as the key problems which must inform intervention strategies: (1) that women failed to stand for public office due to cultural and other constraints; (2) that never having had exposure to campaigning and public office, most women lacked the experience, knowledge, and confidence to compete with men for public office; (3) that the mechanisms and procedures for selecting candidates to fight elections were biased in favor of men; (4) that women's concerns were not regarded as serious political issues by political parties; and (5) that people generally do not consider women as leadership material. The political education program was therefore targeted at the multiple audiences of potential female candidates, the political party structures, and the voting public. The strategy is examined in greater detail below.

The Political Education Strategy

In the first phase of this program, the Emang Basadi Women's Association produced a draft manifesto which set out women's concerns and challenged the political parties to address these. The manifesto had multiple purposes, including concrete documentation of evidence of women's disadvantages, which could be used by political candidates to articulate women's issues, by political parties as a basis for formulating their own political manifestos taking cognizance of women, and by everybody interested in making a positive impact on the quality of women's life. The manifesto covered eight critical areas in which women demanded redress in terms of equality. These were the issues of democracy and political participation, employment, business, agriculture, education and training, health, population, and law. The eighth area was the institutional and policy framework for ensuring that the other areas were adequately addressed. The manifesto noted that equalizing opportunities in these areas could not be achieved by NGOs alone, since they were not the chief architects of development policy and programs. It therefore recognized the need for the government's commitment and directed action.

This manifesto was thoroughly discussed by a range of stakeholders (e.g., women's NGOs, government departments, representatives of educational institutions, financial institutions, the labor movement, political parties, and research institutions). It was also formally adopted by this diverse forum as the "Manifesto of Botswana Women," thus broadening its ownership beyond Emang Basadi. This consultative method created a basis for alliance forming and cooperation in disseminating the information broadly within the country. It also nurtured awareness of a common destiny and purpose among women, which made it easier later to form a NGO coalition and to rationalize the distribution of labor among the various activities of the NGOs in a manner that enhanced their total impact, instead of negating efforts through competition.

As an instrument of political mobilization, the *Women's Manifesto* was the most critical because it concretized the issues in a way that made them accessible to a wide ranging audience. This manifesto is premised on the assumption that whatever differences women have in terms of class positions, education, ethnicity, religion, and other social and economic markers, there are certain things they all share as women, which can be addressed through common strategies and cooperation. The thrust of the strategy, therefore, was to emphasize the areas of commonality and silence the differences. In employment, for instance, the emphasis was on the fact that women generally have fewer opportunities than men in entering the job market, particularly the rural majority and the young and unskilled.

The manifesto highlights those aspects of the employment problem that affect the majority of women, particularly domestics, agricultural workers, service, and informal sector operators. However, it is silent on the peculiar problems that affect minority ethnic groups who, whatever else they may share with other disadvantaged groups, face problems that are directly related to their ethnicity and historically entrenched structural marginalization. Further, the manifesto does not give sufficient recognition of the structural problems that have made employment generation in agriculture and the informal sector difficult to realize, even for men. Thus, it represents a general call for a particular medicine to be extended to women, without interrogating its efficacy. In terms of identifying the broad issues that make women's access to employment opportunities less than equal to those for men, this document succinctly captures the problem. However, there is need to go beyond assuming that the world as it exists for men is the ideal that women should strive for.

This limitation of using the world of men as the yardstick for determining the development of women is consistent throughout the manifesto. In law, for instance, some of the main concerns are: the subordinate position women occupy; lack of recognition of women's inheritance rights; and discrimination with regards to tax. Also included are those laws which do not give women sufficient protection from men in terms of violence and lack of support for children. While the recognition of the need for reform in these areas is crucially important for addressing the most blatant discrimination and violations against women, the concerns do not go substantively deep enough to address the issues of male-female relations.

For instance, most Batswana women are not married or employed. What are the critical areas of law that affect their status besides those dealing with maintenance, tax, and violence? Do laws that apparently favor women, such as those that require only men to pay maintenance and only women to have access to the pensions of their deceased spouses, necessarily enhance women's status? What law reforms and practices would sufficiently address the position of ethnic minorities whose womenfolk have to bear the multiple brunt of marginalization as a group as well as women? As a document aimed at a broad-based appeal, the manifesto does capture the general areas of concern for the majority of women's organizations. It was significant to bring together a coalition of interests and support to form a basis for campaign and political mobilization. On this tangible basis, the political education program entered the phases of actual mobilization and training.

Two levels of training were done, namely, the training of community mobilizers and the training of political candidates. The training of community mobilizers was intended to produce a core of activists who would run voter education workshops within the constituencies, and thus raise awareness on the issues highlighted in the manifesto. The community mobilizers were trained to educate the voting public on the relationship between their vote and the policy and law making processes of government. More specifically, they were trained to sensitize the voters, who were predominately female, on the need to vote for women candidates to represent them in parliament and local government. The project targeted the placement of trained community mobilizers to cover two constituencies during this campaign, and in time for the 1994 elections.

This phase of the project proved somewhat ambitious, given the time factor and the late start of the campaign. For one thing, there was insufficient time to train the mobilizers where they could confidently run workshops and sell the message contained in the manifesto. Many of these activists were themselves still absorbing the issues raised and did not have sufficient time to understand and articulate them before they were called upon to educate others. They were required to master the general issues of women's marginalization as well as those relating to the need to vote for women. Although this effort failed to achieve its broad objective of covering all constituencies or reaching the voting majorities with the message to vote women into power, it served to illustrate that women could mobilize for change and that given their numerical majority, could effectively make demands which had to be taken seriously by those hoping to be conferred with the power to govern. Given the logistical problems of implementing this training program and the general weaknesses of the curriculum, it is clear that the community mobilizers were not prepared sufficiently enough to make a serious impact on the voting public. The lack of impact was partly demonstrated by the voting patterns of the electorate, which will be discussed later.

Candidacy training workshops were even less systematic and directed. This training was meant to arm potential women candidates with campaign management and related skills, and thus help them sell themselves more effectively. Various other crucially needed skills, like fundraising, assertiveness training, debating, issue identification, and research and information skills, were not included in the workshops to any significant degree. The manifesto was expected to give them the substance of the issues on which they could campaign. So, as with the community mobilizers training, this aspect of the program fell victim to time constraints and a limited curriculum.

The manifesto, however, succeeded in demonstrating that women can be trained to take up their rightful positions as leaders. It also provided space for the limited number of female political candidates to realize that as women from different political parties and ideological persuasions, they shared similar problems, including lack of experience, training, support, and opportunities. The experience sensitized them to the fact that they were not alone and had a potential pool of support from women's organizations and other constituencies. This training created space for women to learn, thus demonstrating the fact that participating in the democratic process is itself a learning experience, rather than simply a terminal goal.

In the third phase, the political education project focused on swaying public opinion and voting patterns in favor of putting more women in power. This involved voter education campaigns in the various constituencies, using as content the issues raised in the manifesto. Targeted at the voting public, the campaign used workshops and seminars to reach the communities and make people aware that their voting had a direct relationship to the laws, policies, and programs formulated by elected representatives. The campaigns also aimed to raise public awareness that votes could yield policies, laws, and development programs that reflected their interests. Not only was this intended to teach voters that they could change their destinies by influencing the course of events, but it was also meant to reinforce their right and obligation to demand accountability on the part of those they elect into power. To that end, they could also question those seeking their votes to indicate what they would do to improve the status of women. The manifesto thus served as a source of information for the women to raise issues of concern to them at election rallies.

This political education program was unprecedented in the annals of Botswana's history. For the first time, ordinary people were setting the terms of political discourse in the run-up to the general elections. They were forcing political parties to address issues that concerned them as voters, instead of listening to the usual hyperbole and political posturing of the contending parties. Although not sufficiently planned and executed, this strategy made politicians aware of the extent to which women could mobilize and use their numerical majority to change the course of events. The successful court case against the Citizenship Act both indicated the moral and legal strength of the women's campaign for equality, and enhanced their authority in seeking redress. Together with the mass based political education campaign, this strategy convinced observers and politicians alike that women's concerns could no longer be ignored.

Also, the politicians could no longer afford to dismiss women activists as misguided, foreign educated minorities, who were out of touch with the predominant value systems of Tswana culture and practice. Consequently, there was a greater attempt among the political parties to seek women candidates for political office. For the first time in Botswana's history, four women found themselves in parliament, raising the ceiling from the previous limit of two. The party political manifestoes also reflected a concession to women by including a commitment to addressing their concerns. At the local government level, similar efforts were made to increase female representation. A quota system was used to reach this goal, where the general elections had failed to produce the desired results.

Emang Basadi is poised to take its political education program to the 1999 general elections by preparing early and drawing on the lessons of the campaign in the run-up to the 1994 elections.[12] Its five year strategic plan reflects the concerns of the earlier program of raising the number of elected women representatives, and ensuring that they are sensitive to the concerns of the female electorate. This implies articulating these concerns during the electoral campaign, and doing something to address them after the election. The program will therefore continue to emphasize both practical skill training, issue raising, and sensitization. It will also target the voting public to encourage greater acceptance of female leaders.

Achievements and Limitations

Emang Basadi's political education program must be examined within the broader context of the women's movement in Botswana. The activities of this program go far beyond a single issue, to cover the whole spectrum of women's subordinate position in Botswana society and the need for change. The political education strategy has been in place for too short a time to have made a measurable impact on people's attitudes and behavior — particularly with regards to voting and perceptions of women as voters. As a contribution to the women's struggle for equality, it has added a dimension that has considerably altered the political scene in Botswana from one involving only asking for concessions from those in power, to one where women are demanding concessions as a condition for putting political parties in power.

So far, women voters have been putting their support solidly behind the ruling Botswana Democratic Party (BDP). Since the female electorate accounts for 58 percent of those who normally cast their vote, their votes are decisive in determining who governs Botswana. In the 1994 elections, for instance, the swing of votes to the opposition Botswana National Front (BNF) was overwhelmingly due to the support of the young, male electorate below the age of 35 years.[13] For this trend to be substantial enough to effect a change of government in 1999, the opposition BNF will have to make a serious effort to win the women's vote. Conversely, the BDP will have to fight very hard to maintain the strong female support it has had so far in the face of an increasingly sophisticated voting public, and greater demands for concessions from the women's lobby.

The political education project has set a precedent in political practice in Botswana, with voters determining the issues for debate at political rallies. However, while there are no doubts that the program has been widely supported by NGOs and other groups, its impact will be determined by the extent to which people will vote on the basis of issues. Indications from the 1994 elections suggest that generally Batswana voters do not consider issues,[14] and that the majority may not even know the difference between the two major parties.[15] Z. Maundeni's analysis of the 1994 elections further suggests that even among those who swung their vote to the BNF in 1994, it may not have been so much on the basis of the issues as out of disillusionment with the conduct of the ruling party leaders, who had been involved in corruption scandals. The women's political education program has therefore had the twin problem of making voters consider issues when voting, and raising issues with political candidates.

Women activists can raise issues through lobbying and using the manifesto. Indeed, part of Emang Basadi's 1996-1999 Political Education Strategy is to train female political candidates to articulate gender issues in their parties, as well as in office as parliamentarians and councilors. To that end, Emang Basadi has initiated a multiparty political caucus among female parliamentarians and councilors, which will enhance the impact of the small female representation in government. But to get the voters to consider issues when voting requires greater outreach to, and attitudinal change among, the majority of voters, rather than party functionaries. The curriculum content of the voter education program will be critically important in determining the extent to which the message of change will reach voters. As already noted with regard to the 1994 campaign, this message was mainly concerned with the contents of the *Women's Manifesto*. It did not sufficiently address the question of attitudinal change and more substantial issues regarding the responsibility of voters. For instance, issues of democracy were not dealt with substantively, even though they form the basis, core, and context of women's equality and political participation.

The program has been too narrowly focused on women's issues, and has not linked these to the broader issue of democracy, its processes, problems, institutions, methods, and significance for political life and development in Botswana. For, to have a long-term impact on people's attitudes and behavior, it is necessary to target both formal and informal educational institutions, including literacy programs. The program should also target constituencies on a more informed basis regarding the voting behavior of different categories of the electorate. In the run-up to the 1994 elections, there was little available data on the voting patterns of men and women, or the basis of their voting decisions.

Since then, the University of Botswana's Democracy Research Project has been yielding some baseline data, which could inform Emang Basadi's political education strategy.

This would create scope to both strategize on activity, and to put greater pressure on political parties to make more concrete and substantive concessions to the women's lobby. For instance, the fact that the majority of women vote BDP should be a basis for negotiating greater concessions from the BNF as a major contender for power in 1999. What should they do to win women's confidence? Will the promise of more seats for women, which is the only quantitative demand the *Women's Manifesto* has made, be enough to swing the women's vote? Women's voting power can also be used to negotiate with the BDP for greater concessions. Can they be certain of the women's vote in the changing climate toward issues as a basis for conferment of power? What concessions should they give to retain women's confidence? Emang Basadi's political education program has the potential to make politics interesting and meaningful for those seeking change in Botswana.

To make greater impact, Emang Basadi needs to develop various aspects of its political education program more fully. There is need, for instance, for the program to identify more clearly (1) the target groups that must be reached; (2) the appropriate methods for reaching them; (3) the message or content of its educational and training program; (4) a more systematic capacity both to carry out research or collect data; and (5) the methods for monitoring the programs on a continuous basis. The limitations of resources will also require that greater effort be made toward identifying collaborative partners who can assist with aspects of the political strategy, since it is very broad and unlikely to be adequately done by a single NGO.

What Lessons for Democracy? The Who, What, and Where of Democratic Practice

The activities that make up the campaigns of the women's movement for greater equality have helped to broaden the scope of democratic practice and political life. In the first place, the struggle has highlighted the fact that the subordination of women under male hegemony in the family has consequences for women's rights to equal representation and participation in political processes and other public areas. By so doing, it has helped to extend the definition and boundaries of democracy. As noted earlier, the history of democracy has been one of boundary-setting and an exclusionary and hierarchical distribution of power. What the women's movement has done in Botswana is demonstrate that until democratic practice is extended into family relations and laws governing male-female relations, women will be effectively excluded from participating in the democratic process beyond and above the family. In other words, limiting democracy to the public arena also limits women's access to democracy because they are conventionally restricted to the family as their natural sphere of operation. This has the effect of silencing their voices and experience, as well as the issues that concern them most.

To make democracy more meaningful for women requires the degendering of the division of life between the public and private spheres and the removal of laws and practices that maintain arbitrary conferment of power on men. It also needs the recognition of women's issues and concerns and their processing as political issues that concern at least half the population of the world. On account of the activities of the women's lobby, Botswana has not only begun to recognize the need to have greater female representation in government, but has also actively supported an increase in seats allocated to women since the 1994 election. At the parliamentary level, though the increase from two to four is significant in relation to the history of the preceding five elections, it is still only a third of the minimum recommended by the International Parliamentary Union, of which Botswana is a member. There is, therefore, need to raise women's representation to at least twelve members by the 1999 elections. At the local government level, women's representation still only stands at 8 percent of the seats nation-wide. If it is intended to meet the recommendations of the 1995 World Conference on Women and other international bodies in which Botswana is a member, this country should be aiming to ensure that by the next elections, at least another 120 women are brought into power. Similarly, the captains of industry in Botswana should be compelled to ensure that they increase the representation of women as managers of the Botswana economy to at least 30 percent by the end of the century.

The government has finally conceded to women's demands by promising and taking steps to ensure that all the laws that discriminate on the basis of sex are removed. This, coming after a decade of lobbying and appeal, has helped strengthen Botswana's standing as a liberal democracy. It also serves to demonstrate how this political system can be sensitized to the concerns and interests of voters when the people wake up to exercise their political right as the primary sovereign. Sadly, this is not something that the majority of people in Africa enjoy since their legitimating powers were eroded with the ascendancy of military rule and one-party dictatorships in the very first decade of independence in the 1960s and 1970s.

The Role of Civil Society and the State in Enhancing Democracy

In the context of Botswana's liberal democracy, the women's equality campaign has also shed some light onto the issue of public education and political change. Because multiparty politics is often assumed capable of generating political education through competitive rallies of parties seeking the mandate to rule, there has been a serious gap in the education of the ordinary voter in relation to understanding the new political systems inherited with the demise of colonial rule. In fact, it can be argued that throughout the African continent, those who came to power by way of elections at the end of colonial rule, assumed that the substantial participation of nationals in the electoral process had established an adequate foundation for the new republics. Such mass mobilization as happened was thus merely aimed at furthering the political interests of the contenders for power, rather than building a foundation for the enhancement and maintenance of popular legitimation of power, and thus a basis for competition for the authority to rule.

The lack of mass education led to political degeneration in confrontational party politics, and a situation where the nationals had not yet been welded into nations. Thus, those who found that their hold on power could not be extended by popular mandate, resorted to dictatorship, gross violations of fundamental human rights, and systematic erosion of any and all potential opposition. With Africa now returning to popular legitimation of power, it is necessary to examine the role that education can play in building democracy on a firmer foundation. The experience of Botswana sheds considerable light on these issues because unlike other African states, it has maintained electoral processing of power, the rule of law, multiparty competition for power, and various other structures and procedures associated with democratic governance. Yet this country, because of the neglect of political education for the voting public, has seen the state grow to overwhelming proportions in relation to civil society and its potential power to hold government to account and make significant impact on public decision-making. As a result, Botswana's democracy has been stronger in form that in practice. State power has been greatly consolidated by the fact that the government has successfully managed economic development and ensured that the benefits are distributed in a way that the majority feel they have had a share, inspite of growing income disparities.

When the women of Botswana changed their method of struggle from mere lobbying to political empowerment of the voting public through political education campaigns, they became aware of the need for more informed intervention on the part of the electorate. Until then, the voters had often been railroaded into accepting government policies, even where there were indications of considerable opposition. Such opposition did not entail systematic mobilization of support, and was usually only reflected at meetings called by the government to inform the public. Outside labor union activities, mobilized opposition was seen for the first time in relation to the Southern Okavango Integrated Water Development Project (SOIWDP), when the government sought to dredge the southern reaches of the Okavango river into the world famous Delta. The policy was reversed because local opposition sought international support from bodies like Green Peace.

In the case of the women's political education campaign, however, the threat of women voters actually ushering in a change of government was serious enough to force concessions. This has raised the issue of who really should be responsible for political education of the public? The government of the day, encumbered by the fact that its hold on power relies on being seen as having better candidates than its opponents, and that its intervention may be seen by the opposition as abuse of power through excessive propaganda, is restricted in undertaking comprehensive mass education outside the limits of basic voter education. While a small NGO has taken the lead in initiating mass education, it is clear that this NGO cannot adequately undertake this enormous task on its own — even with the cooperation of other NGOs. The resources required to reach the whole voting public on a sustained basis are considerable.

If the question of voter education is placed within the wider context of the African continent, it raises issues about the role, for instance, of African universities in public education and the consolidation of democracy. Sadly, these leading institutions of higher learning have never played any significant role in the development of democracy outside their walls. Restricting their mandate narrowly to human resources development, mostly for the state sector, these institutions have failed to play a more active role in extending learning in one of the most crucial parts of education and political development — the empowerment of the voting masses. The Botswana women's struggle has shown that it is necessary to educate the public to ensure the development of democracy and just rule. Institutions of higher learning should similarly assume greater responsibility in this development.

Notes

[1] A. Phillips, *Engendering Democracy* (Cambridge: Polity Press, 1991).

[2] It also denied certain ethnic minorities, such as Basarwa (Bushmen), civil and political rights and freedoms. See O. Selowane, "Ethnicity, Development and the Problems of

Social Integration in Botswana: The Case of Basarwa (UNESCO, forthcoming); and R.B. Hitchcock and J.J. Holm, "Bureaucratic Domination of Hunter Gatherer Societies: A Study of the San of Botswana," *Change and Development,* Vol. 24, 1993, pp. 305-338.

[3] L. Letsie (*ed.*), *A Report of the Proceedings of the Women, Law and Development Seminar held in Francistown on June 28-30,1990* (Gaborone: Emang Basadi Women's Association, 1990), p. 89.

[4] Selolwane.

[5] G. Somolekae, "Do Batswana Think and Act as Democrats?" in J. Holm and P. Molutsi (*eds.*), *Democracy in Botswana* (Gaborone: Macmillan Botswana, 1989).

[6] The exception has been with respect to the hunter-gathering ethnic minorities who have suffered political, economic, and social marginalization from colonial times throughout the post-independence period. See A. Mogwe, *Who Was (T) Here First?* (Gaborone: Botswana Christian Council, 1992).

[7] The 1991 Census indicates that the incidence of marriage is highest among the older people (80%+ among those over 55), but declines quite substantially among the younger groups (less than 50% for those in their late twenties to early thirties).

[8] Letsie.

[9] J. Dunn, *Democracy: The Unfinished Journey, 508 BC to AD 1993* (Oxford: Oxford University Press, 1992); and Phillips.

[10] The conceptualization of what is private and what is public has itself evolved and changed, with activities such as production gradually becoming part of the public domain as that activity has become more socializ.d. See Phillips.

[11] These include A. Molokomme, *The Women's Guide to Law* (Gaborone: Women's Affairs Division, Ministry of Labor and Home Affairs, 1985); and Molokomme, *His, Mine or Ours? The Property Rights of Women Married Under Botswana Law* (Gaborone: Women's Affairs Division, Ministry of Labor and Home Affairs, 1985).

[12] Emang Basadi, *Strategic Plan: 1996-2000* (Gaborone: Emang Basadi, 1996).

[13] Z. Maundeni, "Opinion Polls and Electoral Reform: A Report of the Democracy Research Project," Paper presented at the Democracy Research Project Workshop, Gaborone, 1995.

[14] *Ibid.*

[15] Somolekae.

3

Civil Society at Bay in Uganda

Akiiki B. Mujaju

Crucial to any analysis of civil society is a working definition of what it is. For purposes of this study, civil society is defined as the way society is organized outside of the state.[1] When John Locke spoke of the state as a necessary evil, whose powers must be clearly demarcated so that it does not do those things which individuals can do for themselves, he was indirectly speaking of civil society. Of course, at the time, the idea of individuals constituting themselves into groups and associations had not yet arisen, but Locke was clearly talking of protecting individuals against the encroachments of the necessary evil. As society developed and the power of the state increased, Lockean individualism had to be moderated by the acceptance and pursuit of groups as countervailing forces against the state. Interest groups are crucial in our conception of civil society.

For some, political parties are not usually regarded as being part of civil society. However, it is difficult to imagine a force more necessary for the protection of the people against the state. Reference here is being made to multiparty systems, not one-party systems where the political party is an arm of the state. In a society where multiparty systems exist, political parties are intervening organizations which lie between the state and the conventional civil society.

Political parties are important for purposes of aggregating the interests of private associations. As prospectively strong organizations, while one may be controlling the state, others can keep a check on the government of the day. Consequently, political parties must belong to civil society. They should not be relegated to a neutral status, lying between the state and civil society.

The fortunes of civil society vary in accordance with the esteem with which the state is held. In the case of Africa, independence arrived at a time when the state appeared to be quite popular. The New Deal in the United States created a reluctant acceptance of the state as a provider of services. The state became involved in, for example, improving the living conditions of its citizens, providing social security, and later, protecting civil rights. The provision of social and economic services by the state was contrary to Locke's idea of a limited government. In the case of Britain, the formation of the Labour Party at the turn of the century and the work of the Fabian Socialists, forecast a time when the state would be a compassionate institution. Many of the Fabians were lecturers and professors in strategic institutions of higher learning, which were attended by Third World students like Jawaharlal Nehru.[2]

In 1946, after war had ruined the economy of Britain, the Labour Party came to power and introduced the welfare state. The state thus became a friend of the people. The changing role of the state in both Britain and the United States did not necessarily mean, however, that civil society was undermined.

In addition to the above, a new power emerged during World War II, offering a new model for development. The Soviet Union, as it was called, had a charismatic appeal to many Third World politicians. It was an underdeveloped country at the time of the Bolshevik Revolution in 1917. However, following the Revolution, a one-party dictatorship was established, which presided over the most massive industrialization drive ever known in history. By 1947, the Soviet Union had become a strong military and economic power. Third World leaders were impressed by its record, and many of them thought they could emulate the one-party system idea and a planned program of economic development.[3] The details of civil society, in the process, were lost. When many Third World nationalist leaders came to power, the protection of the individual against the excesses of the state received inadequate attention, and the very idea of a civil society was negated.

Within the academia in the 1950s, African nationalists were criticized for not practicing democracy. Political scientists like David Apter, Rupert Emerson and others challenged them.[4] However, during the 1960s and 1970s, these same political scientists swung to the other side and developed sympathy for African leaders. They became more concerned with stability, and, in the process, civil society suffered.[5]

The major focus of this study is on civil society in Uganda since 1986, when the National Resistance Movement (NRM) came to power. Although the NRM promised to democratize Uganda and indicated considerable warmth for the ideals of civil society,[6] the record on the ground has been mixed, and in some cases the government has been out-right hostile to civil society. In order to understand the current attitude toward civil society, it is necessary for the latter's role in Uganda since independence to be placed in historical perspective.

Civil Society in Uganda: The Obote and Amin Regimes

Uganda became independent in 1962 under the government of the Uganda People's Congress (UPC), which had formed a coalition government with the conservative and monarchist party, Kabaka Yekka (KY). The leaders of the UPC were molded in the image of such eminent nationalists as Nehru of India and Kwame Nkrumah of Ghana. The party, particularly its president, Milton Obote, was an ardent admirer of both these two men. Obote wished to emphasize economic planning and establish a one-party system. He did establish a one-party system in 1969, but his government was toppled in early 1971.

There were constraints, however, to the extent to which Obote could implement socialism and a one-party system, since he was sharing power with the KY, which was not supportive of such ideas. However, when it came to the issue of the economy, all political forces in the country agreed that the state had to take a keen interest. There was no intense debate calling for the protection of civil society from the state. Civil society was underdeveloped. For example, there were no independent peasant associations and the cooperative movement of agricultural producers was in its infancy. In any case, with respect to the latter, ethnicity frequently took the upper hand instead of the real interests of the cooperators. This frequently resulted in the movement being censured by public authorities. Nonetheless, civil society did have a voice in Uganda between 1962 and 1979 as evidenced by the activities of cooperatives, trade unions, academics, youth, and women.

Following independence, there were feeble voices calling the state to order, particularly for undermining the multiparty system and the cooperative movement. However, there was no sustained onslaught against the predominance of the state, and from 1967 onwards, there was systematic evidence of the state undermining even the small civil society groups that existed.

In the name of cooperative democracy and efficiency, the state started appointing secretary/managers of cooperative unions on the ground that those appointed by the unions tended to sometimes be corrupt, and frequently stole large sums of money meant to help the purchase of farmers' commodities for export. The Commissioner of Cooperatives subsequently became a big force in cooperative unions, and in 1968, the government established a committee to investigate the abuses by the management committees of the cooperative unions. The committee was under the leadership of S. Arain, a member of Parliament. It identified extensive evidence of abuse by the management committees.[7]

The government responded by reshuffling the committees and appointing its own managers, who were bureaucrats and tended to be equally corrupt. There was no evidence of a systematic educational campaign organized by the state to help the unions operate on the basis of sound cooperative principles, such as providing service to small farmers and implementing democracy. Instead of helping the unions, the state took advantage of the ignorance of the cooperators by expanding its bureaucracy. In addition, the people elected to management committees were frequently local political elites and UPC members who, because of their pre-eminence in the local communities, made it difficult for the unions to change. The small farmer who, in Uganda, is the back-bone of the agricultural industry, remained impoverished, while the elites prospered.

During this early period in the development of civil society, the trade union movement was also in its rudimentary stages, and the working class was only a small fraction of the population. In fact, by 1960, there were only 26,000 trade union members out of a formal working population of 254,000.[8] In any case, the poverty of the trade unions resulted in them being controlled by the International Confederation of Free Trade Unions (ICFTU) based in Europe. The latter was a Western-oriented trade union movement in a world divided between the capitalist West and the communist East. This alliance with the ICFTU was censured by the UPC.

With respect to trade union organizations, confusion reigned. There was the Uganda Trade Union Congress (UTUC) led by H. Luande who, in 1961, became an UPC Member of Parliament. The UTUC was also affiliated with the ICFTU. In turn, the ICFTU was arrayed against the Accra-based All Africa Trade Union Federation (AATUF), which was alleged to harbor communist designs under the guise of African unity. The Uganda Government was weary of the ICFTU Western connection and, like Nkrumah of Ghana, was keen to affiliate the UTUC to the AATUF.

The UTUC steadfastly resisted these efforts, and stuck to the European body. Money was involved in this controversy. The Europe-based trade unions led by the ICFTU during this cold war period, offered substantial economic incentives for the UTUC to reject the intervention of the state and the Ghana-based AATUF, which was not as rich as the European confederation, although it too offered substantial financial incentives. In response, the Uganda Government sponsored its own trade union, the Federation of Uganda Trade Unions (FUTU), which was supposed to eclipse the UTUC and was affiliated to the Ghana-based group. In short, instead of encouraging the UTUC to develop, the government sought to undermine not only the UTUC, but the entire labor movement, which experienced considerable confusion and internal bickering.[9]

In 1968, the government set up a one-man commission of inquiry on the labor movement, with G. L. Binaisa, a former attorney general in Obote's government. On the basis of his observations and recommendations, the government forcibly, by legal designs, abolished both UTUC and FUTU and established a single trade union called the Uganda Labour Congress (ULC). Established through an Act of Parliament, the ULC became a tool of the state which, like trade unions in communist countries, had a lengthy negotiating machinery before a strike could be declared, if at all.

The Ugandan government had, over the years, become weary of strikes. According to the nationalists, strikes were relevant before independence. After independence, however, they claimed that the economy belonged to the people and, therefore, trade unions had little legitimacy for planning strikes.[10] They further argued that strikes were inflicting hardship on people and were ruinous to the national economy. Legal restrictions were therefore imposed on the government-created ULC. It is obvious that a trade union established and controlled by the state is not consistent with the idea of civil society. Therefore, the Obote government undermined the efficacy of civil society. It is only free trade unions that can help in constraining the state, not the other way round.

The situation did not change during the Idi Amin era. There was only a change in the name of the government-sponsored trade union. In 1978, the Amin regime created the National Organization of Trade Unions (NOTU) which, like its predecessor, was controlled by the state, with rigid restrictions on its right to strike. Even when liberation came in 1979 and another UPC government came back to power in 1980, there was no review of the decree which set up NOTU. UPC's most important strategy of controlling the unions and the trade union movement was to set up UPC workers' councils at the factory level. These were literally branches of the UPC. Civil society continued to be on trial.

Civil society at the university level commenced at Makerere University with the University Act of 1970. This Act provided for the establishment of a staff association, with representation on the University Council and the University Senate. Provision was also made for a student association with representation on the University Council. In 1975, the University Act was amended, and provision for a staff association eliminated. Between 1979 and 1985, strenuous efforts were made to reinstate the staff association into the Act. Such efforts were never successful.[11] The staff, therefore, found it necessary to operate a staff association called Makerere Academic Staff Association (MUASA) on the basis of an agreement with the university and the government. In the case of the students, the student association was not deleted from the Act because there was no longer a Makerere students' government in 1975. The Amin regime had harassed its leader, Olara Otunnu, and had forced him to flee the country in the early 1970s. The students refused to elect another leader who, they feared, would be equally harassed or even killed. So, for much of the Amin era, Makerere had no staff association and no student government. Other associations in the country had been muzzled and political parties were, of course, illegal organizations, since political activities as a whole were banned.

With respect to the youth movement, the government, in 1964, established the National Union of Youth Organizations (NUYO) as an umbrella group for all organizations in the country. The NUYO was turned into a government department, with strong ministerial control. Youth officers were appointed to the civil service in order to supervise the activities of the youth.

NUYO was created as a result of the growing rift between the UPC and its youth branch, known as the UPC Youth League. The two disagreed on a number of issues, such as the role of the party in society, definitions of socialism, and the neglect of the party by the older leaders who had assumed state duties at independence. The party considered the youth league a nuisance and argued that it was being manipulated by disgruntled politicians. They wanted to silence it by bringing it under the control of NUYO.[12]

The government policy was unpopular among the youth. The UPC Youth League defied NUYO and was forced underground. Groups such as the opposition youth and Christian youth groups were also not inclined to belong to NUYO. NUYO was kept afloat by the resources of the state. Otherwise, it had little legitimacy. There was also the National Union of Students in Uganda (NUSU), a privately organized body. In fact, it was sponsored by the Makerere Students Guild in 1963, and was financed by an international student organization based in Leiden, Holland. However, between 1968 and 1971, the state had penetrated NUSU and turned it into an instrument of the government. NUSU was in hibernation between 1972 and 1980, since it would not coexist with the Amin regime. It had to be revived in 1980. Afterwards, it was claimed openly that NUSU was an organ of the UPC.[13]

Women in Uganda remained unorganized until 1978, when the Amin regime established the Uganda Council of Women (UCW) in response to recommendations of the United Nations. This was, for all practical purposes, a parastatal organization. The Council was rigidly controlled by the Amin regime and no women's organization was allowed to exist outside its framework.

Looking at the fortunes of civil society during both the civilian and military regimes before the NRM, it can be concluded that the treatment of civil society by Amin's regime was no different from that of the civilian administration. Both indicated considerable insensitivity to the need to protect civil society where it existed, and to foster it where it did not. There was a difference in degree of damage inflicted on society, but not in kind.

Civil Society in the NRM Period (1986-1994)

It is well known that the global environment for domestic politics has radically changed. Such changes resulted in, for example, the disintegration of notorious dictatorships such as Amin, Jean-Bedel Bokassa of the Central African Republic, Mengistu Haile-Mariam of Ethiopia, and Hastings Banda of Malawi. A world-wide movement for pluralism and accountability was triggered off by the collapse of the Soviet Union in 1991. This has been followed by corresponding changes in, for example, Angola and Mozambique. The gist of political debate in domestic politics is to make the state withdraw from active and comprehensive intervention so that political pluralism and private enterprise can take root. The failures of the African state have resulted in an increase in the establishment of civil associations. The NRM, under the leadership of Yoweri Museveni, can be placed within the context of these changes, including the reality that the economic structures of many Third World countries had to be rescued by Western donor agencies. Such agencies began to insist that Third World governments observe democratic rules, be accountable, and banish corruption as a condition for receiving external assistance.

The NRM knew that even if it did not like it, the government would have to sing the song of the International Monetary Fund (IMF) and World Bank in order to have access to funds needed to help Uganda deal with its economic quagmire. To this end, the NRM produced a Ten-Point Program which was, and allegedly continues to be, its ideological blueprint. Key among its main points is the desire to give to Ugandans popular democracy, parliamentary democracy, and a reasonable standard of living. The most important point to note is that the issue of popular democracy was a device for fighting pre-existing political parties, which Museveni wanted to eliminate, as was done in Libya.

Museveni also talked about his desire to stamp out corruption. In addition, he talked of free and fair elections, which, he claimed, had eluded Uganda. The pursuance of such elections, according to Museveni, had forced him to go to the bush and wage a liberation war. He had a quarrel with Uganda's political parties, he said, because they were secretarian and compromised the unity of the people. By 1988, Museveni had said and written enough to indicate his commitment to democracy, as well as his readiness to do something about it.

Under Museveni's leadership, the National Resistance Council (NRC), which serves as the country's parliament, passed a 1987 statute setting up people's committees from the grassroots to the national level. These committees were established at the village, parish, sub-county, county, and district levels.[14] The NRM endowed these committees with powers to deal with local matters and gave them judicial functions to settle family, land, and other minor disputes. There is no doubt that people at these levels feel more efficacious. In 1989, Museveni organized elections of the NRCs through the framework of these committees.[15]

Museveni calls this the process of empowering people. He has also talked of empowering women. At every level of the Resistance Councils (RCs) system, there is a secretary for women who is supposed to take care of women's interests by organizing sensitization programs and civic seminars. In addition, women are now represented on the NRC through elections of district women representatives. They are chosen by electoral colleges composed of members of the District Resistance Councils. Later, women's councils were established, following the model of the RCs system. These are organized at village, parish, subcounty, county, and district levels using the system of indirect elections from the parish level. The women's councils reach the national level where a National Women's Council, composed of representatives of the District Women's Councils, is established. In addition, the National Women's Council elects an executive committee, on which sit one of the two representatives of nongovernmental organizations (NGOs) who sit on the District Women's Council. This is an elaborate arrangement, which is enshrined in an Act of the NRC and was in 1994 used to elect the district women's representatives to the Constituent Assembly (CA) responsible for the new constitution.

In addition, in 1993, a women's umbrella organization for all women NGOs was created. This is supposed to be an independent body where the Ministry of Women in Development performs a facilitating role. The body is known as the National Association of Women's Organizations in Uganda (NAWOU). As of now, there are 14 NGOs which are affiliated to it. These include the Uganda Federation of Women Lawyers, the Uganda Association of University Women, Action For Development, and Uganda Media Women's Association.

As already indicated, a Ministry of Gender and Community Development was created to play the role of a catalyst. Its minister, Specioza Kazibwe, was appointed vice president of the country. There is a feeling that some accomplishments have been attained in the area of empowering women.

With respect to youth, in 1988, the NRM Secretariat, the political, ideological, and mobilizational wing of the NRM party (although at the same time it was a department of government, complete with a permanent secretary), sponsored a student movement.

In conjunction with the relevant ministry, they convened a meeting which established the Uganda National Students Association (UNSA). Created in the mold of NUSU, UNSA may be present in the schools. However, nationally, it has not yet left a mark and is frequently overshadowed by the Makerere Students Guild.

In 1994, the government established Youth Councils, which are a replica of the RCs. Like the RCs, the Youth Councils are organs of the state. Some of their objectives are to: (1) inspire and promote in youth a spirit of unity and national consciousness; (2) provide a unified and integrated system through which the youth may communicate and coordinate their ideas and activities; and (3) initiate and encourage the formation of youth organizations and facilitate communication among them.[16]

The councils, which are financed by the government, are integrated into the government accounting system and are to be audited by the auditor general. The Secretary General of the National Youth Council is appointed by the minister in charge of youth, and his/her terms of employment are a subject of consultation between the ministers in charge of both Youth Affairs and Finance. The minister in charge of youth has other substantive powers, all of which clearly indicate that the youth councils are not much different from the NUYO. The minister also has powers to amend the statute of April 30, 1993, which set up these councils. Such amendments can be done by statutory instrument.

In addition to the above, the government wants to establish the Uganda National Association of Youth Organizations (UNAYO). At the time of writing, the Ministry of Gender and Community Development, which is the ministry in charge of youth, is hosting and coordinating meetings of representatives of NGOs dealing with youth. The intention is to create an umbrella group for all NGOs for young people. The draft constitution describes the goal of the proposed organization as to strengthen the capacity of its members involved in community-based action to help the vulnerable against such problems as AIDS and other diseases, poverty, moral degeneration, and natural disasters.[17]

Among the organizations taking an active part in the meetings designed to establish UNAYO is the NRM Secretariat. It appears that the NRM, which has a youth department, deems itself to be a youth NGO, or at least considers the formation of this organization to be of such importance that it should be involved. UNAYO is supposed to be an independent youth organization. However, the active presence of the Ministry of Gender and Community Development and the government's Secretariat in the founding of this body, makes clear the government's continuing interest and control. Moreover, the Annual Delegates Conference membership for UNAYO shows that both the National Youth Council and the relevant ministry will be represented at this conference, albeit in a non-voting capacity. And there is provision for the Ugandan government to give assistance in the form of grants or loans. On the positive side, the government gave youth four representatives to the Constituent Assembly (CA) and the NRC.

In the area of the trade union movement, the NRM has done some commendable things. The trade union movement has been expanded with the passing of a law making it possible for public servants to join or form trade unions. Previously, only group employees enjoyed the right to belong to a trade union. According to the new law, officers below the rank of U2 are granted this right. This means that permanent secretaries, heads of departments, personnel officers, head teachers of schools, as well as officers of the Bank of Uganda below the rank of the governor, secretary, directors of divisions, and heads of departments, cannot belong to unions.

Civil servants who can join unions bring considerable expertise and experience to the trade union movement. It also endows the movement with considerable leadership potential. The trade union leadership has long been inadequate to the task at hand. It can now recruit new leadership from public servants. The only problem may be that, though highly educated, the new cadres have little experience in trade unionism. As a result of the new changes, three trade unions have been formed and registered. They include the Uganda Public Employees Union, the Uganda Medical Workers Union, and the Uganda Civil Servants Union. The only problem with these new unions is that they are so close to the government that they could become conduits for the state.

In addition to the above, the NRM has provided for the representation of two workers in the NRC, as well as in the CA. This is an important addition to the rights of the trade union movement.[18] It allows workers to be present at centers of decision-making where their input is critically needed. It is an improvement over the 1960s, when Luande, the former President of the UTUC, used to fight lonely battles in the National Assembly. This fact, plus the expansion of the movement which brings in new cadres, should combine to give the movement articulate and influential leadership.

Even though this view of events taking place in the trade union movement is somewhat positive, the overall position of civil society in Uganda is not. With respect to students and youth, for example, the UNSA is not an authentic student organization since it was initiated with the active involvement of the NRM Secretariat. The NRM is fond of complaining about the manipulation of students, and youth in general, by past regimes without realizing that it is doing exactly the same thing. The umbrella youth organization, which the government is in the process of establishing, is the work of the Ministry of Gender and Community Development, as well as the NRM Secretariat, which has now deemed itself a youth movement. Neither in its conception nor in the steps of its initiation, is UNAYO any different from NUYO, set up by Obote's government in 1964. In UNAYO, the NUSU has resurfaced under a new guise.[19]

In the case of women, the state is also actively involved. The matter of the relationship between women's organizations and the state has caused concern. The UCW, established by the Amin regime, was clearly a state organ. Women's groups were unhappy about this and wanted to be independent of the state, although there were some women, particularly in the rural areas, who felt that they needed the assistance of the state.[20]

The women's councils, like the youth, are clearly in the orbit of the state. Although NAWOU, which replaced the UCW, appears to be more independent of the government, in practice, there is collaboration between it, the women's councils, the Commission of Women in the Ministry of Gender and Community Development, and the Women's desk in the NRM Secretariat. Given the fact that NAWOU is in existence, it is difficult to understand why the women's councils, instead of NAWOU, elected representatives to the CA. If the government was serious about civil society, it should have used NAWOU for this purpose. What was needed was for NAWOU to establish branches in the districts. There is no doubt that the councils are not autonomous bodies which can champion the cause of women. With respect to both the women's and youth movements, it appears that the octopus radiating from the NRM Secretariat is hovering over the two movements, clearly neutralizing democracy and autonomy.

As far as the labor movement is concerned, although some positive gains have been recorded, bottlenecks remain. One bottleneck is continued state control over trade unions. This control manifests itself at the level of registration of all trade unions in the country. Through compulsory registration and the fear of deregistration, the government is in a position to victimize militant leaders and others with whom the state does not agree. In order to further control the trade union movement, the law stipulates that for a prospective union to be registered, it must have 1,000 members. This restriction is clearly unhealthy and can be used as a control device against unions not liked by the state. Additional control is maintained through the rather cumbersome dispute-resolution process because the minister can frustrate the work of aggrieved unions by following to the letter the lengthy process of resolving disputes. Such bureaucratic procedures make it virtually impossible for the workers to resort to their ultimate weapon, withdrawal of their labor. This clearly shows that the state is on the side of capital, not labor.

The law also stipulates that the minister responsible for labor has the power to inspect and investigate a trade union to see if it is doing things properly. With respect to this law, it is claimed that the government wants the unions to be accountable. However, this is a dangerous precedent because unions are treated as if they are debating clubs in secondary schools. The membership of the unions is capable of ensuring that trade unionists are accountable to their members. This avenue of control can be used to endanger the autonomy of the movement.

Moreover, the law provides that any funds from outside Uganda donated to any union must have the sanction of the minister of labor. While perhaps such a policy was understandable during the cold war era, when different countries were giving money to different groups, it does not seem that such approval is needed during the post-cold war era.

The Uganda trade union law also prohibits workers from essential services from striking. The list of essential services is lengthy and includes water, electricity, hospital and fire services, as well as customs, fisheries, and food research organizations. In other words, a free, autonomous trade union movement is clearly not in sight in Uganda today.

Finally, with respect to political parties as an integral part of civil society, it is clear that Uganda has a long way to go. The NRM claims that parties are divisive and secretarian and, for that reason, they are not needed. It appears that Museveni's government wants to prop up the NRM, which is in essence a political party. It is not fashionable today to talk of one-party systems, and therefore new methods of concealing them have to be found. The NRM is no different from many one-party systems with which we are familiar. It is in government, has a secretariat which is busy indoctrinating people, and has leaders, although the selection process for such leaders is not transparent.

While the government consists of people who belong to other parties, the NRM government is not a coalition government, since there were no party-to-party negotiations before people were appointed ministers. There is no broad base in the government since individuals do not represent anybody except perhaps their own constituencies. For this reason, it is unfortunate that there is a campaign of slander against parties. While political parties may have problems in this country, they should not be replaced by a one-party system.

Conclusion

From the foregoing, it is clear that Uganda has not reached a stage in which civil society can prosper. Too many institutions are afraid of the state. The state, though weak in absolute terms, is extremely strong and sometimes frightening to civil society. The citizens of Uganda have not yet become differentiated enough to constitute a real base for civil society, which is one reason why it is unrealistic to exclude political parties.

Without parties, civil society will melt and crumble before the state. The fact that the NRM wants to downgrade parties is therefore unfortunate. The general attitude of the current government toward civil society is a cause for worry.

In 1987, the NRM Secretariat convened a Youth Conference in Kyambongo for purposes of establishing a youth movement. The youth became too enthusiastic and wanted to establish a movement which would be independent of the Secretariat and other organs of the state. The government officials were so upset that they unceremoniously adjourned the conference, promising to recall it later. They wanted a youth movement on their own terms, not on the terms of the young people themselves. This was also the case with respect to the women's movement as well as umbrella organizations discussed in this study.

If the youth, women, cooperatives, and trade unions were working efficiently and were autonomous, they could constitute social movements likely to become countervailing forces against the power of the state. By virtue of their size, they could be a check on the state. When opposition parties are added to this array of power, the liberties of the people would be in good hands. There are, of course, other smaller associations such as Action for Development, the Association of Women Lawyers, and the Foundation for African Development, which are scattered throughout the country. They too, are useful, but in the face of a determined state, they are gravely exposed. Therefore, the emphasis on social movements is justified.

Finally, while it could be argued that the NRM is facilitating the development of civil society, the findings of this study point to the fact that the NRM is interested in maintaining control over society. Consequently, under this government, civil society is at bay.

Notes

[1] See Larry Diamond, "Towards Democratic Consolidation," *Journal of Democracy,* Vol. 5, No. 3, 1994; M. Steven Fish, "Russia's Fourth Transition," *Journal of Democracy,* Vol. 5, No. 3, 1994; I. Harik, "Pluralism in the Arab World," *Journal of Democracy,* Vol. 5, No. 3, 1994.

[2] Nehru, who led India to independence in 1947, was a product of the University of London, where he came under the influence of Professor Harold Laski and other British Fabian academics. A prolific writer, his books were read far and wide, with people like Milton Obote of Uganda becoming an admirer of Nehru.

[3] Kwame Nkrumah of Ghana was an admirer of the Soviet Union. Its size, planning experience, and industrialization, inspired Nkrumah to become a passionate believer in African Unity. See Nkrumah's *Ghana: An Autobiography of Kwame Nkrumah* (London: Panaf, 1973).

[4] See David Apter, *Ghana in Transition* (New York: Atheneum 1963); Rupert Emerson, *From Empire to Nation* (Cambridge: Harvard University Press, 1960); David Apter, *The Politics of Modernization* (Chicago: University of Chicago Press, 1965).

[5] See Samuel Huntington, *Political Order in Changing Societies* (New Haven: Yale University Press, 1969); Frederick S. Arkhurst, "Introduction," *Africa in the Seventies and Eighties* (New York: Praeger Publishers, 1970); and H. Wriggings, *The Rulers Imperative* (New York: Columbia University Press, 1969).

[6] See Yoweri Museveni, *The Ten Point Programme* (Kampala: NRM Publications, n.d.).

[7] See S. Arian, *Report of the Committee Appointed to Investigate the Cooperative Movement in Uganda* (Entebbe: Government Printer, 1969).

[8] See J. J. Barya, "The State, Trade Unions and Labour in Uganda: 1962-92," Faculty of Law, Makerere University, 1993.

[9] The UTUC viewed these developments with alarm and its president, who had been a UPC Member of Parliament, quit the party and joined the opposition Democratic Party in 1965.

[10] This argument was particularly stressed by M. Obote who, after introducing the Move to the Left (particularly the Nakivubo pronouncements), claimed that economic enterprises belonged to the unions which should not strike against them. He referred to strikes as "archaic," which should also be abolished. See Barya, p. 12.

[11] Between 1983 and 1988, the present writer was chairman of MUASA and made presentations to the government to reinstate the association into the Act, but all was in vain.

[12] I have gone into these developments in my "Youth Action and Political Development in Uganda," unpublished Ph. D. dissertation, Columbia University, New York, 1972. See also my "The Demise of the UPC Youth League and the Rise of NUYO," *The African Review,* Vol. 3, No. 2, 1973.

[13] We listened to these claims with disgust because some of us played important roles in reviving NUSU in 1966 when we were in the student leadership at Makerere University.

[14] See Yoweri Museveni and NRM, *NRM Achievements, 1986-90* (Kampala: NRM Publications, 1990).

[15] Although Museveni would want to be credited with this innovation, his ideas on popular democracy, peoples' committees, opposition to parties, as well as reservations about parliamentary democracy, are carbon copies of the Libyan experience. See M. Kadhafi, *The Green Book* (Tripoli: Public Establishment for Publishing, Part I, n.d.).

[16] See The National Youth Councils Statute 1993, pp. 4 and 5, in *Uganda Gazette,* Vol. 18, LXXXVI 30/4/93.

[17] See the proposed constitution, Youth Section, Ministry of Gender and Community Development, Kampala.

[18] See J. J. Barya, "Workers Rights in Uganda," Centre for Basic Research, Mimeo, September 1994, pp. 6-8.

[19] See Draft Constitution of the Uganda National Association of Youth Organizations (UNAYO) Ministry of Gender and Community Development, 1994.

[20] Evidence of concern among women groups about the role of the state in the UCW as well as subsequent bodies, is to be found in a brief on "Restructuring of National Council of Women: Recommendations and Suggestions by Women Groups from Kampala and Upcountry" (No author and no date but appears to have been written by the Secretary General of the UCW. Available in the Ministry of Gender and Community Development).

4

Les masses populaires et les préalables d'une transition démocratique au Zaïre (1990-1992)

Mulambu Mvuluya

Aujourd'hui le processus de démocratisation au Zaïre, sept ans après, est bloqué. A la place de la démocratie tant réclamée par le peuple, la dictature lui a substitué la démocrature. Plusieurs raisons sont certes avancées et elles sont d'ordre externe et interne. Il est vrai que les étrangers et notamment de l'Europe Occidentale, sont un obstacle à l'éclosion de la démocratie au Zaïre et en Afrique, ce qui signifierait la fin ou le rétrécissement de la demande qui leur permet d'accroître la production manufacturielle et autre et résoudre la question de chômage qui sévit chez eux. La reprise en main des retombés du discours de la Baule ét du vent de la perestroïka par les forces conservatrices ont permis la résistance du régime dictatorial dont les racines semblent déjà minées. Plus important à nos yeux nous semble la faiblesse de la direction des masses populaires.

En effet, le problème de la participation des masses populaires aux mouvements de protestation politiques se pose au Zaïre à chaque étape de la conquête des libertés politiques ou de la liberté tout court. Il suffit à ce sujet de rappeler, à part quelques exceptions (Demunter, Jewsiewicki, Weiss, Nzongola), la marginalisation pour ne pas dire l'oubli dans la littérature zaïroise sur la résistance anticoloniale, de la participation des masses paysannes et populaires aux mouvements de la décolonisation.[1] Les travaux de Benoît Verhaegen sur les rébellions populaires mis à part, c'est à posteriori qu'on s'est rappelé des mouvements de protestation des masses rurales contre les autorités qui avaient oublié les promesses faites lors de l'accession du pays à l'indépendance (mouvements qualifiés de seconde indépendance).[2] Pendant ce temps, les intellectuels participaient activement à la mise en place des structures d'oppression qui permettront à la couche hégémonique de renforcer la dictature.

Aujourd'hui, comme hier, dans la littérature zaïroise existante, et elle est déjà nombreuse, le rôle des masses populaires dans la conquête de la démocratie semble de nouveau marginalisé. De fait, les ouvrages déjà parus depuis bientôt sept ans sur le processus démocratique reprennent invariablement les thèmes devenus classiques du rôle joué par l'opposition zaïroise, de la clandestinité à son autorisation officielle (opposition des barons et des parlementaires, des humeurs des syndicats ouvriers et des étudiants, etc.).

Dans ces travaux dont l'intérêt est réel, on parle du bout des lèvres du sacrifice suprême des masses populaires pour les exigences de la liberté, pour le départ de la dictature et pour leur soutien sans faille aux véritables forces du changement démocratique. Aujourd'hui plus que hier, il se pose le problème de la direction des masses populaires et d'une nécessaire liaison entre les différents acteurs engagés dans la lutte pour le changement. Les quelques maigres résultats obtenus de 1990 à 1992 correspondent à une période où les masses populaires sont montées à l'avant scène de l'activité politique et ont imprimé leur dynamisme au processus de démocratisation. C'est cette dynamique que les forces du statu quo ont tenté de contrôler et de mâter, d'anéantir par la répression sauvage, par les massacres, par l'insécurité. Elles y sont parvenues par la prolifération des partis sans base sociologique, par le débauchage, par la paupérisation sans borne, créant ainsi la fracture entre la base et le sommet. Celui-ci ayant opté pour la voie du réformisme et non celle du combat. Cela apparaît clairement dans les trois moments du processus de la démocratisation au Zaïre: la lutte pour le pluralisme, pour le gouvernement représentatif et pour une conférence nationale souveraine.

C'est à dessein que nous avons pris la date de 1992 car à notre avis, depuis cette date, le processus démocratique s'est embourbé au Zaïre. La dictature a récupéré à son profit le mouvement des masses populaires qui l'avaient mis en branle. L'opposition s'est depuis lors fait piéger, abandonnant la lutte au profit du réformisme à travers les négociations, donnant ainsi un avantage à son adversaire.

Opposition contre la démocrature au Zaïre (avril 1990-mai 1992)

Partout en Afrique et au Zaïre en particulier, le monopartisme avait servi d'instrument à des dictatures implacables soutenues par les puissances étrangères dans le contexte de la guerre froide, de l'opposition entre l'Europe de l'Ouest et l'Union Soviétique et leurs alliés. Les forces d'oppression diverses (armées, milices, services d'intelligence, etc.) empêchaient que la véritable nature des régimes politiques (dictatorial, patrimonial, tutélarisme, etc.) ne soit publiquement remise en cause. Mais cela ne tarda pas de l'être aussitôt que les langues se délièrent.

En effet, alors que le vent de la perestroïka et de la glanost ne semblait concerner que la seule Europe de l'Est, le Président François Mitterand, dans son discours à la Baule, attira l'attention des Chefs d'Etat africains sur l'urgence d'une démocratisation de leurs régimes politiques et liait l'aide aux mesures qui seraient prises dans ce sens. Aussi le Président zairois Mobutu Sese Seko, qui se croyait aimé par son peuple, se mit-il dès le 14 janvier 1990 à des consultations populaires, dirigées d'en haut. Mais il fut surpris par l'ampleur de la condamnation sans réserve de son système par toutes les couches de la population. Le discours qu'il prononça le 24 avril 1990 pour rendre compte des résultats des consultations fut fort applaudi dans la salle. L'ampleur de ses bonnes intentions était telle qu'il s'était mis à pleurer devant ses barons: *"comprenez mon émotion"*, ajouta-t-il. Ce discours provoqua des explosions spontanées de joie dans les rues de la capitale, en régions et dans les enceintes des universités. Qu' y avait-il donc dit? On retiendra tout au moins qu'il avait pris congé du MPR (Mouvement Populaire de la Révolution), son Parti-Etat, sans en avoir mesuré les conséquences sur le plan constitutionnel.

Beaucoup de choses ont été dites au sujet de ce discours du 24 avril 1990, considéré comme le début du processus de la transition vers la démocratie au Zaïre. Nous pensons quant à nous que trois grandes décisions prises ce jour-là domineront le débat politique au cours de la transition controversée du processus de la démocratisation au Zaïre. Il s'agit d'abord de l'annonce faite par le Chef de l'Etat de la fin du Parti-Etat et l'adoption d'un multipartisme à trois dont une loi devra régir non seulement l'organisation et le fonctionnement mais aussi le financement; la désignation d'un Premier Ministre et la formation d'un gouvernement de transition dont la fin était fixée au 30 avril 1991; enfin la révision de la Constitution en vue de l'adapter à la période de transition ainsi que la mise sur pied d'une commission chargée de rédiger la nouvelle constitution. Celle-ci était censée être approuvée par le référendum pour qu'elle entre en vigueur après le 30 avril 1991.

Ce programme fort chargé et dont l'exécution devait se poursuivre sans faille, telle une charte conçue par un seigneur du Moyen Age pour l'administration et le contrôle de ses sujets, présentait l'ensemble de ces réformes annoncées dans le cadre d'une démocratie octroyée. Mais c'était sans compter avec les exigences des masses populaires. En effet, en optant pour le pluralisme, fut-il limité, le Chef de l'Etat libérait du même coup l'expression populaire. Aussi, très vite, au fur et à mesure que les langues se délièrent et que la torpeur passa, les contradictions apparurent et les faiblesses du schéma présidentiel ne résistèrent à l'analyse critique.

Tout le monde, journalistes, étudiants, masses populaires, émirent des réserves sur la sincérité des réformes annoncées. Aussi l'opposition, composée jusqu'alors de l'UDPS (Union pour la Démocratie et le Progrès Social) d'Etienne Tshisekedi, du PDSC (Parti Démocrate Social Chrétien) de Joseph Ileo et Cléophas Kamitatu, du FCN (Front Commun des Nationalistes) de Gérard Kamanda, du MNC (Mouvement National Congolais) du feu Patrice Lumumba, profitant assez rapidement du soutien populaire, prit à rebours les intentions présidentielles et affirma tout haut que la démocratie ne se donne pas sur un plateau d'argent, mais qu'elle s'arrache. Elle la remit en cause et ne voulut pas d'une démocratie contrôlée.

Pour l'opposition, Mobutu avait démissionné de ses fonctions dès le discours du 24 avril et n'expédiait que les affaires courantes. A ce titre, il n'avait pas à imposer sa volonté comme à l'époque du Parti-Etat dont il venait de prendre congé. C'est pourquoi, au multipartisme à trois, l'opposition revendiqua le multipartisme intégral; au gouvernement du MPR, elle lui préféra un gouvernement représentatif des forces politiques d'une opposition réelle d'abord et issu de la conférence nationale souveraine ensuite. Enfin, à la commission constitutionnelle, les forces de l'opposition réclamèrent à l'instar d'autres pays africains, une conférence nationale souveraine dont les conclusions seraient opposables à tous. Mais croyant ses intentions mal comprises, Mobutu crut bon de faire des clarifications. Ce fut l'objet de son discours à l'Assemblée Nationale en date du 3 mai 1990. Discours qui fut interprété comme une tentative de reprendre d'une main ce qu'il avait donné d'une autre. Il faudra attendre huit mois pour aboutir à la reconnaissance officielle des partis.

La formation du gouvernement représentatif n'a fait que connaître des rebondissements sept ans depuis le discours du 24 avril sans parler de la fermeture des travaux de la CNS (Conférence Nationale Souveraine), le refus de son caractère de souveraineté et sa durée de deux ans au lieu de trois mois escomptés par le pouvoir.

Du multipartisme à trois au multipartisme intégral ou la conquête du pluralisme (1990-1992)

La période qui va d'avril 1990 à octobre 1992 correspond à une période d'intenses exigences des masses pour le pluralisme. En effet, autour de la lutte pour le passage du multipartisme à trois, c'est le pluralisme tout court dans tous les secteurs de la vie nationale. C'est la société toute entière qui voudrait recouvrer sa liberté, dans le domaine syndical, religieux, socio-économique, social, etc. Ce fut la fin du syndicat unique des travailleurs, du seul mouvement de jeunesse, de la presse gouvernementale. Des belles églises qui constituaient le refuge des consciences durant le règne du Parti-Etat vont réclamer leur reconnaissance officielle.

L'opposition demande publiquement au peuple de se défaire de sa peur inoculée depuis des années par la dictature et de descendre dans la rue. Malgré les manoeuvres d'intimidation, la population affronta les forces de l'ordre à Mbuji-Mayi (au Kasaï

Oriental) où il y eut plusieurs morts; à Matadi (au Bas-Zaïre) et dans d'autres villes du pays. Les mots d'ordre en faveur de la désobéissance civile paralysèrent la Fonction Publique et toute l'Administration de l'Etat. La population refusa de payer l'impôt. Bien plus par la pratique des opérations "villes mortes" qui avaient fait leur preuve, le pouvoir fut complètement paralysé. Les associations de défense des droits de l'homme ont dénombré plusieurs victimes. L'opinion internationale fut frappée de torpeur par l'annonce du massacre des chrétiens en février 1992, lors d'une marche pacifique organisée pour réclamer la réouverture des travaux de la Conférence Nationale Souveraine nterrompue par le Premier Ministre Nguz à Karl I Bond. C'est la période de la lutte héroïque des masses populaires pour la démocratie.

Alors que le 24 avril 1990, le Chef de l'Etat avait envisagé le multipartisme à trois, c'est-à-dire le MPR, l'UDPS et un autre parti à créer, sous la pression des événements, il semble avoir eu l'idée d'un multipartisme à quatre en septembre 1990, tandis qu'un mois plus tard, soit le 6 octobre 1990, il accorda le multipartisme intégral de sorte qu'à cette époque déjà, l'on crut à un dérapage. Celui-ci eut effectivement lieu lorsque pour s'assurer d'une majorité numérique à la conférence constitutionnelle d'abord et nationale souveraine ensuite, on vit enregistrés des partis dont le nombre passa rapidement de 19 à 49 puis 77 fin mars 1991 pour atteindre 226 le 18 juin 1991, soit à la clôture des travaux préparatoires de la conférence nationale. Tantôt on crut se trouver en face d'une bipolarisation des forces politiques, tantôt en face de trois, tantôt en face de quatre tendances selon le mode de gestion politique ou la forme de l'Etat.

On distinguait ainsi fin mars 1991 que les conservateurs prônaient un Etat à gestion centralisée avec ou sans décentralisation limitée au plan administratif et économique, les nationalistes avec le groupe MNC à la tête préconisant un Etat unitaire avec un pouvoir fortement centralisé; enfin les fédéralistes avec l'UDPS. Mais les cartels qui vont se former dans la suite révèlent la difficulté d'une construction homogène pour la classification des partis politiques. Ainsi naquirent les partis du consensus, Fronterie de l'opposition, Union Sacrée de l'opposition, Union Sacrée libérale et démocratique, majorité présidentielle, Adeli, Forces démocratiques unies, Mouvance présidentielle, les Forces novatrices de l'Union Sacrée, Collectif des partis progressistes de l'opposition lumumbistes, UFIC (Union des forces fédéralistes), Cartel des 40 avec le FCNR (Front Commun des Nationalistes Radical) créé par Kitenge Yezu, FDU (Forces Démocratiques Unies) créées par l'instigation du Directeur du Bureau du Président, GAMM (Groupes Acquis au Maréchal Mobutu), CODENA (Coordination des Démocrates Nationalistes) formé par les jeunes proches de Beyeye Djema, et j'en passe.

Ces divisions, encouragées et entretenues par le pouvoir, lui ont servi de cheval de Troie pour bloquer la conférence nationale d'abord, la formation d'un gouvernement représentatif ensuite. En effet, la période allant d'avril 1990 à janvier 1991 est marquée par la lutte pour l'adoption du multipartisme intégral, annihilant la volonté du multipartisme à trois, devant sortir des élections primaires qui auraient pu être organisées en janvier 1991.

Refus du multipartisme contrôlé correspond au refus de toute tentative au monolithisme et à l'engagement pour la libéralisation de toute la société. Dès lors que l'idée d'organiser les élections primaires en janvier 1991 est abandonnée, la loi sur l'organisation des partis est rapidement dépassée. Si l'examen des statuts avait bénéficié d'un certain sérieux sous le gouvernement Lunda Bululu, il n'en sera plus questions sous ceux qui vont lui succéder (Mulumba Lukoji, Nguz a Kar I Bond ou Birindwa) où on a assisté à la création effrénée des partis "dits alimentaires". Des scissions au sein des anciens directoires des partis amènent la création des nouveaux tout comme des associations des mutuelles claniques et ethniques, chaque ethnie, chaque clan ou presque poussant les siens à se lancer dans la création des partis, occasion des se positionner sur la scène politique. On a vu lors des travaux de la CNS, toute une famille assister à la CNS, le papa étant président, la maman vice-présidente et leur fille secrétaire générale.

C'était l'avènement des partis sans doctrine ni idéologie, sans projet de société. Aussi a t-on vu les délégués d'un même parti adopter des lignes de conduite différentes. Lors des travaux de la Conférence Nationale Souveraine, sous la pression des masses populaires, les partis politiques alors formés furent obligés à décliner leur position vis-à-vis du processus du changement, leur soutien ou non aux forces du statu quo.

Après la Conférence Nationale Souveraine, l'enregistrement des partis politiques continua de plus belle au Ministère de l'Intérieur avec une légèreté déconcertante de sorte que vers fin juin 1995, on compte plus de 460 partis politiques au Zaïre. Le record jamais atteint dans le monde. Si les masses populaires ont été mobilisées pour l'acquisition du pluralisme, elles ont par la suite manqué de direction pour stopper l'enregistrement anarchique des partis sans aucune base sociologique. S'il est vrai qu'au départ, les grands partis d'opposition d'alors, UDPS, UFERI (Union des Fédéralistes et Républicains Indépendants dirigée par Nguz), PDSC, avaient assimilé le multipartisme à la démocratie, cela a changé dès le début de la CNS. Le multipartisme est favorisé par le régime dictatorial pour fragiliser la conscience populaire et l'opposition. Ces partis d'essence clanique et autres sont du reste financés par le pouvoir en place pour augmenter la majorité numérique de la mouvance présidentielle. Il est d'ailleurs étonnant que sept ans depuis le 24 avril 1990, aucun des partis politiques zaïrois même ceux qui en ont les moyens, n'ait cru bon de convoquer le Congrès pourtant organe suprême des partis.

Il est bon de rappeler que la volonté du pouvoir dictatorial de bloquer l'expression de la volonté populaire par l'interdiction des manifestations publiques liées à l'activité des partis avait abouti à une répression sanglante à Mbuji-Mayi et dans d'autres villes du pays. Le massacre des étudiants de l'Université de Lubumbashi et les marches de protestation qui en suivirent furent pour la plupart noyées dans le sang. Ce sont des martyrs oubliés depuis lors.

Du gouvernement représentatif

La question d'un gouvernement représentatif de toutes les forces politiques a connu des fortunes diverses et beaucoup de soubresauts. En effet, avant même que le discours de Mobutu en date du 24 avril 1990 ait été l'objet d'une critique sévère, sans même qu'une révision de la constitution intervienne, il forma sans tarder un gouvernement dirigé par un Premier Ministre technocrate (Lunda Bululu) et où aucune grande figure connue de l'opposition n'en faisait partie. Il comprenait certes l'une ou l'autre personne ayant collaboré pour un temps avec l'opposition, à un titre ou à un autre.

A part deux caciques du MPR à l'Administration du Territoire et aux Affaires Etrangères, presque pas de grandes figures de la politique nationale des dernières années du monopartisme. Ce fut une équipe de grands inconnus qui, dans l'esprit du Chef de l'Etat, devait conduire sa transition, sans grande expérience du pouvoir, sans jamais avoir eu à lutter sur la scène politique, juste bons pour recevoir les applaudissements lors de l'investiture, comme du temps du Parti-Etat, et qui montra son incompétence aussitôt que l'opposition commença à s'organiser avec les brèches du MPR occasionnées par le départ petit à petit des anciens caciques voulant se repositionner sur la scène politique. On y trouvait un savant dosage dont les proches du Président, les anciens activistes du MPR, quelques têtes d'affiche montantes au Parlement, et quelques inconnus de l'opposition externe et interne.

Pour les milieux de l'opposition, il fallait former un gouvernement d'union nationale et non un gouvernement de transition. Il revenait à l'opposition le droit de former ce gouvernement en vue de préparer la tenue d'une conférence nationale souveraine. L'opposition posa dès ce moment la question de l'alternance du pouvoir, grâce à l'appui des larges masses populaires. Il se posa aussi la question de la légitimité d'un tel gouvernement. Malgré le débauchage par le pouvoir des personnalités infiltrées dans l'opposition, les masses populaires ne les cautionnent pas quelque soit les qualificatifs qui furent données à ces gouvernements. Ainsi en fut-il du gouvernement de transition élargi dirigé par Mulumba Lukoji, du gouvernement de combat par Mungul Diaka, du gouvernement de large union ou large consensus national de Nguz a Karl I Bond ou du gouvernement d'Union Nationale de Birindwa, du gouvernement de transition de Kengo.

Pour les masses populaires, le véritable gouvernement de transition, celui qui incarnerait les aspirations devrait être dirigé par celui qui symbolise leur lutte, Tshisekedi Wa Mulumba. Mais ce gouvernement devait se faire sans compromission, sans peau de banane. Ainsi, lorsque le 21 juillet 1991, la nomination par le Président de Tshisekedi comme Premier Ministre fit l'effet d'une bombe dans les milieux de l'opposition. La permanence de l'UDPS et la résidence de Tshisekedi furent prises d'assaut par une foule de combattants de l'opposition pour empêcher ce dernier d'accepter cette nomination. Pour ceux-ci, *"le Parti doit refuser cette offre qui est un cadeau empoisonné"*. Sous la pression des masses populaires, le 29 juillet 1991, Tshisekedi refusa l'offre de former le gouvernement, car dans l'esprit du Chef de l'Etat, en formant le gouvernement, l'opposition renoncerait à la tenue d'une conférence nationale, dont les travaux préparatoires venaient de se terminer, et adoptera la conférence constitutionnelle.

Le même phénomène se passa lorsque, après les pillages de septembre 1991, Etienne Tshisekedi est de nouveau nommé Premier Ministre le 30 septembre sous la pression des milieux occidentaux. Ce fut la liesse populaire dans les rues de Kinshasa et les messages de félicitations affluèrent de toutes les couches de la population. Cette même population prit d'assaut l'Hôtel du Gouvernement le samedi 19 octobre lorsque les services de sécurité empêchèrent Tshisekedi de se rendre au bureau du fait qu'il avait buffé les mentions "garant de la nation" et "constitution" le jour où il devait prêter le serment, le 16 octobre, devant le Président, à la manière de l'époque du Parti-Etat.

Cette volonté du peuple de conférer la légitimité à l'opposition se manifestera lorsque le 15 août 1992, la séance plénière de la Conférence Nationale Souveraine, par une majorité écrasante, vota Tshisekedi Wa Mulumba Premier Ministre. Jamais de mémoire de Zaïrois on oubliera cette date, toutes les rues de la capitale et des grandes villes de la République furent prises d'assaut, les masses en liesse, les danses, les klaxons de chauffeurs de taxis, etc. C'était leur Premier Ministre malgré les manoeuvres de Mobutu pour empêcher Tshisekedi de gouverner. Malgré le débauchage des personnalités de l'opposition, Mobutu sait qu'aucune autre personnalité n'incarnera la légitimité d'Etienne Tshisekedi comme Premier Ministre de la République du Zaïre pendant la transition. Plusieurs tentatives faites avec les personnalités débauchées à l'opposition et qu'on appelle au Zaïre *"des vagabonds politiques"* n'ont été que des manoeuvres dilatoires auxquelles le peuple ne conférera pas sa caution. Toutes ces personalités ayant été toujours soumises au Président et protégées par ses services de sécurité n'ont jamais inspiré la confiance du peuple. Aussi en fut-il de Mulumba Lukoji, de Nguz a Karl I Bond, de Mungul Diaka, de Birindwa et de Kengo Wa Dondo.

Entre mai-juin 1991, toujours sentant la dynamique de la vraie opposition représentée alors par l'UDPS et le PDSC, beaucoup de caciques du MPR crurent bon de porter son manteau; mais ils n'étaient que des brebis galeuses. Pour diminuer le poids de l'UDPS au Shaba, donc pour fragiliser Tshisekedi dans cette région, le pouvoir initia-t-il l'expulsion des originaires du Kasaï qui en constituaient la base. Ainsi le gouvernement issu de la Conférence Nationale Souveraine aurait difficile de se prévaloir d'unité nationale. Et pour rendre le pays ingouvernable par l'opposition, la dictature décida de faire détruire les seules infrastructures socio-économiques encore en place. C'est ainsi que les pillages éclatèrent les 23 et 24 septembre 1991, ainsi que le 28 janvier 1993. Ils eurent lieu à travers tout le pays. Le pouvoir se mit à acheter les personnalités de l'opposition des autres régions pour fragiliser la vraie opposition. Dès janvier 1991, Faustin Birindwa aurait pu être nommé Premier Ministre, Tshisekedi ayant déclaré lors de sa tournée de décembre 1990 aux U.S.A. qu'il demande le départ pur et simple du dictateur. On lui préféra d'abord Mulumba Lukoji et Nguz a Karl I Bond. Mais les Kasaïens rendirent la "monnaie de singe" à Birindwa. Ils refusèrent de consommer les nouvelles coupures de zaïre-monnaie, comme châtiment de sa traîtrise d'avoir quitté l'UDPS. En effet, Birindwa était passé au camp de la mouvance par sa présence au Conclave du Palais de la Nation qui avait réuni tous ceux qui n'avaient pu ouvrir leur bouche à la CNS sous le regard du peuple souverain. Aussi, pour les masses populaires, un gouvernement d'une véritable transition démocratique doit être dirigé par le Chef de file de l'opposition et non par des individus achetés par le pouvoir. Toutes les décisions prises par ces gouvernements, tous les actes de ces gouvernements ne sont suivis d'aucun effet.

Pour les masses populaires seul un gouvernement dirigé par la vraie opposition est légitime, les autres ne le sont pas. C'est pourquoi, depuis que le Président Mobutu a écarté Tshisekedi de la Primature en décembre 1992, alors qu'il avait été élu à ce poste par la Conférence Nationale Souveraine, aucune autre personnalité n'est parvenue à faire l'unanimité autour d'elle et recueillir le consentement populaire. La décision d'écarter Tshisekedi était considérée illégale, car contraire à un acte de la Conférence Nationale Souveraine.

De la Conférence Constitutionnelle à la Conférence Nationale Souveraine

Dans une étude préparée en 1989, mais parue depuis lors sous l'intitulé "l'Etat et sa structure, quête permanente de la stabilité", nous avions fait ressortir la nécessité d'un débat national afin de définir les nouvelles perspectives pour le devenir national.[3] Seul un débat démocratique plus large pourrait indiquer les perspectives nouvelles, avions-nous écrit. Au Zaïre, il faut pour cela, lutter pour l'instauration d'un régime de large débat démocratique en vue de libérer les énergies et la capacité créative de la société civile. La stabilité des institutions et l'issue du combat pour le progrès économique et social du pays en dépendent. Il était bien entendu qu'un tel débat n'était pas à confondre avec les mémorandums présentés sur demande du Chef de l'Etat et qui n'étaient que des cahiers des doléances. Ce débat, avons-nous dit, prit plusieurs noms: table ronde, commission constitutionnelle pour les uns, conférence nationale tout court, et enfin conférence nationale souveraine, pour les autres. Dès janvier 1990, le mémorandum de fonctionnaires des Affaires Etrangères avait déjà réclamé la tenue d'une conférence nationale. La question de la conférence nationale divisa aussi bien les milieux de l'opposition radicale que ceux du pouvoir.

Quelques semaines après le discours du Chef de l'Etat, les milieux de l'opposition firent clairement comprendre que ce qu'il faut, ce n'est pas une simple commission constitutionnelle mais une conférence nationale à l'instar de celles qui étaient organisées en Afrique, au Bénin notamment; qu'il n'appartenait pas au gouvernement Lunda Bululu de l'organiser, mais bien par un véritable gouvernement de transition formé par l'opposition. Même sur ce sujet, l'opposition tenait à faire remarquer les divergences entre la démocratie octroyée et la démocratie revendiquée. Aussi, dès le 1er mai 1990, l'UDPS par Marcel Lihau interposé, l'un des fondateurs de l'UDPS, déclara lors d'une conférence de presse à Bruxelles, "*l'UDPS et les autres forces de l'opposition à l'extérieur réclament la convocation d'une Conférence Nationale en lieu et place de la Commission Constitutionnelle*". Mais, instruit par l'expérience, le Chef de l'Etat, craignant la convocation d'une assemblée qui viendrait remettre sa légitimité en cause s'y opposa catégoriquement. Lorsqu'il se résolut de confier la formation du gouvernement d'union nationale aux 4 grands partis de l'opposition au mois d'août-septembre 1990, ce fut pour que ceux-ci plaident contre la tenue d'une conférence nationale auprès des formations de moindre importance. C'est à ce moment que des divergences apparurent entre le Chef de l'Etat et certains de ses proches conseillers. En effet, alors que Félix Vunduawe, le directeur de cabinet à la présidence, plaidait pour une conférence des forces vives avec la participation des catégories professionnelles du genre CCPD (Conférence Consultative pour le Développement, sorte de Conseil Economique et Social du Parti-Etat), Nsinga Udjuu, Président Provisoire du MPR, s'y opposait.

La question qui se posait était de la qualité des personnes qui siégeraient dans ce forum étant donné qu'aucun parti n'était pas encore reconnu et qu'aucun d'entre eux n'avait organisé un congrès pour désigner ses délégués à une telle rencontre. Cette position est soutenue par certains milieux de l'opposition proche du pouvoir dont le FCN. Pour ces milieux seules les élections législatives pourraient permettre la formation d'une constituante. Les formations de l'opposition ne sont pas prêtes à accepter les élections qui pourraient être trichées par le pouvoir, lequel contrôlait encore la territoriale. Au cours du dernier trimestre de l'année 1990, toutes les grandes formations politiques prirent position en faveur d'une conférence nationale à l'image de ce qui venait de se tenir au Congo où la conférence nationale avait proclamé sa souveraineté, élu le président du Haut Conseil de la République assumant les charges de l'Assemblée Nationale, et rédigé un calendrier électoral ainsi qu'un projet de constitution à soumettre au référendum populaire. La dissolution de l'Assemblée Nationale est exigée et la session budgétaire d'octobre 1990 est critiquée. Etienne Tshisekedi, qui se trouve au mois de décembre 1990 à l'étranger, refuse même la tenue d'une conférence nationale et exige avant tout le départ du Président.

Le Président envisage alors les élections présidentielles anticipées avant les élections législatives. Ce serait mettre la charrue devant les boeufs, crie-t-on dans les milieux de l'opposition. Alors que la question de la reconnaissance des partis était en train de trouver une solution, celle de la formation d'un gouvernement de transition responsable en vue de convoquer une conférence nationale souveraine se posa dès lors avec une exigence accrue. A ce moment-là, fort des avis des milieux des chancelleries occidentales et des discours des professeurs d'université, Lunda Bululu, comme nous l'avons vu, continue à soutenir la conférence constitutionnelle et non la conférence nationale souveraine à laquelle tiennent toutes les forces de l'opposition. En effet, jusqu'à la fin février 1991, les diplomates occidentaux en poste à Kinshasa, avec en tête les USA, encourageant la tenue d'une conférence constitutionnelle, la seule que connaît leur histoire politique. Au besoin, l'organisation des élections anticipées et la formation d'une chambre d'où sortira la constituante. Plusieurs professeurs d'université mobilisés par le pouvoir montent sur le plateau de la télévision pour expliquer que la conférence constitutionnelle est égale à la conférence nationale. Pour Mobutu, la crise que traverse le pays est avant tout économique et non politique. Le processus démocratique a été initié par le Chef de l'Etat lui-même et qui le mène sur le bon chemin.

Le spectre de ce qui vient de se passer à Brazzaville hante l'esprit du Président Mobutu. Son homologue Sassou Nguessou est privé des véritables pouvoirs républicains. On est allé jusqu'à parler d'un coup d'Etat civil. Le déballage a éclaboussé tous les dignitaires du régime. C'est pour cela que le Président Mobutu tient contre vents et marées à refuser la conférence nationale souveraine, car il sait que son pouvoir va être remis en cause et que les crimes divers commis seront étalés au grand public. C'est pourquoi le Premier Ministre Lunda Bululu interposé, il continue à soutenir le projet de la conférence constitutionnelle alors que l'opposition réclame une conférence nationale souveraine. L'opposition voudrait que le peuple suive tout ce qui se dira. mais dans le but d'en contrôler le déroulement, le Ministre de l'Intérieur enregistre chaque jour des nouveaux partis dont les dirigeants réels ou fictifs sont proches des milieux du Président. Aussi en date du 6 mars 1991, le Président signa une ordonnance instituant une conférence constitutionnelle mais le peuple n'en veut pas.

Mulumba Lukoji, nommé Premier Ministre, se battra malgré l'opposition du Président de la République pour obtenir la souveraineté de la Conférence (15 juillet 1991), à quelques jours de l'ouverture solennelle des travaux (7 août 1991). Ceux-ci traînèrent en longueur, d'abord parce que Mulumba Lukoji suivant l'exemple de Soglo au Bénin, voulait se faire plébisciter Premier Ministre à la Conférence au détriment du leader de la vraie opposition. L'autorité du Chef de l'Etat est mise en cause et beaucoup d'intervenants demandent son départ. Aussi Mulumba Lukoji fut-il remplacé par Nguz. Celui-ci procéda à la suspension des travaux de la Conférence nationale estimant que les participants avaient outrepassé leurs droits.

C'est au cours d'une marche pacifique de protestation pour la réouverture que les chrétiens, dans les rues de Kinshasa, furent massacrés le 16 février 1992 par les hommes en arme. Ce sang des martyrs n'était pas versé pour rien et le Président Mobutu accepta la réouverture des travaux de la Conférence Nationale Souveraine. Celle-ci devrait être un forum de réconciliation nationale. Mais le Président n'en voulait pas car il usa de toutes les astuces pour en limiter la souveraineté. Aussi au lieu d'une constitution révolutionnaire, il amena les participants à un compromis politique global. Il refusa le projet de constitution qui le dépouille de tous ses pouvoirs.

Les débats de la Conférence Nationale Souveraine avaient eu un tel impact auprès des masses populaires que tous les caciques du MPR prirent peur. Ces barons du régime Mobutu vidèrent la salle car ils avaient été tous déballés. Le Président de la République fit tout pour que la lecture en séance plénière des résolutions des Commissions dites sensibles n'ait pas lieu. C'est notamment la Commission des biens mal acquis et celle des assassinats. Et pour liquider entièrement les acquis de la CNS, le Président Mobutu démit de ses fonctions Etienne Tshisekedi, celui qui aurait pu mettre en exécution les actes de la CNS. Le candidat du pouvoir au poste de Premier Ministre, Thomas Kanza, fut battu par le candidat du peuple, Tshisekedi Wa Mulumba.

Et après la CNS

Depuis 1993, le processus de démocratisation s'est embourbé pour ne pas dire est bloqué. La cible a cessé d'être le dictateur et le système autocratique qui a entraîné la désintégration des structures sociales et économiques. Les membres de l'ancienne oligarchie tout comme les jeunes récemment recrutés se battent pour la Primature. C'est le discours de la Conférence Nationale Souveraine qui semble enterré. En effet, la classe politique semble s'être accordée pour le maintien au pouvoir à la magistrature suprême de Mobutu Sese Seko. Elle est anesthésiée par des dispositions constitutionnelles qui font du Zaïre une sorte de monarchie constitutionnelle dans laquelle le monarque règne mais ne gouverne pas. La réalité est pourtant tout autre car Mobutu continue à concentrer entre ses mains l'essentiel du pouvoir notamment par le contrôle de la garde prétorienne, des services d'intelligence et de l'administration territoriale, la répression sanglante des années 1990-1992, une atomisation dangereuse de la société civile avec la résurgence des associations mutuelles régionales, ethniques et claniques sous le vocable de géopolitique, etc.

La lutte pour la conquête de la liberté, libérée dès le discours du 24 avril 1990 avait atteint une dynamique révolutionnaire lors des travaux de la Conférence Nationale. La transmission des débats en direct à la radio et à la télévision avait contribué énormément à l'éveil de la conscience des masses populaires pour un changement du système. On avait cru que la dictature avait basculé dans les ornières de l'histoire et que le peuple allait dorénavant être impliqué au choix de ses dirigeants et à la définition de la politique nationale. La Conférence Nationale Souveraine, ce forum populaire auquel siégeaient les représentants de toutes les forces sociales et politiques sembla avoir marqué le coup d'arrêt. Elle s'était fixée comme mission de faire une relecture de l'histoire du Zaïre afin d'établir les responsabilités et de redéfinir un nouveau projet de société pour l'avenir. Elle croyait avoir rempli cette mission de baliser l'avenir et d'assurer la rupture avec l'ordre autocratique ancien.

Se présentant comme une négation de la société dominée par l'oligarchie de la Deuxième République, la CNS avait connu une participation populaire importante et rempli sa fonction de socialisation et d'éducation politique sans pareille pour notre peuple. Elle rata cependant sa mission de réconciliation nationale. Le Président Mobutu y resta opposé. Aussi n'a-t-il pas cru bon de prononcer le discours protocolaire de l'ouverture solennelle, pas même de clôture. Il continua à l'ignorer superbement. Les caciques de l'ancien Parti-Etat qui en étaient écartés prirent peur du discours révolutionnaire. Aussi se misent-ils à en torpiller les conclusions. En effet, c'est à la CNS même que naquit un courant des opportunistes, regroupant les transfuges de tous bords qui serviront de cheval de bataille pour la reprise en main de la situation par les défenseurs de l'ordre ancien. Cette division de la classe politique et de la société civile a eu des conséquences incalculables pour la marche du processus de démocratisation. Pour eux comme pour le Président Mobutu lui-même, après la CNS égale avant la CNS. Le pouvoir par une politique de clochardisation sans limite a récupéré à son compte presque tous ceux qui se sont faits remarqués par leur critique contre la dictature. L'achat des consciences est devenu une pratique politique qui se fait au grand jour. Si elle est payante au niveau des superstructures institutionnelles, elle convainc au contraire les masses populaires dans la persistance et la continuation de leur lutte.

En effet, Mobutu avait cru qu'avec le limogeage de celui qui aurait pu être l'exécuteur testamentaire des résolutions de la CNS et la distribution des prébendes, c'en était fini.

Bien au contraire. Le combat du peuple, pour le triomphe de sa lutte se fait toujours sentir. Le peuple, dans sa grande majorité, continue à manifester sa confiance au leader de l'opposition, porté au pouvoir par la CNS. Aussi, aucun autre gouvernement de concertations entre les membres de l'oligarchie du Parti-Etat n'a jusqu'à présent reçu son soutien. Ces gouvernements étant dirigés par les hommes débauchés par le pouvoir, des taupes qui s'étaient réfugiées dans les rangs de l'opposition lorsque la dynamique du changement imposé par le peuple avait failli les emporter. Ainsi en est-il du gouvernement de Birindwa et de celui de Kengo Wa Dondo formés à la suite des concertations du Palais de la Nation et du Palais du Peuple (mars 1993 et octobre 1993, respectivement). Pour le peuple zaïrois, ces gouvernements sont formés en violation des dispositions constitutionnelles, donc illégaux et ne peuvent jouir d'aucune légitimité. La vraie transition n'a pas encore commencé.

Actuellement la classe politique s'est divisée en deux, amenant avec elle la société civile. Il y a d'un côté ceux qui défendent les acquis de la CNS, devenue la nouvelle source du pouvoir et de légitimité et de l'autre ceux qui sont des alliés de la dictature qui se fourvoient dans des compromissions avec des négociations parallèles. Par la corruption à large échelle, le pouvoir a atomisé les acteurs de la politique zaïroise. Mais les disponibilités de lutte des masses populaires restent intactes. Il est plus que temps de requalifier le processus de démocratisation tant au niveau des objectifs que des cibles, des stratégies et des acteurs.

Notes

[1] Voir, entre autres, Paul Demunter, *Masses rurales et luttes politiques au Zaïre: le processus de politisation des masses rurales au Bas-Zaïre* (Paris: *Ed.* Anthropos, 1975); Bogumil Jewsiewicki, "Political Consciousness among African Peasants in Colonial Zaïre," *Review of African Political Economy*, No. 19 (1980), pp. 23-32; Herbert F. Weiss, *Radicalisme rural et lutte pour l'indépendance au Congo-Zaïre: le Parti Solidaire Africain (1959-1960)* (Paris: L'Harmattan, 1994); Nzongola-Ntalaja, *Revolution and Counter-Revolution in Africa* (London: Zed Books, 1987).

[2] Benoît Verhaegen, *Rébellions au Congo*, 2 tomes (Bruxelles: CRISP, 1966,1968); Nzongola-Ntalaja, "Le mouvement pour la seconde indépendance au Congo-Kinshasa (Zaïre), de 1963 à 1968", in Peter Anyang' Nyong'o (sous la direction de) *Afrique: la longue marche vers la démocratie* (Paris: Publisud, 1988), pp. 208-252.

[3] Mulambu Mvuluya, "L'Etat et sa structure: quête permanente de la stabilité?" in Kankwenda Mbaya (sous la direction de) *Le Zaïre: vers quelles destinées?* (Dakar: CODESRIA, 1992), pp. 47-87.

5

La démocratie à la base
L'expérience des Parlementaires-debout
Kalele-ka-Bila

Autant la décennie soixante fut celle des indépendances africaines, autant la décennie quatre-vingt dix est celle de l'instauration de la démocratie en Afrique. La nouvelle que l'Afrique allait être démocratisée fut très bien accueillie partout sur le continent. Particulièrement dans ses couches les plus déshéritées.

La raison en est bien simple. Toutes les analyses les plus sérieuses sur les causes du développement du sous-développement de l'Afrique avaient établi la responsabilité fondamentale et prioritaire des régimes dictatoriaux. L'on se rappellera entre autres à ce propos, la célèbre déclaration de François Mitterand au sommet franco-africain de la Baule, relayée par la Banque mondiale et les autres institutions financières internationales: *"Il n'y a point de développement sans démocratie. Et, il n'y a point de démocratie sans développement"*. D'où, vu le degré de l'aspiration africaine au développement, au progrès social, au bonheur et à la liberté, le grand enthousiasme et les espoirs populaires suscités par l'engagement à remplacer lesdits régimes dictatoriaux par des régimes démocratiques.

Très vite cependant, ces espoirs seront déçus. Les dictatures en place, après quelques moments de tangages et de roulis, vont réussir à maîtriser la situation et à orienter les choses dans leur direction à elles: celle de l'instauration des démocratures ou pseudo-démocraties en lieu et place de véritables démocraties. Une reproduction en somme de la triste réalité des années soixante, où le mouvement pour l'indépendance ne réussira qu'à faire transformer le colonialisme en néocolonialisme. Mais ce véritable coup de poker des dictateurs n'étant point digéré, la question qui circule sur toutes les lèvres est celle de savoir comment relever le défi.

Les lignes et pages qui suivent ont pour but de décrire la réponse des masses populaires zaïroises à ce questionnement. Ce qui implique de comprendre dans ce sens-ci, l'intitulé de notre texte. Le concept *"base"* y signifie peuple. Et le concept *"Parlementaires-debout"*, une partie de ce peuple jouant actuellement le rôle de pionniers et d'éclaireurs dans la relance de la lutte pour faire échec au Président Mobutu Sese Seko et à ses complices internes et externes.

Dès lors, les grandes questions auxquelles nous aurons à répondre sont les suivantes:

- *Qui sont les Parlementaires-debout et pourquoi les appelle-t-on ainsi?*
- *Quand et comment a débuté leur mouvement?*
- *Comment sont-ils organisés?*
- *Par quoi se traduit leur lutte pour le triomphe, coûte que coûte, de l'idéal démocratique?*
- *A quelles difficultés ont-ils jusqu'ici eu à faire face et comment les ont-ils surmontées?*
- *Quelles sont leurs chances?*

Signification de l'expression "Parlementaires-Debout", identification de ceux qu'elle désigne et justification de son emploi

S'il existe aujourd'hui, dans le vocabulaire politique zaïrois, un terme qui est très célèbre et qui fait aussi très peur à l'ensemble de la classe politique, c'est bien celui de *Parlementaires-debout*. Cette expression désigne des citoyens zaïrois, hommes et femmes, jeunes et vieux, lettrés et non-lettrés, dont la principale préoccupation et activité consiste, chaque jour, à se rassembler dans différents coins de vente de journaux pour discuter politique et décider des actions à mener pour bien faire marcher les choses. Ils envahissent ces coins dès le lever du jour et y restent jusque vers 15H00! Sur la dixième rue à Limete, à Kinshasa, leur Q.G., ils vont même jusqu'au delà de 17H00.

Ils s'appellent *"Parlementaires-debout"* par analogie. Car, estiment-ils, leur activité, telle qu'elle est décrite ci-dessus, n'est en rien différente de celle de députés ou délégués du peuple qui en défendent les intérêts au Parlement. Aussi appellent-ils mêmement leurs lieux de rencontre *"Parlements"*. Quant à l'épithète *"debout"*, elle leur sert simplement de se distinguer de Parlementaires classiques. En mettant en exergue le fait que, eux ne disposent ni d'un local ni de sièges pour discuter politique. Ils le font plutôt debout et en plein air!

Nous reviendrons plus loin sur les raisons pour lesquelles ils font peur aux hommes politiques. Aussi bien ceux du côté de Mobutu que ceux qui se disent opposants.

Genèse du mouvement

Tel qu'il se manifeste et fonctionne aujourd'hui, le phénomène *"Parlementaires-debout"* date du lendemain de la clôture des travaux de la Conférence Nationale Souveraine (C.N.S.). Il y apparaîtra comme étant la réaction d'un peuple assoiffé de politique, contre l'embargo du pouvoir sur les débats politiques au sein du *HCR* d'abord et du *HCR-PT* ensuite.[1]

Avec la libéralisation de la vie politique au Zaïre le 24 avril 1990 et convaincu que l'avènement de la démocratie allait enfin ouvrir la voie au bonheur, le peuple zaïrois dans son ensemble manifesta un très grand engouement pour la politique. Non seulement en cherchant à suivre de près l'évolution de la situation dans ce domaine au jour le jour, mais aussi en se battant à qui mieux mieux pour être membre actif de tel ou tel parti politique.

Cet engouement atteindra son apogée et opérera une politisation en profondeur chez beaucoup avec l'organisation de la C.N.S. dont tous les débats pouvaient être suivis en direct partout, à la radio comme à la télévision. Mais voyant que de tels débats, puisque mettant chaque jour plus à nu aux yeux de tout le monde ses innombrables méfaits et crimes dans tous les domaines, étaient susceptibles de causer sa perte, Mobutu décida d'y couper court. C'est ainsi qu'il fera enlever et détruire, lors des pillages qu'il commanditera fin 1992 et début 1993, le car de reportage placé dans l'enceinte du Palais du Peuple où se déroulaient lesdits débats.

Il ne restait plus au peuple qu'un seul moyen pour continuer à suivre ce qui continuait à se dire et à se décider sur son sort dans ce Palais. Et ce moyen, ce sont les journaux. D'où, de plus en plus d'attroupements dans leurs coins de vente.

Organisation

Toute l'activité de *"Parlementaires-debout"*, depuis l'apparition du mouvement à Kinshasa, la capitale, jusqu'à son extension progressive en régions ou provinces en passant par son organisation et ses actions sur terrain, pourrait être représentée par ce schéma-ci en forme de triangle.

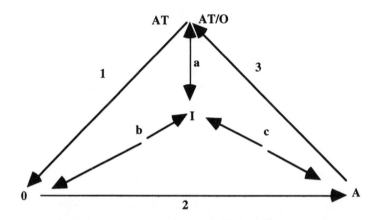

Dans ce schéma, AT   =   Attroupements de départ ou les tous premiers attroupements

AT/O =   Attroupements organisés ou nés par imitation

O   =   Organisation;

A   =   Actions;

I   =   Informations

La flèche No. 1 montre comment l'on est parti des premiers attroupements vers leur structuration ou mise sur pied d'un certain ordre, d'une certaine organisation en leurs seins. La flèche No. 2, de cette organisation à des actions de terrain bien pensées et coordonnées. Et la flèche No. 3, de l'éclat, du succès de ces actions à la naissance, à la multiplication de *Parlements-debout*.

La place de la lettre I au centre du triangle met en exergue l'importance du rôle de l'information dans le phénomène *Parlementaires-debout* à chacune de ses phases; comme le montrent les différentes flèches reliant I aux différents coins du triangle et vice-versa. En effet, la flèche *a* , avec ses deux têtes, a comme signification *"la recherche de l'information"* qui fut à la base de la naissance des Parlements-debout et que c'est sa diffusion qui en explique la prolifération. Quant à la flèche *b*, c'est l'impératif d'avoir et de discuter de manière ordonnée les différentes informations transmises qui dicta la nécessité de la mise sur pied de quelque organisation au sein des attroupements primitifs. Et concernant la flèche *c* enfin, elle indique les conclusions tirées après débat sur l'information reçue, qui déterminent les actions à mener.

Ces commentaires sur le pentacle ci-dessus ainsi faits, nous pouvons passer à la description de l'organisation proprement dite. Il y a lieu, en observant les choses de plus près, de situer cette organisation à deux niveaux. Celui de chaque Parlement-debout ou organisation interne; et celui de l'ensemble de la structure ou la coordination des rapports entre les différents Parlements-debout.

Organisation interne

Chaque *Parlement-debout* comprend à sa tête un président et un secrétaire-rapporteur. Le président joue le rôle de modérateur. C'est à lui qu'il revient d'accorder à tour de rôle la parole à ceux qui ont une information à donner, un commentaire à faire sur telle ou telle information, une proposition sur des actions concrètes à mener. Le secretaire-rapporteur note l'essentiel des différentes interventions. Il en fait la synthèse à la fin pour l'ensemble du groupe. Il en informe aussi les membres des autres Parlements lors des rencontres hebdomadaires.

Pour la transmission des informations urgentes, on recourt à des messagers spéciaux par système de relais. Le Parlement qui a reçu le premier l'information dépêche un de ses membres pour la transmettre au Parlement le plus proche. Celui-ci en fait autant pour le Parlement voisin. Et ainsi de suite jusqu'à atteindre tout le monde au courant de la journée. A leur tour, tous les autres membres ont le devoir de répercuter chaque information apprise au Parlement, dans leurs quartiers respectifs dès qu'ils reviennent à la maison.

Pour leurs déplacements, les messagers spéciaux sont pris en charge par leurs Parlements respectifs, grâce à une contribution spéciale et ponctuelle réunie sur place. A défaut de cette contribution, ils sont transportés gratuitement par des chauffeurs de taxis, taxis-bus ou bus de circuit. Le recours à des cotisations ponctuelles s'explique par l'absence de caisses dans tous les Parlements. L'on a fait exprès de ne pas prévoir le poste de trésorier. Ceci, afin d'éviter des tiraillements voire des éclatements de groupes suite à des querelles de gestion. Mais ces cotisations ponctuelles ne jouent pas que pour couvrir les frais de transport des messagers spéciaux. Il y est également recouru pour acheter certains journaux ou en louer simplement la lecture.

Les journaux sont très nombreux sur le marché. Ils coûtent de plus en plus cher suite à une hyperinflation continue. Par ailleurs, la population est en très grande majorité constituée de chômeurs. Même ceux qui travaillent restent des mois impayés; pour recevoir après de véritables salaires de famine. D'où il est difficile de s'acheter certains journaux en commun ou de verser de petites sommes d'argent aux vendeurs pour se voir autoriser de les parcourir. Dans ce cas, la lecture est faite à haute voix par un membre à l'intention de tout le groupe. S'en suivent des explications et des commentaires en lingala, pour permettre à tout le monde de bien comprendre et de s'exprimer.

Voilà donc de quelle manière des attroupements primitifs ont pu petit à petit se structurer sur le plan interne pour devenir des Parlements-debout. Mais leur nombre augmentant, il fallait résoudre le problème du type de rapports devant les régir ainsi que celui de la coordination de leurs actions.

Organisation de l'ensemble

A l'heure actuelle, les différents Parlements-debout fonctionnent comme un tout dont la représentation schématique est la suivante:

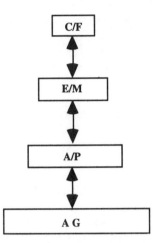

Dans ce schéma, C/F = Coordonnateur en chef
E/M = Etat-major
A/P = Assemblée des Présidents
AG = Assemblée générale ou de tous les membres

Le coordonnateur en chef a la charge de la conception et de la direction générale du mouvement. Il en est le guide suprême. Une fois par semaine, au moins, il se réunit avec les membres de l'Etat-major, au nombre de sept. Ensemble, ils passent en revue les problèmes saillants de l'heure, imaginent les actions à mener et les stratégies correspondantes.

A leur tour, les membres de l'Etat-major se réunissent, une fois par semaine aussi, avec les présidents des différents Parlements. Ils leur font part et discutent avec eux de propositions d'actions et de stratégies arrêtées et en examinent la faisabilité avec le concours ou au niveau de chaque Parlement.

Chaque jeudi, se tient une assemblée générale au cours de laquelle tous les autres membres reçoivent l'information, en débattent et passent directement à l'exécution des actions convenues. L'Assemblée générale a lieu à Limete après le compte-rendu du Conseil du Gouvernement légal dirigé par Etienne Tshisekedi. Plusieurs raisons expliquent le choix, aussi bien de ce moment que de cette zone. Limete est le lieu de résidence de M. Tshisekedi, symbole de la résistance à la dictature mobutiste et Chef de file de l'ensemble de l'Opposition zaïroise. C'est aussi le siège de l'Union pour la Démocratie et le Progrès Social (U.D.P.S.), parti de Tshisekedi, ainsi que de toute cette Opposition.

Le tout premier Parlement-debout est né à Limete. C'est pourquoi on l'appelle *"Parlement-mère"*. Tous les autres Parlements y recourent et s'y soumettent volontiers. A cause à la fois de sa longue expérience et de sa position à la source des informations de l'Opposition. Le jeudi, des centaines de milliers des combattants accourent de vingt-quatre zones de la capitale, pour venir entendre les décisions du Gouvernement du peuple, le seul qu'ils reconnaissent, et en reçoivent des mots d'ordre.

Quant aux contacts avec le Parlements de l'intérieur du pays, ils sont entretenus de manière très suivie par le truchement d'un Secrétaire à l'implantation des Parlements-debout; lequel fait partie du staff dirigeant du Parlement-mère de Limete.

Le Zaïre compte aujourd'hui [c.à.d. en fèvrier 1996] onze Parlements-debout dont huit à Kinshasa et trois à l'intérieur du pays. Il s'agit de Parlements-debout de Kingasani-Masina, Ndjili, Matete, Lemba, Limete, Bongolo, Pont-Kasavubu, Azap, Mbuji-Mayi, Miabi et Kiri dans le Bandundu.

Manifestations de la lutte pour le triomphe de la démocratie

Ces manifestions s'observent le mieux sur un triple plan. Celui des rapports entre membres. Celui de la surveillance et de l'interpellation des hommes politiques. Celui de la participation active à la prise de décisions.

Rapports entre Parlementaires-debout
Les Parlementaires-debout sont constitués par des citoyens zaïrois provenant de toutes les couches sociales. On y trouve en effet, des diplômés d'universités et d'instituts supérieurs; des étudiants et élèves; des analphabètes; des maçons, des menuisiers, des charpentiers, des cordonniers, des domestiques, des sentinelles, des sans-emploi dont principalement des pensionnés civils et militaires.

Nonobstant tout cela, leurs rapports restent fondamentalement des rapports d'égalité et de fraternité. Chacun s'exprime le plus librement qu'il peut et le principe de la tolérance est de stricte observance. Il est interdit à quiconque de faire montre de complexe de supériorité, de chercher à étouffer ou intimider les autres. D'où ce principe quasi sacré dans ces milieux et qui a de plus en plus tendance à gagner tous les autres: *"Personne n'a le droit de faire peur aux amis. Nous sommes tous pratiquement du même âge, parce que tous nés et vivants au XXe siècle"*. L'on ne saurait mieux exprimer l'exigence de l'entretien des rapports de camaraderie en rapport avec le principe démocratique de l'égalité de citoyens!

Surveillance et interpellation des hommes politiques
Autant les Parlementaires-debout tiennent à vivre en camarades et en égaux, autant ils veillent à ce que les leaders politiques de l'Opposition, qui leur servent de guides et de modèles, ne se détournent jamais de l'idéal du changement. Aussi surveillent-ils quotidiennement tous leurs faits et gestes. Aussi vont-ils jusqu'à les corriger physiquement!

Dans le traitement des informations véhiculées par des journaux, des chaînes de radio et de télévision ou circulant de bouche à oreille, une importance particulière est accordée à celles concernant les hommes politiques de l'Opposition: leurs fréquentations, leurs prises de position sur tel ou tel problème d'actualité, leurs attitudes à l'égard de Tshisekedi, symbole du changement voulu par l'ensemble du peuple zaïrois et donc de la lutte contre le régime dictatorial de Mobutu. Question de s'assurer s'ils continuent à demeurer dans cet idéal du changement ou s'ils sont déjà en train de glisser, de rejoindre petit à petit le camp du dictateur.

Dès qu'est établi pareil glissement, son auteur est interpellé publiquement et sommé de s'expliquer. Pour les membres du gouvernement légal, ces interpellations ont généralement lieu le jeudi au moment du compte-rendu du conseil de ministres. La foule, après avoir engagé un débat avec le porte-parole et donné ses avis sur chacune des questions traitées au conseil, cerne le suspect et l'entend dans un interrogatoire très serré. Les non-ministres, quant à eux, sont interpellés soit sur la rue ou carrément à leurs domiciles. Des fois, l'on va jusqu'à organiser des marches de protestation. Ce fut plusieurs fois le cas en juillet et août 1995 contre Frédéric Kibassa, co-président de l'U.D.P.S., devant sa propre maison. Ce qui l'obligea à fuir avec son épouse en Afrique du Sud pendant plus de six mois. Pour tous ces traîtres, la sanction finale est le retrait total de confiance suivi d'un ostracisme politique.

Mais il n'y a point que des renégats de l'opposition qui sont ainsi dans le collimateur des Parlementaires-debout. Il y a aussi tous les gens de Mobutu, lui-même et les pays occidentaux convaincus de soutenir son régime. Les représentants de ces pays, particulièrement ceux de la France, sont conspués à chacun de leurs passages à Limete. Des pétitions contre leurs gouvernements sont régulièrement et massivement signées.

Participation à la prise de décision

Ce triste constat que plusieurs parmi les leaders de l'Opposition trahissent les uns après les autres finit par déterminer les Parlementaires-debout à investir massivement divers organes de prise de décisions. Ceci afin d'amener le peuple à décider lui-même de son sort. Et ce faisant, à appliquer la formule de la démocratie directe.

Mais auparavant, trois importantes décisions vont être prises au cours d'une assemblée générale. Ce sont: l'interdiction d'applaudir tout leader politique autre qu'Etienne Tshisekedi, le combat pour placer les instances dirigeantes entre les mains des candidats du peuple, la suggestion au gouvernement légal des points à inscrire à l'ordre du jour de ses réunions hebdomadaires.

La *première décision* visait à combattre la sentimentalité, à développer l'esprit critique, à éviter de rendre grands des individus dont on n'était pas très sûrs et qui risquaient demain de se retourner contre le peuple.

La *deuxième* se matérialisera particulièrement, mi 1995, lors de la mise sur pied du Secrétariat national de l'U.D.P.S. On verra alors tous les Parlementaires-debout de la capitale se mobiliser et mobiliser tout le peuple en faveur du Dr. Adrien Phongo, du Prof. Kalele-ka-Bila et de Madame Justine Kasavubu, aux postes respectivement de Secrétaire général, de Secrétaire national à l'Organisation et à l'implantation, de Secrétaire nationale aux Relations extérieures. Le même type de mobilisation s'observera et réussira mêmement aux Etats généraux de l'Opposition tenus à Kinshasa du 06 janvier au 20 février 1996, à faire confier la présidence du Bureau définitif à Paul Kapita et celle de l'atelier III appelé à définir les nouvelles stratégies de relance et de radicalisation de la lutte contre la dictature mobutienne, au même Prof. Kalele.

La *troisième* se veut un moyen de pression destiné à emmener le gouvernement légal, l'équipe Tshisekedi, à donner au peuple des instructions claires sur l'attitude à adopter face aux différents comportements de Mobutu et de ses complices, des actions concrètes à mener pour venir à leur bout.

Quant à l'investissement proprement dit dans la prise de décisions, un cas, celui desdits Etats généraux, permet de l'illustrer au mieux.

Dès qu'ils ont eu la confirmation que ces Etats généraux étaient voulus par Mobutu pour disqualifier Tshisekedi au profit d'un Kibassa déjà acquis à sa cause, tous les Parlementaires-debout ont décidé de s'y investir totalement afin de leur imprimer plutôt une nouvelle orientation anti-Mobutu et anti-Kibassa. A cette fin, ils se sont faits membres des divers partis politiques et associations de l'USORAS appelés à participer à ces assises.[2] Grâce à leur nombre et à leur activisme surtout, ils réussiront effectivement à renverser la vapeur. Mobutu sera disqualifié comme Chef de l'Etat et comme candidat aux élections présidentielles. Kibassa perdra son titre de chef de la famille politique USORAS ainsi que tous ses mandats au sein de son parti. Tshisekedi, par contre, verra son pouvoir et son prestige renforcés. Il sera reconfirmé seul Premier Ministre légal et leader maximo de l'ensemble de l'Opposition zaïroise cumulant les titres de Chef de file de l'Opposition et Chef de cette famille politique. Il sera consacré unique candidat de l'Opposition aux présidentielles.

Difficultés rencontrées et stratégies utilisées pour les surmonter

S'étant révélés une grande et très efficace force de redynamisation voire de radicalisation d'une Opposition en perte de vitesse au lendemain de la Conférence Nationale Souveraine, les Parlementaires-debout seront fortement combattus à la fois par Mobutu et des soi-disant opposants à sa solde.

Côté Mobutu, l'on organisera une véritable chasse aux sorcières. Une équipe des militaires commandés par le Capitaine Baramoto, surnommé Zing Zong, sera chargée d'investir les Parlements-debout, pour en disperser les membres à coups de baïonnettes et de crosses; d'arracher et de détruire les journaux; de couper les arbres en-dessous desquels l'on se réunissait.

Mais c'est du côté de la fausse opposition surtout, conformément au principe *"Combattre les opposants par les opposants"*, que les choses seront davantage plus graves. L'on ira en effet d'une campagne de dénigrement savamment orchestrée à des mises en prison, en passant par des mesures d'interdiction, des calomnies et des tortures. Pour tenter de dresser l'opinion contre eux, les Parlementaires-debout seront présentés par certains Fondateurs de l'UDPS, comme *"des bandes de voyous, constituées de jeunes gens drogués et armés de couteaux, de pierres, de tournevis … pour frapper à mort, torturer, et blesser ceux du parti qui ne partagent pas la même opinion que Tshisekedi et ses proches collaborateurs; des irresponsables et d'intégristes"*. Sous prétexte que les Statuts de l'UDPS ne prévoient nulle part un organe appelé *"Parlement-debout"*, le mouvement sera formellement interdit par une décision desdits Fondateurs et une certaine presse mise largement à contribution pour la répercuter.

La mort du co-Fondateur, Roger Gisanga, en pleine réunion du Collège des Fondateurs, de suite d'un arrêt cardiaque, leur sera attribuée.[3] Trois d'entre eux, de passage par hasard sur le lieu en compagnie fortuite d'un membre du MPR[4] inconnu d'eux seront, sur ordre de M. Kibassa, interceptés par sa milice, copieusement battus, torturés et conduits au cachot de la gendarmerie de Limete. L'argent jouant, ils y seront gardés pendant plus d'un mois jusqu'à ce que le Parquet de la même zone se saisisse de l'affaire et établisse leur innocence.

Mais, ni ces actions du pouvoir, ni celles de ses complices dans l'Opposition, ne réussiront point à briser le moral des Parlementaires en question. Bien au contraire! Ils en deviendront encore plus aguerris et continueront, comme si de rien n'était, leur lutte contre la dictature avec davantage de détermination. Ils iront même jusqu'à se doter de leur propre feuillet, *"L'Echo de la C.N.S."*, avec comme devise: *"Débarrassons-nous de faux opposants avant qu'il ne soit tard"*. Ce feuillet, dont la mission est justement d'identifier et de dénoncer ces faux opposants, sera hebdomadaire et de distribution gratuite.

Avenir du Parlementarisme-Debout

Le phénomène *"Parlement-debout"* est promu à un bel avenir. Cette affirmation se fonde principalement sur deux facteurs. Ce sont: la grande aspiration de l'ensemble du peuple zaïrois au changement démocratique d'une part, la maturité politique et la détermination des Parlementaires-debout eux-mêmes d'autre part.

Le peuple zaïrois, qui en a assez depuis longtemps de la trahison de ses leaders politiques parce que retardant sa libération de la dictature mobutiste qu'il déteste à mort, a besoin de gens qui puissent l'aider à se débarrasser d'une telle classe de politiciens. L'action des Parlementaires-debout s'inscrivant dans cette optique, bénéficie de plus en plus de multiples soutiens populaires en provenance, non seulement de tous les coins du pays, mais aussi des communautés zaïroises à l'étranger. Ce fait encourage énormément lesdits parlementaires, leur remonte fortement le moral et les pousse à aller de l'avant.

A cela s'ajoute la confiance grandissante en eux-mêmes, née d'une double démystification: celle de l'ensemble de la classe politique nationale et celle de Mobutu lui-même. Sans oublier la connaissance progressive et approfondie des différentes lois de la guerre.

La découverte, au travers des discussions avec eux, des nombreuses lacunes dans le chef des hommes politiques que l'on admirait et craignait naguère, a fini par convaincre les Parlementaires-debout qu'ils n'avaient aucune raison de continuer à se sentir complexés. Bien au contraire! Ils pouvaient, étant donné la justesse des plusieurs de leurs points de vue telle que démontrée dans plusieurs cas, contribuer positivement à faire sortir le Zaïre de la crise actuelle. Et qu'il était temps qu'ils s'y mettent plus sérieusement encore.

La conviction qu'il y avait bien moyen de vaincre Mobutu et de se débarrasser de son régime, tient aux nombreuses réussites dans la mise en échec de plusieurs de ses plans depuis le début de la transition démocratique au Zaïre.

Le peuple est de plus en plus conscient de ce qu'il a su, sans armes, sans argent, sans stratèges dûment formés et éprouvés, contraindre Mobutu, malgré sa longue expérience politique, ses multiples appuis extérieurs, son argent, ses milices constituées d'éléments les plus sûrs et fidèles, parce que propres frères de région et de clan, des innombrables marabouts venant de tous les coins du globe terrestre, à fuir la capitale pour se réfugier dans son village natal, à céder aux pressions en faveur du multipartisme intégral en lieu et place du multipartisme à trois qu'il défendait lui, à accepter la tenue d'une Conférence nationale souveraine, à capituler devant la détermination kasaïenne de conserver une zone monétaire indépendante de Kinshasa et du reste du pays, à se laisser ravir la direction des Etats généraux de l'Opposition ainsi qu'à laisser ceux-ci évoluer et prendre des décision qui lui étaient entièrement défavorables. Comme quoi, *"ce monsieur"* était point aussi fort qu'on le croyait!

Toutes ces fructueuses expériences dans la lutte contre Mobutu et ses agents infiltrés dans les rangs de l'Opposition ont conduit au dégagement de la vertu d'un certain nombre de comportements que les Parlementaires-debout sont aujourd'hui occupés à s'enseigner les uns aux autres afin de récolter davantage de succès dans la poursuite du combat. Il s'agit entre autres des exigences d'être correctement informé de tout ce qui se passe; de garder haut son moral malgré les injures, calomnies, brimades de l'ennemi; de ne point obtempérer à ses ordres; de persévérer contre vents et marées dans la défense des bonnes causes. Présentées sous la forme d'un catéchisme, ces exigences se formulent comme suit:

- *Un bon Parlementaire-debout est celui qui a l'information; qui la recherche dès qu'il se réveille. Et donc, qui ne passe pas un seul jour sans se rendre au Parlement.*
- *Le Parlementaire-debout doit être lui-même le premier à informer tout le monde de la manière dont il est dénigré par les ennemis. Et il doit le faire en minimisant,*

en tournant en ridicules même, les différents éléments de cette campagne de dénigrement;
- *Le Parlementaire-debout ne doit jamais tenir compte des interdictions faites par ceux qu'il combat. Il doit les passer outre. Il doit les ignorer;*
- *Même s'il est fortement combattu, le Parlementaire-debout doit continuer à défendre ses idées; dès lors qu'il est convaincu de leur justesse et que les faits lui donnent raison.*

Comme on peut le voir, ces recommandations répondent toutes à ces principes-ci de l'art de la guerre:
- *Le pouvoir, c'est l'information ou encore, c'est le savoir qui confère la supériorité morale nécessaire sur les hommes et les événements;*
- *La minimisation de la campagne de dénigrement de l'ennemi en annihile les effets psychologiques, la démoralisation escomptés;*
- *Le pouvoir d'un chef amorce sa descente aux enfers dès que les sujets se mettent à désobéir;*
- *La vérité finit toujours par triompher.*

Hier encore, incompris et boudés par beaucoup, les *Parlementaires-debout* font aujourd'hui la fierté du peuple zaïrois. Ils sont de plus en plus cités comme modèles. Il y a, par conséquent, lieu, au vu de ce qui a été dit dans ce texte, de conclure que l'expérience zaïroise des Parlementaires-debout constitue, pour l'établissement sur le continent africain d'un véritable pouvoir du peuple, par et pour le peuple, un exemple digne de grande attention.

Notes

[1] Il sera créé, pour assurer le suivi et l'exécution des décisions de la C.N.S., un organe spécial. Il s'appelera HCR ou Haut Conseil de la République. Et puis, avec l'incorporation des anciens députés du MPR en son sein, HCR-PT ou Haut Conseil de la Réputblique-Parlement de Transition.

[2] USORAS: Union Sacrée de l'Opposition Radicale, Alliés et Société civile. C'est la famille politique zaïroise opposée à celle de M. Mobutu ou F.P.C. (Forces Politiques du Conclave).

[3] Mr. Gisanga était un cardiaque connu. Il avait même été, en avril 1995, c'est-à-dire quatre mois avant son décès, en soins médicaux en Afrique du Sud. Revenu au pays, il s'est mis à passer outre les prescriptions de ses médecins.

[4] MPR, Mouvement Populaire de la Révolution, le parti de Mobutu.

6

Challenges Facing the Mandela Government

Margaret C. Lee

The peaceful resolution of the South African conflict and the reconstruction of the state not only depends on the removal of the statutory features of the apartheid state, but also on the ability of the ANC to sell its compromises and concessions to its constituency. In other words, a peaceful transition from the collapsed apartheid state to a democratic political order lies not only in allaying the fears of white people, but most crucially, in linking the compromises made to achieve this objective with relief for the social and economic deprivations that the majority of black people have always hoped will be immediately removed by a nonracial democratic state.[1]

Once again a familiar scenario is being played out in Southern Africa. Following the collapse of white political supremacy and the elections for democratic rule, the African majority must resign itself to the fact that socioeconomic change, if it is to happen, will be slow and arduous. Seventeen years after the collapse of the white racist state in Zimbabwe and seven years after its collapse in Namibia, the majority population has yet to benefit from the liberation struggle that gave rise to the new state. While the "new"[2] state of South Africa is in the process of being born, unless there is a radical shift in economic empowerment from the old apartheid forces to the new political structure, South Africa is likely to follow the path of both Zimbabwe and Namibia in terms of limited socioeconomic change.

One of the reasons is the fact that South Africa did not experience a revolution but a negotiated political compromise.[3] It is important to make the distinction between the two, since the former is a term used loosely, especially by whites, in South Africa. Had South Africa experienced a real revolution, a radical change would have occurred. The political and economic structures of the country would have been totally disrupted. Instead, these entities remained intact. With respect to the political structure, an agreement was reached for the black majority[4] to share power with the white minority. The basic political structure, therefore, was not altered. The economic structure of the country remained intact, which means that white economic hegemony (control over the banking industry, financial markets, industry, etc.) was not disturbed. Consequently, once the political transition occurred, the African majority still found itself on the lowest rung of the economic ladder.

As a result of the negotiated compromise, the Mandela government has been left economically impotent. Perhaps the greatest insight into the economic impotence of this government was revealed during Mandela's address opening Parliament on February 17, 1995. Mandela noted that

It is also appropriate that on this occasion we draw the attention of the country to the actual reality that the government has extremely limited resources to address the many and urgent needs of our people ... We are very keen that this real situation should be communicated to the people as a whole. All of us, especially the leadership of political organizations and civil society must rid ourselves of the wrong notion that the government has a big bag full of money. The government does not have such riches ... We must all absorb this reality into our thinking in a cold and dispassionate manner. We must not allow ourselves to be seduced into a world of false hopes leading to unrealistic actions based on the wrong assumption that the government can be coerced to meet demands that it cannot meet, however justified and legitimate these demands might be.[5]

He further stated that

It is important that we rid ourselves of the culture of entitlement which leads to the expectation that the government must promptly deliver whatever it is that we demand. A culture that results in some people refusing to meet their obligations such as rent and service payments or engaging in other unacceptable actions such as the forcible occupation of houses.[6]

It was necessary for Mandela to dispel the widespread notion among the majority population that economic and social gains would be free of charge. During the political campaign, many people were led to believe that socioeconomic improvements (i.e. housing, electricity, education, health care, etc.) would be paid for by the government. According to Warren Krafchik of the Institute for Democracy in South Africa (Idasa), implicit in the ANC's early electioneering was that an ANC-led government would provide free housing, land and electricity. He noted that the ANC did not go out of its way to clarify for people that they would have to pay for socioeconomic development.[7] Rich Mkhondo, a SA journalist, concurs with Krafchik noting that

The ANC did not explain to the people exactly how they're going to get the houses. There are a lot of people who are still confused. Many of them thought that it was going to be like the apartheid era where the government just built a lot of houses and people just moved in and rented the houses on a lease-hold.[8]

The Mandela government is certainly in a precarious position as it attempts to transform the socioeconomic status of the majority population. The problems the country faces as a result of over three hundred years of white domination cannot be wished away. These issues are very serious and, if left unresolved, will disrupt the democratic initiative in the country.

This chapter seeks to discuss the major challenges the Mandela government faced during its first fifteen months (May 1994 to August 1995). They were daunting. For example, the unresolved conflict between the ANC and the Inkatha Freedom Party (IFP), led by Home Affairs Minister Mangosuthu Buthelezi, alone had the potential to wreck havoc throughout the country. The major problem of crime in the country could not be brought under control without enhanced employment opportunities. Such opportunities could not be created without the implementation of the government's Reconstruction and Development Program (RDP), which was in turn dependent on economic growth. Economic growth was largely dependent on investor confidence in political stability. The challenges faced by the government during this period will be discussed in the following order: the conflict between the ANC and the IFP; the implementation of the RDP; the establishment of strong local government structures; crime; the youth; the Truth Commission; institutionalized racism; and illegal immigrants.

Conflict Between the ANC and the IFP

The greatest challenge the Mandela government of national unity (GNU) faced during its first fifteen months was the conflict that existed between the ANC and the IFP. It was considered the greatest challenge because it had the potential to ignite violence throughout the country. This conflict, which dates back to at least 1983, unfortunately, was not resolved prior to the April 1994 elections.[9] In 1994, the ANC-IFP conflict centered around the unresolved issues of the status of the Zulu monarch and the powers of the regions, especially in KwaZulu/Natal. Prior to the elections, Buthelezi

> insisted that the Zulu people had the right to self-determination, that they should be able to draft their own constitution, and that the KwaZulu homeland should not be dismantled until there was a constitutional dispensation acceptable to them … The constitution Inkatha proposed for the KwaZulu-Natal region amounted to secession, making the territory a sovereign state whose laws would take precedence over those of South Africa. The state would have its own president, its own constitutional court, its own autonomous central bank, and its own army. The South African government would not be able to send armed forces there, nor levy taxes without the state's approval.[10]

In order to get Buthelezi to contest the April 1994 elections, both the ANC and the National Party (NP) agreed to resolve these issues through international mediation following the elections.

IFP members denied any secessionist plan. Instead, they insisted they were calling for the creation of a strong federal government, with significant powers being granted to the provinces. The failure of the Mandela government to follow through on its promise to allow international mediation only exacerbated the ANC-IFP conflict. The ANC, some speculated, feared that such mediation would reveal that it had no intention of creating a federal system of government when the final constitution was drafted. Instead, the ANC-led government intended to maintain the current existing system of government.

As a result of the above conflict, the IFP pulled out of the Constitutional Assembly (CA) and "made it plain that it would accept no constitution written in its absence."[11] The writing of the final constitution, however, proceeded without the IFP. Following its withdrawal, the IFP leaked a strategic document that, again, some argued, contained a secessionist strategy. Others suggested, however,

> that the release of the document was an "inspired leak" deliberately engineered by the party to foment just the sort of fears that have emerged from the ANC. The purpose was to indicate the way the wind is blowing inside Inkatha and send a message that the mediation issue needs to be settled, otherwise it will poison relationships.[12]

If, in fact, the latter was the purpose of releasing the document, it began to renew fear in South Africa that a resurgent battle between the ANC and IFP could wreck havoc, not just in Natal, but once again in the townships of greater Johannesburg (Gauteng

Province).[13] While politically related violence decreased tremendously following the 1994 elections, KwaZulu/Natal Province continued to experience serious unrest. In fact, in a thirteen month period following the elections, there were at least one thousand politically related deaths.[14]

In what was deemed by many to be a further attempt to decrease the power of Buthelezi and the IFP, Parliament approved the Remuneration of Traditional Leaders Bill, which would allow the central government to pay traditional leaders[15] and provide them with many of the perks enjoyed by members of parliament (i.e., official residences, cars, and drivers). The Act was controversial because, according to the Interim Constitution, provincial legislatures have legislative authority over traditional authorities.[16] This did not, however, prevent the central government from concurrently paying traditional leaders.[17] Opponents of the Act, including the IFP, argued that it was "a clear political ploy on the part of the ANC to gain political control of the province." The ANC, on the other hand, felt that it would "liberate traditional leaders in KwaZulu/ Natal from the IFP's yoke. 'We are freeing (them) from a particular bondage ... (of pledging) allegiance to a particular political party and not to the province'."[18] In response, the IFP-dominated KwaZulu/Natal provincial cabinet approved two bills that would prevent traditional leaders from accepting central government payments as outlined in the Remuneration of Traditional Leaders Act.[19] IFP leaders also announced plans to challenge the Act in the Constitutional Court.[20] It is estimated that is will cost the government R100 million a year to implement the Act.[21]

KwaZulu/Natal was the only province that did not agree to the central government paying the salaries of traditional leaders.[22] There were those within the province, however, who did support the Remuneration of Traditional Leaders Act. For example, Prince Sifiso Zulu, the spokesman for Zulu King Goodwill Zwelithini's Royal Council noted that

> It is unfortunate that these parties are blinded to the reality of the unique situation in South Africa where we're trying to democratise the entire country. If traditional leaders were going to be stumbling blocks to democracy and development, that would have to be addressed. You can't expect traditional leaders to open up to democracy without some movement toward recognising their importance and difficulties.[23]

Although Mandela was criticized for failing to keep his promise to have international mediation, and for attempting to further usurp Buthelezi's power in KwaZulu/Natal with the Remuneration of Traditional Leaders Act, there did not exist much sympathy in the country for Buthelezi. He, during this period, was viewed by many as being erratic and determined to destabilize the Government of National Unity (GNU) by inciting his followers to violence when he was not pleased with governmental policy. The resolution of the ANC/IFP conflict will require deft diplomatic maneuvering on the part of the Mandela government. A resolution of the conflict is essential for the peace and security of the country.

Implementation of the Reconstruction and Development Program (RDP)

The second greatest challenge faced by the Mandela government following the April

1994 elections was the implementation of the RDP. The cornerstone of the ANC-led government's attempt to change the socioeconomic status of the majority population rests with this program. The RDP, if implemented, is designed to provide land, jobs, electricity, housing, water, transport, a clean and healthy environment, tele-communications, nutrition, health care, and social welfare. When the RDP was first drafted prior to the 1994 elections, the government planned, over a five year period, to "redistribute a substantial amount of land to landless people, build more than one million houses, provide clean water and sanitation to all, electrify 2.5 million new homes, and provide access for all to affordable health care, and telecommunications."[24]

For the majority of Africans, the sole determining factor for whether or not the ANC-led government will be deemed successful in 1999 rests with improvements in their socioeconomic status. Of the 40 million people in South Africa, 17 million (42 percent of households) "live below the poverty line with incomes of no more than $1,800 a year." Seven million of these individuals are homeless. An estimated 12 million do not have clean water and nine million are illiterate. In some areas unemployment is as high as 50 percent, and 63 percent do not have electricity. As a result of apartheid, "about 60,000 Whites own more than 87 percent of the nation's land, producing more than 90 percent of the crops."[25]

Transforming the RDP from an election propaganda document into a program of action is not an easy task. This is especially the case since a large percentage of funding for the program is slated to come from the more efficient use of existing resources. Other funding will come from revenues, issuing debt (e.g., general obligation and revenue bonds), grants, foreign governments, and international investment.[26] At its December 1994 meeting, the ANC announced that the government "will sell state assets to reduce the country's debt and provide more cash for development."[27]

Over a period of five years, it is estimated that the RDP will cost from 26 to 30 billion dollars, and in order for the government to have success in implementing the RDP, economic growth will need to be at least four to six percent. For 1995, the gross domestic product (GDP) was only 3.3 percent. The estimated GDP for 1996 was similarly 3.3 percent.[28]

The ANC has been lauded by many for the compromises it made to maintain fiscal discipline, free enterprise, and economic growth as the engine for development. The latter point is very important, because it signaled that the ANC had given priority to economic outcomes other than the redistribution of the wealth and meeting the basic needs of the masses. Development had become a distant goal. The ANC-led government went to great lengths to convince the white minority that their economic status would not be disrupted. In fact, at its December 1994 meeting, the government came under fire from the 3,000 delegates who said that "it is time to give precedence to the needs of the black majority over the fears of the white minority."[29]

The limited success of the RDP, however, could not be solely blamed on the economic impotency of the ANC-led government and/or slow economic growth. Critics, for example, argued that "an RDP bureaucracy may itself be an obstacle to implementation of the programme," as a result, for example, of "endless policy formulation at the central level" and "the increasing tendency towards attempting to centralise control."[30] Krafchik of Idasa noted that "there is no one in the RDP office that is an expert on project appraisal and no appraisal department is to be set up."[31]

There were some RDP successes during the first fifteen months of the Mandela government. Free health care was made available for pregnant women and children under six, and at least 378,171 homes were electrified. Over 5 million children in more than 12,000 schools were receiving free meals through the Primary School Nutrition Program. Moreover, water had been provided to some areas, and several communities had their land returned to them.[32] The government, however, had a serious challenge before it in the areas of employment, housing, land reform, and education.

Employment

There was perhaps nothing more central to prospects for socioeconomic change among the majority population than enhanced employment opportunities. While the overall unemployment level in South Africa is around 43 percent, in some areas it is as high as 50 percent. The high rate of unemployment in the country has been directly linked to the growing rate of crime, which is having a negative impact on overall economic growth.

The future prognosis for increased employment opportunities does not look promising. One projection is that with a growth rate of three percent, the number of individuals employed in the formal sector would only increase to 8.5 million by the year 2000. Currently, there are just under 8 million employed in the formal sector. "A five percent growth rate would increase formal employment to only around nine million."[33] Annually, nine-tenths of prospective new workers are unable to find jobs in the formal sector.[34]

One of the greatest threats to economic stability during the first fifteen months of the Mandela government was the wave of strikes that hit the country. The conflict between labor and management intensified as an attempt was made for the two entities to reach a compromise on a new labor bill. After two months of hostile negotiations, a compromise was reached between labor, management and the government.[35] This compromise was likely to enhance economic stability, which should lead to increased foreign investment, and prevent the threatened export of local business capital. It is argued, however, that "extra protection for the unionised few ... could mean fewer jobs for the rest."[36]

If South Africa is to attract more investment and increase job opportunities for the unemployed, its industrial sector must become far more efficient. In a research study entitled *Improving Manufacturing Performance in South Africa,* the authors concluded that industry had to become the powerhouse of the economy. This sector, however, is beset with problems, according to the study, including:

> lack of competitiveness, lack of attention to skills training — particularly multi-skilling — and poor work organisation. This is reflected in weak export performance, poor productivity and the fact that industry has not been able to provide enough new jobs to mop up at least some unemployment in a meaningful way.[37]

Housing

By August 1995, not one RDP house had been built, although within a five year period an estimated 1 million houses are to be built. At the height of this building, an estimated 300,000 houses are to be constructed a year. In the 1995 RDP allocation of funds, housing subsidies and infrastructure received the largest allocation, R1.4 billion out of R7.8 billion.

The expectation that 300,000 houses can be built in one year was unrealistic, according to Krafchik. During the best year in South Africa, Krafchik argues, only 30,000 new houses were built, including those built by both the private and public sectors. He further noted that "there is a serious problem in terms of skills, all the way down to artisan skills. In the housing program, for example, in order to build 300,000 houses a year, we need to be training about 1,000 artisans a year. Artisan training has gone down to less than 100 a year for the whole country."[38] Another problem faced by the housing sector during this period was a shortage of building materials.

Land Reform

With respect to the issue of land, Cyril Ramaphosa, former secretary-general of the ANC and former president of the Constitutional Assembly, noted that "Unless we settle the land question, we do not have a country."[39] According to the RDP, 30 percent of arable land in the country is to be redistributed. The government is confronted with both the economics[40] and politics of land redistribution. By early 1995, the Restitution of Land Rights Act was in place. The purpose of the Act is to enable land to be restored to those dispossessed during the apartheid years. A Commission on the Restitution of Land Rights for the purpose of investigating and mediating land claims, and a specialized Land Claims Court responsible for determining restitution and compensation to those who lost their land due to forced removal, were established. In addition, the GNU cabinet approved other bills, including the Interim Protection of Informal Land Rights Bill and the Land Reform (Labor Tenants) Bill.

The purpose of the Interim Protection of Informal Land Rights Bill is to temporarily freeze tenure patterns in the former homelands. The bill "does not change any land titles or provide for expropriation," but instead gave land officials until the end of 1996 to figure out actual residential patterns since formal landholding records are chaotic. Buthelezi criticized the bill saying that "it formed part of a concerted strategy — along with the plan for central government to pay traditional leaders' salaries — to undermine the power of chiefs to administer land in tribal areas."[41]

The Land Reform (Labor Tenants) Bill is more controversial because it is designed to "either give tenants secure title or enable them to buy their own land from farmers."[42] For generations, black families have lived on this land and "now provide free, or virtually free, labour in exchange for a small patch of land for subsistence farming."[43] Eddie Koch, in June 1995, noted that as a result of proposed land reform:

> The most unstable terrain exists ... in parts of KwaZulu/Natal and the Eastern Transvaal where labour tenants and farmers have been waging a low-intensity class struggle over rights to land. Flashpoints are the Colenso/Weenen area and districts around Piet Retief ... In both regions, white farmers, fearful of claims from people who have lived on the land for decades, have been evicting scores of black families, impounding their cattle and burning some of their homesteads. Workers and farm tenants responded by threatening an armed invasion of white-owned land and then by waging a massive labour strike this year. At different stages of these ferocious conflicts, cattle were hamstrung, fences ripped down and there have been cases of farmers being assassinated.[44]

Following the announcement of the bill, white commercial farmers[45] met to discuss it. Surprisingly, many of them accepted the inevitability of redistribution and acknowledged that they would have to change their labor policies.[46] This did not mean, however, that the implementation of the bill would be smooth. In fact, a major problem the government faced was finding the money to buy the land from the commercial farmers. The labor tenants indicated that they "were not prepared to pay for land obtained from white farmers as provided for in the bill."[47]

Governmental land reform was further challenged by the failure of the KwaZulu/Natal provincial government to implement three Land Reform Presidential Lead Projects worth more than R79-million,[48] and resistance by the South African National Defense Force (SANDF) to return unused land back to blacks who were forcibly removed during the apartheid years.[49]

Education

Of the 61 Acts passed by Parliament between May 1994 and May 1995, not one came from the Department of Education. This was interesting since the Department of Education is confronted with a plethora of problems as a result of apartheid education. For example, whites account for 84 percent of those with a college education and blacks account for the more than 90 percent of the population with no formal education.[50]

Although the seventeen apartheid educational departments have been consolidated to form one system, the equalization of education across race will take a long time. While blacks are now allowed to attend better equipped white schools, many cannot afford the cost.[51]

During September 1994, it was reported that tens of thousands of mostly black students were not in school, and that the government needed to build hundreds of new schools and recruit more staff. In addition, many of those who were in school dropped out early, and many schools lacked appropriate discipline among both teachers and students.[52]

The challenge for the government in the educational arena is awesome. On the one hand, the government must attempt to instill a sense of "culture of learning" into students who have developed a "culture of protest," and on the other, struggle to change the system against the resistance of white Afrikaners, who not only still have a considerable amount of power over education, but also are committed to the maintenance of the status quo.[53]

The Establishment of Strong Local Government Structures

The third greatest challenge faced by the government was putting in place strong local government structures. The local governments were significant because heretofore segregated cities, townships, towns, and rural communities were to be joined together in an effort to redistribute wealth and resources. Specifically, according to the Local Government Transition Act, the total restructuring of local government was to take place in order to phase out the current racially based system so that it can be replaced with a single nonracial system.[54] Under apartheid,

> Black townships were flung to the outskirts of rich white towns and cities. While people in the cities had access to electricity, housing, a flowing water supply and tarred roads, almost 90% of townships were unlit and with very poor services. Shack settlements grew around the cities as African people were kept out through influx control ... Rich commercial and industrial areas were included in the white areas and paid their taxes to the white local authorities. Black local authorities were denied a share of this legitimate tax resource and became bankrupt. They were not democratically elected nor could they deliver.[55]

In keeping with the Local Government Transition Act, new boundaries were drawn in order to join heretofore racially exclusive areas together. These new areas were supposed to be designed in such a way that

> they provide the basis for the redistribution of resources from richer areas, middle class areas, to poorer areas, and from white areas to black areas, so that in the city of Cape Town, for example, the local government re-drawing the lines would contain white areas and black areas in the same local government authority.[56]

The resources available for narrowing the gap between the wealthy white suburbs and the poor townships are limited. Nonetheless, according to Andrew Boraine, then Acting Head of the Institute for Local Governance and Development, "We can't afford to maintain the standards of the old white municipalities. We have to cut down."[57] Furthermore, local government experts noted that local authorities would "have to supply the service, regardless of whether communities can pay. Provision of basic services is both stipulated by the interim Constitution and promised by the Reconstruction and Development Programme."[58]

The demarcation of boundaries to join poor and wealthy areas was extremely important if redistribution of wealth was to occur. It was in the major metropolitan areas of Cape Town, Johannesburg, Durban, and Bloemfontein that major demarcation had occurred. These areas had been divided into Transitional Metropolitan Sub-structures (TMS). Each TMS was, in turn, divided into wards. The Transitional Metropolitan Council (TMC) is responsible for the entire metropolitan area.[59]

Stand-alone towns[60] have been divided into wards with one local council.[61] Each province in South Africa is responsible for developing its own local government system based on local conditions. Therefore, different forms of local government are being developed. Most rural areas will have a rural district council with a number of primary local councils.[62]

The establishment of strong local government structures is crucial for the government, especially since much of RDP funding is scheduled to be allocated to local governments. Local governments will also be responsible for resolving the question of the failure of many township residents to pay rent and service fees.[63] The government is dependent on much of this money for reconstruction and development in the townships. Under the new local government system, "the subregions, or local councils, do not have the power to resist paying levies to a metropolitan council; it holds the funds for the entire region."[64] This policy, hopefully, will end the rent and service boycotts of the 1980s and enhance development in the townships.

Crime

A fourth challenge the Mandela government faced was crime. Crime in South Africa is posing one of the greatest challenges to economic development. According to an article in the *Financial Mail* of South Africa:

> Unless the spiral of murders, rapes, armed robberies, carjackings and assaults is reversed, the flight of skills and capital will accelerate, investors will go elsewhere and the RDP will founder in brigandage.[65]

According to police statistics, in 1995, there was a murder in South Africa every 29 minutes, a rape every 16 minutes, a vehicle hijacking every 54 minutes, an armed robbery every 5.5 minutes, an assault with intent every 3.5 minutes, and a burglary every 3 minutes.[66]

The high rate of crime, according to Lloyd Vogelman, Director of the Study of Violence and Reconciliation at the University of the Witwatersrand, is not just a result of poverty. Instead, it is a consequence of the fact that poverty "has been associated historically with an exceptionally high unemployment rate (40 to 50 percent, or higher in some areas), political instability, illegitimacy of government (before last year's election) and a culture of violence — both from the State and its security forces and from the liberation movements and their guerrilla wings." In addition, Vogelman notes, largely as a result of the fact that apartheid brought the law into disrepute, South Africans are known for disrespecting the law.[67]

Poor pay, low morale, corruption, and lack of resources within the South African Police Service (SAPS) does not enhance the proficiency with which police are able to patrol the streets of South Africa. In some townships, for example, reportedly police often do not have vehicles and, therefore, have to use public transportation to investigate cases.[68]

Criminals in South Africa also know that there exists a great probability that they will not be arrested, but if arrested, will likely not be prosecuted for their crime. From 1990 to 1995, according to criminologist Lorraine Glanz, while serious crime increased by 30 percent, criminal convictions declined by 7 percent.[69]

Without increased employment opportunities, South Africa will not see any reversal in this crime wave. In fact, the crime rate will likely continue to increase, posing even greater problems for the government.

Youth

The black youth pose a special challenge to the government because they represent the future of the country. If the youth are to become responsible citizens, the government must replace the "culture of violence" in the townships with a "culture of learning." In addition, the youth must become a central part of the RDP, and the overall quality of their life must be enhanced.

In a study conducted by the Centre for the Study of Violence and Reconciliation, Monique Marks concluded that

> The youth ascribed their involvement in violence to the violent nature of the security forces in the townships. Their active participation in violence, in turn, made them vulnerable to attacks by the security forces. The youth were subjected to an array of repressive measures such as mass arrest and detention and indiscriminate shootings. They were harassed in the streets, during rallies and funerals and in schools ... they justified their acts of violence against the police as retaliation. They rationalised their violence as defensive and not offensive.[70]

The escalation of violence in the townships was a result of the inequalities of apartheid, and violence was perceived as a means of changing the status quo. Marks further notes, according to township youth, "A perception that violence was a necessary part of transition gave rise to the glorification of casualties and the mounting of tensions."[71] Much of the political violence that was initially directed at the security forces and justified as a means of ridding the country of white racist rule, has become an integral part of township life as criminal violence. Most of the victims of such violence are other township residents.

Many of the youth who are currently involved in criminal violence sacrificed their education in order to heed the call of the ANC during 1984-86 to make the townships "ungovernable." The majority of them have no formal skills, are unemployed, and feel marginalized from society at large. Many are also angry that they, unlike ANC members in government, have not benefited from the political transition. If the youth are going to be a stabilizing force for the government, a creative way must be found to make them a major part of the RDP. Employment opportunities must be made available, including skills development. Township education and the quality of life in the townships also must be improved, because, as Marks notes, "township conditions promote violent inclinations among the inhabitants. This is more so among youth especially because recreational facilities are lacking."[72]

The need to tackle the problem of black youth is made especially more urgent by the findings of a study assessing the conditions under which children live in South Africa. The study, which was conducted by the National Institute for Economic Policy (NIEP), concluded that largely as a result of apartheid:

> Almost four out of every 10 children under the age of 16 live in the poorest 20 percent of households ... This imbalance is reflected in an unacceptably high incidence of malnutrition and mortality among children in the poorest sections of society, which in turn is a result of complex processes in society ... Infant mortality is ... most acute in the African community, where 125 children out of every 1000 die before reaching the age of five. The average rate for the whole country is estimated at between 115 and 120 ... Based on NIEP findings, South Africa would rank among the 35 worst countries in the world.[73]

Truth Commission

Another challenge for the government is the Truth Commission. It is perhaps one of the most delicate political issues for the entire country. Created for the purpose of probing "human rights abuses committed in the course of the political struggles,"[74] many fear that the Commission could turn into a "witch hunt." Instead of enhancing unity and reconciliation, the country would become more divided and angry.

The Truth Commission was officially established by the Promotion of National Unity and Reconciliation Act. According to the Act, amnesty was to be given to individuals who committed offenses before December 5, 1993. Such offenses, however, would have to have been committed for a political purpose, with the nature of such offenses bearing some resemblance to the stated political purpose.[75] Those granted amnesty "would not be liable in civil court for damages nor would the state or any organisation they represented."[76] Numerous families of victims of apartheid era crimes pronounced their opposition to the amnesty provision of the Truth Commission and instead called for the prosecution of assassins of political activists.[77]

It is anticipated that as the offenses committed by individuals during the apartheid era are revealed, top governmental officials, including members of the ANC, IFP, and NP, will be implicated in sinister activities. As a result of the impact that the Truth Commission will likely have on the GNU and the society at large, many question just how much of the past needs to be revealed if the country is to move forward. On the other hand, others argue that the country cannot move forward until the sins of the past are revealed. Hopefully the Commission will be able to realize its objective without further polarizing the country.

Institutionalized Racism

The seventh challenge identified in this study concerns institutionalized racism. In a society that has been polarized by race, it is impossible for racism not to exist. Although the apartheid laws have been removed from the statute books, many whites still retain the notion that they are superior to other racial groups in the country. Consequently, many whites feel that blacks are not capable of doing jobs that once were reserved for whites. Ironically, this notion of white supremacy is often reinforced by blacks who similarly feel that whites are more competent than blacks, and often seek the assistance of whites instead of blacks.[78] The notion of white supremacy will certainly continue to affect socioeconomic development within the black community, since many blacks are dependent on whites for employment in a country where the wealth remains in the hands of the white minority. A large percentage of blacks, therefore, will continue to be marginalized economically as a result of institutionalized racism.

Racism within the ANC, however, is more perplexing, in light of the stated nonracial policy of the party. As long as the ANC was fighting the apartheid regime, the issue of racism within the party was ignored. Since the 1994 elections, however, the problem of racism has surfaced. As a Western Cape parliamentarian noted:

Regardless of the April elections' emphatic African stamp for the ANC, the minorities (whites, Indians and coloureds) have a disproportionate influence ... We are prisoners of non-racialism. It's just a concept. We have not unpacked it ... If Cabinet Ministers who are supposed to know that the majority of Africans come from a disadvantaged background advertise jobs in their departments for people with five years' experience in the public sector or experience in handling budgets worth billions of rand, what are they saying? ... Let's have a standard which will make it possible for Africans to be involved ... ANC members must be catalysts for non-racialism and the ANC must be seen to be a home for us all.[79]

During 1994, racism reportedly was reflected in the way some ministers hired in their departments. Mac Maharaj, Minister of Transportation, for example, was accused of hiring only Indians. Prior to his death, Minister of Housing, Joe Slovo, was accused of hiring only whites, while Kader Asmal, Minister of Water Affairs and Forestry was similarly accused of hiring only whites.[80] Complaints were also raised within the Department of Foreign Affairs where allegedly ANC members who had been trained abroad in foreign affairs had not been able to get jobs in the department, although the Minister of Foreign Affairs, Alfred Nzo, is African and a member of the ANC.[81]

The alleged perpetuation of racism by some ANC governmental officials speaks to a fundamental contradiction within the party. The party, therefore, needs to address the issue and rectify it in order to prevent further disunity within the ANC, and among the society at large. Furthermore, it will be fundamentally impossible for the ANC-led government to address the larger issue of white supremacy as long as the perception exists among ANC members that Africans are discriminated against by the party.

Illegal Immigrants

The last challenge identified in this study is the issue of illegal immigrants. This issue has caused such a controversy in South Africa that the South African National Defense Force (SANDF), in June 1995, "called for a 3 000-volt electric fence along the country's border with Mozambique to be switched on to lethal mode to deter thousands of illegal immigrants."[82] Between 1986 and 1989, the 62km fence was on lethal mode during which time 94 people were electrocuted.[83] The army wants to extend the fence another 108km.[84]

It is estimated that there are from two to eight million illegal immigrants in South Africa.[85] During the first five months of 1995, more than 10,000 people crossed the electrified fence.[86] Most immigrants attempt to cross the fence in search of a better economic life. In 1993, some 96,600 illegal immigrants were expelled to 39 countries, mostly to Mozambique, Zimbabwe, and Lesotho. The cost to the government of providing housing, education, police, and medical care just to Mozambicans, who make up the largest number of illegal immigrants, is extremely high. The estimated cost for 1995 was R270 million and by 2000, it is estimated that the cost could be R1 billion.[87]

Among many people in South Africa, a xenophobia has developed about illegal immigrants. They are accused of grabbing low-wage jobs, undercutting prices, and aggravating unemployment and crime. In Alexandra township, allegedly some immigrants were able to get false IDs which allowed them to receive RDP assistance. It is feared that ethnic antagonism and civil conflict would be sparked in townships as a result of this.[88]

In terms of crime and violence, toward the end of 1994, police border control specialist Colonel Van Niekerk estimated that as much as 14 percent of it involved illegal immigrants. They are mainly involved in gunrunning, drug trafficking, car theft, and armed robbery.[89]

Not all South Africans are xenophobic about illegal immigrants. Wilmont James, Executive Director of Idasa, for example, suggests that "South Africa should debate whether foreigners take jobs from South Africans or whether they fill jobs South Africans don't want to perform." James proposes that the answer to the problem of illegal immigrants does not rest with pouring more money into border patrol. Instead, he argues that "we need collaboration on an effective regional policy for border control operation, not to hunt down people as they cross but to develop controls consistent with human rights."[90]

The issue of illegal immigrants has reached a crisis state in the country, and during 1995, reportedly some immigrants were attacked in townships. Anti-immigrant sentiment is strong and has the potential to become extremely volatile as the struggle over the resources of the country intensifies.

Conclusion

This chapter has discussed eight challenges faced by the Mandela government during its first fifteen months. The three greatest challenges included the conflict between the ANC and the IFP, the implementation of the RDP, and the establishment of strong local government structures. Other challenges included crime, the youth, the Truth Commission, institutionalized racism, and illegal immigrants. Although this chapter has examined these issues separately, several of them are interconnected.

To date, the government has had limited success in improving the socioeconomic status of the majority population. It is important that this lack of success be examined within the context of the compromises the ANC-led government made on the eve of the establishment of a new political dispensation in the country. Perhaps the most significant compromise was to allow white economic hegemony to be maintained. This has left the Mandela government economically impotent. Socioeconomic change in the country will continue to be slow unless there is a shift in economic empowerment from the old apartheid forces to the new political structure. By the end of the current transitional period in 1999, the ANC-led government will only be deemed successful by the majority population if socioeconomic change takes place. In addition to enhancing the living status of the majority population, the Mandela government is challenged to maintain political stability and enhance the democratic initiative. This is particularly difficult in a country that has been polarized by both ethnicity and race.

In the final analysis, as one scholar noted, "South Africa's transformation has created popular expectations that would be difficult for even the most popular, practiced, and gifted government to satisfy."[91]

Notes

[1] Sipho Shezi, "South Africa: State Transition and the Management of Collapse," in William Zartman (*ed.*), *Collapsed States: The Disintegration and Restoration of Legitimate Authority* (Boulder: Lynne Rienner, 1995), p. 199.

[2] I use the term "new" state of South Africa to only refer to the changing of the guard from the old apartheid political structure to the transitional phase now underway.

[3] Much of the literature talks about a "negotiated revolution," and numerous whites whom I spoke to stated that they felt a revolution had occurred, while blacks I spoke to did not share this sentiment. On the "negotiated revolution," see, for example, Allister Sparks, *Tomorrow is Another Country: The Inside Story of South Africa's Negotiated Revolution* (Wynberg, Sandton: Struik Publishing Company (Pty) Ltd, 1994); and Heribert Adam and Kogila Moodley, *The Negotiated Revolution: Society and Politics in Post-Apartheid South Africa.* (Johannesburg: Jonathan Ball Publishers, 1993).

[4] Black majority here is used to refer to non-whites in South Africa.

[5] Address of President Nelson Mandela on the Occasion of the Opening of the Second Session of the Democratic Parliament, Cape Town, February 17, 1995.

[6] *Ibid.*

[7] Interview with Warren Krafchik, Idasa, Cape Town, June 12, 1995.

[8] Interview with Rich Mkhondo, Reuters, Johannesburg, June 29, 1995.

[9] For a history of the conflict see Sparks, pp. 164-178; Rich Mkhondo, *Reporting South Africa* (London: James Curry, Ltd, 1993), Chapter 6; Martin J. Murray, *The Revolution Deferred: The Painful Birth of Post-Apartheid South Africa* (London and New York: Verso, 1994), pp. 95-100.

[10] Sparks, pp. 220-21.

[11] *Financial Mail,* June 2, 1995.

[12] *Ibid.*

[13] The Interim Constitution divided South Africa into nine provinces: Gauteng, Northern Transvaal, Eastern Transvaal (now Mpumalanga), NorthWest, Free State, KwaZulu/Natal, Western Cape, Northern Cape, and Eastern Cape.

[14] Paul Bell, "No Wishing Him Away," *Leadership,* Vol. 1, No. 2, 1995, p. 24.

[15] Chapter 11 of the South Africa Interim Constitution is entitled "Traditional Authorities." I.M. Rautenbach and E.F.J. Malherbe in *What does the Constitution say?* (Auckland Park, South Africa: Rand Afrikaans University, 1994), p. 55, offer the following explanation of traditional authorities.

"Before the first European settlements in South Africa, the indigenous inhabitants were already organised in a variety of government institutions ... The existence of institutions such as tribal authorities, captains and chiefs and of indigenous law has long been officially recognised and particularly in rural areas it is still a reality in the daily lives of millions of people. In chapter 11 of the transitional constitution *traditional authorities* and *indigenous law* are recognised and it is provided that traditional authorities who apply indigenous law and have previously been recognised by law, shall continue to exist."

[16] Rautenbach and Malherbe, p. 48.

[17] *The Star*, June 16, 1995.

[18] *Mail and Guardian*, June 30 to July 6, 1995.

[19] *Mail and Guardian*, July 21 to 27, 1995.

[20] *Mail and Guardian*, July 7 to 13, 1995.

[21] *Sunday Times*, June 18, 1995.

[22] *The Star*, June 15, 1995.

[23] *Mail and Guardian*, June 23 to 29, 1995.

[24] ANC, *The Reconstruction and Development Programme: A Policy Framework* (Johannesburg: Umanyano Publications, 1994), pp. 7-8.

[25] Mkhonto Mkhondo, "Rebuilding A Nation," *Emerge*, June 15, 1995, pp. 28 and 31.

[26] Margaret C. Lee, "South Africa: The Long and Arduous Road to a New Dispensation," in George A. Agbango (*ed.*), *Issues and Trends in Contemporary African Politics: Stability, Development, and Democratization* (New York: Peter Lang Publishers, 1997), pp. 237-272.

[27] Rich Mkhondo, "ANC Advocates Sale of State Assets to Reduce Debt," Reuters, December 20, 1994.

[28] *Mail and Guardian*, June 23 to 29, 1995.

[29] Rich Mkhondo, "ANC to Stress Needs of S. Africans," Reuters, December 19, 1994.

[30] *Mail and Guardian*, June 9 to 14, 1995.

[31] Interview with Warren Krafchik.

[32] *The RDP*, Ministry of the Office of the President, April 27, 1995.

[33] *Mail and Guardian*, July 14 to 20, 1995.

[34] *The Economist*, July 22 to 28, 1995.

[35] *Ibid.*; and *Mail and Guardian*, July 21 to 27, 1995.

[36] *The Economist*, July 22 to 28, 1995.

[37] *Mail and Guardian*, June 23 to 29, 1995.

[38] Interview with Warren Krafchik.

[39] *The Christian Science Monitor*, September 14, 1994.

[40] It is estimated that land redistribution will cost an estimated R10 billion. While the Constitutional Bill of Rights allows the state to expropriate the land, it must provide "fair and equitable" compensation.

[41] *Mail and Guardian*, June 30 to July 6, 1995.

[42] *Ibid.*

[43] *Mail and Guardian*, July 7 to 13, 1995.

[44] *Mail and Guardian*, June 30 to July 6, 1995.

[45] Most commercial farms in South Africa are owned by white men and they provide five to six million poor people in the countryside with the only means of survival (see *Mail and Guardian,* July 7 to 13, 1995).

[46] *Ibid.*

[47] *Mail and Guardian,* June 30 to July 6, 1995.

[48] *Mail and Guardian,* June 23 to 29, 1995.

[49] *Mail and Guardian,* June 9 to 14, 1995.

[50] Mkhondo, "Rebuilding a Nation," p. 31.

[51] *Ibid.*

[52] *Financial Mail,* September 9, 1994.

[53] *Mail and Guardian,* July 14 to 20, 1995.

[54] Rautenbach and Malherbe, p. 53.

[55] Project Vote, *Voter Education: Manual for Trainers* (Cape Town: Project Vote, 1995), p. 10.

[56] Wilmont James, "Building on Democracy in the New South Africa," Lecture at the Southern Center for International Studies (SCIS), Atlanta, GA, September 22, 1994.

[57] "Cash Crunch Coming: Local Level Last in Line," *Negotiation News,* No. 18, September 12, 1994, p. 1.

[58] *Ibid.*

[59] Project Vote, p. 13

[60] Stand-alone towns are not located near a metropolitan area. The majority of South African towns fall under this category.

[61] Project Vote, p. 14.

[62] *Your Guide to the Local Elections.* (Cape Town: INGLOV and Project Vote, n.d.), p. 11.

[63] Non-payment of rent and services grew out of protests during the apartheid years. The current government is having a very difficult time trying to convince many township dwellers that they must now discontinue this practice and assume responsibility for the economic development of their communities.

[64] *Your Guide to the Local Elections.*

[65] *Financial Mail,* June 2, 1995.

[66] *Ibid.*

[67] *Ibid.*

[68] *New Nation,* June 30, 1995.

[69] *Financial Mail,* June 2, 1995.

[70] *New Nation,* June 15, 1995, p. 13.

[71] *Ibid.*

[72] *Ibid.*

[73] *New Nation,* June 15, 1995.

[74] *The Star,* June 29, 1995.

[75] *Ibid.*

[76] *New Nation,* June 15, 1995.

[77] *Ibid.*

[78] Interview with Rich Mkhondo.

[79] Lizeka Mda, "A House Divided," *Tribute,* December 1994, p. 45.

[80] *Ibid.,* p. 47.

[81] *Mail and Guardian,* June 9 to 14, 1995.

[82] *The Star,* June 29, 1995.

[83] *Ibid.*

[84] *The Star,* July 3, 1995.

[85] *Mail and Guardian,* June 23 to 29, 1995.

[86] *The Star,* July 3, 1995.

[87] *Financial Mail,* September 9, 1994.

[88] *Ibid.*

[89] *Ibid.*

[90] *Mail and Guardian,* June 23 to 29, 1995.

[91] Kenneth Grundy, "South Africa: Putting Democracy to Work," *Current History,* April 1995, p. 173.

7

New and Old Political Allegiances in the Eastern Cape Province, South Africa, and the National Implications Thereof [1]

Geoffrey Wood

Based on an extensive survey of potential voters in the main urban belt of the Eastern Cape Province (Port Elizabeth-Grahamstown-East London), this study explores political allegiances, participation, aspirations, and attitudes toward South Africa's fledgling democracy in the period immediately following South Africa's first democratic elections. Particular attention is accorded to voters' expectations of the new political order, their support thereof, the extent of political competition, and the national implications thereof.

Method

The research method employed was a survey of adult (18 years or over) potential voters resident in the two primary (Port Elizabeth and East London) and a secondary (Grahamstown) urban centers in the Eastern Cape Province. Sample size represents a product of not only the overall size of the population, but also deviation in responses.[2] An estimate of the latter was obtained and the final sample size computed after a pilot study was conducted through simple quota sampling.[3] In addition, the pilot study greatly assisted in the formulation of the final interview schedule, and resulted in the elimination or modification of ambiguous or difficult-to-comprehend questions. The final survey was conducted through probability sampling, by means of the area sampling method. Area sampling involved an element of systematic sampling, where each unit constituted a collection of elements. The advantage afforded by the systematic sampling was that the final sampling frame was drawn up during, rather than prior to, the interviewing process. This is of particular advantage in lower income areas, where accurate lists of the population are generally not available.

Interviews were therefore conducted at the level of place of residence, rather than in terms of selected respondents' names.[4] The overall population was divided up into a series of readily identifiable strata (upper-middle, middle, and lower income formal settlements as well as informal settlements), defined in terms of different residential areas, in order to encompass a range of income levels. These constituted the primary sampling unit. Thereafter, trained interviewers (all senior students in Sociology) selected respondents' dwellings systematically.

It should be noted that the sampling method used does have certain inherent limitations. Firstly, as places of residence, and not individuals' names were used, there was the remote possibility of the same respondent being interviewed twice. To reduce the possibility of this occurring, interviews were conducted in as short a time as possible, during a week in August 1994. Secondly, each stratum was to be sampled representatively. This led to upper income (mostly white) voters being somewhat over-represented, although this difficulty can be obviated by comparing the views of members of different strata with regard to key issues, making use of statistical tests.

The interviews were conducted by trained interviewers, fully conversant with the vernacular language, enabling respondents to answer questions in the manner in which they felt most comfortable.[5] Following the survey, the data was inputted into the computer, using the Statgraphics Program, to enable the generation of graphs and cross-tabulations and the performance of limited statistical tests, including the chi-squared test (a test of association) and Lambda (which reveals the strength of the relationship).

A serious limitation to making use of the chi-squared test is that "chi-squared" curvers represent only an approximation of the true chi-squared distribution. This is usually acceptable if expected frequencies in all cells (in a contingency table) are five or greater. In some cases, greater than three is acceptable. In this research, where individual cells in a cross-tabulation were empty, or more than a certain number less than five, response categories were collapsed in a revised matrix, most notably in the case of political allegiances and language categories, where only the relationship between the larger (and more important) categories were explored. Where appropriate and necessary, Yates' Correction was used. It is generally accepted that in the case of 2 x 2 contingency tables, where a fairly large sample is used (such as was the case in this study), the use of Yates' Correction can enhance reliability.

Political Party Support

Figure 1 depicts the degree of support for the major political actors in the region. The relatively high number of respondents who refused to reveal their political views (16%), can be seen as a sign of uneasiness regarding the experience of democracy among many people. A significant group of people regard it as unwise to expose their political affiliation, and this phenomenon underlines the fact that any form of political socialization needs to emphasize the guarantee of the secret ballot.

As can be seen, the African National Congress (ANC) was by far the most popular party in the region. The ANC enjoys a high degree of legitimacy among many South Africans, on account of the prominent role it assumed in opposing the previously-dominant apartheid ideologies. Although the former ruling party, the National Party (NP), was the second most popular party, it is interesting that the Democratic Party (DP) remained a significant force among the respondents in this poll, despite its poor election showing. However, it should be borne in mind that the liberal DP has traditionally had a significant presence in the region, most notably in the English-speaking upper income areas, and, to a lesser extent, in certain Colored areas. The Pan Africanist Congress (PAC), the "other" former liberation movement, committed to an Africanist ideology, seems to have virtually disappeared as a political force, contrary to a number of opinion polls conducted prior to the elections. Relatively few respondents supported any of the other minor parties, the most popular of the latter being the African Christian Democratic Party (ACDP).

There is a statistically significant relationship between home language and support for political parties.[6] The overwhelming majority of Xhosa speakers supported the ANC. Only a small minority of Xhosa speakers supported the DP (1%), Inkatha Freedom Party (1%), NP (1%) or the PAC (2.5%). Meanwhile, the ANC seems to have a surprising amount of support among Afrikaans and English speakers (54% of the respondents who gave either as their home language), although closer analysis revealed that this grouping was mostly resident in traditionally Colored areas. The survey revealed that the NP is perhaps less politically hegemonic among the Colored grouping than is commonly assumed. Although the NP seems to have majority support among Coloreds in the Western Cape, this is definitely not the case in the Eastern. This could be due to the harsher implementation of racial discrimination in the Eastern Cape Province, as well as some past benefits and protection in the Western Cape as a result of the former Colored labor protection policy.

It is interesting that with the exception of the ANC, the political parties in the Eastern Cape Province which currently enjoy a significant degree of support, have traditionally been predominantly white. This reflects the persistence of political divisions between supporters of the old dogma and those who favor change, which remain largely on racial grounds. However, it should be noted that a large proportion of whites (particularly Afrikaners) held relatively privileged jobs within the bureaucracy, and support for the old order reflected not only racial concerns, but also the desire to protect a certain economic status.

It also makes for a highly constrained political marketplace. For example, dissatisfied ANC supporters will most probably have to turn to parties which have had radically different political histories, and which are dominated by members of a conspicuously economically privileged grouping. Neither the DP nor the NP have comprehensive alternative policies for social upliftment should the Reconstruction and Development Program (RDP) fail. The other liberation movement, the PAC, had significant pockets of support in the region prior to the elections (roughly 12% of respondents to an earlier survey),[7] and it is possible that this organization could experience something of a renaissance should there be widespread disillusionment with ANC rule.

Against this must be considered the fact that the PAC never succeeded in breaking out of a handful of traditional strongholds, and is beset by leadership problems, chronic internal divisions, and an organizational and funding crisis. Consequently, the major opposition to ANC governance will probably come from within its ranks, from members of rival factions. The ANC represents an extremely broad coalition of interests, and has subsumed much political competition into internal debate.

Democratic Participation

Most respondents believed that their **vote** was secret, although a large minority (23%) were uncertain, or believed this not to be the case (Figure 2). This finding is of considerable importance, in that its reveals a future role for voter education programs. Although the election revealed that most residents in the region were quite capable of performing the business of democracy, concerns about the secrecy of the ballot, for whatever reason, could make it extremely difficult for new alternative political organizations to emerge. There seems to have been widespread exposure to voter education programs, but it should be noted that many of these programs were organized by political parties, and focused around the basic procedures of casting a vote. However, very few respondents felt that they had been unduly influenced into voting for a particular political party.

When questioned as to what the characteristics of democracy were, most respondents identified traditional liberal criteria, most notably free expression, equality before the law, tolerance, and representative government where majoritarian parties have the major say (Figure 3). The majority of respondents saw freedom of speech as of particular importance. However, 32% of respondents believed that democracy was also about free facilities. This percentage is not unexpected, particularly if some of the populist rhetoric in the run-up to the election is considered. It seems, however, that the traditional conception of democracy has taken deep root in the Eastern Cape.

In the period just before the election, one of the major issues in the Eastern Cape Province was over regional boundaries, and whether the region should, in fact, be divided into two. The implications of such a division would mean the emergence of a somewhat wealthier Port Elizabeth-oriented subregion, and a region centered around the Border corridor, but demographically dominated by the former Ciskei and Transkei homelands. The ANC came out in favor of a single region, in contrast to the NP's ambivalence and the DP's support of a division. However, the survey revealed that there was no relationship between political party support and views on regional divisions.[8] Similarly, there seems little connection between age and views on regional division, and political affiliations and views on regional division. Interestingly, supporters of all the major political parties were deeply divided on the issue, including ANC supporters. The latter split could partially be explained by the then internal ANC debate over the future regional capital.

The ANC leadership originally favored greater King William's Town (including the former Ciskeian capital of Bisho). However, the powerful Transkeian lobby forced the reopening of the debate. Umtata is relatively remote to say, Port Elizabeth, but would be far more centrally located relative to a region composed of the former Kei homelands. This could lead to ANC supporters coming from the Transkei region favoring two sub-regions. Furthermore, ANC supporters in Port Elizabeth could be in favor of regional divisions precisely to avoid having their capital situated in an impoverished and remote rural backwater, which would reduce accountability to the Port Elizabeth constituency. DP and NP supporters in the Border-Kei region could prefer to be linked to the more prosperous center of Port Elizabeth, while those resident in the latter center may fear the economic implications of being twinned with some of South Africa's poorest districts.

Prior to the elections, it was the ANC that had the most effective voter education apparatus. There is a statistically-significant relationship between support for various political parties and exposure to voter education programs.[9] In general, the ANC supporters were far more likely to have been exposed to voter education than supporters of any other political party. A sizable component of the ANC support is among the more economically and educationally disadvantaged. It was precisely this grouping that was most targeted by party political and independent voter education programs. Therefore, since the ANC probably had the most effective voter education network in the region, this could well have affected party support.

Accountability and Representativity

There seemed to be considerable confidence in the voting process as a means of participation in political life. A majority of respondents believed that their vote affected what the government did (see Figure 4). This contrasts sharply with the apparent cynicism among voters in the Western world, with, often, low turnouts at the polls. This research finding is also borne out by the far higher turnout in the recent South African elections than in most elections in the developed world. On the one hand, it is possible that this was due to the relative novelty of the voting process in South Africa. On the other, and more likely, it reveals confidence in the efficacy of participative democracy. It also demonstrates that, despite the limited nature of political competition in the region, it is likely that a political party that does not meet the needs of their supporters may be brought sharply to account in the next elections. However, it is possible that, as a "halo effect" from the elections, many saw the electoral process in a highly idealistic fashion. Should the new government fail to provide meaningful social upliftment, it is possible that members of this grouping may simply withdraw from the political process and not cast their votes in future elections.

Not only was there a high degree of confidence in the voting process, but it was also widely held that public representatives were issued with a rather narrow and strictly defined brief. Most respondents believed that MPs should report back on their decisions in parliament (see Figure 5). While 32% felt that this was only necessary when major decisions were made, only a tiny minority (2%) felt that they need not report back to their constituencies. Thus, the major political actors clearly face demands from their constituents to report back and consult on their activities in parliament. Interestingly, research of trade union members by Maree and Wood[10] revealed that workers expect a similar degree of accountability from their workplace representatives. The unions have a deep-seated and highly functional internal democracy, and it is indeed interesting that similar notions of accountability are held by the general public.

Questioned as to what measures could be taken if the government does not fulfill popular demands, a wide range of strategies were chosen. Interestingly, it was again traditional liberal-democratic methods of bringing a government to account that were the most popular: press exposure, legal action, demonstrations, voting for another party and/or petitions (Figure 6). However, other measures favored by a sizable minority included mass action, boycotts, and strikes. Very few respondents said that they would do nothing if the government failed to fulfill their wishes. It is clear that, despite the relatively constrained political market place, the government will face (and indeed is already facing) a range of pressures from the populace to fulfill their expectations and demands.

Most respondents strongly believed that the salaries of public representatives were too high. Given the expressed desire of most respondents to call the government to account should it fail to fulfill their wishes, it is evident that the government cannot deal with this issue simply through excuses, as was too often the case in the past. Although it is unlikely that the salaries of public representatives are, alone, an issue which would cause voters to shift political allegiance, it is evident that, when combined with the issue of accountability, it could prove to be an important issue in the next elections.

There is a statistically significant relationship between party support and the willingness to switch political allegiances if the government does not do what is desired.[11] Although it was only the ANC and the NP which had cabinet representation and a significant presence in the Eastern Cape Province (making it unlikely that supporters of, say the DP would switch political allegiance should they be displeased with the government's actions), certain trends were apparent. A sizable proportion of the ANC and the NP supporters indicated that they were displeased with the government's actions. Given the radically different nature of these two groupings' constituencies, and the fact that they both constituted parties in the government (albeit that the NP was only a junior partner, and had some pretensions to being an opposition), it is somewhat unlikely that dissatisfied voters would move between the two. In particular, it is in the predominantly black areas where there is a political vacuum as far as effective opposition parties are concerned. While, as noted earlier, much political debate has been subsumed into the rank of the ANC, the willingness of voters to cast votes for a different party intensifies pressures for this seeming lack of outright competition between political parties to be ended.

Reconstruction and Restitution

When questioned as to in what areas of life respondents expected to see an improvement in the quality of their lives prior to the next elections, most believed it was in the provision of basic services, although many also felt that more jobs should be provided (Figure 7). The latter is hardly surprising in view of the high unemployment in the region, and the centrality of the employment issue in the ANC's campaign in the region. Indeed, there was a widespread perception, particularly among the young, that jobs will be created for all by the new government. Surprisingly, the land issue was of somewhat lesser importance, and, to many respondents, land was primarily desired for living, and not farming space. Despite the high incidence of rural poverty in the region, it seems that the government faces far more pressures to provide basic housing than to redistribute land. Although the grossly unequal distribution of land nationwide will have to be resolved, and that the desire for land is probably far higher in the former homeland areas, the findings suggest that this is a somewhat lesser concern as far as a large grouping of ANC supporters are concerned.

It is evident that the RDP is extremely popular among respondents. Indeed, even among the sizable grouping of respondents who do not have an in-depth knowledge of the initiative, many supported it. Certainly, the RDP has become something of a "buzz word," and may well be seen as a key to economic salvation, rather than as a focused program of social upliftment. Similarly, most respondents felt that it would solve the problem of poverty in the region. It is clear that the concept has captured the imagination of the region. However, it is evident that it is in a number of material areas of life that improvements are expected (Figure 7), and that the RDP is seen as a means whereby social life can be improved, and not simply as a symbolic rallying point.

The survey revealed that affirmative action was most popular among the unemployed (with 62.5% support), unskilled (92%), and blue collar workers (71.4%). This is of particular interest in that, to date, much of the debate around affirmative action has centered around relatively skilled, white collar workers. The survey reveals that it was among the least privileged, even within the Xhosa-speaking group of respondents, that the concept of affirmative action was the most popular. In the lower occupational categories, affirmative action would not simply be about ruthless head-hunting and the bending of job descriptions. It would not only entail fulfilling quotas, but include educational empowerment. Indeed, most respondents, across all age groupings, believed that education was a basic human right and should be available free of charge. Demands for affirmative action should be seen as part and parcel of the desire for improvement in social conditions, as also reflected in previous figures. Again, it is evident that material progress in promoting the interests of the disadvantaged is expected by the electorate.

There is a statistically-significant relationship between political allegiance and the belief that the new government will create jobs for all.[12] In particular, it is among ANC supporters that the highest number of respondents believed this to be the case. Given the announced intention of voters to hold their public representatives to account, and their willingness to consider voting for an alternative political party, it is clear that the ANC will face ongoing pressures from its supporters to improve job prospects in the region. This will prove to be an extremely difficult task when the region's poor economic performance and history of labor militancy is considered.

Outlook on the Future

There is not a statistically-significant relationship between respondent's home language and degree of confidence in the future,[13] although it seems evident that Afrikaans-speaking respondents are, proportionately-speaking, somewhat more undecided as to what the future may bring. This may well be the result of the fact that traditionally, relatively large numbers of Afrikaners have been employed in the public service, and that the government is committed to affirmative action in that sector, and will probably face pressures to radically change employment practices therein. They also have concerns over the future status of the Afrikaans language.

Most respondents believed that racism was still a very real social phenomenon, although ANC supporters were somewhat more hopeful that racism had indeed passed when compared to supporters of other political parties. It is evident that South Africa has a long way to progress on the road toward true reconciliation, given responses to this question, and the continued demarcating of political allegiances on cultural, ethnic, and linguistic lines.

There is a statistically-significant relationship between home language and the belief that minority rights will be protected.[14] In particular, it was Xhosa (40.6% felt this would not be the case), and then Afrikaans-speaking respondents (21.7%) that were most pessimistic in this regard. In the case of the former, and given the belief among many ANC supporters that racism was a thing of the past, it may be the case that it is held that such protection is undesirable, and contrary to the spirit of reconciliation and nation-building. In the case of the latter, it could well reflect concerns over the continuation of statutory protection for the Afrikaans language, as well as, perhaps, over the future of civil service employment. However, it should be stressed that the majority of respondents, regardless of language, were confident that minority rights will be protected in the future.

Political Participation in Transition

The survey revealed the positive and negative features of South Africa's new democracy. On the one hand, there is a high degree of commitment to the democratic process, to participation in the voting process, and to holding public representatives to account. As Carol Pateman notes, "we learn to participate by participating."[15] In other words, participation in democratic structures is a self-reinforcing phenomenon. Those socialized in a participative environment are indeed more likely to actively participate in, and have enthusiasm for, South Africa's first democratic elections. It is a most positive start, and will encourage similar participation and democratic commitment in the future.

On the other hand, there are some grounds for concern. Firstly, it is evident that political allegiance is still largely on linguistic and ethnic grounds. There is a lack of effective opposition grouping in traditionally black areas. While much political discourse and competition in such areas has been subsumed into internal contests within the ANC, the willingness of voters to seek alternatives should their chosen party not fulfill their demands highlights a definite political vacuum. As Hannah Arendt notes, an initial wave of grassroots participation in an organization, although founded on democratic practices, will not always ensure lasting accountability and representativity.[16] It cannot be assumed that internal competition within a political organization will always be resolved in a satisfactory and inclusive manner. Furthermore, political choices are not only limited on account of continued ethnic divisions, but also in terms of the very nature of South Africa's sociopolitical transition.

South Africa's transition should be seen as the product of a pacting process between political elites, during which extremists on both sides were marginalized.[17] In the short term, the lack of completely open political competition may make for stability. Both radicals within the ANC and reactionaries within the NP have little option other than to stay within their respective political organizations, if they wish to wield political influence and have access to adequate resources to dispense political patronage. There are few alternative organizations which could provide suitable platforms for them to pursue their objectives. It is thus likely that the major opposition to the emerging new order will come from within the major sociopolitical actors. Such opposition is likely to be tentative, however, and remain constrained by the desire to preserve organization unity.

Meanwhile, it is likely that other key sociopolitical actors are likely to be accommodated within the new order, rather than becoming open opponents of it. As Adnan Przeworski notes, in a time of socioeconomic transition, the reformist government is faced with the choice of mobilizing support from the unions, opposition parties, and other broadly based organizations, or actively seeking to undermine them. The latter option will have adverse consequences for new democratic institutions.[18] In addition, as noted above, the senior governing party, the ANC, itself represents a broad coalition of interests, and any recourse to the latter option would jeopardize its own viability. In the end, it is likely to be only fringe political groupings, with limited popular appeal, which will not be accommodated within the new order. Sociopolitical groupings are only in a position to participate in pacts if they are relatively strong, broadly based, and politically influential.[19]

Furthermore, those working for social change at the grassroots level may have little impact if "not connected to institutionally imminent possibilities."[20] Social relations represent structures within which individual and collective actors choose alternatives and select courses of action, albeit with differing degrees of knowledge of the alternatives. While social relations constitute a structure of choices, what individuals and groupings choose will have a reciprocal impact on social relations.[21] In other words, it is possible that key groupings at the grassroots, or indeed entire communities, could have little impact in affecting the decisions of regional and national governments. The nature of elite pacting necessitates a partial demobilization of key support groupings (particularly those with radical tendencies) in the interests of national level reconciliation. There remains considerable support for, and optimism surrounding, the new order. However, the lack of political alternatives may result in widespread disillusionment with democratic processes, particularly should the new government fail to deliver on its promises.

Conclusion

While the survey revealed considerable support for the new political order in the Eastern Cape Province, most respondents indicated that they intended to hold the new government to its election promises. However, continued racial divisions in political party support, and the very nature of South Africa's transition, has led to a vacuum in political alternatives. This vacuum must be filled for the health of South Africa's fledgling democracy, either through the emergence of new political actors, or the revitalization of old, to maintain faith in the electoral process. Organizations dedicated to change tend to have high levels of democratic commitment and practice. Fairly soon, however, this becomes subsumed by the desire to ensure organizational stability and continuity.[22] This desire can inhibit both internal democracy and the capacity to effectively engage in collective action in the future.

Should this vacuum persist, voters are willing to resort to other, extra-constitutional methods, such as a return to mass action. While such action may have a place in providing an additional channel for bringing the government to account, this should not be at the expense of constitutional methods. Perhaps, as Pateman suggests, there may be a linkage between the types of decisions made and the degree of participation.[23] In other words, there may be a greater willingness to participate in democratic structures, if the primary focus is on issues of more immediate concern to voters. Ultimately, it is on whether the initial focus on social upliftment is maintained, and if tangible improvements in day-to-day living are brought about, that the future of South Africa's fledgling democracy hinges.

FIGURE 1
Political Party Support

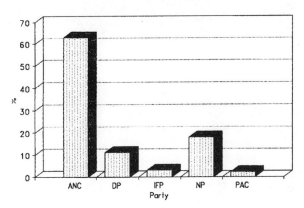

FIGURE 2
One's vote was secret

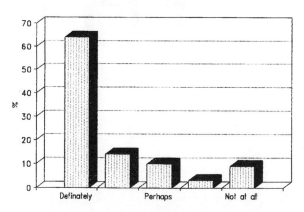

FIGURE 3
Characteristics of democracy are

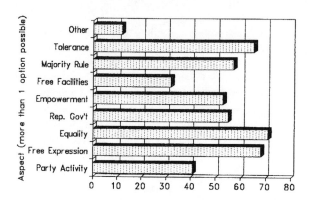

FIGURE 4
Vote affects what the government does

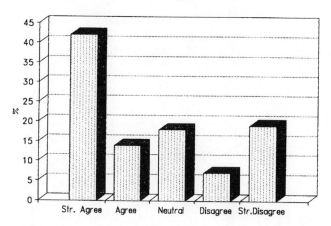

FIGURE 5
Parties must report back on decisions

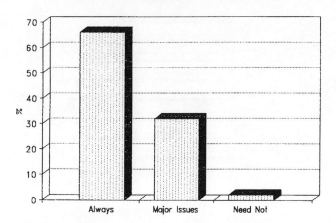

FIGURE 6
Gov't can be made to follow people thru'

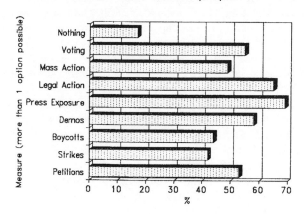

FIGURE 7
Expect improvement in 5 years in

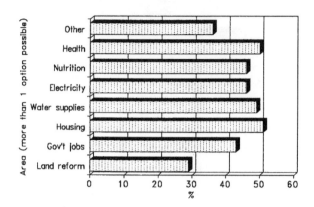

Notes

[1] The contribution of Professor Jan K. Coetzee is acknowledged and appreciated.

[2] K.D. Bailey, *Methods of Social Research* (New York: The Free Press, 1987), pp. 84-92.

[3] Total sample size was 220 respondents. Probability theory assures that a relatively small sample size can be adequate, although it should be recognized that small samples can leave a very small margin for error in coding and related areas (Bailey, p. 84). Sample size depends not only on the size of the population, but also of the heterogeneity of variables within the population. The greater the heterogeneity in responses to an individual question, the larger the sample size (*Ibid.*, p. 102). Standard deviation summarizes the average deviation from the mean. The greater the standard deviation, the larger the sample size must be for the sample mean to be an accurate estimate of the population mean (*Ibid.*, p. 103). The sample size was estimated following the conducting of a pilot study. The standard deviation in responses to key questions for the actual survey ranged between 0.308015 (whether respondents voted) to 1.48306 (political party support). It can be concluded that the sample was representative of the population.

[4] Bailey, pp. 87-88.

[5] The authors are extremely grateful to the following senior students in the Department of Sociology who participated in the questionnaire construction and data collection: L. Hector, T. Mcuba, C. Majola, N. Mpapha, J. Ngqument ana, H. Smith, C. Jameson, G. Dean, Z. Africa, J. Don-Wauchope, K. Beukes, M. Ntleki, S. Wood, and D. Mitchell.

[6] Chi-square = 67.7488; D.F. = 2; Significance = 2.00E-15.

[7] G. Wood and J. Coetzee, "How the Vote Will Go: A Survey of African Potential Voters," *Politikon*, Vol. 20, No. 2, 1993, pp. 25-45.

[8] Chi-square = 3.298; D.F. = 2; Significance = 0.19.

[9] Chi-square = 5.644; D.F. = 1; Significance = 0.02.

[10] J. Maree and G. Wood, "Trade Union Development," Paper presented at the Annual South African Sociological Association Conference, Pietermaritzburg, July, 1994, p. 5.

[11] Chi-square = 23.947; D.F. = 2; Significance = 6.30909E-6.

[12] Chi-square = 38.674; D.F. = 2; Significance = 3.99E-9.

[13] Chi-square = 9.036; D.F. = 4; Significance = 0.06.

[14] Chi-square = 31.859; D.F. = 4; Significance = 2.04E-6.

[15] C. Pateman, *Participation and Democratic Theory* (Cambridge: Cambridge University Press, 1970), p. 104.

[16] H. Arendt, *On Revolution* (Harmondsworth: Penguin, 1965), p. 218.

[17] G. Adler and E. Webster, "Challenging Transition Theory: The Labour Movement, Radical Reform and the Transition to Democracy in South Africa," Paper presented at the Albert Einstein Initiative Workshop, University of Witwatersrand, Johannesburg, 1995.

[18] A. Przeworski, *Democracy and the Market* (Cambridge: Cambridge University Press, 1991), pp. 182-183.

[19] *Ibid.*, p. 185.

[20] A. Giddens, *The Consequences of Modernity* (Cambridge: Polity, 1990), p. 155.

[21] A. Pzreworski, *Capitalism and Social Democracy* (Cambridge: Cambridge University Press, 1985), p. 96.

[22] Arendt, p. 219.

[23] Pateman, p. 83.

8

The National Question, Ethnicity, and the State: Some Insights on South Africa

Cheryl Hendricks

Of late, there has been a renewed academic focus on the nation-state, ethnicity, and identity in general. Central to this focus is the questioning of the conceptualization of these phenomena as primordial "givens," and/or, in the case of ethnicity, as a set of social interactions deemed to disappear with the advent of modernization. There now appears to be a convergence on the idea that these identities are socially constructed phenomena: a cue taken from the works of F. Barth, B. Anderson, E. Hobsbawm, and others.[1]

This chapter attempts to discern how "the nation" and ethnicity have been conceptualized, generally, before contextualizing them first with respect to Africa and then to South Africa. There are six underlying contentions to my argument. The first is that we need to move beyond the debates of primordialism versus instrumentalism and constructivism,[2] to a level in which we seek to determine the impact of different methods of consolidating statehood and the conflicts they produce: ethnic, class, race, and gender. That is, we need to analyze the conditions under which, and the processes by which, ethnic identities and solidarities become activated and converted to political conflict. As such, we seek to analyze behavior and structure, rather than determine authenticity.

The second contention is that we need to recognize that the state is not merely an arbitrator in disputes; it is both a contributor to, and the manager of, ethnic conflict. As such, the role of the state should form an important component of studies on ethnic conflict.

Contention three is that there is a necessity to depart from the "false consciousness" paradigm by which we construe ethnic conflict as simply being the consequence of imperialism, class domination, or colonial stereotypes. This is particularly important regarding the African context. These factors undoubtedly play a role, but they are not sufficient explanatory variables. Ethnicity is used by the dominant and the subjugated constituents of the state as both a means of domination and resistance. It is also the fabric that binds sections of the ruling elite to those of civil society. As such, this intertwining makes dichotomous stereotyping implausible and simplistic. Post-modernists are among those who have widened our theoretical lenses so that we are now able to conceptualize identities as "multiple, interlocking, and conflicting." This should move us to explain what is, rather than launch into a tirade against all practices which do not conform to the models of society that we have devised.

The fourth contention, which follows from the above, suggests that we need to refrain from seeing ethnic identity as "in and of itself" reactionary and counterproductive. It is the context that determines what form ethnic mobilization will take, either politically, and thus potentially conflictual, or socially.

Contention five is that we need to focus on intraethnic conflict as well as interethnic conflict. Ethnic groups are not homogenous entities. Ethnic identity may vary markedly in terms of class, gender, and the extent to which ethnic identification is salient in the lives of individuals. The political significance of this is that some people within a group would have more interests than others in asserting their identity. This needs to be determined through analysis, with respect to what is at stake and for whom?

How to govern diversity is at the heart of our debates on issues of nationalism and ethnicity, and is therefore the final contention. Thus we need to be open minded and determine the multiple avenues through which legitimacy and authority can be obtained.

Conceptualizations of the Nation, Ethnic Identity, and Ethnicity

The Nation
J. Degenaar has identified at least four uses of the term nation: an ethnic use, which refers to common ancestry; a legal use, which refers to statehood; a political use, which links ethnic culture and political power [congruency]; and a second political use which refers to a common loyalty that transcends ethnicity.[3] I would reduce this classification to primarily two conceptualizations of a nation — as a cultural unit and as a political unit. This overlaps with the construction of a nation as primordial versus those who see it as a modern construct.

According to Joseph Stalin, a nation "is a historically constituted, stable community of people, formed on the basis of a common language, economic life, and psychological make-up manifested in a common culture ... It is only when all these characteristics are present together that we have a nation."[4] Similarly, Anthony Smith sees an enduring *ethnie* as providing the foundation of the modern state.[5] Max Weber projects a different image of the nation. For Weber, nations are too varied to be defined in terms of any one criterion. Instead, his definition hinges around a common political project: the nation as a community of sentiment likely to produce a state of its own. Whereas Stalin laid stress on objective characteristics, Weber's definition brings in the element of subjectivity. Modernists like E. Gellner, Anderson, and Hobsbawm, stress the modernity of nations.[6] These authors claim that nations are invented phenomena, primarily for the expediency of capitalism and/or the state. They therefore note the discontinuous (as opposed to linear) nature of the nation-building exercise. John Brueilly clearly emphasizes that the nationalist project is one for control of state power — it has very little to do with the preservation of culture.[7] Nationalism is thus the ideology used to gain control of state power and to maintain it, and as such, it legitimates state power.

What we glean from the modernist perspective is that the nation and the state are purely contingent phenomena, not universal necessities. Despite this depiction, we still live in a world in which the nation-building exercise is at the forefront of political agendas. We have seen a proliferation of nation-states in the 1990s in Eastern Europe. There is still the belief that a state should "bring in train a unitary lineage of culture, tradition, ethnicity ..."[8] As such, we need to analyze how the state implements its nation-building exercise and how the population responds to it.

Ethnic Identity and Ethnicity
Two conceptualizations of ethnic identity seem to prevail. There is a narrow definition stressing cultural attributes — language, customs, and origins — and which places emphasis on objective criteria and authenticity; and a broader definition which lays emphasis on political behavior. From the standpoint of the second definition, ethnic groups reveal themselves the best only in interaction with other groups. This is to say

that which of their cultural and/or other markers become important is dependent upon the nature of the conflict.[9] Authors adopting this latter definition usually stress the socially constructed nature of ethnic identity and its relational character. Ethnicity is seen as a process of politicizing ethnic identity. Thus one usually speaks of ethnicity in the context of contestation between particular ethnic groups, and/or between ethnic groups and the state.

The debate on primordialism versus instrumentalism tends to replicate itself within the literature on ethnicity. Primordialists like Edward Shils, Clifford Geertz, and Pierre van den Berghe, view ethnic identity as a historical given, a static identity rooted in a historical past.[10] They tend to emphasize cultural and psychological aspects of group identity, seeing these as natural, rather than as acquired through social interaction.

For modernization theorists, this "naturalness" was, however, only seen as relevant for "backward" societies and would thus disappear with the process of urbanization. For authors like Peter Gutkind, ethnicity, through the absorption into a national culture, would eventually fade away in favor of more "rational" forms of political identity.[11] Education, urbanization, and industrialization were to be among the key components in the conversion of ethnic identity to national identity. This kind of conceptualization was challenged when empirical evidence suggested that ethnicity was as much an urban phenomenon as a rural one. Ethnic identity was malleable enough to incorporate aspects of modernization and hence transform itself accordingly.

Theories of cultural pluralism became quite popular in the 1970s. According to van den Berghe, pluralism "refers to a property or set of properties, of societies wherein several distinct social and/or cultural groups coexist within the boundaries of a single polity and share a common economic system that makes them interdependent, yet maintain a greater or lesser degree of autonomy and a set of discrete institutional structures in other spheres of social life."[12] Characteristic of this approach was the idea that people "mix but do not combine."

One of the pitfalls of this approach is that it tends to see cultural cleavages as permanent within the society and the mere existence of plurality/difference appears to account for conflict. The primordialists' perspective is useful for alerting us to the persistence of ethnic ties. However, they have a deterministic and static view of ethnic behavior. These theorists downplay the political and economic aspects of ethnicity. Bernard Magubane, as far back as 1969, noted that they allow ethnic and racial conflicts to play themselves out in a social vacuum.[13] Ethnic identity is also given primacy above all other forms of identification. Moreover, they fail to take account of the state as a main actor in ethnic conflict.

Instrumentalists stress the dynamic, voluntary, situational, and pragmatic nature of ethnicity. Ethnic conflict is not reduced to a primordial need to belong, but rather to efforts on the part of either elites or groups, who mobilize ethnic symbols, in order to achieve access to social, political, and material resources. Rational choice and critical theory tend to dominate the instrumentalist paradigm. Both approaches agree that ethnicity is instigated by scarce resources. However, critical theorists stress that ethnicity masks class exploitation.

Rational choice theorists contend that ethnic conflict will occur when two or more ethnic populations come to compete for the same valued resources.[14] Robert Bates asserts that because members of ethnic groups tend to cluster together in space (and colonialism distributed rewards unevenly), one logical consequence is that competition for the benefits of modernity becomes structured along ethnic lines.[15]

Critical school theorists emphasize the interconnectedness between class and ethnicity.[16] Thus, Okwudiba Nnoli states that "we cannot fully comprehend the ethnic phenomenon in Africa without an adequate understanding of its historical origin and class character ... "[17] Theorists within this school attempt to attribute ethnic mobilization to a particular class which desires to either gain or maintain political primacy in the postcolonial order. The instrumentalists bring an important dimension to the debate on ethnicity — it is not mere cultural distinctions which initiate conflict, but the economic and political structures within society have a contributory role. This school, however, like the primordialists, retains an essentialistic and deterministic perspective. Whereas the primordialists endow all ethnic competition with a cultural motivation, critical theorists endow it with an economic motive. Eghosa Oshaghae notes that, "to say that ethnicity does not exist outside of the class context is to deny it any amount of relative autonomy."[18]

Constructivists, like Leroy Vail, place more emphasis on decoding the notion of ethnic group itself.[19] These theorists stress that ethnicity is socially constructed — how, why, and when it arises is contingent, and thus ethnic identity itself is in a continual state of flux.

Whether ethnic identity is real or imagined does not prevent it from having tangible political and human consequences. Too many people have already sacrificed their lives in ethnic conflicts. As such, this debate on authenticity needs to be refocused. M. Esman, in *Ethnic Politics,* concretely helps us in this regard. For him, ethnicity is shaped by the environment, by the threats and opportunities it affords. Furthermore, he notes that ethnicity is not normally only one of several equal identity choices. The more politicized ethnicity becomes, the more it dominates other expressions of identity. More importantly, the role of the state is brought in as a central actor in ethnic relations. How the state attempts to accommodate ethnic demands, i.e., the kinds of opportunities it affords, is a determinant for the outcome of ethnic relations within a given country.[20]

Africa

In Africa, there has been an obsessive concern with "national integration." This concern stems from the desire to conform to the world nation-state system and a belief that nation-building would bring both stability and prosperity. This was because nationalism was the ideology used to overthrow colonialist rule and to legitimate the role of new modernized elites in state formation. Thus, the nationalist project was simultaneously one of attaining independence, creating a nation, and jettisoning a modern elite into power. State crafters sought unity at all costs — an attempt to counter the divisive divide and rule politics on the one hand, and to bolster their own tenuous hold on the state, on the other.

The generation of statesmen of the 1960s were assisted by scholars who adopted a unilinear model of development — deemed modernization — and therefore decried ethnic affiliation as outmoded forms of political association. Ethnic identity was viewed as part of a backward past that had to be eradicated in favor of a national identity. These two forms of identity, ethnic versus national, were often viewed as mutually exclusive.

There is nothing intrinsically wrong with attempting to construct a nation. However, often the methods used to bring about this construct lead to domination and/or violence. The recent "ethnic cleansing" exercises in the Balkans is testimony to the scourges that can accompany this process. In Africa, too, the way in which nations have been constituted has not gone unchallenged. Often this is a result of ethnic groups feeling that the state has not protected their particular interests or is unduly favoring another group.

We do not have to interpret every conflict in Africa as an ethnic problem (as is so often portrayed in the Western media). However, we should also not engage ourselves in the politics of denial. There needs to be a sober reassessment of how best to govern diversity. Simply negating ethnically based political parties is not the solution. If ethnicity represents the easiest way in which to mobilize people — given that it is a ready made resource — it will be used despite bans on it. Rather, recognizing subnational identities and finding equitable ways in which to accommodate them, appears to be a more appropriate exercise.

South Africa

In South Africa, the role of the state as a central actor in promoting ethnicity has long been recognized and this, ironically, has led to studies of ethnicity being tabooed forms of scholarly inquiry. To discuss ethnicity was seen as tantamount to legitimizing the state's exercise. Race, class, and gender have been the predominant social science foci of interpretation for the society.

South Africans, having only recently gained nationhood status, are still enjoying the euphoria of nationalism. Thus reconciliation, unity, non-racialism, and the "rainbow nation," are the catch phrases of the day. Differences of race, class, gender, and ethnicity are consequently being temporarily submerged. However, as the constitutional process unfolded and various regional governments sought to augment their power bases, ethnicity was once again placed on the agenda.

Before looking at some present day issues in the country, it is noteworthy to see how South Africans have conceptualized the national and ethnic question. For the white Conservative Party (CP) and National Party (NP) supporters, until the early 1980s, ethnic identity was seen as the primary identity, not only for social interaction, but the basis upon which to structure the state. This primordialist interpretation rendered each group a nation or potential nation which had the right to express itself politically within its own state (an ethno-state conceptualization).

This was the basis of the Bantustan policy, which was designed to maintain white supremacy through ethno-nationalist self-determination. The apartheid regime therefore actively contributed to and enforced the creation of ethnic politics. It created ethnically based governments (itself included), and in so doing provided the incumbents of those governments with a stake in the system. The KwaZulu Bantustan is a case in point. Mangosuthu Buthelezi, leader of the Zulu-based Inkatha Freedom Party (IFP), was used by the state to counter the national liberation movement. Although he ostensibly espoused non-racialism, he mobilized around ethnicity. However, as is usually the case with collaborators, once the government decided to negotiate with the ANC, Buthelezi became dispensable. He, however, was not about to be outmaneuvered, and in his pursuit of maintaining power, the country experienced increased violence. As a result of the violence, which was state-supported, Buthelezi became indispensable to the creation of a new political dispensation in the country.

Countering the apartheid regime's interpretation of the nation was a nationalist movement which sought to constitute a non-racial, unitary state in which race and ethnicity (if they were to persist) would at best be secondary forms of identification — with loyalty to the South African nation being paramount. Heribert Adam states that, "the ideology of non-racialism rejects an ethnic nation in favour of a civic nation, based on equal individual rights, regardless of origin, and equal recognition of all cultural traditions in the public sphere. The civic nation is based on consent rather than descent."[21] These two differing conceptions of the nation, ethno versus civic, still dominate, as depicted by right wing demands for their own "Volkstaat."

Within academia during the 1960s and 1970s, the liberal paradigm imbibed the cultural pluralist perspective, seeing incompatible cultural institutions as the basis for conflict in the country. As the model came under criticism for being ahistorical and static, and for justifying actions of the state, a new shift in thinking occurred espousing a more modernizationist perspective where it was thought that industrialization would break affective ties. In the late 1980s, however, there was a reemergence of a pluralist perspective drawing on the works of A. Lipjhart and D. Horowitz, who have devised elaborate constitutional engineering models to deal with ethnicity — "consociational democracy" and "alternative voting" models, respectively.[22] The primary problem with these models was that they assumed a fixed ethnic positioning, resulting in ethnicity being furthered entrenched.

Most studies of race and class in academia largely dismiss ethnicity as either invented or as an epiphenomenon. For example, as Paulus Zulu notes:

> Successive [SA] governments ruled Africans as a common group and no distinct regional or ethnic groupings mobilized against white rule on any significant ethnic ticket. Liberation movements such as the ANC and PAC organized on a non-ethnic or non-racial basis. It was the National Party that created and rewarded politicized ethnicity in order to sustain it. Cleavages which arise out of this form of social engineering are, therefore, not natural but contrived.[23]

While one can agree with the above conceptualization, it does not negate the practice of ethnic politics; it merely identifies one source thereof.

The debate on the national question has received much more scholarly attention. Whether South Africa consisted of four nations, two nations, or if a nation was yet to be created, formed the essential component of the debate. However, this debate has disappeared and the conceptualization of one nation appears to have entrenched itself. Sam Nolutshungu states that

> matters debated with great passion in the past — as to how many nations there are, who constitutes the nation, or what the class destiny of such a nation must be — will not be solved by philosophical inquiry or scientific demonstration, if they ever could be, but by the fait accompli of state power and interest, and by the convergent practices of those strata close to the state, truly functioning, in this regard, as ideological state apparatuses ... The call for "national unity" will be made by the state as part of its work of "nation building."[24]

The forces at play in the South African political arena were such that a compromise package was settled for, which resulted in the creation of the Government of National Unity (GNU). The GNU is now in the process of state consolidation; a process in which the various coalitions seek, through the amount of power they wield, to leave their imprint on the formation of the state. Central to this exercise were the constitutional making process and the interplay between central, regional, and local governments.

How the state is constituted, its nature and strength, how it deals with issues of redistribution and identity, are all crucial elements in determining the level of ethnic conflict which will persist.

With regards to the constitution, it is noteworthy that South Africa had one of the unique opportunities to devise a constitution which is sensitive to the major current international issues (gender and ethnicity being among them), both in terms of process and content. Even before the process was completed, the constitutional principles governing the exercise took race, gender, and ethnicity into account. Thus, for example, with regards to ethnic relations, the diversity of language and culture, collective rights to self-determination, and the institution of traditional leadership were to be protected.

Discernible from the above were political forces that demanded that these principles be included. This testified to the accommodating behavior forced upon the ANC, which would not otherwise have so readily incorporated these principles. This confirms a general rule of politics that, the stronger the opposition, the more one has to accommodate its demands. These principles were being put to the test as Inkatha called for the right to self-determination for the KwaZulu/Natal Province.

By not closing off the avenue to ethnic groups who seek self-determination, and instead, to assert that they need to show proven support, the state effectively accommodated ethnic demands without running the risk of every ethnic group seeking secession. It is this type of maneuvering by the state that shows how central it is in either fostering or impeding ethnically based revolt. An intransigent state is likely to come up against resistance.

Although the principle of a unitary state has prevailed, the question of federalism versus unitarianism remains a controversial issue in South Africa. The debate on federalism is intimately bound up with ethnicity. South Africa's regional boundaries largely correspond to ethnic settlements. Natal and Western Cape, from which calls for federalism have echoed the loudest, have a concentration of Zulu and Colored groups, respectively. The Afrikaners are still attempting to discern where they could possibly locate themselves. If we agree that ethnicity is primarily a political issue, then it plays itself out in the case of Western Cape and Natal. Here, two political parties, Inkatha and the NP, have used ethnic identification to not only muster political support, but also to guarantee themselves access to power. They have succeeded in being the dominant political forces in the two regions, and a federal option would give them the necessary power base they need.

Paul Brass provides us with the theoretical insight to see the role of marginalized elites, such as the NP and IFP leaders, within the process of ethnicity.[25] These elites can remain in power only if they are able to dispense rewards to their followers. The point here is not to make the claim that this is foul play, but to suggest instead that it is part of the very exercise of political power play. As such, the interests of these elites cannot be simply willed away. More interesting is to question at which particular juncture ethnicity lends itself as a viable political resource tool? When is it able to constitute the dominant form of opposition politics, as opposed to other forms of representation?

Another interesting phenomenon, in the South Africa context, is the role accorded to traditional leadership and the contradictions this entails. South Africa appears to acknowledge a dual system of authority (although this remains contested) prevalent in the country, whether or not invented or sustained, by the previous government. The GNU feels the need to afford these "traditional leaders" some form of representation, and has thus drafted them into the governing process. The problems which emerge are the following. Firstly, what kind of representation do you afford them and on what basis? Secondly, given the unevenness of traditional practices throughout the country, with the system of chieftaincy being weak or non-existent in some areas, do you create chiefs in order to achieve uniformity in presentation? And thirdly, how do we reconcile a progressive stance on gender with a patriarchal institution of chieftaincy?

Tandabantu Nhlapo recently suggested that traditional practices are not static and thus the whole practice of chieftaincy can be transformed to accommodate the concerns of the women's movement.[26] I would agree. The emphasis here is not on tradition but on the best method by which to incorporate the largest number of constituencies into the governing process. We should use institutions that have served communities rather than seeing them as rivals to the nation-building enterprise, and specifically to an elite which has yet to earn the right to wield authority over the population at large. South Africa has a long and tedious way to go in the process of nation-building and state consolidation. There are, and will be, many stumbling blocks. At least there is enough willingness to not foreclose issues merely because they do not correspond with a particular ideological framework.

Finally, with respect to the question of identity, studies on ethnic conflict have largely seen identity as rigid — you are born into a particular ethnic group and will forever remain bounded to it. Early nationalism, on the other hand, assumed that one could shed one's ethnic identity in favor of a nationalist one. It is now more apt to assert that people have multiple identities: gendered, racial, ethnic, national, religious, and others. These identities coexist, are constantly changing, and the identity that gains ascendance is largely determined by circumstance. Contradictory identification can exist within the same individual without an inevitable conflict or choice having to be made. However, it is when identities become politicized that they constitute a potential point of confrontation: that is, when I can only gain access to resources because of a particular identity, be it racial, ethnic, or gendered. This is a phenomenon that seems dominant worldwide, and hence the intense struggles that emerge around identity and/or representation.

Conclusion

In conclusion, it appears as though, thus far, the Government of National Unity has succeeded in maintaining a semblance of cohesiveness. In the process of state consolidation, the government has to a large extent remained fairly flexible on the question of ethnicity. In its nation-building exercise, it has sought to at least provide a hearing for those who express fears on the nature of the future South African state.

If we take heed of history, however, we need to be aware that in the rest of Africa, and indeed within the apartheid era as well, state perpetuated ethnicity became pronounced once the incumbents were confronted with opposition. Successive governments resorted to ethnic based support in order to maintain themselves in power. It is too soon to tell which direction the new government will take once threatened with heightened opposition. In South Africa, however, due to historical factors, it appears more likely that race will provide the constitutive base for the state.

If Africa is still caught up in the process of the "nation state in the making," to use Ibbo Mandaza's phrase,[27] let it at the very least seek to constitute its political communities on the basis of principles and policies acceptable to all those who have to abide by them.

Diversity can be a power base or it can be a destabilizer, depending entirely on how these human resources are managed.

Notes

[1] F. Barth, *Ethnic Groups and Boundaries: The Social Organization of Cultural Difference* (Boston: Little, Brown and Company, 1969); B. Anderson, *Imagined Communities* (London: Verso, 1983); E. Hobsbawn and T. Ranger, *The Invention of Tradition* (Cambridge: Cambridge University Press, 1983).

[2] Although constructivism and/or the new post-modernist conceptualizations are insightful, they merely present us with a different view of how identities are shaped. They do very little in terms of assisting us to understand when and how conflict manifests itself. For this, we need to look at sociopolitical and economic processes — not merely at identity construction.

[3] J. Degenaar, "The Myth of the South African Nation," Paper presented at a conference on Ethnicity, Identity, and Nationalism, Grahamstown, South Africa, 1993.

[4] J.V. Stalin, *Marxism and the National Question (1913)*, in J.V. Stalin, *Works,* Volume 2 (Moscow: Foreign Languages Publishing House, 1953), p. 307.

[5] A. Smith, *The Ethnic Origins of Nations* (London: Basil Blackwell, 1986), pp. 17-18.

[6] In addition to Anderson, and Hobsbawm and Ranger, see E. Gellner, *Nations and Nationalism* (Ithaca: Cornell University Press, 1983).

[7] John Brueilly, *Nationalism and the State* (UK: Manchester University Press, 1982).

[8] R. Nixon, "Of Balkans and Bantustans," *Transition*, Vol. 3, No. 2, 1993.

[9] See M. Esman, *Ethnic Politics* (Ithaca: Cornell University Press, 1994).

[10] E. Shils, "Primordial, Personal, Sacred, and Civil Ties" *British Journal of Sociology,* Vol. 8., 1957; C. Geertz, *Old Societies and New States* (New York: The Free Press, 1963); and P. van den Berghe, *Race and Racism* (New York: John Wiley, 1967).

[11] P. Gutkind, "Preface: The Passing of Tribal Man in Africa," *Journal of Asian and African Studies*, Vol. 5, No. 1, 1970.

[12] P. van den Berghe, *The Ethnic Phenomenon* (Westport, CT: Greenwood Press, 1981).

[13] B. Magubane, "Pluralism and Conflict Situation in Africa," *Africa Social Research,* Vol. 7, No. 1, 1969.

[14] S. Olzak and J. Nagel, *Competitive Ethnic Relations* (New York: Academic Press, 1986).

[15] R. Bates, "Ethnic Competition and Modernization in Contemporary Africa," *Comparative Political Studies,* Vol. 6, No. 4, 1974.

[16] See O. Nnoli, *Ethnic Politics in Africa* (African Association of Political Science Book Project Series, No. 1, 1989); and Y. Barongo, *Political Science in Africa* (London: Zed Books, 1983).

[17] Nnoli, p. 14.

[18] E. Oshaghae, "Ethnicity in Africa or African Ethnicity: The Search for a Conceptual Understanding," in U. Himmelstrand *et al (eds.)*, *African Perspectives on Development* (London: James Currey, 1994), pp. 137-157.

[19] L. Vail, *The Creation of Tribalism in Southern Africa* (Berkeley: University of California Press, 1989).

[20] See note 9.

[21] H. Adam, "Ethnic versus Civic Nationalism: South Africa's Non-racialism in Comparative Perspective," *South African Sociological Review*, Vol. 7, 1994.

[22] A. Lijphart, *Democracy in Plural Societies* (New Haven: Yale University Press, 1977); and D. Horowitz, *A Democratic South Africa: Constitutional Engineering in a Divided Society* (Berkeley: University of California Press, 1991).

[23] P. Zulu, "The Melting Pot: Bridging Divided Societies," *Indicator South Africa*, No. 15, 1992, p. 27.

[24] S. Nolutshungu, "Reflections on National Unity in South Africa: A Comparative Approach," *Third World Quarterly,* Vol. 13, 1993, pp. 607.

[25] P. Brass, *Ethnicity and Nationalism: Theory and Comparison* (New Dehli: Sage, 1991).

[26] T. Nhlapo, Talk on Traditional Leadership presented at the International Roundtable on Democratic Constitutional Development, Pretoria, July 17 to 20, 1995.

[27] Ibbo Mandaza (*ed.*), *Zimbabwe: The Political Economy of Transition* (Dakar: CODESRIA, 1986).

9

Political Scientists and the Subversion of Democracy in Nigeria[1]

Jibrin Ibrahim

Authoritarian leaders in Africa have been devising methods of subverting the democratic struggles and aspirations of their people. In Nigeria, the military administration of former President Ibrahim Babangida initiated its program of return to civilian rule in 1986 with the determination of tightly controlling, and indeed subverting the process, thereby frustrating the objective of democratization. The state not only imposed a two-party system, but also formed the parties, wrote their manifestoes, and financed them. The country's political class was destabilized through a constant process of banning and unbanning of politicians and the disqualification of nominated popular candidates at the last instance. In addition, a primitive and palpably anti-democratic system of open ballot elections, in which voters queued in the open in front of the symbol of their choice, was imposed.

Virtually all the anti-democratic measures were devised and implemented by leading members of the political science establishment recruited from Nigerian universities. For all practical purposes, political scientists played the role of a competent technocracy that was a willing accomplice of the military in subverting the democratic struggles and aspirations of the people. Each blockage of democratic space, each device for defeating democratic forces, and every refusal to keep to the schedule of power transfer to elected candidates, was vigorously defended by a coterie of political science professors working for the military dictatorship. This involvement poses serious problems of deontology, which we explore in this chapter.

Political Science and Political Practice

This study is not about political scientists who opt to go into politics and become politicians and act as such. It is about those who offer their services to politicians as academics and technicians of political science. Establishing what should be the relationship between political science as an academic discipline and political practice has always been a contentious issue. A debate on the issue was initiated in Nigeria by Sam Oyovbaire, who contended that

> The essential role of political science is to sensitise and socialise, it is not to legitimise or subvert. The latter role belongs to the realm of practical politics — to actors who may be politicians, regime experts and revolutionaries. While there is a supportive relationship between scholars and actors in the form of "committed scholarship" or of actors and scholars taking cues from each other, the distinctive role of one must not be confused with the other.[2]

Separating the roles of sensitizing and socializing from those of legitimizing and subverting is not an easy task. As Bala Usman argued in his response to Oyovbaire, the knowledge and information the political scientist has, could constitute central aspects of practical political activity, and when the knowledge involves value perceptions, it could impact on the core of political practice.[3]

In addition, as Eme Awa contends, professionals, by virtue of their training, are concerned about positively advancing the objects of their professions — doctors about curing the sick, economists about getting rid of inflation:

> Political scientists everywhere are concerned to ensure the emergence of the good state, defined in some specific way. For instance, for most Americans, the good state is a capitalist democracy predicated on the doctrine of competitive politics in a two party system. For Russians, the good state is a Marxist state predicated on the doctrine of controlled competition ... Political and other social scientists who possess specialised knowledge in these matters are obliged by the nature of their training to give advice regarding the choices to be made. To do otherwise is to abdicate responsibility to society.[4]

We therefore agree with Usman and Awa that the deontology that governs the profession of political science goes beyond sensitizing and socializing the public. It is about ensuring that there is a good state and good governance. However, since there is no agreement within the discipline on the core values constituting the good state and good governance, and the best means of achieving them, the professional and practical engagement of political scientists cannot but reflect these differences.

As Gabriel Almond has argued, the history of the discipline is one of separate tables at which are seated different and contending schools and sects. There has been no "political science" that has stood above issues of ideological commitment.[5] Awa evokes in the citation above the different responsibilities of American and Russian political scientists, which, as we all know, marked the discipline until the fall of the "really existing communist" systems in Eastern Europe in 1989. There is virtual agreement in the discipline that the changes that occurred in those societies were the result of internal subversion. Both empirically and in value orientation, subversion cannot but be a central commitment of many political scientists. The liberal turn that occurred in the Soviet Union and Eastern Europe has led some scholars to suggest that the end of ideology has arrived. Such scholars are palpably wrong. The authoritarian one-party communist model has collapsed, but the central ideological issues of our epoch, relating to imperialist control of world resources and rising inequality in the national and international levels, remain. Ideological struggles can only take new forms; they cannot "end." However, one cannot but agree with Lucian Pye[6] that political scientists can say with some degree of confidence today that there is a crisis of authoritarianism and that the stigma of failure marks every form of tyranny, whether of the one-man or one-party variety. Out of this failure is emerging a consensus that plural democracy is a universal element in enthroning the good state, and good governance, and is therefore a core value of the discipline.

The central issue that arises in the debate about political science and political practice is not whether members of the academy should enter the arena of practice, but about scholars accepting to be misused by politicians for the purpose of subverting the good state and good governance. As Harry Eckstein argues, those in power seldom need the scientific advice of academics:

Even if they use academics, they too often ignore them or else recruit only people who are, so to speak, pseudo-academics in search of political careers or people willing to say what the practitioners want to hear.[7]

The majority of political scientists who offer their services to politicians do so in a manner that consciously subvert their training and professional commitment. Their major activities are sycophancy and the use of their skills to enable their bosses to acquire and use power to subvert the good state and good governance, and in so doing, they subvert the professional integrity of the discipline.

As Chinua Achebe argues in his novel *Anthills of the Savannah,* dictators are not born, they are made by sycophants. Sam, the President in the novel, did not scheme to be President, and he was open and sincere in the beginning of his rule, till the sycophants got him.[8] It has been argued by Kwesi Prah[9] that African social science should take up the study of sycophancy more seriously as many of the most intelligent members of society perfect the art of bootlicking. In the 1960s and 1970s, Africanist political science devoted a lot of time to the study of "charismatic leadership," thereby falling victims to the propaganda of the sycophants, who had inundated the literature with claims about the greatness of their respective heroes. Dictators are partly made by their sycophants, who continue to repeat into their dumb brains that:

The people have spoken, their desire is manifest. You are condemned to serve them for life.[10]

Of course, the sycophants also end up being victims of the monster they have helped create:

Worshipping a dictator is such a pain in the ass. It wouldn't be so bad if it were merely a matter of dancing upside down on your head. With practice, anyone could learn to do that. The real problem is having no way of knowing from one day to another, from one minute to the next, just what is up and what is down.[11]

So, while the dictator repeats over and over that he did not want to rule for ever, his sycophants must be able to read his mind and appeal to him to please save humanity by agreeing to rule for ever. The era of what A.H.M. Kirk-Greene described as "His Eternity, His Eccentricity, or His Exemplarity: His Excellency, the African Head of State,"[12] has become so characteristic of the African political scene. The greatest victims are, of course, the ordinary people, who in their ignorance, opt for rationality rather than sycophancy, and pay the price. The people of Abazon are the example Achebe uses to make this point:

The people who were running in and out and telling us to say yes, came one day and told us that the Big Chief himself did not want to rule for ever but that he was being forced. Who is forcing him? I asked, and their eyes shifted from side to side.[13]

So the people of Abazon obeyed the "wishes" of the dictator and voted against his ruling for ever. In return, the dictator showed his appreciation by closing their boreholes in the middle of a major drought. That is when authoritarianism loses its rationality and becomes self destructive. The king forgets the people have to survive for him to be able to rule them.

Anthills raises serious issues about academics and political practice and evokes painful parallels for those who follow the Nigerian situation. Numerous intellectuals are engaged in an intensive competition to "achieve" the status of the greatest sycophant. The business of government was carried out without any respect for the economic and social needs of the people. Five years after the publication of *Anthills*, the Association for A Better Nigeria (ABN) was formed to campaign for perpetual rule by President Babangida, and leading political scientists on the payroll of military politicians were already working for the same goal.

The Babangida Regime and the Role of Political Scientists

Nigerian political scientists never played a prominent role in the country's political process before the advent of the Babangida regime in 1985. Preceding regimes, both civilian and military, tended to rely on learned members of the legal profession for their political technicians. In fact, a recurring corridor topic of debate in the annual conferences of the Nigerian Political Science Association was the so-called "failure" of the profession to get a frontline role in the process of political engineering, in the manner in which the leaders of the Nigerian Economic Society were playing a prominent role in economic policy formulation and implementation. The Babangida regime, from its very inception, decided to recruit leading members of the professions — medical, economy, political science, information — to formulate and implement government policies.

A fairly large proportion of the leading professors and scholars of political science were recruited to design and implement Babangida's transition program (BTP), which was supposed to lead the country to civil and democratic rule. Babangida established a Presidential Advisory Council (Kitchen Cabinet) that had three leading political science professors — Jonah Elaigwu, Ali Yahaya, and the late Yahya Aliyu. The initial design of the BTP was awarded to the Political Bureau, composed mainly of academics (13 out of 17), while the professional rivals of political scientists, the lawyers, were completely excluded from the body. A number of leading political scientists, including Professors Eme Awa, A. D. Yahaya, Oyeleye Oyediran and S. E. Oyovbaire, were members. Other members included Drs. Bala Takaya, Tunde Adeniran, and Haroun Adamu. The report of the Political Bureau was reviewed by a nine-man panel composed mainly of senior military officers, under General Paul Omu. The panel was to draft a White Paper, with the assistance of two political scientists — Jonah Elaigwu and Yahya Aliyu. After the adoption of the Omu Draft White Paper, the transition timetable was established by the Special Adviser to the President on Political Affairs, Tunji Olagunju, who worked in conjunction with two other political scientists, Sam Oyovbaire and Tunde Adeniran.

With the constitution in preparation, other political scientists were recruited into the various implementation bodies. Professor Eme Awa[14] took control of the National Electoral Commission (NEC), with Adele Jinadu, Tony Edoh, and others. Among those drafted to the Constituent Assembly were Professors Amoda and Oyediran, Drs. A. Jalingo, B. Takaya and H. Adamu. Two organs, the Centre of Democratic Studies and the MAMSER, the agency for mass mobilization, were supposed to instill the new democratic culture in Nigeria's new breed politician. They were staffed by a fairly large group of political scientists, led by Professors Omo Omoruyi and Tunde Adeniran. Almost all the eminent political scientists were recruited into the various transition bodies.[15]

The political scientists that were closest to General Babangida and played the most prominent roles were: Oyovbaire, Political Adviser to the Chief of General Staff, Adeniran, Director-General of MAMSER, Omoruyi, Director-General of the Centre for Democratic Studies, Olagunju, and Elaigwu.

Most of these political scientists devoted themselves to two principal activities, sycophantic praise singing in favor of General Babangida, or IBB as they called him, and devising tactics and strategies for perpetuating his repressive rule. In their profile of IBB, Olagunju and Oyovbaire shamelessly describe the tyrant as

> A Professional, courageous and devoted soldier of the good old days; a military intellectual and strategist; a man with great personable disposition, charm and humour; a very brilliant and witty person; a man of robust heart with tremendous African humanism; a person of manifest devotion to family and friends; a leader with profound knowledge, grasp and appreciation of history, who skillfully combines his visions and dreams with realism and pragmatism in the cause of history; the "Maradona" of Nigerian politics and master tactician; a statesman with abidingly immense convictions and faith in the unity and greatness of Nigeria and in her destiny in world affairs.[16]

The strings of adjectives of adulation and hero worship are certainly not the normal verbal baggage of serious political scientists.

The theme that Babangida had arrived on Nigeria's political scene with a great historical mission recurs in many of the writings of the IBB professors. Jinadu contends, for example, that the work of IBB:

> Reflect a deep concern with the human condition in Nigeria and how to improve upon it. They represent the thought of a patriot and nationalist, of a statesman who, *acting out a historical role* and contending against great odds, is working strenuously with his colleagues and compatriots to *bequeath a legacy* of which future generations of Nigerians will be proud.[17]

In their book on *Transition to Democracy in Nigeria,* Olagunju, Jinadu, and Oyovbaire reaffirm that:

> The book is a testimonial to, and an appreciation of the vision *and historical significance (in the Hegelian sense)* of President Ibrahim Babamasi Babangida and his colleagues in the Armed Forces Ruling Council for their commitment to and dogged pursuit of the democratization of political and socioeconomic structures and processes in Nigeria.[18]

Our sycophantic professors of political science, of course, failed in their mission of convincing their countrymen that their IBB was a great man.[19] They forgot the essential value elements necessary for the emergence of a historical individual:

•   A commitment concerning these values must be made by the historical actor;

         whose conduct is the ultimate datum of historical investigation;
- These values cannot be purely personal or private. They must express the general concern of a culture;
- These values must be objective in the sense that an unconditional general validity can be ascribed to them; and
- Historical investigation itself cannot take a position on these values. Rather, it must relate them to the individual in a purely theoretical fashion.[20]

The core values that governed the life of General Babangida have been personal ambition, scheming for power, and the embezzlement of public resources. These are certainly not the type of values that make a Hegelian historical individual.

As has been the pattern in similar attempts to "fabricate" a historical figure such as Nicolae Ceausescu in Rumania, the IBB professors devoted themselves to the writing of texts that falsified their hero's politics so as to give the impression that he was the stuff of a great man. According to Jinadu, for example:

> Underlying his (IBB) approach to governance is the view of government as a trust ... First, there should be accountability. Secondly, there should be consultation and participation. Thirdly, due process must be followed, except for reasons of state. Fourthly, fundamental human rights must be secured, protected and guaranteed.[21]

These are virtually the exact opposite of what is known about the Babangida regime. To attribute these values and commitment to Babangida is therefore nothing short of telling damn lies in an attempt to create a myth.

On the issue of human rights, it will be recalled that President Babangida had claimed at the commencement of his regime that he took over power to protect human rights. We are told by one of his professors that:

> President Babangida's enunciation of human rights as a cardinal aspect of his regime is not merely accidental or an opportunistic rationalization to take advantage of the opprobrium in which the Buhari regime was held and thereby win popular acclaim. Rather, it runs deep in his liberal and populist convictions and is based on a reasoned and well-thought out conceptualisation of the military role in African politics.[22]

The Babangida regime turned out to have the highest level of human rights abuses in the history of Nigeria.[23] It is revealing that while the IBB professors[24] attacked the Muhammadu Buhari regime, from which the Babangida regime emerged in a palace coup of tyranny and authoritarianism, they mention nothing in their various books about the even more atrocious human rights abuses of the Babangida regime.

The IBB professors claim that Babangida was committed to promoting Nigerian federalism[25] and that he was a committed liberal democrat who was acting as "the last bastion of democracy in the country."[26] They also claim that the problem of kleptocracy was only the fault of political parties.[27] What they tried to hide was that the major crime of their administration was the final destruction of Nigerian federalism, the transformation of corruption into the "raison d'état," and the subversion of the struggle for liberal democracy in Nigeria.

What the Professors Tried to Hide: The Reality of the Babangida Regime

The first military ruler to consciously and deliberately break the tradition of collective military rule and establish a one-man tyranny in Nigeria was General Babangida. He was the first military leader to take the title of "president," and he clearly embarked along a trajectory of personal, as opposed to military rule. For example, he dissolved and reconstituted the ruling military council at will, and informed his military colleagues of his decisions rather than consult with them in the official decision-making bodies.

The Nigerian military have transformed the country's body politic in a very significant manner. In the first place, the military have entrenched the culture of public corruption established earlier by civilian regimes. In the past, corruption was corruption — unethical or illegal advantages procured through official positions. Under the Babangida administration, what used to be known as corruption became the art of government itself. There was a complete prebendalisation of state power and virtually all acts by public officials involving public expenditure or public goods of any kind led to the appropriation of state finances or property by officials. The routine operations of government were being subjected to prebendal rules. It is widely known, for example, that officials of state governments and parastatals had to pay, as they put it, "up front" a percentage of their statutory allocations to the Presidency, Ministry of Finance, and Central Bank officials before their allocations were released. They, in turn, simply took their own share, "up front," from the so-called government coffers.

Contractors who used to bribe officials for government contracts were completely sidelined. The president, military governors, ministers, etc., simply allocated contracts to their own front companies, which did not even have to pretend they were doing the job because few would dare pose questions. Under Babangida, the country's major resource, petroleum, was allocated to individuals who then sold their allocations to petroleum companies. All the major drug barons arrested by the agency set up to fight against the narcotics business under Babangida were released, or rather, allowed to escape, by their captors, and most of the seized drugs "disappeared" from government security depots. There was even a major struggle between different military and security agencies for the control of the lucrative "drug prevention" business. IBB succeeded in transforming corruption from a deviant activity by public officials into the "raison d'être" of the Nigerian state.

Secondly, the military have succeeded in destroying Nigerian federalism, sacrificing it on the alter of over-centralization. The country's geopolitical realities have been completely modified. The tripartite structure which had become quadripartite with the creation of the Mid-West in 1963, has changed drastically as a result of the multiplication of states, whose number, under Babangida, was raised to 30. The multiplication of states has produced a Jacobean effect, in which miniature states can no longer contest or counterbalance federal authority. Nigeria thus finds itself now with a federation that is for all practical purposes a unitary system with some devolution of power to the states. This tendency was reinforced after the decision by former President Babangida on October 1, 1988, to scrap ministries of local governments and establish a directorate in the Presidency to directly control local governments, thus bypassing the state structure of the federation.

At the level of the transition program, General Babangida, with the help of his professors, acted like a voluntarist architect, who drew a plan for a complete transformation of the Nigerian body politic. His program covered a long transition period during which a group of political scientists drew up a program of "political crafting" that was supposed to create a new democratic political culture. General Babangida was indeed like an experienced trapeze artist determined to use the political skills at his disposal to complete the patrimonialisation of Nigeria's political culture, to ensure that only rapacious political entrepreneurs that have looted the nation's wealth, have the slightest chance of ever coming to power.[28] The method he used involved an elaborate process of political engineering in which the popular forces were successively excluded from the transition program through arbitrary and ever-changing rules, and corruption was entrenched as the only instrument for the acquisition of political power.

The first element of the process was the systematic destabilization of the country's political class, beginning with the ban of "old" politicians, in September 1987. The totality of those who had held political office in all previous civilian and military regimes were prohibited from participating in the political transition process. A new breed of "grassroot politicians" were to be created and they were to operate, not in a multiparty framework, but in two new political parties registered by the state. To determine the two political parties to be registered, the National Electoral Commission (NEC) and the government imposed very expensive and virtually impossible preconditions that only the upper section of the bourgeoisie, or old politicians with established networks, could have afforded or met. In three months, the parties were to establish well equipped offices with at least three paid staff in all the 435 local government areas in the country. In addition, they were to supply 25 membership lists of their parties comprising the names, photographs, and personal details of at least 200 members from each local government in the country (marketing at least 87,000 individual membership files per party), to the NEC. For good measures, prospective parties were to submit their applications with a registration fee of 50,000 naira. In spite of these draconian measures, 13 parties were able to submit their files before the deadline.[29]

In a broadcast to the nation on October 6, 1989, the Head of State in a perfect *Catch 22* scenario used the argument that the "impossible" preconditions had not been perfectly adhered to as a justification to refuse to register any of the parties. The political parties, he said, had

> failed to comply with key conditions in the guidelines such as documentation on members, declaration of assets and liabilities of individual members of the national executive committees. . most of them [parties] had operated underground prior to the lifting of the ban on politics on 3rd May 1989 ... [and] had deep roots in the party politics of the First and Second Republics. There were very strong indications of the wealthy individuals in the executive committees of the associations that confirm fears that they were being hijacked by money bags.

Babangida acted as if any mass party in the world could give exact and detailed information on all its members at any point in time, or as if politics could suddenly be cut off from historical connections to past leaders, networks, and issues, or that people with money could or should be barred from the politics of liberal democracy!

Be that as it may, the government decided to dissolve all the thirteen parties and create two new ones for the "ordinary people" — the Social Democratic Party (SDP) and the National Republican Convention (NRC), with the former leaning "a little to the left of the centre" and the latter leaning "a little to the right of the centre." In addition, the government drew up the manifestoes of the two parties, and decided to fund and staff them, before calling on individuals (as opposed to organized groups) to sign up. It is clear from the transition program that the military government of General Babangida decided to define and apply each "democratic" step on behalf of the people. They were not willing to allow the people to take democratic decisions on how they were to be governed.

Apart from imposing manifestoes and constitutions on the two parties, excessive powers were given to government-appointed administrative secretaries to organize their take-off and to *exclude* undue radicals, socialists, anti-Structural Adjustment Program agitators, as well as ideological and religious extremists, from them. In addition, Decree 48 of 1991 gave the NEC wide ranging powers to disqualify any political aspirant whose action was "likely to disrupt the process of grassroots democracy," and the law was amended with Decree 6 of 1992, which widened these powers by absolving the NEC of the duty of explaining or giving reasons for disqualification. This law enabled the NEC to disqualify thirty-two aspirants who had already won their party's nominations for the Senatorial and House of Assembly elections in July 1992. The threat of the NEC ax was used to scare away many presidential candidates that were not close friends of the military hierarchy.

The most dramatic aspect of the transition, was, however, the commercialization of the nomination and electoral process through the use, or rather abuse, of the open ballot or queuing system, in which the secret ballot was disallowed and voters queued up in public behind the party symbol of their "choice."[30] The direct effect of the system was that candidates paid people to vote for them and party aides could directly observe and ensure that people who have been "bought" joined the queue of the aspirant who had paid for their vote. Not surprisingly, the state governors who were elected in 1991/2 were considered the most corrupt and notorious elements of the nouveaux riches, including a well known cocaine dealer and somebody who had been found guilty by a judicial tribunal of bankrupting a state owned national supply company by stealing its resources. They were political entrepreneurs who had decided to invest in the political game to make more money. It has been estimated, for example, that no serious presidential candidate spent less than fifty million naira (US$ 2.5 million) for his campaigns.[31]

The first set of leading presidential candidates for the two parties were disqualified by the NEC for using money rather that ideals. At that time, the handover date to an elected administration had been postponed from October 1990 to October 1992, and then to August 1993, while Babangida and his political science gurus "crafted" the new breed politician. In a last ditch attempt to get the General to hand over power, the two parties nominated close personal friends and business associates of Babangida as their presidential candidates — Moshood Abiola for the SDP and Bashir Tofa for the NRC. After a lot of procrastination by the government and determined protest against another postponement by the people, the presidential election was finally held on June 12, 1993. The candidate of the SDP won neatly in an election that was generally considered free and fair. The election was above all a referendum in which Nigerians voted *out* Babangida, but he would not take *no* for an answer. He cancelled the election and tried to initiate yet another round of "political crafting," but there was so much mass protests against the cancellation, that he had to leave power in haste. He handed power over to an incompetent and powerless civilian, without any mandate, creating the basis for yet another coup d'état in November 1993 by his second in command, General Sani Abacha, who is now continuing with the type of antics he inherited from Babangida.

Conclusion

In their book *Transition to Democracy in Nigeria: 1985-1993,* Olagunju, Jinadu, and Oyovbaire, some of the leading IBB professors, claim that what they have written:

> Is a testimony to our own stewardship in the transition programme of the Babangida Administration, and of our own commitment as intellectuals, to the cause of freedom and social action or praxis to bring it about.[32]

While they certainly bear responsibility for their stewardship of Babangida's kleptocratic and anti-democratic politics, they have not lived up to the reputation they had previously built of responsible and respected professors of political science. The professors of political science who designed a transition program aimed at frustrating the democratic aspirations of the Nigerian people and enabling President Ibrahim Babangida to perpetuate his tyrannic and corrupt rule for eight years, have clearly betrayed the deontology that guides their discipline. They have consciously and actively schemed against the evolution of the good state and good governance in their country. They have used their skills to thwart popular demands for a genuine democratic pluralist regime in the country. The Nigerian people have suffered enormously under the policies that they have formulated and they bear responsibility for that. We agree with René Lemarchand's argument that the scholars who built the intellectual base that sustained the tyrannic regime in Burundi bear direct responsibility for the massacres subsequently carried out by the regime.[33] Our own IBB professors also bear responsibility for the major reversals of Nigerian federalism, public ethos and democratic aspirations suffered under their tutelage.

Notes

[1] In writing this chapter, I have drawn on the 1988 paper written by Ibrahim Muazzam and myself on the same theme, and benefited from subsequent discussions with him.

[2] Sam E. Oyovbaire, "The Responsibility of Political Science in Nigeria," *Nigeria Journal of Political Science,* Vol. 2, No. 2, 1980, p. 9.

[3] Bala Y. Usman, "The Elementary Responsibilities of Political and Other Sciences in Nigeria," *Nigerian Journal of Political Science,* Vol. 2, No. 2, 1980, p. 24.

[4] Eme Awa, "The Responsibility of Political Science in Nigeria," *Nigerian Journal of Political Science,* Vol. 2, No. 2, 1980, p. 61.

[5] Gabriel Almond, "Separate Tables: Schools and Sects in Political Science," *Political Science and Politics,* Vol. 21, No. 4, 1988.

[6] Lucian W. Pye, "Political Science and the Crisis of Authoritarianism," *American Political Science Review,* Vol. 84, No. 1, 1990, p. 5.

[7] Harry Eckstein, "More About Applied Political Science," *Political Science and Politics,* Vol. 23, No. 1, 1990, p. 55.

[8] Chinua Achebe, *Anthills of the Savannah* (London: Heinemann, 1987).

[9] Kwesi Prah, "Africa's Heritage, Populism and the Contemporary Democratic Process in Africa," Paper prepared for CODESRIA General Assembly Conference on Democratization Processes in Africa, Dakar, 1992.

[10] Achebe, p. 5.

[11] *Ibid.,* p. 45.

[12] A. H. M. Kirk-Greene, "His Eternity, His Eccentricity, or His Exemplarity: A Further Contribution to the Study of H. E. the African Head of State," *African Affairs*, No. 90, 1991.

[13] Achebe, p. 126.

[14] Eme Awa was one of the few principled political scientists to resign immediately after it became clear that the political transition program was a fraudulent one. He was replaced at the head of the Commission by another professional colleague, Humphrey Nwosu.

[15] As far as I know, the notable exceptions who resisted incorporation were Professors C. Ake, O. Nnoli, O. Oyediran, and A. T. Gana.

[16] T. Olagunju and S. Oyovbaire (*eds.*), *Portrait of a New Nigeria: Selected Speeches of IBB*, Volume I (London: Precision Press, 1989), p. IX.

[17] Adele Jinadu, "Introduction," in Olagungu and Oyovabaire (*eds.*), p. 29. Emphasis mine.

[18] T. Olagungu, A. Jinadu and S. Oyovbaire, (*eds.*), *Transition to Democracy in Nigeria: 1985-1993* (Ibadan: Safari Books, 1993), p. 24. Emphasis mine.

[19] Widespread comments in the media and in public fora about the hidden agenda of Babangida and about the excessive corruption of his regime clearly indicate that almost nobody took the eulogies being reeled out by these professors seriously. Essentially, they were not writing to make any scientific or professional point, but to prove their loyalty to Babangida.

[20] Guy Oakes, "Max Weber and the Southwest German School: Remarks on the Genesis of the Concept of the Historical Individual," *International Journal of Politics, Cultures and Society*, Vol. 1, No. 1, 1987, p. 126.

[21] Jinadu, "Introduction."

[22] *Ibid.*, p. 8.

[23] See Jibrin Ibrahim (*ed.*), *Expanding Nigerian Democratic Space* (Dakar: CODESRIA, forthcoming).

[24] Olagungu *et al*, p. 25.

[25] *Ibid.*, p. 50.

[26] *Ibid.*, p. 32.

[27] *Ibid.*, p. 37.

[28] Jibrin Ibrahim, "The State, Accumulation and Democratic Forces in Nigeria," in Lars Rodebeck (*ed.*), *When Democracy Makes Sense: Studies in the Democratic Potential of Third World Popular Movements* (Uppsala: AKUT, 1992), pp. 105-129.

[29] It was political farce at its worst. Nigeria ran out of photographic materials and polaroid films in the stampede to produce photographs of party members, and emergency imports had to be made while people were paid to have their photographs taken. The parties had to hire lorries to carry hundreds of thousands of the hurriedly prepared membership files to the NEC.

[30] The secret ballot is an elementary condition for the conduct of free and fair elections, yet the IBB professors rivaled themselves to "prove" the contrary.

[31] For some detailed examples of the types and scale of the expenses incurred, see "The Money Game," *African Concord*, September 21, 1992.

[32] Olagunju *et al*, p. 22.

[33] René Lemarchand, *Burundi: Ethnic Conflict and Genocide* (New York: Woodrow Wilson Center Press and Cambridge University Press, 1995), p. 33.

10

The Two Political Parties and the Electoral Process in Nigeria: 1989-1993

Said Adejumobi

The transition to civil rule program of the Nigerian state (1986-1993), under the Ibrahim Babangida administration, was characterized by strict regimentation or what Richard Joseph described as extreme political engineering.[1] This was aimed at promoting a "guided democracy,"[2] in which there is a gradual opening up of the political space, conceived as essential to evolving the requisite political framework and democratic processes, and for resolving the intractable problem of leadership succession and change in Nigeria. For its authors, the transition program was seen as a learning and design project, through which democratic values, nuances, and behavior were to be foisted by the regime and subsequently transmitted to, and internalized by, the political elites in particular, and the political community in general.[3] On this Babangida posits:

> From our past experience, our political programme must be gradual, purposeful and effective, it must aim at laying the basic foundation of a new socio-political order. We must create a new set of values — a new set of political attitudes or political culture aimed at ushering in a new social order. For this administration, this is a duty we owe future generations yet unborn.[4]

The pernicious political pathologies of the civilian political elites constitute the underlying rationale of the transition to civil rule project. This is what George Kieh and P.O. Agbese aptly referred to as the "pathological elite thesis."[5] The logic affirms that it is the preponderance of anti-democratic values and practices, or what Samuel Finer called, "a low level political culture,"[6] especially among the civilian political elites, which defines the "debilitating cycle of political renewal and decay in Nigeria."[7] Central to a reversal of this trend are three major political changes or reforms. First is the psychological reorientation of the political elites toward democratic norms. Second is the creation of an appropriate party system to moderate political behavior and institutionalize a framework for promoting healthy political competition, and third is the evolution of a credible structure and process of elections. The structure of elections suggests the machinery for the administration of elections, while the latter denotes the electoral process.[8]

Complimentarily, the transition to civil rule program was organically linked with the economic reform process of the Structural Adjustment Program (SAP), with the latter believed to strengthen and reinforce the former. The SAP emphasizes a reduction in the role and scope of the state in the economy, which has the capacity to attenuate the "entrepot"[9] character of the state, and thereby regulate politics and its prebendal nature[10] in Nigeria. In other words, economic liberalization is viewed as the flip side of political democracy.

Essentially, a critical hub of the transition to civil rule project was the reform of the party system and the electoral process. Thus, fundamental and radical chaos were introduced in this regard. A two-party system was introduced as a means of domesticating political competition and removing the inherent instability involved in a multiparty framework.[11] Also, an electoral commission was reconstituted and granted enormous powers. Similarly, the electoral process was also significantly overhauled.

This study analyzes these changes in the party system and the electoral process in Nigeria under the transition to civil rule program of the Babangida regime. Its aim is to explicate their nature, implications, and essence, and to examine how such reconstituted democratic politics could vitiate the deleterious and fanatical passions and struggle for political power in Nigeria.

Political Parties in the Electoral Process in Nigeria

To the extent that political patrimonialism defines the essence of the state in Africa, access to state power has been a major source of capital accumulation and the fulcrum of social privileges by the local bourgeoisie. In a patrimonial state, the domain of the "private" and the "public" are blurred, a fact which Claude Ake described as the non-autonomization of the state,[12] and the personal will of the ruler often predominates. The state, according to Thomas Callaghy, forms the major avenue of upward mobility, status, power and wealth.[13] Indeed, the control or access to state resources constitutes a potent instrument in the process of class formation and reproduction.

The patrimonial state in Africa has its origin in the colonial era. The appropriation of state offices and rents was a peculiar feature of the colonial regime. It was this factor which determined the constitution of politics and the logic of electoral competition among the political parties, at the dawn of self-rule in the postcolonial era. During decolonization in Nigeria, when political power was gradually being devolved to the nationalist politicians, the institutionalized means of social appropriation by the state were the regional marketing boards. The marketing boards provided the regional political potentates with the necessary funds to finance party political activities, line their pockets, accumulate money capital, dispense such to business, political, family and kinship cronies, and also finance industrial development, either directly or indirectly.[14] In the postcolonial era, particularly after the Nigerian Civil War, oil rents became the major source for the creation of public and private wealth and political patronage.

In this context, the way of doing politics, in the words of Max Weber, is not to live for it, but to live from it.[15] Politicians, therefore, assume the role of political entrepreneurs who invest heavily in politics, with the aim of claiming super profits and dividends in the ruthless appropriation of state resources. In other words, politics is viewed only in terms of the allocation of resources, that is, who gets what, when, how and, how much — a political game which inevitably assumes a consumerist dimension.[16] Thus, political parties serve as nothing but political instruments for the continuation at all costs of an electoral warfare, in which the end justifies the means, fair or foul.[17] In this regard, political parties are conceived as analogous to a private army or militia organized to fight an ominous electoral battle. Neither the constitutive nor regulative rules of politics or elections are valued or respected. Extra-legal means become the permissive rule of elections. Billy Dudley puts it poignantly, noting that the

> Election did show that for the political elite, power was an end in itself and not
> the means to the realisation of some "greater good" for the community and

whatever instrumentalities employed in the pursuit of power, such instrumentalities were legitimate. It follows from this, that any talk about "rules of the game" must be irrelevant. For to talk about rules of the game is to presuppose some end or ends which rules are intended to subserve but there can be no such ends since power has been taken as an end in itself. The only possible kind of ethics thus become that of privatisation, the pre-occupation of the individual with his personal rather than his social solution.[18]

In essence, political morality was largely eschewed from competitive electoral politics in Nigeria. Political brinkmanship and fissiparous tendencies marked the activities of the political parties in the electoral process. The main features of the party system in Nigeria include the trappings and manipulation of ethno-religious factors as veritable elements of political mobilization and party support; large scale electoral malfeasance; institutionalized elements of bitterness, thuggery, and violence; personality fetishism of the party leaders, rather than adherence to set ideas, programs and principles; and factionalism within the parties.

Richard Sklar, in his classic study of Nigerian political parties during the First Republic, analyzed the nature, origins, and features of the party system.[19] The parties had ethnic fixations, which was a result of the system of administration (indirect rule), and divisive politics promoted by the colonial regime. To be sure, ethnicity provides an organic solidarity among a group of people, but its instigation for political action makes it a highly conflictual phenomenon.[20] Sklar rightly argued, however, that although the ethnic bases and coloration of political parties are historically rooted, their consolidation and the ensuing conflict in Nigerian national politics actually "marked a more complex struggle between interests that were non-ethnic in nature."[21] For him, the ethnicized political parties only provided a convenient and potent vehicle in the contest over the social surplus appropriated by the state:

> In every region, political leaders exercised authority and dispensed patronage to build support for themselves and discourage or repress opposition. Thus did regional Government become the fount of privilege and the fulcrum of social control.[22]

The argument is that the basis for the fierce struggle between the political parties in the electoral process is basically economic, not ethnic. It is an attempt by the various fractions of the ruling class, either directly or otherwise, to augment their weak material base, through the control of state power, which the relatively undeveloped private sector cannot facilitate.

The three major political parties in the colonial and immediate postcolonial era, namely, the Northern Peoples Congress (NPC), the Action Group (AG), and the National Council for Nigerian Citizens (NCNC), corresponded with the three then regions of the country, North, West and East, respectively, where they were rooted and exercised control. Indeed, the first two, the NPC and the AG, arose primarily as cultural organizations, the *Jamiyyar Jama' ar Arewa* and the *Egbe Omo Oduduwa,* respectively. The development of the political parties followed the pace of the constitutional reforms, which were also stimulated by nationalist pressures. The constitutional changes which promoted the policy of regionalism, encouraged essentially a three-party system in Nigeria based on these regions. These parties also had mobilizational leaders, in petty bourgeois nationalist figures Tafawa Balewa, Obafemi Awolowo, and Nnamdi Azikwe, who rallied overwhelming political support in the various regions. The attempt of the NPC to break the power hegemony of the AG in the West, by sponsoring a splinter group, the Nigerian National Democratic Party (NNDP) led by Ladoke Akintola and bent on hijacking political power from the AG, precipitated a debilitating political crisis in the region in 1965, which served as a prelude to the military intervention in Nigerian politics on January 15, 1966.

The structural characteristics of the parties in the Second Republic (1979-1983) showed the dominance and re-emergence of the pre-1966 patterns, personalities, and styles.[23] Although five parties were registered for the 1979 elections by the Federal Electoral Commission (FEDECO), namely, the Peoples Redemption Party (PRP), the Great Nigerian Peoples Party (GNPP), the National Party of Nigeria (NPN), the Unity Party of Nigeria (UPN), and the Nigerian Peoples Party (NPP), the latter three were the dominant parties, which were a political reincarnation of the major parties of the First Republic, with a strong ethnic background. Although the NPN attempted to make some claim to a national spread and outlook, as it coopted some commercial capitalists and disaffected politicians (of other parties) from other parts of the country into its fold, the party maintained a "northern primacy."[24]

The class character and the logic of electoral competition by these three main parties were essentially the same. They were capitalist parties, whose ideological orientation varied from the commitment to free market principles to a social welfarism of a mixed economy. The operation, internal organization, nature of membership, and purpose of these parties were not significantly different. Perhaps it was the outstanding record of political corruption and financial recklessness of the NPN, which distinguished it from the two other parties.

The activities of these parties and their damaging consequences on the growth of liberal democracy in Nigeria, have been well analyzed.[25] Suffice it to note that the political tendencies which proved to be the Achilles heels of the First Republic were also set at play. Massive election rigging, thuggery, violence, and arson were characteristic features of party activities in the electoral process, especially during the 1983 general elections. The police, FEDECO, and other state agencies concerned with the conduct of the elections, were less than neutral in the roles they played. They were manipulated at various levels — federal, state, and local — depending on who controlled what. However, the ruling party at the federal level, the NPN, had overwhelming control and manipulation over these organs as they were largely federal agencies. In fact, the Nigerian Police Force, under the leadership of Sunday Adewusi, the Inspector General, became a terrorist organization, which suppressed the political opponents of the NPN and facilitated the "landslide" electoral victory of the party, particularly at the presidential polls. The report of the Babalakin Commission of Inquiry set up by the Muhammadu Buhari administration in August 1985, unraveled the incidence of large scale electoral fraud which marked the 1983 general elections. The nature of the electoral abuses ranged from falsification of election results, illegal printing and use of voters cards, compilation of fictitious names on the voters register, voting by the underage, harassment of candidates' agents and voters, and the inflation of the election figures.[26] The result of all this was the de-legitimation of the civilian regime, which paved the way for a military coup on December 31, 1983.

It was against this background of persistent political failures and the collapse of democratic experiments, that the Babangida administration inaugurated the Political Bureau on January 13, 1986 to "produce a blueprint of the new political model"[27] for the country. Indeed, the activities of the Political Bureau constitute the background to the formulation of the Babangida transition to civil rule program. The Bureau reviewed the Nigerian political economy, which included the party system and the electoral process, and made far reaching recommendations. In its report of March 1987, the Bureau argued that for a stable democracy to evolve in Nigeria, fundamental changes had to be introduced into the party system and the electoral process. It suggested a two-party system for the country, which was to be foisted and substantially funded by the state. These parties, the Bureau continued, must be geared toward a new national philosophy of government, namely, socialism.[28]

On elections and the electoral process, the Bureau submitted that three basic reforms had to be carried out. Firstly, an honest, competent, non-partisan, and autonomous electoral body had to be established, which, it suggested, should be named the National Commission on Political Parties and Elections. Secondly, politics had to be reconstituted to allow for the strict adherence to the rules of electoral competition. Thirdly, an independent judiciary had to be promoted, which would impartially interpret electoral laws. In addition, the Bureau approved the continuation of the single member constituency system.[29]

To institutionalize a culture of consultation and responsive governance in the polity, the Political Bureau suggested that the use of referenda and the power of recall should be encouraged in the political process and be made part of the constitution. Indeed, in the view of the Bureau, the draft constitution engineered during the transition process should be subjected to a popular test through a referendum, before it was finally adopted.

The government in its white paper[30] on the Bureau's report, accepted all the recommendations made by the Bureau, except two. First, although it accepted the idea of a bipartisan polity, and the logic of state foisting and funding of the two parties, it rejected the socialist philosophy. In the same vein, although the recommendations on referenda and the powers of recall were accepted, the use of the former to determine the acceptability or otherwise of the draft constitution prepared under the Babangida transition process, was rejected. Thus, the Bureau's report was so emptied of its serious content that its ultimate essence was lost.

Consequent to the acceptance of a two-party system by the state, it was given legal sanction with the promulgation into Law of the 1989 Constitution through Decree No. 12 of 1989, the Constitution of the Federal Republic of Nigeria (Promulgation) Decree. Clause 220 (1) of the 1989 Constitution recognized the institutionalization of the two-party system in the country. Also, on the electoral process, a new electoral body was established in 1987, the National Electoral Commission (NEC), while the electoral rules and procedures were significantly reformed.

Earlier, the Babangida regime, in its attempt to change the texture of politics in Nigeria, sought to reconstitute the political class. It imposed a blanket ban on certain categories of past public office holders, mostly politicians, who served in the First and Second Republics. They were disqualified from contesting for elective public office. Although this policy was highly contested in the civil society as unfair and unjust, its purpose from the regime's viewpoint was to promote a group of "new-breed" politicians, untainted by the political ills of the past. How effective this proved to be will be made clear with an analysis of the two-party system and the electoral process.

Constructing the Two Political Parties

The ban on partisan politics was lifted on May 3, 1989. During his broadcast to the nation, General Babangida made it abundantly clear that his administration would closely scrutinize and monitor the party formation process. According to him:

> The present administration will watch every step, monitor every move and follow every action to ensure that everything is done according to the rules of the game. The National Electoral Commission is hereby ordered to release the main guidelines for the formation of the two political parties, no violations of the guidelines or the rules of the game will be tolerated.[31]

This is indicative of the paternal nature of the regime's policies on the transition process, and it set the tone for excessive political control by the state.

Shortly after the President's speech, the NEC released the guidelines on party formation, which outlined the conditions that political associations seeking registration as political parties were to fulfill. The conditions were quite arduous and extremely demanding. Moreover, the requirements had to be fulfilled within two months. The requirements included that each association be well established at the federal, state, and local levels of government, be well staffed at each level, and present a complete list of registered members with relevant personal data, including name, age, and residential address. Registered members had to be issued membership cards with photographs, to be submitted to the NEC for the purpose of verification. The association's assets and liabilities had to be declared. The constitution and rules of the association had to guarantee the election of the executive committee of the party every three years, and at all levels of organization, the association had to reflect the federal character principle. In addition, banned politicians had to be excluded from the activities of the political associations, and the political program of each association had to address a host of socioeconomic and political problems facing the country. The associations had to specify how they wished to tackle such problems. Finally, each political association was required to pay an application fee of 50,000 naira.[32]

The pent up enthusiasm of the civilian political class for partisan activities, which had been suppressed for six years, prompted the mushrooming of political associations shortly after the ban on politics was lifted. Within the two months period allowed for the filing of registration documents by the political associations to the NEC, no less that 49 political associations responded.[33] However, the guidelines proved rather tough and daunting for most of the associations to fulfill. Only 13 of these associations actually filed their registration papers with the NEC.

It is important to highlight the prevailing political context in which the party formation process was conducted, which underscores the nature of the political associations which evolved. Essentially, it was a militaristic and highly anti-democratic political environment in which human rights and political liberty counted for little. Most active civil associations, trade unions, and professional groups in the civil society, which should have played crucial roles in the party formation process, were suppressed. The Academic Staff Union of Universities (ASUU), the National Association of Nigerian Students (NANS), among others, had been banned. In addition, the elected national leadership of the central labor organization, the Nigerian Labor Congress (NLC), had been dissolved in 1988, and an enfeebled and pliant leadership had been enthroned by the state. Although the suborned leadership of the NLC attempted to float a political party and get it registered, its efforts in this regard were largely unsuccessful. Three factors militated against labor in the formation of a strong political party. First, the labor law, Decree No. 13 (1973), Section 15, prohibited the formation of a political party by trade unions. This Decree hounded labor and opened up the possibility, once again, of its repression by the state. The second constraint was the tenuous hold of the new leadership over the organization, and the third was the electoral regulation which stipulated that civil servants had to resign their appointment before they could participate in politics. This was a very risky option which most civil servants could not contemplate.

In addition to the above, and as previously noted, the old politicians of the First and Second Republics were barred from the process of party formation. The net effect was that those left on the political turf, tagged the "new breed" politicians, were mainly composed of the business and political clientele of the Babangida regime. They consisted mostly of currency speculators, oil bunkerers, commissioned agents, retired military officers and later, some of the former political personnel of the regime, all of whom benefited enormously in material terms from the regime's economic policy (SAP).[34] It was these groups of people who formed, funded, and led the political associations.

The NEC conducted the verification exercise of the claims of the political associations from August 1 to 30, 1989, through the social science research methodology of a stratified random sampling technique. The result was a serious indictment against the political associations, with all receiving a score of below average. The NEC accused these associations of routing in old political alliances, loyalties and parties; making false claims in terms of fictitious names and addresses of their membership; the prevalence of serious factionalism within the association centered on the struggle for power and leadership; religious and ethnic bickering; and poor organization at the three levels of government, particular at the grassroots or local level.[35] On these disturbing signposts, Babangida noted:

Some of the most disturbing aspects of the political process during the pre-registration period were indeed sonorous echoes of our historical experience. Old lines of cleavage — ethnic, geopolitical, religious and class — surfaced in bold discomfort in the new political associations, these "newbreed" associations, which were expected to transcend those lines of cleavage and promote issue based politics, instead relapsed into debilitating infighting, each group within itself. Most worrisome was the fact that the political associations paid little attention to organisational structures at grassroots levels. In short, the people were, once more, taken for granted and no premium was placed on their views which the political aspirants simply brushed aside and assumed to be of little consequence. The associations merely revolved around certain leaders and personalities.[36]

The overbearing political fraudulence of the political associations was facilitated by three factors. First, was the inadequate time frame given the political associations to prepare and submit their registration documents. Second, was the politics of exclusion promoted by the Babangida regime in the party formation process, which delinked a large proportion of the articulate segments of the society from the political process. This included those who could possibly have provided both the reasoned logic and ideas on how to handle the registration exercise, including contesting the burdensome registration conditions and embarking on the task of mass mobilization for the associations. Third, the registration conditions stipulated by the NEC required enormous financial commitment which only the rich in the society could afford. Akinola Aguda, a highly respected international jurist, likened the NEC conditions to the art of performing magic, which can only be attempted by the rich.[30] For example, one of the political associations, the People's Solidarity Party (PSP), estimated that it cost 31.1 million naira only to obtain the passport size photographs of its registered members. What this suggests is that it was only the rich, particularly those earlier identified as the business and political clientele of the Babangida regime, who could form and fund political parties. The consequence was a departicipation of the majority of the Nigerian people — who were mostly living below the subsistence level — from the political process. The political associations therefore had to use financial inducements to buy membership, which logically encouraged an avalanche of fraudulent practices.

The ranking of the 13 political associations in terms of their performance, according to the NEC's report, is shown in the table on the next page.

Despite the dismal performance of all the political associations, the NEC recommended the top six to the Armed Forces Ruling Council (AFRC), the ruling military body, to select any two to be registered as political parties. The AFRC considered the option unacceptable and ultimately chose to impose two state-created political parties. Babangida justified the decision as follows:

> The AFRC is convinced that something revolutionary in our thinking needs to be introduced, given the context of the failure of all our experiments. Only ... the grassroots democratic two party system provides the kind of revolutionary departure we need for establishing a mass two party system.[39]

On October 7, 1989, General Babangida announced the formation of the two government-sponsored political parties, the Social Democratic Party (SDP) and the National Republican Convention (NRC). These parties were to be substantially funded by the state. The objectives of forming the two parties were to reduce the salience of ethnic and religious differences in the political process, bridge the political gap between the urban and rural areas of the country, and make impossible the privatization of politics around ethnic barons and "moneybags."[40] In addition, the parties were to provide a platform for the emergence of a new leadership and give equal rights to all Nigerians. In other words, there were to be no "founders," only "joiners."

Subsequently, the constitution, manifesto, and program of each party were drawn up by the state. Party secretariats were established for them at all levels of government and the offices were staffed by the state. Mostly civil servants were deployed at inception to manage these parties. Membership recruitment as well as funding of all party activities were also done by the state.

In theory, the formation of political parties by the state, as Jean Blondel argues, often finds expression in the desire to introduce new goals and values into the polity, or preserve existing ones, something that the natural process of party formation may not guarantee. However, Blondel admits that imposed parties usually face serious legitimacy problems, which poses a challenge to the state foisting it.[41] In the event in which the political regime undertaking the project lacks legitimacy or possesses a tenuous one, the problem of party imposition becomes heightened, as the Nigerian example suggests. Many of these parties collapse even before achieving legitimacy. Maurice Duverger, however, sharply disagrees with Blondel on the issue of party imposition, and points out, quite correctly, that political parties as expressions of social forces, cannot be created

National Electoral Commission — The Overall Performance of the Political Associations in Order of Priority

Association	Membership		Admin. Org.		Manifesto	Total	Ranking
	Size 25.00	Spread 25.00	Staff 15.00	Spread 15.00	20.00	100	
Peoples Solidarity Party	8.70	5.30	9.30	8.10	12.50	43.90	1st
Nigerian National Congress	4.30	7.80	9.70	8.50	12.30	42.60	2nd
Peoples Front of Nigeria	5.20	5.20	9.40	7.90	13.50	41.20	3rd
Liberal Convention	2.50	5.10	9.00	7.20	10.20	34.00	4th
Nigerian Labour Party	.10	.90	4.20	3.60	9.10	17.90	5th
Republican Party of Nigeria	.50	2.10	3.10	2.90	8.40	17.00	6th
All Nig. Peoples Party	.07	.30	2.10	1.50	7.80	11.77	7th
Ideal Peoples Party	.03	.14	.94	.77	7.60	9.48	8th
United Nigerian Democratic Party	.03	.17	1.68	1.39	5.80	9.08	9th
National Union Party	.01	.02	.00	.02	7.88	7.93	10th
Peoples Patriotic Party	.03	.02	1.10	.90	4.60	6.83	11th
Patriotic Nigerian's Party	.00	.00	.09	.07	3.30	3.46	12th
Nigerian Peoples Welfare	.00	.02	.24	.17	0.00	.44	13th

Source: *Newswatch*, October 23, 1989, p. 17.

by a simple act of legislation.[42] Indeed, if a political party is conceived as a form of political organization constructed on the basis of set ideas, principles, and policies around which the struggle for power and state offices through the electoral process is conducted, then the logic of party imposition is precarious and unacceptable. It is simply an attempt by the state to coercively impose its will on society, which is antithetical to the logic of democracy.[43]

The two state created political parties, the SDP and the NRC, were basically identical. They were centrist parties, one a "little to the right" of the center (NRC) and the other, a "little to the left" of the center (SDP), both parading a liberal capitalist ideology. The NRC, in its manifesto, advocated the philosophy of market forces, while the SDP settled for welfarist capitalism, with the euphemism of a mixed economy. The manifestoes and programs of the two parties overtly expressed a commitment to the continuation of the polices of the Babangida administration, especially its economic reform package of the SAP. For example, the SDP manifesto stated:

> We of the Social Democratic Party will take off from these recent reforms which are progressive in intention and strive to improve upon their operation.[44]

Likewise, the NRC manifesto stated:

> We of the NRC believe that there is need to continue with and strengthen the present reforms that have been put in place over the past few years.[45]

These provisions tended to lend credence to the argument that the parties were created in order to provide an appropriate political platform for perpetrating the economic policy of the SAP.[46]

The two parties lacked clear constituency support, political focus, direction, and mass orientation. The artificial nature of the party organization, as Peter Lewis observed, only exacerbated the internecine struggle among aspiring politicians, as parties served mostly as isolated arenas of elite fractional competition.[47] The demand for political pluralism, which an heterogeneous society like Nigeria calls for, was ignored, and a two-party system was created by fiat, with the potential danger of the disparate interests of groups in the society not gaining accommodation. These state-created parties also had the potential to evoke a debilitating in-fighting.

In a party system in which all are "joiners" and none are "founders," except the state, the tendency is for party commitment to be close to nil and the adherence to principles to be non-existent. The theory of the "two publics," put forward by Peter Ekeh,[48] supports this assertion. According to the theory, amoral behavior often characterizes the relationship of the citizenry to institutions created by the state, in this case, the two political parties.

The state denied autonomy to the two parties and related to them as part of the coterie of its bureaucracy. In this regard, both the NEC and the government suffocated the parties with controls, guidelines, directives, and decrees. Indeed, the Transition to Civil Rule (Political Parties Registration and Activities) Decree of 1989 conferred enormous legal powers to the government and the NEC over the political parties. Retired General Olusegun Obasanjo, Nigeria's former Head of State, argued that it was in fact too charitable to describe these parties as part of the government bureaucracy or parastatals, noting that

> Those who call the two Government created parties as parastatals are even being generous. Parastatals at least have effective and accountable Chief Executives who can enforce order and discipline. The same cannot be said about the Government created parties. And yet they are the vehicle through which it is hoped that a stable democracy will be built and nurtured. We delude ourselves.[49]

Thus, rather than build credibility and legitimacy for the two parties, the state further undermined them. In the final analysis, these parties lacked public respectability and legitimacy, membership commitment, internal cohesion, and clear political perspectives. The lack of these factors greatly marked the parties' role in the electoral process.

The Reformed Electoral Process

The reform of the institutional mechanism of elections in Nigeria, namely, the electoral body, constituted the first major step taken in the reform of the electoral process. Such reform was undertaken with the realization that effective electoral administration is central to the preservation of the integrity of elections. Against the background of the reports of the Babalakin Commission of Inquiry and the Political Bureau, it became palpable that the setting up of an independent and credible body to manage elections was imperative.

As previously noted, the NEC had been established in 1987 through Decree No. 23, which was amended by Decree No. 8 of 1989. Its functions were as follows:

• Organize, conduct and supervize all elections and matters pertaining to elections into elective offices;
• Provide clear guidelines, rules and regulations for the emergence, recognition, and registration of the two political parties;
• Register the two political parties (this power was later transferred to the AFRC through Decree No. 8 of 1989);
• Monitor the organization, conduct, financing, and political campaigns of the two political parties, and provide for rules and regulations which shall govern them;
• Recommend to the Federal Military Government the amount of public funds required for the organization and conduct of the affairs of the two political parties;
• Arrange for the annual examination and auditing of the funds and accounts of the parties;
• Provide rules which shall govern the qualification to vote and be voted for at elections; and
• Carry out such other functions as may be conferred on it by law.[50]

Later, the NEC's powers and responsibilities were expanded through various decrees to include the screening of party candidates to determine their eligibility for elective office and, with near absolute powers, to control the activities of the two political parties. Indeed, NEC's former chairman, Humphrey Nwosu, admitted that the NEC was given more powers than any previous electoral body in Nigeria's political history.[51] In order to make the NEC functional, the structural defects of the former electoral body, FEDECO, were rectified. For example, the chairman of the commission was made the chief executive and the accounting officer, in contradiction to the arrangement under the FEDECO, where the secretary to the commission exercised executive powers. The latter arrangement created role ambiguity and a situation of responsibility without power for the chairman. Also, in what could be described as the "unitarianisation" of the NEC, it was made a unified organization, or "an all Nigerian agency," empowered to conduct elections at all levels of government. State electoral commissions were abolished and substituted only with state offices of the NEC. The intent was to allow for a unity of purpose and effective coordination of elections by the Commission. Adele Jinadu paradoxically, but questionably, referred to this as the "federalisation" of the NEC.[52]

In addition, the NEC was granted enormous financial resources by the state in order to allow it to perform its assigned responsibility of election management. Between 1987 and 1991, the budgetary and extra-budgetary allocations made to the body amounted to 2.6 billion naira.[53]

Other political infrastructure or institutions were established to facilitate the conduct of free and fair elections. These were, the Directorate for Social Mobilization (MAMSER) and the Center for Democratic Studies (CDS). MAMSER was set up primarily to create political awareness among the people and reorient them toward the values of political tolerance, accommodation, and fairness in the electoral process. The CDS, on the other hand, had a specialized audience. It was aimed at providing formal political training through fora such as workshops and seminars to members of the political class toward accepting democratic norms and nuances. The philosophical conception of the transition to civil rule process as a learning and design project, gave expression to these institutional innovations.

With respect to the electoral process, the rules governing elections and election campaigns were reformulated. The legal provisions on the latter are contained in Decree No. 27 of 1987, Section 25-34, which seeks to forestall political rancor and violence in election campaigns. The measures stipulated include the prohibition of the possession of "offensive weapons or missiles" such as guns, rifles, cutlass, knives, tear-gas, corrosives, and other sharp objects which may inflict injury on people at political rallies; political campaigns on the basis of sectional, ethnic, or religious factors; the use of slanderous, abusive, or intemperate language likely to provoke violent emotions at campaigns; and the recruiting, hiring, or maintenance of any private security organization.[54]

Also, changes were made regarding the arrangements and modalities of elections. The NEC made extensive preparations in terms of logistics for the conduct of elections, and it worked in close collaboration with federal (including the army, police, and air force), state and local government agencies, and, in some cases, the organized private sector.[55] With respect to modalities, reforms introduced included the "open voting" system, which was highly controversial. It was a system in which voters were expected to queue up behind the portrait of the candidate of their choice. Voting and counting of votes was done openly. The NEC claimed that the system was an antidote to the endemic problem of election rigging in Nigeria. Open voting was credited with the advantage of preventing impersonation, multiple voting, stuffing and swapping of ballot boxes, and the use of fake ballot papers.[56] In fact, the open voting system neither required ballot paper nor the ballot box.

The open voting system came under virulent and pervasive criticism by civil society groups.[57] Firstly, it was considered as a crudity and highly retrogressive electoral model, incompatible with the demands of a modern electoral system. Secondly, the act of voting openly created potential fears of political intimidation and harassment of voters. Thirdly, it promoted de facto disenfranchisement of certain groups of people who, in the "public interest," were barred from voting. These included those occupying political offices, like the president, ministers, governors, and commissioners, who were portrayed as neutral and members of a non-partisan regime. Traditional rulers and the electoral officials were also involuntarily disenfranchised.

Conceptually, what underlines the notion of political preferences in a democracy through free and fair elections is its element of secrecy. This is a protected civil and political right in a democracy. To expunge the element of secrecy from elections is to make a mockery of its object and essence. As a consequence of the stiff opposition against the open voting system within civil society, it was later revised to what the NEC described as the open secret ballot system, which was only used for the June 12, 1993 presidential election.

Another reform consisted of the streamlining of voting. Voting was scheduled from 8:00 am to 2:00 pm, and restrictions were placed on the movement of people during voting hours. However, this electoral regulation had an economic cost, as industrial production and commercial activities were suspended for the duration of the voting period, which no doubt, had a negative effect on national production.

Furthermore, a residency clause was introduced into the electoral regulation, which made it mandatory for a prospective political aspirant to have lived in the area in which he or she wished to contest elections for at least twelve months before the elections. What the regulation meant to promote is what I refer to as the "locality principle," which means that those who live in a locality will exercise political power there. Absentee political representatives would thereby be discouraged. This residency clause was applied during the 1987 local government elections. However, it was later relaxed in subsequent elections, due primarily to the opposition to it from members of the political class, who mostly lived in cities, but contested elections in rural areas.

From this analysis, it may appear that much was done to engender free and fair elections in Nigeria. However, two tendencies revealed the lack of commitment to the ideals of the reforms by the Babangida regime. In the first place, over 1,000 electoral laws[58] were enacted, with the Babangida regime randomly changing, modifying, and remodeling the electoral regulations according to his whims and caprices, and subjecting the important issues to the logic of patrimonial rule. The judiciary was emasculated as ouster clauses were inserted in virtually all the electoral laws and decrees, abrogating the power of the courts to adjudicate on electoral matters. The power was then shared between the AFRC, the elections tribunal, and the NEC, all of which were controlled by General Babangida. In the second place, the autonomy which the Babangida regime purportedly claimed it yielded to the NEC was only in theory. In practice, the NEC operated as an agency of the Babangida regime, which determined what funds it got, its powers and limits, and the appointment of its personnel. On the autonomy of the NEC, Ema Awa, a professor of political science and the initial chairman of the NEC, clarified the issue:

> I was aware of the conflict between the search for autonomy for NEC and the military attitudes. The military could not imagine why an agency set up by them should not be under their control.[59]

Moreover, the perversion of the NEC's autonomy can be seen in the way the government handled the Commission's chief officers and dealt with the 1993 election results. Both Awa and Nwosu were ignominiously removed from office in 1989 and 1993, respectively, for having divergent opinions with the regime on critical issues. For Awa, his stout defense of the autonomy of the NEC was considered an anathema by the regime. Nwosu's "offense" was his apparent reluctance to cooperate with the military junta, in its diabolical plot to subvert democracy, by stalling the June 12, 1993 presidential election. As for the election itself, the manner in which it was scuttled by the Babangida regime was a clear and disgraceful negation of the relevance and autonomy of the NEC to the management of elections.

The Two Political Parties and the Electoral Process

The role of the two political parties, the SDP and the NRC, in the electoral process will be viewed from two levels. The first is at the level of electioneering campaigns and intraparty elections, or party primaries. The second concerns the activities of the parties during the general elections, or interparty elections, and their aftermaths.

There was a wide gap between the precepts and practice of election campaigns in the transition process. There were two phases of the campaign. The first was at the level of securing the party nomination by the political aspirants, which is usually an intraparty affair. The second was at the level of contesting for elective political office in a general election. However, the pattern was essentially the same in both cases. The trend was to de-emphasize program issues and policy options by the candidates. This was due to the bankruptcy of ideas within the two political parties and to the militaristic nature of the transition, which compelled candidates to be extremely mindful of what may offend the sensibilities of the Babangida regime. In the absence of a program based political campaign, coupled with the fact that the parties lacked a clear constituency, political aspirants mostly had to rely on the political network, organization, and support base of the banned politicians to wage their campaign and mobilize support. For instance, in the Lagos State SDP primary elections in October 1991, the two major contenders for the governorship nomination, Femi Agbalajobi and Dapo Sarumi, had to rely on the political network of two banned politicians (though later unbanned), Lateef Jakande and Shehu Musa Yar'Adua, respectively.

In the event in which political aspirants mostly served as proxy for the banned politicians, the consequence was that the nature of the electoral campaigns followed the same old patterns. Its features included political brigandage, thuggery, violence, monetized politics, and the reliance on primordial values, namely ethnicity and religion. In terms of violence, for example, during the 1990 local government elections, violent clashes occurred in Okene, Kwara State, between the supporters of the two parties.[60] In Gongola State during the 1991 governorship election campaign, assassination attempts were made on the lives of some of the NRC candidates. In Rivers State, the NEC office in the Brass Local Government area was blasted with dynamite by political hoodlums acting at the behest of one of the candidates who was bent on forestalling the elections.[61]

An astonishing example of the use of money and ethnic sentiments during the electoral campaign is best represented by events that took place in Edo State during the December 1991 election campaign. With respect to the issue of money, Lucky Igbinedon, the gubernatorial candidate of the NRC, was reported to have rounded up his supporters at the New Benin and Oliha markets in the Oredo Local Government area by throwing money indiscriminately into the air. This resulted in gruesome scrambles in which some people were injured.[62] This was representative of what occurred in virtually all the political campaigns, although in various forms and degrees. With respect to ethnicity, Igbinedon alleged that the Benin Chief Priest, Nosakhare Isekure, used the name of the Oba of Benin to campaign against him, hence the massive support of the Benin people for his opponent, John Oyegun, who eventually won the governorship elections in the state. The issue precipitated internal bickering and some intergroup dissensions within the Benin traditional institution.[63] This was a case of traditional and ethnic ties being manipulated and compromised in electoral politics.

The manipulation of religion as a veritable tool of political campaign by the two parties seemed to have reached its apogee during the 1993 presidential election. The NRC accused the SDP of seeking to promote the hegemony of Islam in Nigerian politics, thereby undermining the secular nature of the Nigerian state. The fact that both the presidential and vice presidential candidates of the SDP, Moshood Abiola and Babagana

Kingibe, were Muslims, was interpreted by the NRC as an attempt by the SDP towards the "Islamisation of politics" in Nigeria. The response of the SDP to this apparent political blackmail by the NRC was to hit back in the same direction. Bashir Tofa, the presidential candidate of the NRC, was alleged to be an "Islamic Fundamentalist," who had in the recent past called for the launching of a "jihad" against Christians. Reference was made to an article Tofa contributed to the August 1991 edition of a magazine, the *Pen Magazine*, in which he made these insinuations. According to the publication, Tofa allegedly remarked that "Christianity is an idle culture ... it is time to begin an offensive (i.e. by the moslems), it is time to claim our unnegotiated rights and freedoms."[64] Tofa did not refute the allegation, but only chose to rationalize it. The unraveling of this religious issue, which was quite emotive at the time, probably had damaging consequences for the electoral fortune of the NRC at the presidential polls.

There were five party primaries between 1989 and 1993. They included the 1990 local government primaries, the 1991 governorship and State House of Assembly primaries, the 1992 National Assembly primaries, the botched August presidential primaries, and the 1993 presidential primaries. In all these party elections, two common features were prominent — large scale election rigging and the monetization of the electoral process. The political tricks used by the political aspirants to perpetrate electoral fraud included the compilation of fictitious names, illegal compilation of separate voters lists, abuse of voters registration exercise, voting by the underage, renting of voters, and the falsification of election results.[65] These fraudulent practices were clearly evident in the October 19, 1991 governorship primaries and the August 1992 botched presidential primaries. In both cases, the internal conflicts and fission generated in the parties threatened the existence of the parties, such that on both occasions, the NEC and the federal government had to intervene to disqualify some candidates and cancel the primaries. Similarly, in the August 1992 presidential primaries, all the political aspirants were disqualified, the primaries canceled, and the banned aspirants barred from participating in the rescheduled exercise. In addition, the executive committees of the two parties at all levels were dissolved.[66]

For the general elections, which were managed by the NEC, the situation was slightly better. Most of the elections were relatively peaceful and orderly, but were generally marked by apathy and indifference on the part of the electorate, except for the June 12 presidential election. The Civil Liberties Organization (CLO), a prominent human rights group in Nigeria, estimated that in the December 1990 local government elections, only 10.57 percent of registered voters voted.[67] However, another source claimed that 22 percent of the registered voters voted.[68] What is important to note is that the ratio of voters was quite low and the trend continued in subsequent elections.

Three reasons may account for the political lethargy of the people in the elections. There was, first of all, the inchoate open voting system, which evoked political harassment and intimidation. The second reason was the militarization of the electoral process. Indeed, the level of the mobilization and preparation of the security agencies for elections was worrisome. The CLO noted that the mood of the Nigerian police in the preparation for the elections was like that of a force preparing for war. For example, on November 4, 1990, at Akure in Ondo State, the Mobile Policemen, while rehearsing their role for the December 8, 1990 local government elections, tear gassed a court in session and the town's central market, injuring several judges, lawyers, and pregnant women.[69] This situation left people wondering whether the elections would be entirely a civil affair. Thirdly, electoral regulations were legion. This prompted fears and skepticism as to what constitutes an electoral offence during the elections. The safe option was not to vote.

There were allegations of election rigging in virtually all the elections conducted by the NEC. For instance, in the governorship elections, both parties accused each other of election rigging. The NRC chairman, Tom Ikimi, shortly after the results were released, stated that his party had come to the inevitable conclusion that the elections were rigged in four states — Edo, Delta, Jigawa and Taraba — in favor of the SDP.[70] Similarly, the SDP chairman, Babagana Kingibe, alleged that the NEC officials, in collaboration with the NRC, rigged the elections in ten states. These were Katsina, Cross River, Adamawa, Enugu, Kebbi, Akwa Ibom, Bauchi, Kano, Imo, and Rivers.[71]

The election results for the two political parties showed a new trend in voting behavior in Nigeria. Both parties had national spread in terms of their electoral performance, although the SDP was more entrenched in the southwestern part of the country and the NRC in the north. Nonetheless, transethnic electoral results were also visible. For instance, the results of the 1990 local government elections showed that both the NRC and the SDP had good performance in the north. While the NRC won 18, 6, and 11 chairmanship seats in Bauchi, Niger, and Gongola States, respectively, the SDP performed better in Benue, Katsina, and Plateau States, with 15, 14, and 10 chairmanship seats, respectively. In the governorship elections, while the NRC won some governorship seats in southern states like Lagos, Enugu, Imo, and Cross River, the SDP also did well in the middle belt and the northern states. It won the governorship elections in Borno, Jigawa, Plateau, and Benue States. The presidential election, which was annulled by General Babangida, could have provided a much better picture of the shifting political alliances in Nigerian politics, which seem to transcend ethno-religious considerations.

What appeared to be a hazy, but significant shift in the voting pattern in Nigerian politics, if even achieved at the cost of political regimentation, was, however, scuttled by the Babangida regime, when, with crude viciousness and perfidy, it annulled the June 12, 1993 presidential election. The election, which was preceded by extensive preparation by the NEC, was acclaimed by both local and international election monitoring observers and the Nigerian people as generally peaceful, free, and fair. But the trajectory of the political events and processes ignited by the regime in its political conspiracy to perpetuate itself in power, led to the annulment. The highly contemptuous and illogical reasons which the military regime gave, left little doubt that the annulment was a heinous act, done to perpetuate the personal rule of General Babangida.

It is important here to note the significant role played by the two political parties in the treacherous act to subvert the electoral process and democracy in Nigeria. Firstly, prominent members of these parties constituted the cream of the nefarious pro-military organization, the Association for Better Nigeria (ABN), which, at the behest of the Babangida regime, hatched the plan to forestall the election and perpetuate the regime in power. Indeed, the leader of the organization, Arthur Nzeribe, was a prominent member of the SDP. The ABN not only engaged itself in a tenacious "Babangida must stay" public campaign, but also went ahead to secure two dubious court injunctions from the Abuja High Court (one shortly before the election, on the night of June 10, 1993, and the other after the election — when the results were being released — on June 15, 1993), granted by Justices Bassey Ikpeme and Dahiru Saleh. Since an electoral law, Decree No. 13 of 1993, empowered the NEC to disregard any court injunction or ruling in the conduct of the presidential election, the NEC ignored the former court injunction and proceeded with the election. The NEC, however, was forced to obey the latter injunction and suspend the announcement of further election results, because of pressure by the Babangida regime.

Secondly, even after the election had been annulled, the two parties easily traded off the goal of democracy for political opportunism. The leadership of the two parties, in one form or the other, later supported the annulment. For the NRC, the annulment was an opportunity to have another trial at the presidential election, while material inducements and parochial power and political considerations defined the attitude of the SDP leadership. Claude Ake captures the issue clearly:

> The National Republican Convention (NRC) decided to abandon democracy for a chance of getting into power at another election ... Most leaders of the winning Social Democratic Party (SDP) heartily supported the annulment of their victory. A few of the most powerful among them did so on the calculation that the annulment would allow them to resume their presidential bid. Many more supported it in order to corner some of the fortunes on offer. Others did so fearing a trend which could destroy the parochial basis of their political power.[72]

The leadership of the two political parties was actively involved in the contrivance of the illegal political arrangement called the Interim National Government (ING), which replaced the Babangida regime and which was designed primarily to further scuttle the realization of the June 12, 1993 presidential election and stultify the goal of democracy in Nigeria. In essence, the venality and bankruptcy of these parties was a major factor in the subversion of the electoral process and the subversion of democracy in Nigeria under the Babangida regime.

Conclusion

The concept of transition to civil rule suggests a process of political decentralization or liberalization, and an eventual transfer of power to elected civilian governors. However, while there were pretentious claims of opening up the political space under the Babangida transition project, what was in reality promoted was the concentration of political power in the hands of a patrimonial ruler — General Ibrahim Babangida. Babangida operated like a *Kabiyesi* (an imperial king), who exercised enormous and decisive powers over the state. He had the power to constitute and dissolve the highest ruling body under his regime, the Armed Forces Ruling Council (AFRC) and later, the National Security and Defense Council (NSDC); to create, shape, control, and formulate political institutions, including the two political parties, the NEC, MAMSER, and other bodies; determine the rules of electoral and political competition; ban and unban political aspirants; harass and intimidate pro-democracy organizations and activities; and suborn the judiciary.

In other words, the elements of a democratic transition or an evolving democracy, which include respect for due process and the rule of law; political liberty as expressed in the right of dissent, association and representation; and political pluralism, where all ignored and undermined by the Babangida regime. In addition, the political infrastructure germane to the process of democratic renewal was squandered. Both the transition to civil rule project and the economic reform program (SAP) of the regime, were considered to be national dogmas. Alternative views or positions on them constituted "sabotage" from the perspective of the regime, and those who expressed such views were treated as "saboteurs," to be ruthlessly dealt with. Clearly, what the Babangida regime constructed with its transition to civil rule project was a patrimonial political machine, which revolved around him as the chief patron.

The tenuous legitimacy and fragile existence of the two state-created parties were a result of two basic contradictions. The first was the essence of the transition itself, which through its own internal logic and contradictions, engendered political authoritarianism. The second was the character of the state. Although the SAP was meant to redefine the role and scope of the state in the nation's political economy by vitiating statism, the management of the policy, which was characterized by high fiscal indiscipline and economic clientilism, only perpetuated statism. In addition, the social consequences of the SAP on poverty and social hardship was also arduous.[73] The net effect was that the state continued to be the locus of economic and political largesse, with elements of corporatism and neopatrimonialism predominating. The premium placed on the capture of state power, therefore, remained very high and priceless.

Notes

[1] Richard Joseph, "The Challenge of Democratization in Africa," in the Carter Center, *African Governance in the 1990s* (Atlanta: Carter Center, 1990), p. 18.

[2] See Tunji Olagunju, Adele Jinadu and Sam Oyovbaire, *Transition to Democracy in Nigeria, 1985-1993* (London: Safari and Spectrum Books, 1993).

[3] Said Adejumobi, "The Structural Adjustment Programme and the Transition to Civil Rule Project in Nigeria (1986-1993): A Shrinking of the Democratic Agenda," (*mimeo*), 1995.

[4] General Ibrahim Babangida, Text of an address to the nation on the occasion of the formation of the two political parties on October 7, 1989. See Tunji Olagunju and Sam Oyovbaire (*eds.*), *For Their Tomorrow, We Gave Our Today: Selected Speeches of I.B.B.*, Volume II (London: Safari Books, 1991), p. 2.

[5] P.O. Agbese and G.K. Kieh, Jr., "Nigeria: Transition to Democracy and the Pathological Elite Thesis," *Zest*, Nos. 15&16, 1992, pp. 18-24.

[6] S. E. Finer, *The Man on the Horseback: The Role of the Military in Politics* (London: Pall Mall, 1962).

[7] Richard Joseph, "Class, State and Prebendal Politics in Nigeria," *Journal of Commonwealth and Comparative Politics*, Vol. 21, No. 3, November 1993, p. 30.

[8] Adele Jinadu, "Electoral Administration in Africa: A Nigerian Case-Study Under the Transition to Civil Rule Process," in Said Adejumobi and Abubakar Momoh (*eds.*), *The Political Economy of Nigeria Under Military Rule 1984-1993* (Harare: SAPES, 1995).

[9] On the concept of the entrepot state, see Terisa Turner, "Multinational Corporations and the Instability of the Nigerian State," *Review of African Political Economy*, No. 5, 1976, pp. 63-79.

[10] On a discussion of prebendal politics in Nigeria, see Richard Joseph, *Democracy and Prebendal Politics in Nigeria: The Rise and Fall of the Second Republic* (Ibadan: Spectrum Books, 1991).

[11] Sam Oyovbaire and Tunji Olagunju (*eds.*), *Foundations of a New Nigeria: The I.B.B. Era* (Lagos: Precision Press, n.d.), p. 24.

[12] Claude Ake, "The Problem of Implementation of the Two Party System," *Nigerian Journal of Policy and Strategy*, Vol. 2, No. 1, June 1987, p. 67.

[13] Thomas Callaghy, "Politics and Vision in Africa: The Interplay of Domination, Equality and Liberty," in Patrick Chabal (*ed.*), *Political Domination in Africa* (Cambridge: Cambridge University Press, 1986), p. 36.

[14] Gavin Williams, *State and Society in Nigeria* (Idanre: Afrografika, 1980), p. 33.

[15] Max Weber, cited in Jibrin Ibrahim, "Democracy and the Crisis of the Rentier State: Across Patrimonialism and Political Recomposition in Nigeria," Paper and book proposal for CODESRIA/Rockefeller Reflections Program, April, 1994, p. 7.

[16] Said Adejumobi, "Political Leadership and Political Decay: A Synopsis of Post-Independent Nigeria," in S.G. Tyoden (*ed.*), *Leadership, Democracy and the Poor* (Jos: NPSA, 1991), pp. 110-134.

[17] Oyeleye Oyediran and Adigun Agbaje, "Two-partyism and Democratic Transition in Africa, " *The Journal of Modern African Studies,* Vol. 9, No. 2, 1991, pp. 219. Also Oyeleye Oyediran, "Democratic Electoral Process: Can Nigeria Make it this Time Around?" *Nigerian Journal of Electoral and Political Behaviour*, Vol. 1, No. 1. September 1990, pp. 15-24.

[18] Billy Dudley, *Introduction to Nigerian Government and Politics* (Lagos: Macmillian, 1982), p. 70.

[19] Richard Sklar, *Nigerian Political Parties* (New York: Nok Publishers, 1963).

[20] On the political import of ethnicity and on ethnic pluralism, see Okwudiba Nnoli, *Ethnic Politics in Nigeria* (Enugu: Fourth Dimension Publishers, 1980); Onigu Otite, *Ethnic Pluralism and Ethnicity in Nigeria* (Ibadan: Shaneson Limited, 1990).

[21] Sklar, p. xiii.

[22] *Ibid.,* pp. xiii-xiv.

[23] Sam Oyovbaire (*ed.*), *Democratic Experience in Nigeria: Interpretative Essays* (Benin: Omega Publishers, 1987), p. 187.

[24] Joseph, *Democracy and Prebendal Politics in Nigeria*, pp. 129-140.

[25] See, in addition to Joseph, Toyin Falola and Julius Ihonvbere, *The Rise and Fall of Nigeria's Second Republic, 1979-1984* (London: Zed Books, 1985); Victor Ayeni and Kayode Soremekun, *Nigeria's Second Republic* (Lagos: Daily Times, 1988).

[26] On the report of the Babalakin Commission of Inquiry see, *Newswatch,* July 10, 1989, pp. 20-16; *The African Guardian,* May 8, 1989, pp. 16-17; National Electoral Commission, *Transition to Civil Rule, Laws and Materials on the Electoral Process* (Lagos: NEC, 1990), pp. 313-339.

[27] General Ibrahim Babangida, Text of an address delivered at the Inauguration of the Political Bureau, January 13, 1986. See Tunji Olagunju and Adele Jinadu (*eds.*), *Portrait of a New Nigeria: Selected Speeches of I.B.B.* (Lagos: Precision Press, n.d.), pp. 27-33.

[28] *The Report of the Political Bureau* (Abuja: MAMSER, 1987), pp. 126-136.

[29] *Ibid.,* pp. 137-142.

[30] *Government Views and Comments on the Findings and Recommendations of the Political Bureau* (Abuja: MAMSER, 1987).

[31] See Olagunju and Jinadu, *Portrait of a New Nigeria*, p. 83.

[32] National Electoral Commission, *Main Guidelines, Formation of Political Parties* (Lagos: NEC, 1989).

[33] Adigun Agbaje, "Party Formation and the Transition to the Third Nigerian Republic," *Research Report Submitted to the Social Science Council of Nigeria and the Ford Foundation* (Ibadan, 1990), pp. 42-44.

[34] Adejumobi, "The Structural Adjustment Programme and the Transition to Civil Rule in Nigeria."

[35] See National Electoral Commission, *Report and Recommendations on Party Formation* (Lagos: NEC, 1989).

[36] See Olagunju and Oyovbaire, *For Their Tomorrow*, p. 5.

[37] See *Newswatch*, July 17, 1989, p. 15.

[38] See *The African Guardian*, June 26, 1989, p. 21.

[39] See Olagunju and Oyovbaire, *For Their Tomorrow*, p. 19.

[40] Tunji Olagunju, "The Party System and the Creation of Two Political Parties," in Okon Uya (*ed.*), *Contemporary Nigeria* (Buenos Aires: Edipuba, S.A., 1992), p. 54; Olagunji and Oyovbaire, *For Their Tomorrow*, p. 28.

[41] Jean Blondel, *An Introduction to Comparative Government* (New York: Praeger Publishers, 1969), p. 19.

[42] Maurice Duverger, *The Idea of Politics: The Uses of Power in Society* (London: Mathven and Co., 1978), p. 14.

[43] For a critique of the two party system in Nigeria, see Anthony A. Akinola, "A Critique of Nigeria's Proposed Two Party System," *The Journal of Modern African Studies*, Vol. 27, No. 1, March 1989, pp. 109-123; Anthony A. Akinola, "Manufacturing the Two Party System in Nigeria," *The Journal of Commonwealth and Comparative Politics*, Vol. 28, No. 3, November 1990; Abubakar Momoh and Said Adejumobi, "The Two Political Parties and the Shrinking of the Democratic Space in Nigeria: A Retrospective Analysis, 1989-1993, " Paper presented to the 1994 Annual Conference of the Nigerian Political Science Association, Obafemi Awolowo University, Ile-Ife, Nigeria; Claude Ake, "The Problem of Implementation of the Two Party System," *Nigerian Journal of Policy and Strategy*, Vol. 2, No. 1, June 1987.

[44] *Manifesto of the Social Democratic Party* (SDP, 1989), p. 3.

[45] *The Manifesto of the National Republican Convention* (NRC, 1989), p. 5.

[46] See Yusuf Bangura, *Crisis, Adjustment and Politics in Nigeria* (Uppsala: Akut, University of Uppsala, June 1989); also his "The Crisis of Underdevelopment and Transition to Civil Rule: Conceptualising the Question of Democracy in Nigeria," *Africa Development*, Vol. 13,, No. 1, 1988; Abubakar Momoh, "The Philosophical and Ideological Foundations of the Transition to Civil Rule in Nigeria," in B. Caron, A. Gboyega and E. Osaghae (*eds.*), *Democratic Transition in Africa* (Ibadan: Credu, 1992), pp. 141-165.

[47] Peter M. Lewis, "Endgame in Nigeria: The Politics of a Failed Democratic Transition," *African Affairs*, Vol. 93, 1994, p. 313.

[48] Peter Ekeh, "Colonialism and the Two Publics in Africa: A Theoretical Statement," *Comparative Studies in Society and History*, Vol. 17, January 1975.

[49] Olusegun Obasanjo, Text of a proposed speech at the aborted National Council of States meeting, November 1992, p. 5.

[50] See Humphrey Nwosu, "Mechanisms for the Successful Conduct of Elections in Nigeria: 1992 and Beyond," *Nigerian Journal of Electoral and Political Behaviour*, Vol. 3, No. 1, March 1992, pp. 12-13.

[51] *Ibid.*

[52] Adele Jinadu, "Elections, Party Politics and the Transition in Nigeria," *Nigerian Journal of Electoral and Political Behaviour*, Vol. 3, No. 1, March 1992, p. 22.

[53] See Olagunju *et al*, *Transition to Democracy in Nigeria*, p. 255, Addendum A.

[54] Transition to Civil Rule (Political Parties Registration and Activities) Decree, otherwise known as Decree No. 27 of 1989. See National Electoral Commission, *Transition to Civil Rule, Laws and Materials on the Electoral Process* (Lagos: NEC, 1990), pp. 42-45.

[55] Jinadu, "Elections, Party Politics and the Transition in Nigeria," p. 25.

[56] *The Nigerian Interpreter*, November/December 1990, p. 9.

57 For a public critique of the open voting system, which is often erroneously referred to as the open ballot system, see "Open Ballot: The Dangers Ahead," *The African Guardian*, October 22, 1990; and Bilikisu Yusef, "Open Ballot, Open Apathy," *Citizen* (Kaduna), December 17-23, 1990, p. 36.

58 See Itse Sagay, "Disappearing Act: Nigeria's Bumpy Road to Democracy," *Liberty*, Vol. 4, No. 1, January - April, 1993, pp. 10-11.

59 Eme Awa, "Why I was Sacked," *The African Guardian*, October 18, 1993, p. 22.

60 See Said Adejumobi, "Local Government Elections Since 1950," *National Concord*, November 29, 1990, p. 3.

61 *The African Guardian*, July 29, 1991, pp. 119-125.

62 See *Tell*, November 25, 1991, p. 13.

63 See *Newswatch*, August 17, 1992, pp. 20-23.

64 *The Guardian*, June 9, 1993, p. 5.

65 Peter Ishaka, "As it was in the Beginning ...," *Tell*, November 4, 1991, p. 11.

66 For detailed information on the electoral malpractice of the August 1992 presidential primaries and their consequences, see *Newswatch*, August 17, 1992.

67 Civil Liberties Organisation, *Report on the Local Government Elections of December 8, 1990* (Lagos: CLO, December 1990), p. 17.

68 S.O. Fajonyomi, "A Review of the December 8 Local Government Elections in Nigeria," *The African Review*, Vol. 18, Nos. 1 & 2, 1991, p. 4.

69 Civil Liberties Organisation, p. 25.

70 See Jide Ogundele, "Ikimi Rejects Poll Results," *The Guardian* December 18, 1991, p. 1.

71 Sina Osubambo, "S.D.P. Rejects Results in 10 States," *The Guardian*, December 20, 1991, p. 2.

72 Claude Ake, "The 1993 Guardian Lecture," *The News*, November 21, 1994.

73 See Said Adejumobi, "The Impact of Structural Adjustment on the Economy and Society in Nigeria," in Adejumobi and Momoh, *The Political Economy of Nigeria*.

11

The Annulment of the Presidential Election in Nigeria and the Shrinking of the Political Arena

Abubakar Momoh

Chief M.K.O Abiola has been in detention since June 22, 1994. The military dictatorship alleged he committed treason when Abiola declared himself president following the Sani Abacha regime's refusal to acknowledge the mandate given to him through the June 12, 1993 presidential election.

The election itself has elicited varying responses, depending on the interests — class, economic, religious, ethnic, or geographic — or sentiments involved. According to one scholar, this multiplicity of sentiments could indeed become a risk to the whole campaign for upholding the verdict of the ballot box. As he puts it:

> There is a strong tendency that the emotional response to the annulment of June 12 presidential election may overshadow the real problem of transfer of power and political succession that it raises.[1]

The objective of this chapter is twofold: to attempt to put the June 12 issue in its proper perspective and grapple with the reasons Nigerians struggled for upholding the electoral results; and to examine the contending perspectives on the annulment. In looking at these issues and their deeper political and historical implications, the study attempts to assess the feasibility of democracy in Nigeria.

Why has June 12 become a controversial issue in Nigeria? First of all, because a ban was placed on certain categories of citizens by the military regime. In this way, credible individuals could not contest elections. Instead, a gulf was created between the so-called "old-breed" and "new-breed" politicians. The latter were a creation of the military as a counterweight to the influences of the former. They were to be used as beneficiaries of the political transition program (PTP) to complement General Babangida's strategy to remain in office. The new-breed politicians were uniformly irascible, opportunistic, and unprincipled.[2]

Secondly, because two political parties were created by the state and foisted on the people. The parties had no endogenous character and were not rooted in the people. Funded and run by the state, both parties were identical ideologically. They were regulated by the state through the supervisory role of the National Electoral Commission (NEC), which was given unrestricted powers. At times, the state directly intervened in the day-to-day activities of the parties, even dissolving them at will.

In the third place, June 12 became a controversial issue because the political process was being monopolized by the elites. Those close to the state apparatus were allowed access to the agencies and institutions that managed the transition. In this way, state ideology was imposed as a political culture and the people's interests were marginalized. The people had little or no representation on the Political Bureau, the Constitution Review Committee, the Constituent Assembly, and other transitional organs.

Closely related to this was the fourth problem, the fact that the cost of political participation was made so enormous that only wealthy individuals could participate. It was no accident that the eventual two contestants in the June presidential election, Moshood Abiola and Bashir Tofa, were billionaires.

The fifth reason for the controversy over June 12 was that the over-supervision of the PTP by the government gave the latter an opportunity to disqualify candidates at will, without recourse to due process. This made the PTP unattractive to decent people. Indeed, at the time Tofa and Abiola declared their intention to run in the presidential election, the two parties had no credible candidates who could provide a meaningful challenge to these men, and therefore make the nomination within each party genuinely competitive. Credible candidates had either been banned and disqualified or were not personally interested in the whole process. As one of the old breed politicians, Bola Ige, noted, many of them had adopted a *siddon look* or amusing detachment as the best attitude toward the transition charade.

In the final analysis, since the military is an intrinsically authoritarian and palpably anti-democratic institution, it would be a paradox for soldiers to supervise a successful and meaningful transition to democracy project.

Nigerian military leaders claim that they alone are best qualified to save the nation from drift and chaos, and determine the pattern of a peaceful and orderly political transition. They thus felt justified in taking over the reigns of power. Once in office, however, the military became as highly corrupt as the civilians before them. Consequently, they reneged on promises of returning the country to civilian rule. Under General Babangida, "guided democracy" was introduced as a militarized transition program designed to discourage people from participating in the political process.

The Politics Leading up to the June 12 Election

When Babangida disqualified all the 23 presidential aspirants of the two state-created political parties, the National Republican Convention (NRC) and the Social Democratic Party (SDP), he requested that the NEC make fresh proposals and options for another presidential primary. This was the same tactic he had used in 1989 when he disqualified the 13 political associations that sought registration as political parties. The NEC served as a tool for providing the intellectual rationalization of the shortcomings of the PTP. The Commission eventually came up with eight major options, one of which Babangida and his cohorts decided to choose. This was later known as option A4. Under this option, delegates to national party conventions were selected on the following basis:

- Delegates elected for that purpose at their state congresses on the basis of five or six delegates per local government;
- All state legislators who are members of the party;
- All national legislators who are members of the party;
- All governors and deputy-governors of states in which the party formed the government;
- A maximum of seven commissioners and three special assistants in states in which a party formed the government; and
- All members of the State Executive Committees.

The entire process, from the ward level to the national convention of the two parties, was marked by excessive bribery and corruption. Babangida designed it in such a way that he could have an excuse for further scuttling the PTP.

The presidential aspirants of both parties sponsored candidates and gave money to delegates to vote for them at the party conventions. The Civil Liberties Organization (CLO), a civil rights campaign group, monitored the presidential conventions of the two parties. According to its report:

> In relation to eliminating or minimizing the corrupt use of money to influence electoral behaviour, which was one of the main raison d'être for the introduction of option A4, the system failed rather woefully. Virtually all the candidates, with the possible exception of a few whom delegates maintained did not offer them money, offered money to delegates for their votes while delegates on their part had a field day collecting the monies from every candidate that offered the same although they could not vote for all of them ... the results of the elections conducted during the conventions of the two parties can be described as a triumph of money politics and ethnic sentiments.[3]

The report, in another comment, pointed out that

> The conventions were organised in a way that did not encourage a programme-oriented contest. Candidates for the presidential primaries, if they had any programme, were not given adequate time to present them to the delegates ... within the minutes they were given during the ballot, none of the candidates showed any good grasp of the problems of the country.[4]

However, it is the caveat the CLO puts on its findings that is most interesting, especially since the report was published before the presidential election in June 1993:

> We must emphasise that the presentations in this report are not meant to provide the military government with the excuse *which it may possibly be looking for to justify another cancellation of the primaries and a further extension of the transition programme.* Rather, strict notice must be taken of the fact that the conventions were organised by government-appointed caretaker committees and not the parties per se.[5]

The two political candidates that emerged, Abiola and Tofa, were not strangers to Nigerian politics. Ironically, when they declared their intention to contest the presidential election in December 1992, neither of them had fulfilled the statutory requirement of being a party member for at least one year. Interestingly, on May 21, 1990, Tofa placed an advertisement in the *Daily Times* urging Babangida to remain in power until 2000. And on June 12, 1993, Tofa could not even vote because he had not registered.

The relationship between Babangida and Abiola was even more curious. In an interview following the annulment of the election, Abiola commented that

> Babangida is my friend. We have been friends for quite a long time. The first time he started this democratic race of his, I asked him whether indeed there was a vacancy since I do not like applying for a job which is not vacant. I was not convinced by the answer he gave. For that reason, I decided to remain on the

sidelines and watch. I saw that it was a futile gesture. I decided not to make hide and seek with my life. I stayed on the sidelines because I know one thing: all the people who were there are people he could tell to go and sit down. Nobody tells me to go anywhere and sit down. Nobody. I asked Babangida several times whether he was genuinely intent on quitting. Each time he swore on the Koran. I was not satisfied with that, so I sent the Emir of Zaria to go and find out. I told him, he cannot ask me to go and sit down.[6]

After Abiola resigned from the National Party of Nigeria (NPN) in 1982, he swore never to take part in partisan politics again. On several occasions during the Babangida PTP, Abiola repeatedly told journalists that he was not interested in politics. Further, Abiola had been very close to Babangida, close enough to have openly defended, on many occasions, the policies and programs of the government. Such was Abiola's presence as a friend and defender of Babangida that a well-known pro-democracy activist and one of those Nigerians who has had a life-long running battle with the military, Gani Fawehinmi, described Abiola as the de-facto vice president of Nigeria at a public symposium at which Abiola himself was present. When Abiola's magazine, *African Concord*, in its April 13, 1992 edition, published materials which were critical of the Babangida regime, the magazine's premises were sealed off by the security forces. Rather than challenge this in court, Abiola took the rather private step of tendering a personal apology to his friend. This prompted many of the magazine's journalists, responsible for the offensive story, to resign in protest.

There is no doubt that Abiola allowed this private relationship to permeate his political attitude toward Babangida, which resulted in his being taken for granted by the General. As Abiola himself noted with respect to chosing his vice presidential running mate:

Babangida was suggesting that I should pick Pascal Bafyau, the Nigeria Labour Congress president (as running mate). Well, Bafyau comes from an area where the local council is dominated by NRC, effectively controlled by them ... if he were influential in his area and he's a strong member of our party, why didn't he get the local council of the area for our party. Any way, I picked Babagana Kingibe to please the eleven governors who were backing me up and thereby unite the party as well as to satisfy the people of the North.[7]

Continuing, he disclosed:

I phoned the president at midnight before the announcement, and told him that out of courtesy, I must let him know that there is no way I can pick Bafyau. I was going to announce Baba Kingibe in the morning. Before the phone went dead, I asked "are you still there?" He said "Yes." I said "have you heard me?" he said "Yes." I said "thank you very much, and good night Mr President." He said "Good night and God be with you." That was the beginning of a long silence. Since then, any more calls put to him he won't pick up. If he hears my voice, he gently puts the phone back.[8]

Why did Abiola rely or confide in Babangida so much as to want to inform him of a political decision of such magnitude? Why did Babangida prefer Bafyau when he knew he was a political nonentity, although an adroit supporter of the government? The answer is simple. Babangida wanted Abiola to fail, or at least expected a stalemate, and he knew that for that to happen, he needed a Trojan horse the like of Bafyau. It is important to note that Bafyau, as president of the Nigerian Labour Congress (NLC) at the time, did attempt to demobilize the Nigerian workers from full participation in the struggles that ensued after the annulment of the election.

Following the vice presidential nomination crisis, several other things happened to the Abiola campaign. First, an orchestrated grumble about "Muslim-Muslim SDP ticket" rented the air, obviously directed at Abiola and his running mate, Kingibe. Second, the government suddenly declared that the candidates of the two political parties, together with their running mates, would have to be screened by the NEC. It was not until late May that the NEC announced that everyone had passed. Meanwhile, the two candidates had less than three weeks to campaign, while the government withheld the money due to them until one week before the election. All these were stalling strategies by Babangida.

In a curious development, two days before the election, a group known as the Association for Better Nigeria (ABN), petitioned the courts for an order to stop the election from proceeding as scheduled. The ABN was created after the primaries by a military front-group sponsored by security agencies. It was, however, ostensibly under the public leadership of Arthur Nzeribe, supposedly a maverick politician. By late March, the ABN had started its own "Babangida Must Stay" campaign. In response to their request for an order to stop the election from proceeding, a court was hurriedly created in Abuja, the seat of the Federal Government. The presiding judge, Bassey Ikpeme, was taken from Port-Harcourt, reportedly from the private chambers of the then chief government lawyer, the Attorney General of the federation, Clement Akpamgbo. The ABN action was the first case heard by Justice Ikpeme's court.

On June 9, several of Babangida's loyalists within the army met in Minna. Their main agenda was to consider the implications of an Abiola victory in the election, especially for the northern interest in the army. Among those present were Colonel Abdul-Muminu Aminu, commander of the National Guard; Colonel Abubakar Umar, Commandant, Army Armored Corps Center and School, Bauchi; plus Colonel Chris Abutu Garba, Colonel John Madaki, and Brigadier John Inienger. During this meeting the idea was conceived to filibuster the election. NEC chairman Humphrey Nwosu was brought into the arrangement. The main objective was to ensure that either the election did not occur, or, if it did, the results would be questionable.

Some members of the military clique proposed an outright extension of military rule. On June 10, the National Defense and Security Council (NDSC) met to deliberate on the impending election and the Ikpeme judicial stone-walling. They found a convergence of interests in a judicial maneuver to be executed by Ikpeme. Although it was said that the majority of the NDSC members preferred that the election be held, a stalemate was declared. No one doubted that Abiola was by every criterion possible a better candidate, and, therefore, most certain to beat Tofa.

On June 11, as the nation looked forward to voting the next day, Justice Ikpeme granted the injunction sought by the ABN to stop the election from proceeding. However, on the same day the Vice President, Augustus Aikhomu, promptly evoked Decree No. 13 of 1993 which states in section 19 (1) that

No interim or interlocutory order or ruling, judgement or decision made by any court or Tribunal before or after the commencement of this Decree, in respect of any inter-party dispute or any other matter before it shall affect the date or time of the election or the performance by the commission or any of its funding and this Decree or any guidelines issued by it in pursuance of the election.

Then Nwosu, the NEC chairman, appeared on national television to announce that the election would be held as scheduled. Quoting from relevant decrees, he said that the injunction granted by the Justice Ikpeme Court was not enough to stop the election at this crucial stage. Indeed, Decree 52 of 1992, section 16 prohibited any

Court proceedings with respect to matters done or purported to be done by any agent of the Federal Government in the process of realising the objectives of the transition programme.

Notwithstanding the above, as soon as the decision of the Abuja Court was announced, human rights groups, like the Committee for the Defense of Human Rights and the CLO, filed urgent actions at the Lagos High Court to compel the NEC to conduct the election as scheduled. The election was held, of course, with conflicting signals as to whether the electorate should or should not vote in light of Justice Ikpeme's ruling. Fourteen million votes were reported to have been cast, and both local and foreign observers attested to the fairness of the election.

Post Election Politics

By Sunday, June 13, the election results had started trickling in officially and through party agents. The method adopted for vote collation was such that the result would have been known by the end of the day. Votes in every polling booth were counted and declared before each candidate's agent. The two agents and the electoral officer in charge of the polling booth were expected to sign a copy of the election results as written down on a prescribed form. This was to be the certified copy. On June 13, the NEC declared the election results in 12 states. Abiola led convincingly in seven of them, while also securing the mandatory one-third of the votes cast in the remaining five. In fact, the BBC announced the results from 27 of the 30 states, with Abiola as the clear winner. On June 14, the NEC headed for the Court of Appeal in Kaduna to raise objections to the case brought by the ABN. Its main point was that the association had no jurisdiction for the action it filed. But, on June 15, the Chief Judge of the Federal Capital Territory of Abuja, Justice Dahiru Saleh, instructed the NEC to suspend its release of the election results. This order was given in spite of the case being heard by the superior court of appeal. On June 16, Nwosu of the NEC, announced the suspension of the election results, reportedly after he was summoned to the presidency in Abuja to explain why he did not cause a stalemate in the election. Nwosu explained as follows:

In the light of the current development, the commission has in deference to the court injunction and other actions pending in court, decided to stay action on all matters pertaining to the presidential election until further notice.[9]

Nwosu's decision raises several questions. Why did Nwosu now suddenly decide to obey the Justice Ikpeme court order not to hold the election until the ABN case had been heard? Was this necessary when that order was about the holding of the election and not the declaration of its results? What about the counter ruling by the Lagos High Court to Justice Ikpeme's order which effectively asked the NEC to continue with the election? What about those decrees whose provisions were clearly in support of every action the NEC had taken to ensure that the election went ahead? Finally, were all these not substantial grounds for proceeding with the announcement of the results?

On the same day that Justice Saleh of Abuja was asking the NEC to discontinue the announcement of the results, another judge, J.O. Sadoh of Benin High Court, gave a counter-ruling that the results should be released. This followed the hearing of an application filed by Matthew Egbadu, a member of the Edo State House of Assembly. A similar application was filed in Lagos by two citizens, Sumbo Onitiri and Babatunde Adejumo. It was heard by Justice Moshood Olugbami, who also directed that the results of the election be released.

The Babangida regime was later to blame its annulment of the election on the "politicisation of the judiciary" and the need to rescue it from "public ridicule." This was contained in an unsigned press statement distributed by Nduka Irabor, the press secretary to the vice president, on June 23, 1993. Apparently aware that this excuse was neither tenable nor acceptable with the majority of Nigerians, Babangida himself changed the reason claimed for the annulment in a national broadcast on June 26. He claimed that the election had been massively rigged by the two candidates, who had allegedly expended an estimated 2.1 billion naira. He added that officials of the NEC had been bribed. Finally, he alleged that the candidates had interests which conflicted with the national interest. The NDSC, he said, had confidential evidence of all these allegations.

Certain questions inevitably arise from all of the above, which were trenchantly asked in the days following the broadcast. If it was true, as Babangida alleged, that the judiciary was politicized, could this be blamed on either Abiola or the NEC? If there were elements of malpractice in the election, or conflict between the interests of the candidates and that of the nation, why could this not be addressed by the Electoral Tribunal which was authorized to deal with such issues under the transition decrees? And, perhaps more fundamentally, why did Babangida usurp the powers of the NEC at the last minute?

From June 13, several military formations in Lagos, Kaduna, Jos, Ibadan, and Lagos were already making phone calls to one another to confirm their preparedness to launch a military offensive in case Abiola became president. In Abeokuta, the capital of Ogun State and Abiola's birthplace, soldiers took up positions at the state-owned television complex, the state-owned radio station, and the premises of the federally-owned Nigerian television station.

As previously noted, the NRC candidate and Abiola's sole opponent in the election, Tofa, was not a registered voter and was therefore unable to vote. On June 13, the public relations officer of the NRC, one Mr. Izoho, appeared on television to say that Abiola had violated the electoral laws by wearing a dress in his party's colors with the symbol of SDP emblazoned on it. For this reason, he said, Abiola should be disqualified. By June 14, the state machinery had been put to work, as rent-a-crowd protesters took to the streets in the capital of some northern states. In Minna, the capital of Niger and Babangida's home state, the protesters went to the palace of the local emir and the office of the state governor. Accompanied by state-employed television cameramen and journalists, the protesters demanded that the election results be canceled, since, they argued, the majority of the voters had been confused by the ruling of the Abuja High Court suspending the election.

Even Tofa, who had told journalists on June 12 that he was willing to concede defeat in the election provided his campaign team was satisfied that it was free, made a sudden U-turn on June 16, after an audience with Babangida. He began to suggest that the election had not been fair. On June 17, however, the western caucus of the NRC, including the party's national chairman, sent a message of congratulation to Abiola, saying he had won in a free and fair contest. Two prominent members of the party from the north, Adamu Ciroma and Umaru Shinkafi, who were also among presidential aspirants disqualified in the earlier stage of the PTP, expressed similar sentiments, noting that Abiola should be installed as president. The northern caucuses of the NRC, however, dissociated themselves from the congratulatory message of their western regional counterparts, saying it had been ethnically inspired. Following this, Ciroma and Shinkafi, also, became ambivalent regarding the election. Then the governors elected on the NRC platform in the eastern region of the country began to organize meetings calling for the annulment of the election altogether.

Within the SDP, elements like Shehu Musa Yar'Adua and Sule Lamido, who had declared that Abiola won the election, also began to shift grounds. The State House in Abuja, Aso Rock, now became the Mecca of several political pilgrims, as those jockeying for power, money and patronage, trooped to the presidential palace supposedly to associate themselves with Babangida's wisdom. If ever there was a moment that reflected how deeply Babangida had penetrated all the segments of Nigerian society and institutions, this proved to be it. The state propaganda machine was set against Abiola. He was denigrated, pilloried and ridiculed. Uche Chukwumerije, the Secretary (minister) for Information perfected and carried out this task in the methods of the Nazis of old.

Babangida blackmailed the opportunistic political class into accepting an interim government. He had actually gone to the National Assembly on August 23, 1993 hoping that he would get approval to head this interim government. The two political parties readily approved of it, as did prominent politicians and so-called statesmen. As Yar'Adua, one of the politicians most active in the ensuing haggling noted, it was a game of hide and seek and everybody seemed bent on playing it. According to him:

> SDP called another forum ... They said I should speak. I said I couldn't contribute at all. I said we had 12 June people with us at that meeting, where we reached the resolution ... all accepted that SDP should go for the interim government ... It was Baba Kingibe, when the resolution was read ... who called me to attention ... He said don't you think there is a lacuna in this resolution? I said what lacuna, Baba? He said what about June 12? So I said, Baba, you see that these people are protecting their jobs. He said do something about it. I replied why don't you? That resolution did not say anything about 12 June. All the governors were there, so were the senators and so on. Nobody had any objections.[10]

General Olusegun Obasanjo, a former head of state, was among those who had spearheaded the campaign for the military to leave power. In a personal letter to Babangida on November 14, 1992, he wrote that:

> Any prolongation of military rule in the form of diarchy or any other arrangement will bring the armed forces into utter disrepute, it will amount to a declaration of

war against the sovereign rights of the people of Nigeria to choose their own leader and conduct their affairs in accordance with the constitution.[11]

In a speech delivered in Harare a few weeks after the June 12 crisis began, General Obasanjo seemed to have changed his whole perception of democracy. He was reported to have said that Abiola was his classmate in secondary school, hence he could be said to know him very well. On this basis, Obasanjo indicated he was sure that Abiola lacked leadership qualities and was therefore an unreliable candidate for the presidency. Elsewhere, he disclosed that he had personally approached Babangida and asked him to constitute an interim government. His basis for all this was that he would not stand by while Nigeria was disintegrating as a consequence of the June 12 crisis. "Having fought for the unity of Nigeria, I cannot be a party to its disintegration," he was quoted as saying.

The Interim National Government (ING) was formed and a businessman who had retired as chairman of United Africa Company (Nigeria), Ernest Shonekan, was appointed to head it. Shonekan was the head of a much taunted but ineffectual group of technocrats earlier invited to head government ministries as part of the transition process. Shonekan also hailed from Abeokuta, the home state of Abiola. The objective of forming the ING was said to be to "diffuse tension" over the June 12 issue. However, the rest of Nigerians saw it differently. It was business as usual among despicably unprincipled power opportunists. Their view was aptly summarized in a newspaper:

> Prominent among several personalities who thronged the corridors of the presidential villa to lobby for the appointment of their favoured candidates into the interim national government were General Shehu Yar'Adua, Chief Tom Ikimi, former national chairman of the NRC, Governor Ada George of Rivers State and Governor Okwesileze Nwodo of Enugu State. On Yar'Adua's insistence, Dr. Patrick Dele Cole was dropped in favour of Chief Dapo Sarumi as communications secretary.[12]

Among the other political elites who now became ambivalent over the June 12 election, the position of Emeka Ojukwu, the former secessionist leader, was both remarkable and interesting. Ojukwu, who in the early days of the political transition program had chastized the Babangida regime over the length of the transition saying, "if you want to hand-over to a civil government, you don't need so many years for it," suddenly began to describe June 12 in such sordid terms as "trash" and "national aberration," among others. According to him, "June 12 is a non-event because somehow, we seem to have forgotten the antecedent to June 12." Ojukwu was later elected as a delegate to the National Constitutional Conference, which many people have dubbed a talking shop for the lackeys and apologists of the military. Compared to the 14 million votes cast at the presidential election, the constitutional conference election attracted only 300,000 voters nationwide. Ojukwu, nonetheless, went ahead to describe himself as having a superior mandate, superior, that is, to Abiola who was elected president:

> once he (Abiola) had been detained and put into the judicial system, particularly because I'm in the process of writing a constitution, I cannot permit our

constitution to rise from the ashes of crime. There must be in our nation a concept of treason that makes it really the supreme crime.[13]

As the crisis began to unfold, a string of criticism and tough-talking by the international community began to hurt the Babangida regime. Therefore, the Transitional Council, which succeeded the regime, sent a high-powered lobby group to the US Congress, ostensibly to explain the June 12 crisis, but no doubt to spread the false information that was being peddled locally. According to Alao Aka-Bashorun, a distinguished Nigerian lawyer and former chairman of the Bar Association who was in exile at the time, the lobby group was led by a politician, Nduka Obaigbena and Nigeria's Ambassador to the US, Ahmadu Kazaure. In Aka-Bashorun's words:

> Kazaure briefed three lobbyists at a cost of $1.5 million each. On the whole he paid $4.5 million to all of them. So they began lobbying the Republicans. He got one Gregory Copley to present a 15-page paper where he told them Nigeria needed a dictator like Babangida who will whip Nigerians into line. Copley told the Congress that Abiola put N50.00 notes in loaves of bread meant for voters. Ambassador Kazaure sat down there and watched how facts were distorted. But of course, Copley did what he was paid to do. Kazaure paid Copley about a million dollars for that 15-page paper.[14]

None of the people mentioned by Aka-Bashorun, including Obaigbena, Kazaure, or Copley, has attempted to deny that the incident took place as alleged. It was to counter this and other external propaganda being put out by the Babangida regime and its moribund successor, the ING, that Aka-Bashorun, the Nigerian born writer Chinua Achebe, and other concerned Nigerians in the US, invited Abiola abroad to explain his case to the international community. Abiola left the country in August 1993 unannounced, except, perhaps, to a few of his lieutenants. This was in the midst of a second round of protests called by the Campaign for Democracy (CD). The government and its dirty propaganda minister, Uche Chukwumerije, immediately seized on this trip to say that Abiola had abandoned his supporters at home. The language and tone of the anti-Abiola and anti-June 12 campaign became, from then on, very hostile, insidious, and alarming. The military high-handedness in suppressing protests, particularly in Lagos, Ibadan, and Benin, where protesters were shot, was blamed on Abiola. It was Abiola, the propagandists said, who frivolously caused children of innocent Nigerians to be killed while his own children never stepped out of their father's house to join the solidarity marches and protests. The Somali crisis was turned into a cliché as rumors of an impending war was mindlessly peddled. As a result of all this, the biggest ethnic migration since the Nigerian Civil War was witnessed. Many Nigerians moved their personal belongings and families from the economically active city of Lagos back to their ethnic bases.

From Europe, Abiola established contacts with the head of the ING, Chief Shonekan, and its leading military members, Generals Abacha and Oladipo Diya, all of whom gave him assurances that they were pro-June 12. However, he was advised to delay his return to Nigeria until his safety could be guaranteed. When eventually he did return, Abiola was treated to a red-carpet welcome. This heightened his illusion that power would be handed over to him. Rather than promoting the continuation of the resistance started by popular forces, Abiola chose to dialogue with those in the government and the politicians who joined in the annulment of the election. As part of his reconciliation program, he was seen publicly with Yar'Adua, Nzeribe, and Bafyau, among others. The popular forces who had rightly expected that Abiola would assume leadership and take them into the counter-offensive against the ING, were demobilized. Even Abiola himself admitted to having stopped the popular protests when he said:

> One hundred and sixty (people) were shot at the back running away. Not a single apology has been given. They are human beings. I was saddened by that and did everything I could to stop it and I have since stopped it. That is why I went to court. To take the issues from the streets to the process of the law courts.[15]

Abiola went to the Supreme Court and lost. Meanwhile, there was information about Abiola hobnobbing with people in the government, while at the same time still dallying with Babangida. *Tempo* magazine published a letter he wrote to the latter after his "stepping aside" from the government. The letter revealed that both had been in some sort of secret contact and were plotting a strategy which would exonerate Babangida from blame over the annulment. In addition, the letter revealed that both did not want the affair to affect their friendship. When this letter was published, Abiola made no qualms in rationalizing his action. The popular forces were all shattered.

The military wing of the ING, headed by General Abacha, finally shoved aside its civilian wing, headed by Chief Shonekan, to assume effective control of the government on November 19, 1993. The belief then was that this faction was pro-June 12. However, no sooner did the regime settle into office that it began to dismantle what was left of the democratic structure, thereby fueling speculation that it nursed its own private agenda. This was widely confirmed when two senior members of the regime, the Chiefs of Army and Naval Staff, said to be the most insistent that the military should honor the June 12 mandate, were retired.[16]

The military had indeed manipulated the most vocal wings of the pro-June movement, including Abiola himself, into believing that it would de-annul the election and enthrone Abiola as president. When the pro-June 12 campaign was most vociferous, for instance, the Babangida regime had detained some familiar faces in the anti-military coalition. Among them were Gani Fawehinmi, Femi Falana, Baba Omojola, and Segun Maiyegun. Not only were these campaigners released by the interim government, but they were also courted to support the ING, something which they refused to do.[17] Instead, they openly demanded an overthrow of the ING, in the hope that the military, based on the contacts already established with the pro-democracy movements, would restore the June 12 mandate as a necessity. It was for this reason that the leadership of the CD became enthusiastic initially when the military announced that it would sponsor a National Constitutional Conference, which would serve as the anchor for its democratization program. The CD believed, erroneously, that this was going to be like the sovereign national conference, which it had repeatedly demanded. The appointment of Olu Onagoruwa, a vocal member of the anti-military coalition, and one of those who had been detained repeatedly by the military, as the new Attorney General of the Federation, indeed buoyed the confidence of the CD that the new military junta would be truthful to the assurances it had given them. It was for a similar reason that Abiola had embraced the coup and visited Abacha when the latter assumed power. However, things started to take a totally unexpected turn, according to the perception of those in the pro-democracy movement.

Abiola was reportedly asked to produce a paper on how best the June 12 mandate could be actualized. This was before the coup. The paper was titled "The Way Forward" and was to be handed over to General Diya, who in turn was to brief Abacha. The go-between in all this was Bola Tinubu, a senator in the parliament, which was abolished by Abacha. Saying that "Abacha deceived us," Tinubu disclosed how they were led to believe that the military wanted to resolve the crisis:

> They used 12 June to buy support of the people for the take-over. Lt General Oladipo Diya who consulted with us appeared very resolutely committed to the cause of 12 June, describing it as a travesty of justice ... Even Abacha told us that their mission was to restore 12 June. That was even as far back as the coup.[18]

According to Tinubu, Abacha's maiden speech was to have contained most of the issues in Abiola's blueprint, including a statement that the annulment of the June 12 election was unjust and would therefore be set aside. Nwosu, the NEC chairman, would have been recalled to declare the remaining results and, subsequently, the winner installed. As Tinubu further noted:

> Chief M.K.O. Abiola and myself, in company of Dr Jonathan Zwingina, visited Abacha to ask him why he changed the broadcast. The fact that General Abacha's maiden broadcast was not consistent with the highlights I enumerated earlier immediately gave the game away that he had come not to intervene and resolve the crisis in favour of June 12, but seize power for himself.[19]

Abacha, however, claimed that he did not get the blueprint sent through Diya, hence he could not incorporate it in his maiden broadcast. Diya, on the other hand, claimed that the blueprint was delivered to Abacha. Abacha had tried to persuade Abiola to drop his campaign for the June 12 mandate, telling him that he intended to form a government of "big names" like General Yakubu Gowon did when he appointed the late Chief Obafemi Awolowo and others to a crisis cabinet following the coup d'état of July 1966 and before the outbreak of the Civil War. Some of the big names canvassed by Abacha were those of Abiola's running mate, Kingibe, and Lateef Jakande, a former populist governor of Lagos State in the Second Republic. Once Abiola heard this, his reply was:

> let me call my people who supported me throughout the country and ask them whether they want me to abandon the mandate. "No," he (Abacha) said, "Once the military do a coup, that is the end of the whole thing" ... Kingibe knew that our agenda was to actualise my mandate without bloodshed. And part of the agenda was that this guy will take over the government and finish what is left of the interim government by the end of March in the meantime while we form our own government.[20]

Abiola then called a meeting of the SDP leadership where, according to him, he asked:

> Do we surrender our mandate? Those in favour of surrendering our mandate should raise up their hands. Nobody did. Those who want us to uphold the mandate? Everybody did including Kingibe himself.[21]

As it turned out, this did not stop a preponderant number of pro-June 12 SDP members from joining politicians from the NRC to accept ministerial appointments from Abacha. Kingibe's rationale for accepting his ministerial job was the most intriguing of all. According to him, the inability to actualize the June 12 mandate was a collective failure of the political class. With respect to his acceptance of a ministerial appointment, he said:

> a correspondent of the FRCN (Federal Radio Corporation of Nigeria) called me on my cellular (phone) and said congratulations. I said on what? "We have just seen your name on the list of ministers, and you have been made the minister of foreign affairs." I am experienced enough not to tell him that oh, I never knew. And before I reached Chief Abiola's house, the BBC correspondent again phoned me and asked what did I think of my appointment? Again, I am experienced enough not to tell them (sic) that I knew nothing about it. I then reached Chief Abiola's house with the background information.[22]

Kingibe then continued on a different note:

> I expected that by the time I entered, he (Abiola) would smile and say we have heard of your appointment. And then we could discuss the implications rather than to be quiet about it, to be quiet with his discussions with the head of state and skip around those issues. The moment I realised what was up, I also decided to play along ... it became obvious that we had both been wasting our time once the deed had already been done.[23]

These various acts, which no doubt left Abiola in the cold, caused him to lose faith in his political confidantes, the political class, and the military. For example, he lamentably remarked about General Abacha that, "why wouldn't he want to rule when he could become a General without passing the staff college." This remark set the general's blood on the boil.

Popular Forces and the Struggle Under the Abacha Junta

The relationship between the CD, which spearheaded the anti-military coalition, and Abiola, was based, at best, on mutual tolerance, since both shared the same objective, which was to get rid of the military. However, contact between the leadership of the CD and the military prior to the overthrow of the ING caused a row within the organization. This row became a rupture at the February 1994 convention of the organization, when a faction staged a walk-out over the refusal by Beko Ransome-Kuti, CD chairman, to apologize for taking the organization into an alliance with the military. The CD waged its campaign on a popular platform in the belief that if the mandate was actualized, they could get Abiola to form a national government made up of broad interests, including professional associations, and trade unions. When this proposal was submitted to Abiola, however, he rejected it. He also rejected the CD's demand that a sovereign national conference be convened to discuss the national question and similar issues regarding Nigeria's future. All that Abiola wanted was to give financial assistance to the various groups involved in the June 12 campaign so they could intensify their efforts, presumably to actualize his mandate.

Abiola's position generated tensions within the CD and was partly responsible for the breakaway by a faction which later constituted itself into the "Democratic Alternative" under the leadership of Aka-Bashorun. This was the same faction that staged a walkout at the February 1994 convention. They wanted the CD to severe its relationship with Abiola following his rejection of the organization's agenda. However, there were two other views. One was that the CD should maintain a friendly collaboration, by accepting Abiola's financial support for CD activities, especially the prosecution of the June 12 struggle. The second view was that the collaboration should be full, meaning that the CD should accept Abiola's terms and a few positions in his government whenever the June 12 mandate was actualized. The question has been asked whether it was the CD that gave June 12 credibility or vice versa.

The argument being made is that the June 12 struggle, which the people waged between June and November 1993, was compromised by Abiola himself. Hence, the struggle he resuscitated when he proclaimed himself president a year later, had a different philosophy and agenda behind it. It was seen as not worth the struggles that had been waged over a whole year. For example, it was contended that Abiola could have made his declaration when a judge of the Lagos High Court, Justice Dolapo Akisanya, declared the ING illegal,[24] but that he faltered because he wanted the matter resolved as a fight among bosom friends. There is also the argument that the post-August 1993 struggles over June 12 did not take a popular, but petty bourgeois character, in which power seekers, both military and civilian, attempted to resolve the political impasse peacefully. The failure to achieve such a peaceful settlement, however, led them to elicit the support of the popular forces as a last resort. In the address read by Abiola while declaring himself president on June 11, 1994, he stated that:

> Our patience has come to an end, as of now. From this moment, a new government of national unity is in power throughout the length and breadth of the Federal Republic of Nigeria, led by me, Bashorun M.K.O. Abiola, as president and commander-in-chief. The national assembly is hereby reconvened. All the dismissed governors of the states are reinstated. The state assemblies are reconstituted, as are all local government councils. I urge them to adopt a bi-partisan approach to all issues that come before them.[25]

This declaration came as a surprise to the general citizenry, which had stopped taking Abiola seriously in view of his compromise-seeking negotiations with both members of the political class, who had campaigned openly against the June 12 election, and the military. In the one year between the election and Abiola's self-proclamation as president, June 12 was stripped of its social force. Even worse, the CD, which had mobilized the popular protest, had been hit by internal wrangling and squabbles over strategies and vision. These two events led inexorably to the formation of the National Democratic Coalition (NADECO), on whose platform Abiola renewed the struggle for the actualization of June 12. NADECO was a hotchpotch or amalgam of political associations with divergent, and at times, conflicting purviews. It was relatively unknown until it announced itself with an ultimatum to General Abacha to hand over power by the end of May 1994, or face a series of political actions. Because NADECO was unknown beyond the circle of politicians and the political interest groups which founded it, its ultimatum was regarded as an empty threat.

As soon as he finished proclaiming himself president, Abiola went into hiding. He appeared four days later to address a political rally in central Lagos. On June 22, 1994, the Abacha junta ordered the arrest of Abiola. There were public protests and criticism, but the on-going 1994 World Cup finals in the US, in which Nigeria was participating for the first time, provided a temporary, but effective diversion. Nigerians are soccer loving and they were particularly pleased to see their national team featuring in these prestigious finals, hence they adopted a wait-and-see attitude to Abiola's detention, while savoring the pleasure of watching their Super Eagles on television. When Nigeria was kicked out by Italy, however, the Abiola affair again became the issue of the moment.

Abiola was soon brought to court and charged with treason. However, while Abiola was being driven to the Abuja Federal High Court, in the notorious *Black Maria*, a specially designed van with poor ventilation used by Nigerian police to convey criminals to and from court (the use of the van was outlawed in 1977 when scores of suspects were suffocated to death, but the police have not desisted from its use), the same national television which showed the picture of his humiliation also showed Umaru Dikko, once the most wanted political criminal in Nigeria, being welcomed back from exile by high officials of the state. Dikko fled Nigeria in 1983, after a military coup announced by Abacha. Labeled as the most unconscionable politician in the ill-fated Nigeria's Second Republic, Dikko had sought and received political asylum in the United Kingdom. A sinister attempt to abduct him by Nigeria in 1984 was foiled by the British police and led to a diplomatic row between the British and Nigeria governments. In a bizarre reversal of fortunes, Dikko was flown back to Nigeria in a presidential jet and given a rousing welcome, which included a motorcade procession to the government house in Kaduna, his home state. He was then nominated by the government as a representative to its Constitutional Conference in Abuja. These two events, Abiola being taken to court in the *Black Maria* and Dikko being flown to the country in a presidential jet, offended public sensibility and heightened sentiments.

The Constitutional Conference election attracted a low voter turn-out in many parts of the country. In the southwest, it was boycotted by nearly all the important and acknowledged politicians, leading to the emergence of what is now euphemistically referred to as "the second-eleven" politicians from the southwest. Apparently in search of credibility, having been chosen in an election in which four out of every five voters refused to vote, some of these southwest "second eleven" attempted to table the June 12 issue as an item of discussion at the conference. But the matter became ethnicized and effortlessly sidelined.

Some members of the Nigerian political class have joined the military in chorusing that the June 12 election was not annulled by the Abacha regime, hence it could not be held liable for it. There is also the view that the annulment was the result of judicial recklessness. Ethnic organizations such as the Afenifere (an assembly for mainly Yoruba welfarist politicians), suddenly began to champion the June 12 question and several Yoruba Obas made representation to Abacha. Some fractions of the entrenched northern bourgeois class began to claim that June 12 was not the first annulment to take place in Nigeria, hence Nigerians should stop making an issue out of it. According to this view, the first military coup in January 1966 was also an annulment as was the coup of December 1983. Therefore, the argument goes, to insist on the recognition of the June 12 mandate is to reawaken the sad experiences of 1966 and 1983.

The Ndigbo and Eastern Mandate, purporting to be representing the interests of the Igbo people of the southeast, argued that the Ibos have been marginalized in Nigerian politics. For this reason, they pushed very hard at the Constitutional Conference forum for the inclusion of a rotational presidency clause in the new constitution, an objective which they appear to have achieved. They have also argued that the first president under the next civilian dispensation should come from the eastern part of the country. As it turned out, the June 12 issue was killed at the conference.

The humiliation of Abiola by the military, and the politicization of his trial, led once more to a series of civil actions. Two trade unions in the crucial oil sector, NUPENG and PENGASSAN, spearheaded a national campaign to demand the installation of Abiola as president. The two unions called out their members on a strike, which brought the nation to a virtual standstill for two months. Properties belonging to key supporters of the Abacha regime, such as Augustus Aikhomu, Babangida's Vice President, and Samuel Ogbemudia, Abacha's Minister of Labor, were vandalized in their home state of Edo in retaliatory violence. It was Ogbemudia who had propounded the catchy phrase, *FFF — find, fix, and finish* — as the formula for containing the June 12 demonstrators. Although it was broken eight weeks later, through a series of repression, intimidation, and outright violence by the government, the strike was a surprising but well-received rekindling of the spirit of open struggle and defiance. This was the case because the two unions had soldiered on without any help from the central labor union, the NLC, the attitude of whose leadership regarding the June 12 crisis was, from the beginning, manifestly dubious. Other popular forces had either become too weakened, disillusioned or rankled by internal contradictions to give effective backing to NUPENG and PENGASSAN.

The international community used this as an opportunity to call on the Abacha regime to democratize. Several emissaries, among them former US President Jimmy Carter, Nelson Mandela, Jesse Jackson, and Salim Ahmed Salim, visited Nigeria in an attempt to persuade General Abacha to release Abiola and seek dialogue with the opposition, to no avail. Several humanitarian and medical groups raised alarm over Abiola's failing health, after he was denied medical attention. The Abacha regime, however, did not budge. Meanwhile, Abiola's trial was becoming entangled in technicalities. It was argued that since his alleged offense was committed in Lagos, he ought to have been tried in Lagos, and not in Abuja. This would have been in compliance with Section 44 of the Federal High Court Act. It was contended that the Abuja High Court, to which he was charged, was illegal as there was no statutory instrument creating it. Indeed, Justice Babatunde Belgore, the Chief Justice of the Federal High Court, said that the Abuja court was a unit of the Jos Judicial Division. All these technical flaws were used to highlight the political and indeed vindictive nature of Abiola's trial. This in turn decreased the probability of his getting a fair trial. While all these arguments were going on, the presiding judge at the Abuja High Court, Abdulahi Mustapha, further muddied the water by saying that he wanted to consult with "higher quarters in Sokoto" before he could make a ruling on the important issue of jurisdiction. The public reaction to this remark forced the judge to withdraw himself from the case. Announcing his withdrawal, the judge said:

> I have decided that in order to rekindle the confidence of the accused person and sceptics, I will now ask the Chief Judge to excuse me from this trial and assign another judge of the Federal High Court to handle the case. I have noted with great concern the connotations, innuendoes and interpretations given to my recent accidental slip.[26]

But while regretting his own mistake, Justice Mustapha ruled that his court had jurisdiction and could therefore hear the case. He added that there was evidence to show that there was an attempt to "overthrow" the Abacha regime. Mustapha's ruling was challenged at the Federal High Court of Appeal in Kaduna, where the presiding judge, Muri Okunola, declined to participate in the case on the ground that Abiola was a personal friend of his. Two other judges were later to withdraw from the Abiola trial for one reason or another. The successor to Justice Okunola granted Abiola bail in self-recognition, but the government did not release him from prison. At the Abuja High Court, a new judge, Christopher Selong was brought in to replace Mustapha. He too had to withdraw when Abiola's counsel drew attention to the fact that he was an interested party in the case, having been joined as co-respondent with Mohammed Yussuf, the Police Commissioner for Abuja, and one Lawal Katsina, in Abiola's case at the Appeal Court. In the midst of all this, the Federal High Court in Lagos declared Abiola's arrest and detention "illegal, irresponsible and embarrassing." Even such strong words were not enough to secure the release of the politician.

In the final analysis, the question that remains is, can June 12 still be actualized? A lot will depend on two variables. The first is the balance of social forces, together with the vibrancy of the civil associations. The second is the disposition of Abiola himself and his supporting faction of the political class.

Conclusion

The arguments for and against June 12 are now legion. Some take the view that because of Abiola's class background, it was a mistake to have fought so determinedly to actualize his mandate. Those opposing this perspective argue that Nigerians did not set out to fight for Abiola, but for the principles and ideals his cause symbolized. A third perspective is that the democratic struggle in Nigeria cannot be fixated on June 12 because events have made it lose its meaning and originality. Finally, a fourth perspective is that the election was neither free nor fair and therefore must be rejected in its entirety because the process that gave birth to it was neither legitimate nor credible.

No matter which perspective is canvassed, three issues will always remain apparent around the June 12 debate. The first is that the whole crisis threw up a plethora of social forces and gave added vibrancy to civil society. The second is that the way the June 12 struggle was misdirected tells much about the character of the Nigerian ruling class, especially its political fraction. The third issue is that June 12 may be exploited in a very dangerous manner that could lead to separatist agitation in Nigeria. For as long as it remains unresolved, June 12 will always be an albatross round the neck of the political class. This is because the annulment of the election represents intra-class injustice. It does not matter if it is the bourgeoisie that is depreciating itself.

The crucial questions here are why the military cannot allow the law to apply without manipulation, and why the June 12 issue cannot be decided by a properly constituted court of law? In light of the politicization of both the June 12 question and the judiciary, there is little hope that a satisfactory judicial settlement is now possible. The issue can only be resolved politically, and this will depend on the balance of forces. We can only hope, however, that this will not be at the risk of the stability and territorial integrity of the Nigerian nation-state. No doubt the Abacha junta is having a field day at the moment, with increased patrimonialism and militarism. The political space has become highly contrived, and it has shrunk alarmingly.

Notes

[1] Lai Olorude, *M.K.O. Abiola on June 12 Mandate* (Lagos: Rebonik Publications, 1993), p. 12.

[2] For an elaboration on this category of the political class, see Abubakar Momoh, "The Political Economy of the Transition Process," in Said Adejumobi and Abubakar Momoh *(eds.), The Political Economy of Nigeria Under Military Rule,* (Harare: SAPES, 1995).

[3] Chima Ubani and Emma O'Mano Edigheji, *Report On the Conventions of the Social Democratic Party (SDP) and the National Republican Convention (NRC) on March 27 to 29,* (Lagos: CLO 1993), p. 5.

[4] *Ibid.,* p. 3.

[5] *Ibid.* Emphasis mine.

[6] M.K.O. Abiola, Interview, in "The June 12 Question," *Liberty* , Vol. 4, No. 3, p. 4.

[7] *Ibid.,* p .6.

[8] *Ibid.,* p. 7.

[9] "Conspiracy: Desperate Attempt to Abort Democracy," *The News,* June 28, 1993, p. 20.

[10] "Shehu Yar'Adua, "Why I Couldn't Help Abiola," *The News,* January 31, 1994, p. 18.

[11] Cited in "Stolen Presidency," *Tell,* July 5, 1993, p. 13.

[12] "Puppets take Over," *Tempo,* September 6, 1993, p. 8.

[13] Cited in *The News,* October 31, 1994, p. 5.

[14] *Ibid.*

[15] *Ibid.*

[16] For details, see "The Fall of June 12 General," *The News,* September 5, 1994, pp. 18-19.

[17] See interview with Gani Fawehinmi in *The African Guardian,* September 13, 1993.

[18] See interview with Bola Tinubu, "Abacha Deceived Us," *The News,* June 13, 1994, p. 22.

[19] *Ibid.*

[20] Interview with Abiola, "I Won't Disappoint Again," *The News,* June 6, 1994, p. 18.

[21] *Ibid.*

[22] Interview with Kingibe, "Why I Dumped Abiola," *The News,* May 2, 1994, p. 15.

[23] Gani Fawehinmi, *The Illegality of Shonekan's Government* (Lagos: Nigeria Law Publications, 1993).

[24] *Ibid.*

[25] Address to the People of Nigeria by Bashorun M.K.O. Abiola, June 12, 1994.

[26] *The News,* July 18, 1994, p. 14.

12

Decentralization in Africa: Appraising the Local Government Revitalization Strategy in Nigeria[1]

Dele Olowu

African states are centralized, at least formally, whereas their societies are relatively decentralized, and in many cases, dispersed. The centralized state, once touted as the key to hastening the process of modernization by both sides of the ideological spectrum, is now regarded as part of the African problem in evolving appropriate and acceptable governance structures and enhancing economic production. Africa continues to lag behind the rest of the world in all measures of economic and social progress, and the conditions of its people seem to be worsening. Concentrated power structures have led to wars and ethnic violence (Somalia, Liberia, Sierra Leone, Ethiopia, Rwanda, Burundi, Angola, and Nigeria, for example), or party or military autocracy, and all the ills associated with it: inappropriate allocation of resources to arms instead of health and welfare; economic mismanagement; state corruption; human rights abuses; and money laundering. The impoverishment of potentially rich economies by corrupt, but determined, political leaders in countries such as Zaire and Nigeria, remind the serious student of Africa that centralized state rule is a major cause of Africa's economic and political ruin, as well as state "softness."[2]

There are several explanations for Africa's current centralized state — historical, political, and economic. However, in the post-cold war era, there is serious dissatisfaction with this state of affairs, both from within and outside Africa. There is consensus that decentralization to empower ordinary citizens is desirable. As a result, some African countries have opened up to genuine decentralization. The best example is South Africa, where the debate on the nature and extent of decentralization and democratization at central and local levels has continued since 1990, when Nelson Mandela was released from 27 years in jail, to become president of an independent and powerful post-apartheid state. Other examples include Mozambique, Zambia, Malawi, Angola, Ethiopia, and, possibly, Uganda, which are working out credible ways for genuinely empowering the people and correcting the colonial and postcolonial imbalance between state and society. On the other hand, in the majority of African states, commitment to decentralization is like it has always been — phony.[3]

The strengthening of local government is regarded in particular as crucial to political and economic reforms on the continent. Local governments in Africa are much less developed politically, institutionally, and financially than other public sector organizations or local governments in other continents[4] (see Table 1).

Within the last decade, several national governments, multilateral financial and development institutions, as well as donor agencies, have made efforts to "strengthen" local governments in Africa, in the belief that this is essential for economic and social progress. In 1989, for instance, the World Bank organized two sets of workshops for senior African policy makers, experts, and major donor agencies in Poretta Terme, Italy, on "Strategies for Strengthening Local Governments In Africa."[5] UN agencies such as the United Nations Department of Economic and Social Development, the United Nations Children's Fund (UNICEF), the United Nations Development Programme (UNDP), the World Health Organization (WHO), and the Food and Agricultural Organization (FAO), are also supporting capacity building efforts aimed at strengthening local governments.[6]

The problem with the recent decentralization initiatives sponsored by African governments is that, like the ones before them, they fail to produce the expected outcomes, including greater citizen participation and empowerment, and local development. Yet, these reforms are often linked to the processes of democratization, and, therefore, are quite explicit about their overriding goal of empowering the people. In this chapter, I wish to suggest that one explanation for this problem is the failure of the new round of reforms to sufficiently differentiate between the key components of decentralization. This makes it easy for African political leaders to continue to use decentralization as a ploy to buy legitimacy for themselves and acquire aid support from international donor agencies, while they further concentrate more powers in central state initiatives. The rhetoric of decentralization is strong, but the reality of decentralization is hollow. The argument is not anti-central government, because the center has important roles to play in economic and social change. The problem is one in which the center continues to assume that it alone can promote social and economic development. A detailed case-study of Nigeria is provided below to illustrate the argument.

Objectives and Dimensions of Decentralization

One author has noted quite appropriately that "decentralisation is a slippery term."[7] The conventional manner in which it is defined is to distinguish *deconcentration*, or delegation to bureaucratic agencies, from *devolution*, or delegation to autonomous public or lay agencies outside the bureaucracy.[8] However, these distinctions are often not very helpful, especially when government authorities (especially in Africa) deliberately label what is evidently intended to be the reform of field administration institutions (which is often quite necessary and useful), as the reform or strengthening of local governments. The deliberative, or supposedly autonomous agency of the local authority, remains part and parcel of the state civil service with its budget, for example, largely being provided from central sources. Likewise, the "political" representatives are appointed, just as administrative officials, by the central government. Yet legally, at least, they possess the "attributes" of local government.

In order to analyze the concept and policies relating to decentralization, I have devised, with the help of the available literature on the subject, a fourfold typology of decentralization dimensions and expected outcomes (Table 2).

Political decentralization refers to the opening up of the political space to accommodate civil and political liberties, the existence of genuine institutional pluralism, and political competition through fair and free elections. It entails a movement away from a monocentric to a polycentric structure of political power. Political decentralization also incorporates the creation and/or strengthening of institutions for enhancing vertical and horizontal decentralization, or in fact, non-centralization. The latter would include institutions for promoting the separation of powers and the accountability of the executive for its actions and inactions to other public bodies, such as legislatures and the courts. Finallly, political decentralization refers to the creation and strengthening of institutions designed to promote vertical decentralization of power through local government structures. The objectives of political decentralization are greater citizen participation and higher levels of accountability of the political system to citizens, leading to positive governance norms such as institutional responsiveness and reduction in governmental corruption and waste.

Economic decentralization, on the other hand, refers to reduction of state dominance in the economic domain, the stimulation of economic pluralism through such initiatives as deregulation, privatization, and support of private sector and informal sector growth. The objectives of economic decentralization are higher rates of production, competitiveness, fiscal solvency, and economic diversification.

Administrative decentralization refers to the strengthening of field administrative units of the civil service operating in a country. It may also include efforts at capacity building at national and local levels.

Finally, financial decentralization refers, among other things, to the transfer of financial resources from the central government to autonomous local agencies. These resources may be transferred directly or through tax powers to enable the decentralized agencies to undertake responsibilities already transferred to them. This may also involve efforts at financial deregulation and deconcentration of financial institutions away from the major capitals, and the efforts at mobilizing credit from the informal sector, such as through the Grameen Bank of Bangladesh, the *tontines* of Cameroon, or the Community Banks of Nigeria.

Ideally, all of these forms of decentralization should accompany a genuine process of democratization. The reality, of course, is usually different. It is possible to have one without the other, but each of these possibilities has significant effects on the feasibility or non-feasibility of overall state decentralization. This is the theme I intend to pursue in the analysis that follows.

The thrust of my argument in this chapter is that state decentralization (Ds) has four major dimensions — political (Pd), economic (Ed), administrative (Ad), and fiscal (Fd). What this means is that for a successful effort at strengthening local government, there must be decentralization in all four areas, and particularly in the political and economic fields. In summary form, the argument can be explained as follows:

$$(1) \quad Ds = Pd + Ed + Ad + Fd$$
$$(2) \quad Ds = Pd + Ed$$
$$(3) \quad Ds = Ed + Fd$$
$$(4) \quad Ds \neq Pd + Ad$$
$$(5) \quad Ds \neq Pda$$
$$(6) \quad Ds = Pdb$$
$$(7) \quad Ds \neq Pd,Ed,Ad,Fd$$

Where: Ds = State Decentralization
      Pd = Political Decentralization
      Ed = Economic Decentralization
      Ad = Administrative Decentralization
      Fd = Financial Decentralization
      Pda = Political Decentralization from above
      Pdb = Political Decentralization from below
           = Positive value; $\neq$ Negative Value

(1) Decentralization is realizable ideally where it occurs on all four dimensions. This ideal is represented by most of the countries of the OECD (Organization for Economic Cooperation and Development), where the various dimensions of decentralization mutually reinforce one another.

(2) Nevertheless, even where there is only decentralization along the political and economic dimensions, the result will ultimately be substantial state decentralization as the political and economic forces, once liberated, force through institutional and fiscal decentralization, or neutralize centralization in those areas. The best European examples are France and the Netherlands, where there is considerable administrative and financial centralization, respectively. Botswana is a good African example.

(3) Where only economic and financial decentralization have taken place, it is possible to have effective state decentralization, even where there is no political and full administrative decentralization. The experience of most of the Asian tigers (Singapore, Korea, Taiwan, Hong Kong, Thailand, Indonesia, Malaysia) and Japan is of this variety. Their political systems, until recently, have remained centralized, but they enjoy relatively high levels of economic and financial decentralization.

(4) It is, however, difficult to have a situation in which financial and administrative decentralization occur without putting political and economic decentralization in place. Ad, Fd are the product of Pd, Ed. Even if it was possible to have financial and administrative decentralization, there would be little or no state decentralization because it is difficult, if not impossible, for administrative and financial decentralization to bring about political and economic decentralization. Most of the effort at local government reform in African countries is of this variety, as will be shown below.

(5) In the same manner, decentralization along only one of the dimensions cannot bring about real local autonomy. Perhaps the single exception is political decentralization. Although political decentralization in itself will not bring about state decentralization, it is an open question whether a thorough-going political decentralization program, one that is galvanized by pressure from below rather than concessions from above, can in turn decentralize the economy as well as administrative and financial systems. The experience of the former socialist states (and a few African countries including South Africa), is instructive in that the attainment of political democracy is leading to the successful achievement of institutional decentralization, although decentralization of the economy and public finance systems remains difficult.

In this case, $Pd = Ad, Fd; Pd + Ad + Fd = Ds$. However, in most African states, political decentralization is a concession from above, usually to satisfy donors or particular segments of the society (e.g., the military constituency of military rulers, elements in the ruling party, or traditional rulers). The ruling authorities decide the nature, pace, and dimensions of political decentralization with the result that this process cannot bring about any other form of decentralization, whether economic (because the political leadership tends to wield tremendous economic power and influence), institutional, or financial. This explains why the practice of multiparty politics and/or elections in several African countries has not led to institutional pluralism and strong local governments.

(6) Hence, we need to distinguish various forms of political decentralization, whether it is from above (Pda) or from below (Pdb). The implication is that:

(a)   Pda ≠ Ed, Ad, Fd ≠ Ds; and
(b)   Pdb = Ed, Ad, Fd = Ds.

When political decentralization is initiated from above by those who wield executive power, and without any substantial inputs from civil society, the impact on state decentralization, or any of its dimensions (economic, administrative or financial), is likely to be minimal. The reverse is likely to be the case if pressure for political decentralization is from below, and if civil society takes an active part in defining the elements of the reform.

(7) Since Pda may not bring about state decentralization, neither can any of the other forms bring it about on its own.

The efforts of the multilateral financial institutions to encourage or compel African countries into economic decentralization through structural adjustment programs (SAPs), is widely recognized as having failed.[9] This led to the articulation of "good governance" norms which can be equated with demands for some form of political decentralization. The experience to date indicates that donors and international financial institutions (IFIs) are likely to have impact where they have a leverage on the government concerned (i.e., where the government is heavily dependent on these organizations for financial support). Countries such as Zaire and Nigeria have shown that they can safely ignore these institutions, and even countries such as Kenya, Zambia, and Malawi are showing that they can manipulate donor pressure. Multiparty elections in any of these countries have not led to genuine empowerment of the masses at the grassroots.

In the case study below, it will become obvious that neither administrative nor financial decentralization, nor a combination of both, can bring about state decentralization in a milieu in which all the initiatives for political decentralization come from above (Pda).

Institutional/Fiscal Decentralization Without Political/Economic Decentralization: The Nigerian Case

Nigeria is Africa's most populous country and has considerable human and natural resources. A former British colony, Nigeria became independent in 1960 as Africa's only federally-governed nation in view of her large population (approximately 100 million today), geographical size (940 km^2), and diverse ethnic composition (estimates range from some 250 to 400 groups). Civil government was brought to an abrupt end by the military in January 1966, and they have virtually ruled the country ever since, although not without a promise to return the country to full civil or democratic governance. In fact, in 1979, the military handed over power to the civilians, but came back again after only four years. Perhaps the boldest and seemingly most genuine initiative to return the country to civilian authorities took place in 1975. After the country experimented with different types of local administrative systems, the military authorities embarked on an ambitious program of revitalizing the nation's local authorities as part of their five-point program of re-civilization or democratization. Local government reorganization or reform was part of the five-point program (the others included creation of states, creation of political parties, reform of the election machinery, and the launching of a constitution).[10] Local government reform was launched in 1976.

The major components of the 1976 reform were largely institutional and financial and can be summarized as follows:

- Creation of local government units on a uniform population criteria of 150,000-800,000 throughout the country, and with a uniform political/administrative structure (the councilor model).
- Local governments were to be democratically elected by the same electorate for other units of government in the federal system.
- Local government responsibilities were articulated and divided into mandatory and optional.
- Local government revenue sources were to comprise the traditional sources, such as rates, fees, and fines, but also annual transfers from the federal and state governments. Specifically, urban local governments were to develop property rates in several cities where they had not been developed.
- Senior personnel of local governments were to have similar conditions of service as those of the state government. Special training programs were mounted for local government senior management personnel in three of the nation's federal universities (Ife, Nsukka, and Zaria).

Virtually, all of these provisions were incorporated into the nation's 1979 and 1989 constitutions.

According to the authors of the 1976 reforms, the major objectives of local government must be to: (1) make appropriate services and development activities responsive to local representative bodies; (2) facilitate the exercise of democratic self-government close to the local levels of our society, and encourage initiative and leadership potential; (3) mobilize human and material resources through the involvement of members of the public in their local development; and (4) provide a two-way channel of communication between local communities and government (both state and federal).[11]

In the 1980s, further efforts were made to consolidate these reforms. The most important initiatives included direct payment of federal transfers to local governments rather than through the state governments; the progressive increase of the federation account allocation to local governments from 3 percent to 10 percent and subsequently to 15 percent and 20 percent; and the creation of many more local government councils to bring the total to 549. These local councils were later to become constituencies for the election of federal and state government representatives. Other measures included the change over from a weak to a strong mayoral system, with a separate council, to resemble the presidential structures at federal and state levels. Efforts were also made at increasing the capacity of local governments, and some economic decentralization initiatives were undertaken to mobilize financial resources from the rural sector. Banks were compelled to open rural branches, and new credit institutions such as the People's Bank and the Community Banks, were opened to mobilize credit from the informal sector.[12]

A lot has been written already about these reforms and the Federal Government of Nigeria has conducted official periodic reviews of the reform program.[13] It is difficult to dismiss the reforms as an outright failure. Local governments today dispose of a little over 20 percent of the nation's public expenditures, up from about 2 percent in 1975. This is a remarkable achievement when compared with other African and Third World countries (see Tables 3 and 4). They are responsible for important services, such as basic health care and primary education (which they pay for, but do not manage), roads and town planning, markets, and motor parks. The quality of the political and administrative leadership is quite high, and, in the few times when citizens voted for councilors, the level of community participation (measured by voter turnout) was comparable to that for elections for the highest political office at the national level.[14]

On the other hand, the local governments have neither become democratized nor are they sustainable without large inflows of federal transfers. For most of the period between 1976 to the present, both under military and civilian politicians, local governments were filled by appointments made by state government authorities. Throughout this 21-year period, local governments were run by elected officials for less than half of the period (1976-78; 1987-90; and 1991-92).

Moreover, the senior administrative and professional staff is managed by state-based local commissions throughout the country. When these commissions were abolished in 1992 and local governments were given a free hand to manage their own staff, this innovation lasted only six months before it was reversed by the national government out of fear that local government functionaries could abuse these powers. Many people believe that the heavy hand of the state, which brought about the uniform structure of local government, failed to make necessary concessions for cultural and economic diversity (e.g., between the urban and rural areas and between areas of strong non-governmental activity and those without).

Local governments are being managed largely by the state, rather than the citizens. Even though the federal government dissolved state ministries of local government because they were stumbling blocks to the progress of local government devolution, it created a ministry at the national level which required local governments to send their budgets to it before implementation. This ministry has now been transformed into a department in the office of the head of state at the federal level. The citizen has practically no input into how local governments are run. Most of the initiatives come from the center. Even when some reform efforts were made to enhance the autonomy of local governments beginning in 1988, they only made the local government chief executives (politicians) more unaccountable and irresponsible in the absence of effective institutions to hold these local officials accountable to the citizens. The local legislatures have been largely ineffective, and state governments' supervision of local governments has been virtually eliminated by the administrative and financial autonomy granted to the latter by the federal government.[15]

One of the reasons why it has been so easy for the national government to dominate the process is that there is no political decentralization — the military has been in power for 27 out of the nation's 37 years of independence. Another important reason, however, is the fact that most of the funding available to local governments comes from federal transfers. While this has enabled local governments to become important players in the intergovernmental arena, it has made them heavily and increasingly dependent on central government funding. A final reason, not unconnected with the first two, is that there are few civil society or non-state institutions that have focused on decentralization as a worthwhile objective — enough to subject the key issues affecting local government to critical scrutiny from the point of view of democratization. Most of the human rights groups (the only oppositional voice on the political spectrum) are focused exclusively on the national level for good reasons. Those few non-state actors which are interested in local government matters, tend to focus on their own narrow interests, e.g., the National Union of Local Government Employees (NULGE) or the traditional rulers. The status of Nigeria's local government reform can be summed up as follows:

- Local governments are highly dependent on federal and/or state governments for policy initiatives and program development.
- Local government capacity to generate its own revenue sources has been hampered as internally generated revenues have fallen in relative and absolute amounts. Several cities as yet do not rate property and most are still heavily dependent on the flat rate (paid only by those with incomes less than 600 naira) for their internal revenues.
- Local government accountability to the people has weakened. This is further aggravated by the fact that several local governments prefer not to tax the people so that few questions will be raised about public monies.
- Local government sustainability is endangered as the national economy is heavily dependent on oil resources (for up to 90 percent of public revenues) which are subject to the vagaries of the international economy.
- Local governments' ability to carry out developmental activities have been impaired as they have been overburdened with responsibilities such as primary education, which are assigned to them, but which they are not capable of financing from available sources, as well as other services which are given ad hoc by central agencies to local governments (for example, women's development, population, security, agriculture, and employment).

In addition, they have not been compelled to carry out reforms of their internal administrative organization because of the relative ease with which federal funds are available. Most of the councils pay a large proportion of their budgets as recurrent (personnel) costs, although some do not even have enough to cover such costs. The result is that there is very little left for development project expenditures.

In short, even though there has been a continuous drive toward institutional and financial decentralization for almost two decades, local governments have not been strengthened, and decentralization is far from being a reality. Local governments, like state governments, are heavily dependent on the federal government for cash, carriage, and initiatives.

In fact, the Nigerian state has become ever more centralized and the present military authorities have reversed the concessions earlier made toward political and economic decentralization. All the "democratic" structures created under the previous military regime (democratic local governments, elected state authorities, and national legislature) have been proscribed. Many independent mass media organizations have been shut down, and human rights and political pressure group leaders have been detained. Similarly, the economy has been brought under new controls, with, for example, privatized banks and enterprises being returned to the public sector. The result has been increased economic stagnation as a result of hyperinflation, capital flight, and low-capacity utilization. The country's health and educational institutions are also collapsing as professionals leave the country in the hordes. Yet, the regime claims to be committed to political decentralization and democratization, albeit on its own terms.

In Table 5, an attempt is made to assess the effectiveness of the Nigerian local government system on a seven-point scale. The system scores above average (3 to 5 on a maximum scale of 5) with respect to communication between governments and contribution to a more equitable distribution of basic services. On the other hand, it scores low (0 to 2) on such indices as: responsiveness and accountability of services; participation; development of leadership potential; resource mobilization; economic development; and administrative efficiency. While the local government system is widely perceived as incompetent for developmental initiatives, the community-based institutions are gaining respectability for their remarkable ability to promote a variety of developmental, social, and administrative activities.[16] In sum, there is very little state decentralization, even though there has been a continuous stream of reform activities in favor of stronger systems of local government over a period of about two decades, most importantly in the area of fiscal decentralization.

Conclusion

The central message of this chapter is fairly straightforward. The decentralization of the African state is desirable, if only because it will help reduce the present gulf and tension between state and social institutions. Also, the strengthening of local governments is a worthwhile strategy for bringing about state decentralization. Nevertheless, it is doubtful if local governments can be strengthened without a simultaneous attainment of decentralization on at least two important dimensions examined in this study: the political and the economic. Alternatively, if political decentralization was fueled from below, it alone has the possibility of bringing about economic, administrative, and fiscal decentralization. In addition, local government structures should be built on what already exists and is valuable to the people, rather than attempting to create new structures which are derived from state structures.

The case study reviewed in this chapter may perhaps not be representative of all African experiences, but it is instructive that after two decades of attempts to revitalize or strengthen local governments, the opposite results have occurred, with the state becoming more centralized, both politically and economically. Furthermore, the local government system is completely dissociated from local development organs, which have been carrying the burden of development in many communities across the continent.

The Nigerian experience compares negatively with the South African experience. Apartheid South Africa was also highly centralized. However, within a much shorter period of time, the country has made impressive strides in all the four dimensions of decentralization. The pressure for decentralization is as strong at the center as it is in the localities, particularly the urban centers of South Africa. It has overtaken earlier central initiatives and preference for concessionary reforms. The contrast between Nigeria and South Africa underscores the critical importance of political reforms and the democratic transition in bringing about the decentralization of administrative and financial structures out of which devolved governments can emerge.

Table 1. Non-Agricultural Sector Employment (%) By Level of Government and Region (1980 Data)

	OECD Industrial Countries	Developing Countries			
		Total sample of countries	Africa	Asia	Latin America
Central Government	34.9	58.7	65.5	43.3	65.0
State and Local Government	48.6	12.4	5.5	17.7	15.6
Non-Financial Public Enterprises	16.5	28.9	29.0	39.0	19.4
Total Public Sector Employment	100	100	100	100	100
No. of Countries in sample	14	18	10	4	4

Source: Heller and Tait, *Government Employment and Pay, Some International Comparisons,* Washington D.C, International Monetary Fund, 1983, p. 9.

Table 2. Dimensions and Goals of State Decentralization

POLITICAL DECENTRALI- ZATION	ECONOMIC DECENTRALI- ZATION	ADMINISTRATIVE DECENTRALI- ZATION	FISCAL DECENTRALI- ZATION
Emphasis	*Emphasis*	*Emphasis*	*Emphasis*
Political Rights	Reduction of State Dominance in the Economy	Delegation of Responsibilities to Field Agencies	Allocation of Responsibilities to Decentralized Agencies
Civil Liberties	Stimulation of Private Initiatives	Strengthening Field Agencies (Personnel, Authority)	Allocation of Resources to Decentralized Agencies
Institutional Pluralism (Multiparties, NGOs, Local Governments & CBOs)	Deregulation, Privatization, Credit Reforms	Reform of Administrative Organs/Capacity Building for Decentralized Organs	Financial Deregulation or Credit Mobilization
Pluralism In Policy Choices	Support for Informal Sector		Creation of IGR Agencies
Expected Outcome	*Expected Outcome*	*Expected Outcome*	*Expected Outcome*
Greater Citizen Participation	Higher Economic Productivity	Greater Administrative Efficiency	Revenue Adequacy
Higher Levels of Accountability	Economic Pluralism & Promotion of Competitiveness	Efficiency of Services Delivery	Sustainability
Institutional Responsiveness	Fiscal Solvency & Economic Diversification	Responsiveness	Allocative Efficiency
Political Integration	Reduction of Poverty and		Improved Budgets and
Reduction of Bureaucratic Corruption & Government Waste	Governmental Indebtedness		Program Delivery

Table 3. Share of Each Level of Government in Total Public Sector Expenditure for Selected Years, Nigeria 1955-1991 (in Percentages)

Year	Federal	State	Local
1955	44.1	43.0	13.0
1965	44.5	44.7	10.0
1976	57.3	40.7	2.0
1985	64.8	29.8	5.4
1991	67.6	23.1	9.3

Sources: Central Bank of Nigeria, Annual Statement of Accounts; D. Olowu, *The Nigerian Conception of Local Level Governance*, Ibadan, NISER, 1990.

Table 4. Importance of Local Government in Selected Countries

Countries	Local Government Expenditure as % of Public Spending (1988)
A. Industrialized/Rapidly Industrializing	
Japan	47
Denmark	45
Sweden	41
Korea	33
Poland	27
U.K	26
Netherlands	23
Switzerland	22
U.S.A	21
France	18
Germany	17
Canada	16
Belgium	12
B. Underdeveloped/African	
Zimbabwe	22
Algeria	14
South Africa	10
Brazil	8
Kenya	4
Pakistan	4
Ghana	2
Côte d'Ivoire	2

Sources: United Nations Development Programme, *Human Development Report 1993*, New York, Oxford University Press, 1993; D. Olowu, *African Local Governments as Instruments of Economic and Social Development*, The Hague, International Union of Local Authorities, 1988.

Table 5. An Appraisal of Nigerian Local Government Reforms, 1976-1995

Reform Goal	Score	Remarks
1. Responsiveness/Accountability of Services Administration	1	Basic health and education services devolved but not responsive to the public
2. Participation	0	Minimal involvement of the public in political administrative matters
3. Development of Leadership Potential	1	Political leaders appointed and changed at will by state/federal governments
4. Resource Mobilization for Economic Growth	1	LGs highly dependent
5. Communication between/with Governments	5	High intergovernmental communication
6. Equity in Basic Services	3	Reform encouraged regional equity up to 1981
7. Administrative Efficiency/ Funds or Discretion	2	LGs have more responsibility than they used to have but less resources

Source: Nigeria, *Guidelines for Local Government Reforms in Nigeria*, Kaduna, 1976.

Notes

[1] Opinions expressed here are those of the author, who is currently a Public Administration Officer in the United Nations Economic Commission for Africa, and do not represent those of UNECA.

[2] D. Rothchild and N. Chazan (eds.), *The Precarious Balance: State and Society in Africa* (Boulder: Westview Press, 1988).

[3] D.A. Rondinelli, J. R. Nellis and F. S. Cheema (eds.), *Decentralization in Developing Countries: A Review of Recent Experiences*, World Bank Staff Working Paper No. 581 (Washington: World Bank, 1994).

[4] D.C. Rowat, "Comparing Bureaucracies in Developed and Developing Countries: A Statistical Analysis," *International Review of Administrative Studies*, Vol. 56, No. 2, 1990, pp. 211-236.

[5] World Bank, *Strengthening Local Governments in Africa: Proceedings of Two Workshops*, Economic Development Institute Policy Seminar Report No. 21 (Washington: World Bank, 1989).

[6] See, for example, United Nations, *Senior Policy Seminar on Decentralization and Strengthening of Local Government in African Countries,* Banjul, Gambia July 27 to 31, 1992 (New York: Department of Economic and Social Development, DESD/ SEM. 93/1).

[7] Richard Bird, *Financing Local Services: Patterns, Problems and Possibilities,* Report No. 31 (Toronto: Centre for Urban and Community Studies, University of Toronto, 1995).

[8] See R.E. Wraith, *Local Administration in West Africa* (London: Allen and Unwin, 1972); and B.C. Smith, *Decentralization: The Territorial Dimension of the State* (London: Allen and Unwin, 1985).

[9] World Bank, *Continent in Transition: Sub-Saharan Africa in the Mid-1990s* (Washington: World Bank, 1994).

[10] See O.O. Oyelakin, "Local Governments in Nigeria and the Federal System," *Journal of Nigerian Federalism*, Vol. 1, No. 1, 1995.

[11] Federal Republic of Nigeria, *Guidelines for the Reform of Local Government* (Kaduna: Federal Government Printer, 1976).

[12] Alex Gboyega, "Local Government Reforms in Nigeria," in P. Mawhood (ed.), *Local Government in the Third World: The Experience of Tropical Africa* (Chichester: John Wiley, 1983), pp. 225-248; Oyelakin; A.M. Awotokun, *New Trends in Nigerian Local Government* (Ile-Ife: Obafemi Awolowo University Press, 1995).

[13] L. Adamolekun and L. Rowlands (eds.), *The New Local Government System in Nigeria: Problems and Prospects* (Ibadan: Heinemann, 1979); Alex Gboyega, "Decentralisation and Local Autonomy in Nigeria's Federal System: Crossing the Stream While Searching for the Pebbles," Research Report, Ibadan, 1994; L. Adamolekun, "The Idea of Local Government as a Third Tier of Government Revisited: Achievements, Problems and Prospects," *Quarterly Journal of Administration*, Vol. 18, Nos. 3 & 4, 1984, pp. 92-112; D. Olowu, "Achievements and Problems of Federal and State Transfers to Local Governments in Nigeria Since Independence," in L. Adamolekun, R. Robert and M. Laleye (eds.), *Decentralization Policies and Socio-Economic Development in Sub-Saharan Africa* (Washington: World Bank, 1990); Federal Republic of Nigeria, *White Paper on the Report of the Committee on Local Government Administrative System* (Lagos: Government Printer, 1985).

[14] D. Olowu, *The Nigerian Conception of Local Level Development* (Ibadan: Nigerian Institute of Social and Economic Research, 1990).

[15] Awotokun and Oyelakin.

[16] D. Olowu, B. Ayo and B. Akande, *Local Institutions and National Development in Nigeria* (Ile Ife: Obafemi Awolowo University Press, 1991); Gboyega, 1994; and D. Olowu and E.J. Erero, "Governance of Nigeria's Villages and Cities Through Indigenous Institutions," *African Review of Rural and Urban Management* (forthcoming).

13

Overdrawing the Nation: The National Question in The Political Theories of Ghanaian Constitutions[1]

Amos Anyimadu

In this study, the resources of the making of written constitutions in Ghana will be used as a basis for reading certain fundamental aspects of the relationship between and within state and society in Ghana. This will be done with particular reference to the intentional attempt to build a Ghanaian nation in an engineered manner through constitutional mechanisms. The nub of the presentation concerns an attempt to read the texts of Ghanaian constitutions "backwards:" a genetic, intentionalist explanation with a view mainly to deciphering the founders' intentions. The particular aspects of the discussion will provide a vantage point for a more general perspective on the notions of the intensity and lineaments of political communities and states in African studies. My axial concept would be the set of issues which many analysts have referred to as the concept of "the integral state."[2]

The concept of an integral state summarizes a lot of the early academic and nationalist impressions of state-led transformation of society. In simple terms, the concept refers to the degree of political integration deemed necessary and the extent to which multiple collective solidarities are deemed appropriate in a polity. The concept assumes a very high degree of integration and few bases of collective solidarity. It is a pleasant view in which social divisions, especially ethnic divisions, are underrated and, even then, seen as challenges to be overcome. The concept of the integral state was central to the practical drive for, and academic concern with, modernization, in its orthodox as well as neo-Marxist forms. Ghana can claim some internationally significant credit for the practical articulation of this view. Nkrumah's slogan "Seek ye first the political kingdom ..." was, above all, a brutal articulation of the ideal of the integral state. In the Ghanaian context, there have been attempts to restrict this kind of extreme nationalism to the Convention People's Party (CCP).[3] It may be more accurate to see it as a wider expression of practical Ghanaian political thought.[4] The concept is now invoked largely in a negative vein.[5]

Although constitutions do not fully reflect the reality of political systems, they are an important aspect of such systems. The perspective that a constitution exudes or refracts on the state is important for real and analytic purposes. It is useful to consider constitutions along two major dimensions. We may talk of rights provisions and structural provisions. Rights provisions can be construed as referring to "softer," cultural aspects of a constitution whereas structural provisions deal with "nuts and bolts" institutional issues. Rights provisions are usually designed to "fence off certain areas from majoritarian control" and structural provisions "are usually intended to minimize the pathologies associated with one or another concept of democracy."[6] The notion of constitutional culture is one which has been applied to the current, expanded wave of constitution-making.[7] It also reflects new approaches to the connection between culture and politics in political science which see the significance of culture in political affairs in more than instrumental terms.[8]

There is a long tradition of concern with the way in which structural aspects of constitutions affect ethnic diversity. Arguments on federalism have always had relevant hues and Arend Lijphart has very successfully promoted the idea of consociationalism. Constitutional cultures are also important for ethnic diversity. Disadvantaged ethnic groups, especially those which are permanent minorities in their polities, can either have their solidarities protected by rights guaranteed in a constitution, or the constitution can provide a basis for attacking the roots of their disadvantage. A focus on constitutional culture and the structural aspects of constitutions does not exhaust issues which are relevant to ethnicity in this context. However, it covers a fair ground, especially if emphasis is more on concepts than implementation.[9]

I shall deal with the substantive issue identified above under the headings of constitutional culture and structural aspects of constitutions. There is a close connection between the degree to which a constitution is influenced by the concept of the integral state and its usefulness in managing ethnic differences. A constitution which is suffused with the concept of the integral state is unlikely to take a general posture conducive to the protection of minority rights. It is also unlikely to provide for political structures which are intentionally designed to accommodate, rather than overcome, ethnic divisions.

The Integral State in Constitutional Cultures in Ghana

From the discussion above, we can consider various indications of constitutional cultures. The preamble to a constitution often provides a cryptic formulation of this. As noted above, the conception of rights in a constitution also provides a strong signal of its culture. What has become known in recent Ghanaian constitutions as the Directive Principles of State Policy, a charter which all constitutional agencies are to follow, provides elaborate texts for understanding the cultures of the constitutions they relate to.

The preamble to the draft 1979 Ghanaian constitution contained the most explicit advocation of an integral state. Its most important clause announced that Ghanaians were

> Anxious to establish institutions which will promote the maximum unity and stability of our country and the full exploitation of our resources for the benefit of all the people.

This clause reflected important aspects of the history of the production of that constitution. The effort began as an attempt to incorporate into the constitution General Kutu Acheampong's Union Government concept, which harped as much on the general need for unity and consensus in Ghanaian political life as on the particular union of the army, civilians, and the police, from which the name Union Government emerged. Although the preambles to the other Ghanaian constitutions were not so clear advocates of an integral state, the background discussions on which they were based, especially the opening debates on General Principles Underlying the Constitution in the Constituent Assemblies and their equivalent, bore marks of arguments for the integral state. The preamble of the 1969 constitution, for example, reflecting the strong abhorrence of Nkrumah's legacy, was exclusively concerned with the need to protect against dictatorship. However, as our discussion of other indicators would soon show, sentiments similar to those captured in the 1979 preamble underlay the 1969 constitution. It must also be noted that because preambles are couched in special prose, acknowledged experts among those involved in the production of constitutions have a big advantage in determining their content.

Directive Principles of State Policy have been a prominent feature of the last two Ghanaian constitutions. In the constitution-making project for the Second Republic, the idea of such a charter was explicitly rejected. In December 1966, the Akuffo Addo Constitutional Commission was persuaded, in a way that bears the full impress of its chairman, that "the future constitution of Ghana should take the form of a legal document rather than a 'Charter' to make it easy of legal interpretation and understanding by the ordinary citizen," although it

> agreed in principle that whilst the Constitution should take the form of a strictly legal document as short and as concise as possible to meet Ghana's special circumstances, this consideration should not preclude the inclusion in the Preamble to the Constitution of reference to certain general directive principles and sentiments. Where a constitution is profuse with a declaration of directive principles, there was always the danger of judges finding difficulty in interpreting it.[10]

Nonetheless, a valiant but unsuccessful attempt was made in the Constituent Assembly to include such a charter.[11] In seconding the motion which sought to achieve the objective, Dr. Susana de Graft-Johnson, who emerged as the major force behind the attempt, cited the need to "equalize economic conditions for all regions and sections of the community," an intonation of an integral state, as one of the prime objectives to be enshrined.

In contrast to the difficulties in 1969, the introduction of Directive Principles in the Constitution of the Third Republic was easy. The principle was accepted in the expanded Constitutional Commission without debate.[12] The recommendation of the Constitutional Commission was enthusiastically carried by the Constituent Assembly.[13] The Constitution ordained that:

> The Government shall actively encourage national integration. It shall take all appropriate steps (a) to foster a feeling of belonging and of involvement among the various peoples of Ghana to the end that loyalty to Ghana shall override sectional, ethnic or other loyalties.

The 1992 constitution of the Fourth Republic expanded the Directive Principles, although the drafters of the constitution made it clear that the principles were not justiciable.[14] This was in contrast to the enthusiasm of the 1979 Constituent Assembly which passed a motion that sought to make the chapter on Directive Principles in the 1979 constitution justiciable. This motion had been moved as a counter to a motion by a senior judge who had sought to make it clear that the Directive Principles were not to be justiciable "because only political courts could interpret them ... courts should not be drawn into the political arena."[15] Also, in 1992, the extent to which the Directive Principles enunciated the idea of an integral state was somewhat watered down. Although national integration is still maintained as a dominant objective, there is a more sympathetic treatment of other bases of collective solidarity. For instance, a new clause enjoins the state to "achieve reasonable regional and gender balance in recruitment and appointment to public offices."[16]

All in all, that Ghana's constitutions have taken on a charter character, that they have become increasingly more detailed guides to public action as opposed to mere loose frameworks for the structure of core governmental machinery, has had, in the first place, important rhetorical effects which have strengthened the pursuit of an integral state and made the anti-political nature of official intentional development a little more manifest. The most obvious factor is the ordination of national development planning. Now, it can be argued that such planning need not be centralizing. However, in spite of the advocation of decentralized planning during the making of the last two constitutions and by the governments that have been established under them, the development plans produced so far have, in my view, been centralizing.[17]

As noted above, there is likely to be an inverse relationship between the degree of advocacy of an integral state and the security of minority rights in a constitution. The preceding paragraph can in fact be seen as a discussion of rights insofar as the Directive Principles of State Policy are principally about economic and social rights, which have become known as second generation rights. Minority rights cover what some analysts now call third generation rights.[18] The issue that has come to distinguish this category is the idea that, if minorities are going to be well protected and/or to enjoy suitable affirmative action — for instance if states accept multiculturalism rather than attempt to steamroll a "national culture"— there is a need for the protection of group as well as individual rights.[19] For what I consider misleading reasons, Africa has become well associated with this idea.[20] Our concern with the conception of rights in Ghanaian constitutions would be based on the idea that to be effective in ethnic management, rights provided for in a constitution must be able to support group rights, at least on the basis of enlightened judicial interpretation.

Perhaps the most seminal public policy in Ghana concerning the conception of rights and the management of ethnic differences is the Avoidance of Discrimination Act of December 1957. This law invoked the Universal Declaration of Human Rights in the unlikely case of banning organized political action "substantially for the direct or indirect benefit or advancement of the interests of any particular community or religious faith." In spite of changes in the Ghanaian political situation, this law remains the fundamental norm for postures toward political representation in Ghana. Thus, the Ghana Bar Association, which we must consider one of the bastions of liberal thought in Ghana, positively invoked this law in the context of the politics of the making of the present constitution.[21] Also, the Christian Council of Ghana, whose political positions at the time of the making of the Avoidance of Discrimination Act were critical of it,[22] similarly positively invoked the Act in its contribution to recent constitutional debates.[23]

There can be little doubt, however, as the 1968 Constitutional Commission pointed out, that the real aim of the Avoidance of Discrimination Act was "solely to stifle opposition to the then Government."[24] The law had been presaged by a resolution of the congress of the CPP — the governing party — soon after independence, "to ask the government to ban parties based on tribal or religious allegiances."[25] Positively, we now know that the invocation of the Universal Declaration of Human Rights was merely opportunistic. When the Act was discussed in the cabinet, it originally went under the more informative label of "Prohibition of organisations, parties or societies restricted to tribal, racial or religious groups" and it had the more accurate short title of "The

Political Parties (Restrictions) Act." The opportunistic symbolism of the presentation of the Act as an instrument for human rights protection can be seen from the following explanation of the name change recorded in the paper the relevant minister presented to the cabinet:

> it is proposed that the short title which my colleagues earlier agreed should be "The Political Parties (Restrictions) Act" should be changed to "The Avoidance of Discrimination Act." It is considered that the latter title is more consistent with the principles of the Universal Declaration on Human Rights ...[26]

The genetic explanation given above should not belittle the fact that perhaps the most important concern of Ghanaian public policy with group rights has been to restrict them. It is true that there has been a tremendous improvement in the conception of rights in Ghana's constitutions. However, overall, progress has mainly been in the field of first generation rights. The 1969 Constitution put these rights center stage. The chapter on rights was entitled simply "Liberty of the Individual." It is true, and it will soon be outlined, that the 1979 and 1992 Ghanaian constitutions have sought to give some prominence to economic and social rights. However, I shall imply that in spite of the rhetorical significance of these rights, in the founders' intentions, and even more so in the ways in which the constitutions are likely to be construed in politically effective ways, this regime of rights must be considered to be of an inferior sort in Ghanaian constitutional thought.

In the draft constitution produced by the 1969 Constitutional Commission, the only itemized right which could be construed as a group right was that which offered "Protection of Freedom from Discrimination," but the commissioners indicated that they did not expect that it would be used as a major basis for protecting ethnic minorities, for, as they joyfully indicated, "in Ghana tribalism has never been a danger in politics."[27] At the Constituent Assembly stage, a right which sought to protect the welfare of the family was added. This was meant to mainly cover children within the context of intestate succession and not as a microcosm of group rights as some modern human rights instruments try to achieve. The only difference in the scheme of rights in the 1979 Constitution was a small change in this article, with the provision of separate articles for the protection of the rights of women and children. The present constitution, crafted with a number of world-class experts on rights, and within the context of the interpenetration of humdrum diplomacy and high domestic politics in the good, if not necessarily free, government/governance push, has a very elaborate scheme of "fundamental human rights and freedoms." However, as in 1979, most of the changes are accounted for by the expansion of second generation rights. A provision for "cultural rights and practises" may butt into group minority rights, but it is qualified in the constitutional text as well as its background.[28]

The Integral State and Structural Aspects of Ghanaian Constitutions: Devolution of Administrative Responsibilities to the Regions

As noted above, the spatial organization of the state is of critical importance to the concept of the integral state. Political structures concerning the geographical distribution of power were, as is well known, inestimably central in constitutional debates surrounding independence in Ghana. However, it would seem that a firm settlement has been reached, at least within practical political thought, in Ghana for what the 1960 Republican constitution proudly called a "sovereign unitary republic." Even in the making of the constitution of the Second Republic, the idea of federalism, or indeed anything close to it, was not given much of a hearing.

The submissions that were made to the Constitutional Commission for the Second Republic were overwhelmingly in support of a unitary state. Even in Asante, a series of coordinated memoranda from various chiefs and traditional bodies supported this position.[29] Ironically, Baafour Osei Akoto of the National Liberation Movement settled for deconcentration, although he called it devolution:

> It was our experience during the last regime that certain administrative matters which were formerly dealt with at the local or regional level were gradually concentrated in the Ministaries (sic) at the seat of Government. This policy led to unnecessary delays in the handling of matters ... When policies ... have been established by the Central Government, there is no reason why their implementation should not be entrusted to the appropriate officials in the Regions.[30]

The Constitutional Commission agreed with these centralizing ideas. For instance, it excoriated Arthur Lewis's consociational ideas.[31] It, however, tried to attenuate the centralizing impulse of the submissions made to it by trying to boldly "rationalize" chieftaincy by integrating it fully into the official local government system.[32] This attempt was defeated at the Constituent Assembly stage. All clauses in the draft constitution which sought to make the boundaries of local councils usually coterminous with those of traditional councils were rejected. In place of the integration of traditional and local councils, a National House of Chiefs was created as the main forum for chiefs. Without secure political control of their localities, the new chiefs' national forum could not but be, as the National House of Chiefs has become, a tempting symbolic resource for an attempt at galvanizing an integral state by ideationally challenged national regimes. In effect, the 1969 Constitution enunciated a highly geographically centralized political structure.[33]

The treatment of local government in succeeding constitution-making projects in Ghana has not been very different. Reflecting on the 1978-1979 process, in which he had taken a prominent part with a view to influencing the 1992 exercise, the late Professor Folson stated:

> The 1979 attempt at making the Third Republican Constitution development oriented was vitiated by one defect. So traumatised were all by the Acheampong experience that our gaze was firmly fixed on the central institution of government, in trying to make the constitution development oriented we paid scarce attention to local/district level institutions ... In this the constitution did not go beyond the 1969 constitution, it even distracted somewhat from the 1971 Local Administration Act.[34]

It suffices to say, with the benefit of hindsight, that the 1992 Constitution did not considerably enhance the legal decentralization of government in Ghana.[35] Today, the president almost exclusively determines the creation of new districts and he is the biggest influence in the appointment of political heads of all districts in the country. Although the operation of the district assemblies is the subject of much official hype and propaganda, any careful evaluation would show that "the district assembly concept" has not yet been translated into reality.[36]

The connection between the distribution of powers within the central political institutions and the integral state is less obvious. It would appear that a parliamentary as well as a presidential system can be pressed into the service of the idea of the integral state. In Ghana, there has been an obvious trend toward presidentialism. In 1979, as well as 1992, we ended up with an American-style presidency. In 1969, the Constitutional Commission recommended what, in my judgment, amounted to a French Fifth Republic style "split executive" or semi-presidential system.

In spite of the difficulty of making a general link between presidentialism and the propensity toward an integral state, it can be said that in Ghana the trend has been clearly underpinned by such a linkage. The explanation of a change to the executive presidency in Ghana in the memorandum of the Constitutional Commission in 1979 centered on the protection of personal liberties through the operation of the separation of powers. This did not accurately reflect the balance of opinion in the deliberations of the Commission. The need to provide strong leadership at the political center was almost as important, and certainly the more important factor before the Commission was expanded following the overthrow of Acheampong. Thus, before the expansion of the Commission, B.S.K. Kwakye, who was to become the head of the National Police, supported the executive presidential system because, according to him, "by our traditions and set up," if the polity was to be stable, there was a need for a "benevolent dictator ... somebody who must be a man who can command the country and not be commanded." In a similar vein, Mumuni Bawumia, now Chairman of the Council of State, stated, "the President could be dictatorial. We want somebody who will be very firm."[37]

In the Constituent Assembly in 1979, the two strands of argument were often combined. However, the argument that an executive president would be a more effective "father" of the nation was very strong. It was felt, as one of the most articulate advocates put it, that "the Presidential system is bound to do away completely with tribal politics because the President belongs to the whole country."[38]

Discussion of the question of the executive in the process leading to the present constitution was somewhat diverted by the instruction of the constitution drafting committee to provide for a French-style split executive. I have argued elsewhere that this proposal was not well thought through.[39] Its defenders argued that the split executive could combine the advantages of the presidential as well as parliamentary systems.[40] The extreme centralization of the French political system was not a big issue in the debate surrounding the proposal. The Consultative Assembly voted against the proposal because many of the district assembly representatives in it projected the difficulties in the relationship between the district secretaries and the presiding members, or chairpersons of the district assemblies. In any case, the presidency in Ghana today is very imperial: seemingly arbitrating above politics; "granting audience" to the deserving; and lining up chiefs for "educational rallies."

Conclusion

All in all, it must be clear that the concept of the integral state is firmly ingrained in Ghanaian constitutions. It is detectable in the institutions they provide for, as well as in the thought they exude. One direct implication of this is that the extreme centralization of governmental operations in Ghana, which several analysts and official commissions have bemoaned, is not simply pathological. Real decentralization would obviously help healthy interethnic relations in Ghana, but it has to confront a deep system of thought. It would appear that Ghanaians have consistently overdrawn their nation to important consequences.

From a more general perspective, we may say that the constitutions have been no more than aspirational poems. We may contend that the integral state is an ideational mirage which contributes to the marginalization of the state in action, especially through the "exit" of its supposed citizens. We may mistake an amoral familism for "civil society" and celebrate that grand, oblique concept as a critique of the state. I have been arguing, in a more particular way, that we must be cautious on these popular points.

Moreover, we must reckon the impact of new "decentered" perspectives which attack over-patterned views of the relationship between states and societies.[41] The impact of these views on, for example, Albert Hirschman's concept of "exit" as one modal form of response to dissatisfaction in organizations, which has been very influential in the analysis of state-society relationships in Africa, can be devastating. In this particular example, these decentered views lend conceptual support to the concept of "neglect," which has been noted to be an important omission from Hirschman's seminal framework of exit, voice, and loyalty.[42] Agents can become entrapped in organizations without good access to loyalty, voice, or exit. They can be simply "neglected" and yet remain organizationally outflanked and constrained to cooperate in important domains of social existence. Many states are able to organize such entrapment. If this is so, then states would seem much more resilient than the contemporary celebration of civil society suggests. The ideological representations of their strategies of entrapment deserve attention. Constitutions, as an important part of the formal aspects of the institutional basis of states, deserve recognition as significant resources for political understanding.

Notes

[1] A version of this paper was presented to the Centre of African Studies, University of Edinburgh's Conference on "Ethnicity in Africa: Roots, Meanings and Implications." I am grateful to all who commented on the paper then, especially Terence O. Ranger and Carola Lentz. The paper has also benefited from the help of Gareth M. Austin, F.K. Drah and E.V.O. Dankwa. I am further grateful to the staff of Balme Library, Legon, especially those on the CD-ROM for Development project.

[2] For perspectives on the concept of the integral state, see Crawford Young, "In Search of Civil Society," in John W. Harbeson, Donald Rothchild and Gnome Casein *(eds.)*, *Civil Society and the State in Africa* (Boulder: Lynne Rienner Publishers, 1994), pp. 33-50; Crawford Young, "Zaire: The Shattered Illusion of the Integral State," *The Journal of Modern African Studies*, Vol. 32, No. 2, 1994, pp. 247-263; and Jean-Francois Bayart, *The State in Africa: The Politics of the Belly* (London: Longman, 1993), Chapters 7 and 9. Both authors invoke the work of Christian Coulon.

[3] See, for example, Kwame Ninsin, "The Nkrumah Government and the Opposition on the Nation State: Unity versus Fragmentation," in K. Arhin *(ed.)*, *The Life and Work of Kwame Nkrumah* (Accra: Sedco, 1991).

[4] R. Rathbone, "Politics of Hope," in J. Mayall and A. Payne *(eds.)*, *Fallacies of Hope* (Manchester: Manchester University Press, 1991).

[5] Perhaps most stridently is the recent reflective work on Basil Davidson. See, for

example, Mahmood Mamdani's review of Basil Davidson, *Black Man's Burden: Africa and the Curse of the Nation-State* (New York: Times Books, 1992), "Book Review: Africa and the Curse of the Nation-State," *Monthly Review,* Vol. 45, No. 3, 1993. It is noteworthy that Davidson first used his arresting notion of "Black Man's Burden" in relation to Ghana. See Basil Davidson, *Black Star. A View of the Life and Times of Kwame Nkrumah* (London: Allen Lane, 1973), pp. 97-102. For a broader perspective of Mamdani's views on the set of issues summarized under the integral state rubric see M. Mamdani, "Pluralism and the Right of Association," in M. Mamdani & J. Oloka-Onyango *(eds.), Uganda: Studies in Living Conditions, Popular Movements and Constitutionalism* (Vienna: JEP Book Series, 1994).

[6] Cass Sunstein, "Constitutions and Democracies: an Epilogue," in Jon Elster and Rune Slagstad *(eds.), Constitutionalism and Democracy* (Cambridge: Cambridge University Pres: 1988), p. 327.

[7] R. Teitel, "Post-Communist Constitutionalism: A Transitional Perspective," *Columbia Human Rights Law Review,* Vol. 26, No. 1, 1994, especially pp. 168-169; and Ben Nwabueze "Legal and Institutional Mechanisms for Democratic Transition", in B. Caron, A. Gboyega and E. Osaghae *(eds.), Democratic Transition in Africa* (Ibadan: CREDU Documents in Social Sciences and Humanities, 1992).

[8] John Street, "Review Article: Political Culture — From Civic Culture to Mass Culture," *British Journal of Political Science,* Vol. 24, 1993, p. 103; and, more generally, but in a Ghanaian context, T.C. McCaskie, *State and Society in Pre-colonial Asante* (Cambridge: Cambridge University Press, 1995), Chapter 1.

[9] For a comprehensive outline of the range of possible public mediated action, see Edmond J. Keller, "The State, Public Policy and the Mediation of Ethnic Conflict in Africa," in D. Rothchild and V. Olorunsola *(eds.), State versus Ethnic Claims: African Policy Dilemmas* (Boulder: Westview Press, 1983). For a rounded case study see J.A.A. Ayoade, "Ethnic Management in the 1979 Nigerian Constitution," *Canadian Review of Studies in Nationalism,* Vol. 14, 1987.

[10] National Archives of Ghana (Records of Ghana Project), Accra, NLC/CC6, *Minutes of the Second Plenary Meeting of the Constitutional Commission, 28/12/1966.*

[11] *Proceedings of the Constituent Assembly. Official Report,* col. 2762-2775; col. 3214-3229.

[12] *Proceedings of the Constitutional Commission,* 33rd Meeting, 15 September, 1978, p. 21. Mimeo graphed copies of the Proceedings are in the Law Library, University of Ghana.

[13] This was obvious from the initial debates on the General Principles of the Constitution. Although certain predictable patterns could be discerned on the patterns of support on this issue — the representatives of labor and students were very much in support — there was considerable across the board support. Even Professor K. G. Folson, who had written the paper which formed the basis of the 1968 Constitutional Commission's decision against Directive Principles, in his long contribution to the debate in the 1979 Constituent Assembly, strongly supported the idea of clear Directive Principles. See *Proceedings of the Constituent Assembly. Official Report,* 15 January 1979, col. 218-230.

[14] Republic of Ghana, *Report of the Committee of Experts (Constitution) on the Proposals for a Draft Constitution of Ghana,* 1991, p. 49. However, some of the Directive Principles which were deemed very important are repeated in the Chapter on rights where they are "more precisely elaborated as rights" and, therefore, perhaps deemed justiciable *(Ibid,* p. 65).

[15] *Daily Graphic,* February 3, 1978, p. 3. In spite of the outcome of the debate in the Constituent Assembly, the text of the constitution did not say that the Directive Principles were justiciable. Legal opinion in Ghana tended to the view that they were indeed not. This is not surprising in view of the dominance of a statutory approach to interpretation in Ghana. The episode is one example of the way in which expertise, supposedly in draftsmanship, in many instances subverted democratic decisions in the process of producing constitutions in Ghana. For an example of a heated discussion of such subversion on the floor of a Ghanaian Constituent Assembly, see Republic of Ghana, *Proceedings of the Constituent Assembly. Official Report,* 30 April 1968, col. 1555-1558.

[16] *Constitution of the Republic of Ghana,* 1992, Article 35 (b).

[17] The Limann government, the only government constituted under the constitution of the Third Republic, in delayed compliance with a constitutional requirement, submitted a Development Plan to Parliament, but it was not passed before the overthrow of the Third Republic. The plan is available in the National Archives of Ghana, (Records of Ghana Project), Accra, RG6/7/30 and also through the International Labour Office's LABOURDOC document delivery system. In his 1995 annual address to Parliament, President Rawlings introduced a new Development Plan, *Ghana Vision 20/20,* which, in keeping with the symbolic unpopularity of development planning in the present condition, is not officially called a development plan.

[18] For example, George Shepherd, Jr., "Global Majority Rights: The African Context," *Africa Today,* 1st/2nd Quarters, 1987, p. 13.

[19] Nigel S. Rodley, "Conceptual Problems in the Protection of Minorities: International Legal Developments," *Human Rights Quarterly,* Vol. 17, 1995, pp. 48-71.

[20] The association is linked to two main factors. First, the presence of the notion of people's rights in the Banjul Charter — see J.K.N. Blay, "Changing African Perspectives on the Right of Self-Determination in the Wake of the Banjul Charter on Human and People's Rights," *Journal of African Law,* Vol. 29, No. 2, 1985, pp. 147-159; and Etienne Mbaya, "Relations Between Individual and Collective Human Rights: The Problem of Rights of People," *Law and State* (Tubingen), Vol. 46, 1992, pp. 7-23. Second, the idea that African traditional values emphasize the group and consensus — see, for example, Kwasi Wiredu, "An Akan Perspective on Human Rights," in A.A. An-Naim and F.M. Deng *(eds.), Human Rights in Africa: Cross-Cultural Perspectives* (Washington: Brookings Institution, 1990), especially pp. 250-252. But see also "Moral Foundations of an African Culture," in K. Wiredu and K. Gyekye *(eds.), Person and Community: Ghanaian Philosophical Studies, I,* CIPSH/UNESCO, 1992, especially pp. 200-202.

[21] Ghana Bar Association, *Comment of the Ghana Bar Association on the Report of the Committee of Experts (Constitution) on Proposals for a Draft Constitution of Ghana,* The Association, 1991, p. 30.

[22] James Anquandah, *Together we Sow and Reap - the First Fifty Years of the Christian Council of Ghana* (Accra: Asempa Publishers, 1979), Chapter 6.

[23] Christian Council of Ghana, *Christian Council's Response to Ghana's Search for a Democratic System: Memorandum from Heads of Churches to the Government,* The Council, 1990, pp. 13-14.

[24] Republic of Ghana, *Memorandum on the Proposals for a Constitution for Ghana,* 1968, p. 69.

[25] Jean Marie Allman, *The Quills of the Porcupine: Asante Nationalism in an Emergent Ghana* (Madison: University of Wisconsin Press, 1993), p. 186.

[26] "Memorandum from Minister of Interior," Cabinet Agenda for Cabinet Meeting of 5/11/57, National Archives of Ghana, Accra, ADM .13/2/42.

[27] *Ibid.*

[28] Article 26 (1) "Every person is entitled to enjoy, practise, profess, maintain and promote any culture, language, tradition or religion subject to the provisions of this Constitution." In the experts' memorandum this right is significantly further restricted in relation to 'the national interest'." Republic of Ghana, *Report of the Committee of Experts (Constitution) on the Proposals for a Draft Constitution of Ghana,* 1991, p. 82.

[29] The chain of memoranda originated from the Joint Houses of Chiefs, signed by the Asantehene. National Archives of Ghana (Records of Ghana Project), Accra, NLC/CC/32, Memoranda from Ashanti Region.

[30] National Archives of Ghana (Records of Ghana Project), Accra, NLC/CC/32, Memoranda from Ashanti Region. Baafour Akoto's demand for local political control appears to continue to go down. In his interesting autobiography, he argues that the PNDC decentralization program is a vindication of his Federalist agitation. See *Struggle Against Dictatorship: Autobiography of Baafour Osei Akoto* (Adum, Ghana, 1992), p. 96. Joe Appiah makes a similar point in his autobiography.

[31] National Archives of Ghana, (Records of Ghana Project), Accra, NLC/CC6, *Minutes of the Fifth Plenary Meeting of the Constitutional Commission,* 01/06/1967 and *Minutes of the Sixth Plenary Meeting of the Constitutional Commission,* 02/06/1967.

[32] Republic of Ghana, *Memorandum on the Proposals for a Constitution for Ghana,* 1968, Chapter 22.

[33] Many writers have criticized the Local Administration Act of 1971, which the Busia government passed to give full effect to the 1969 Constitution's provisions on Local Government, for being too centralized and perhaps unconstitutional. See David Harris, "Central Power and Local Reform: Ghana During the 1970s" in P. Mawhood *(ed.),* *Local Government in the Third World* (New York: John Wiley, 1983); and J. Ayee, *An Anatomy of Public Policy Implementation: The Case of Decentralization Policies in Ghana* (Aldershot, UK: Avebury, 1994), p. 83 ff. However, many of the controversial aspects of that law, especially the role of the central government in appointing the heads of local government, was permitted by the letter of the constitution. From what has been argued above, it would appear to be legitimate in terms of the spirit of the constitution as well.

[34] K.G. Folson, "The Constitution and Development." *People's Daily Graphic,* 25 January 1992, p. 7.

[35] Compare PNDC Law 207 and the new Local Government Law, Act 462.

[36] See the guarded evaluation in World Bank, *Ghana 2000 and Beyond: Setting the Stage for Accelerated Growth and Poverty Reduction,* Africa Regional Office, The World Bank 1993, Chapter 7.

[37] *Proceedings of the Constitutional Commission,* 1978, 23 August 1978, p. 21, p. 63.

[38] M. Atadika, "The Cornerstone of the Constitution: The Executive President" *Daily Graphic,* February 9, 1979, p. 5. Mr. Atadika was a member of the Constituent Assembly.

[39] "A Pessimistic View of the Split Executive Proposed for Ghana's Fourth Republic," in F.K. Drah, and K. Ninsin *(eds.),* *Ghana's Transition to Constitutional Rule* (Accra: Ghana Universities Press, 1991).

[40] See, for example, Maxwell Owusu, "Constitutional Choices: A Dual Executive," *West Africa,* October, 1991, pp. 14-21.

[41] For a recent, critical overview see Charles Tilly, "To Explain Political Processes," *American Journal of Sociology,* Vol. 100, No. 6, 1995, pp. 1594-1610.

[42] See Albert Hirschman, "Exit, Voice, and the State," *World Politics,* Vol. 31, 1978, pp. 90-107, for a more political application of his well known framework. The notion of neglect has been developed largely in the context of social psychology. See M. Withey, and W.H. Cooper, "Predicting Exit, Voice, Loyalty and Neglect," *Administrative Science Quarterly,* Vol. 34, No. 4, 1989, pp. 521-539.

14

Governability in Portuguese-Speaking African Countries: A Real or a False Concern?[1]

Carlos Lopes

Pessimistic views are increasingly being expressed about governability in Africa. In the specific case of the African countries whose official language is Portuguese, this debate is clearly related to the crises in these states and their recent transitions to parliamentary democracy. Thus, the parameter to be analyzed appears to be that of the structure of the state. What, then, are the issues relating to the structure of democratic states in Africa? Immediate prominence needs to be given to four issues: (1) the applicability of the concept of liberal democracy in the African context; (2) the erosion of the role of the state; (3) the international context and the debate about nationalism ; and (4) the capacity to construct an alternative development model. A brief analysis of these parameters will be presented, followed by relevant theoretical and methodological issues.

Liberal Democracy in the African Context

The current debate about governability in Africa is a manifestation of not only the crisis of the state, but also of the crisis of democracy and concepts of development. The growing international pressure regarding human rights and the single-party system coincided, from the mid-1980s, with the evolution of unsustainable internal contradictions resulting from the application of economic programs that were increasingly disastrous for the vast majority of Africans.

A holistic analysis of the problem would lead to the conclusion that the external struggle (against international pressures) and the internal struggle (against population pressures) differ in scope. Nevertheless, common denominators between the two can be found.

Just as during the struggle for liberation the aim of attaining independence united various interest groups within the country, in this second transition, a union of forces has also taken place. Specifically, during this second transition, it appears that those who were in the middle had the fundamental role of interpreting what needed to be done to save the situation. It became clear that the only solution to the problem was to embark on a political transformation capable of recognizing the reality of the 1990s. As always happens in nation-building, the recourse was to adopt simplistic imitations of models and concepts.

During the transition of the 1990s, such models and concepts were mostly juridical, with strong political and economic overtones. Fortunately, countries held elections, and policies were implemented that resulted in the separation of the powers between the legislative and executive branches of government. Also, autarky was implemented, and parliamentary factions and other representative groups were formed in the image of what exists in the liberal democracies, commonly referred to as the Western countries. The new constitutions that have been adopted are serving as a backdrop for the settlement of institutional conflicts in Sao Tome and Principe and Cape Verde, while in Guinea-Bissau and Mozambique, the recent electoral processes are backed by promises of support from the international community.

Without engaging in polemics about the merits these processes undeniably possess, it is more important to draw attention to the need to review the experience of the democratic transition in Africa. Following such an exercise, it is not difficult to recognize that, under the cover of the liberal democratic model, the pressure imposed on countries to implement changes has differed. Such differences have depended on the countries concerned and the interests involved. Thus, Gabon has been different from Kenya, Zaire from Togo, and Angola and Mozambique from South Africa. The reason for these differences lies, according to many, in the nature of the international pressures much more than in the identity of the political forces involved. In this context, Angola appears to offer the most obvious instance of excessive interventionism. Such interventionism tends to be greater the richer the country is, but perhaps more importantly, the more disorganized its internal forces are in terms of constructing their own models for change.

The main features of Western democracies, alternation and legitimacy of representation, are today seriously in question as a result of historical experience. While there are exceptions, the predominant trend is towards: (1) a narrowing of the distinctions between the economic models proposed by various schools of thought in the Western countries; and (2) an increasing decline in voter turnout, particularly in the United States, Japan, and Switzerland, where it has reached around 30 per cent.[2]

This usurpation of political representativeness has extremely serious consequences. It permits the voters to legislate the exclusion of others, and they exhibit an increasing lack of restraint in doing so. In the specific case of the Portuguese-speaking African countries, clearly the syndrome is still far from attaining such proportions, but the importance of democracy accordingly appears to lie in the elections and not in the rest of the liberal model, a situation which to some may appear paradoxical.

The Erosion of the State

A logical explanation for the imitations of the liberal model is readily to be found in the erosion of the state. Although the phenomenon is not confined to the Portuguese-speaking African counties, or to Africa in general, the situation is taking on disturbing contours in the former.

The basic principles of state authority exhibit a marked international dependence. Where state revenues are concerned, the International Monetary Fund (IMF) and the World Bank are dictating tax policies in Sao Tome and Principe, Guinea-Bissau, and Mozambique. The temporary halting of assistance to Tanzania until the minister in charge of tax revenues was replaced, is a clear warning sign of the new aid conditionality.

In the military sphere, the establishment of national armies in Angola and Mozambique is governed by international agreements. In education, it is international organizations or foreign agencies that are taking the lead in drawing up programs and textbooks. They are also financing operations under programs to remedy the deterioration of social services caused by structural adjustment programs.

Lastly, the external debt of the Portuguese-speaking African countries, including most recently Cape Verde, places these countries in a vulnerable situation in any economic negotiations, because of the current parameters of macro structural equilibrium, which readily leads to a guarantee of dependence. Thus, the state in the Portuguese-speaking African countries is incapable of ensuring its economic survival without massive external intervention in the cases of Sao Tome and Principe, Guinea-Bissau, and Mozambique, without remittances from emigrants in the case of Cape Verde, and without an urgent rescheduling of the debt in Angola.

This erosion of the state makes it an increasingly less important factor for the population, while the threats to its political role are on the increase with the appearance of new actors on the scene of the transition to democracy.

The International Context and Nationalism

The end of the cold war and the Soviet model had a considerable impact on the Portuguese-speaking African countries owing to the historical proximity of regimes associated with the model of the people's democracies. In the history of modern African regimes, reference is frequently made to "African Socialism," which, according to Armando Entralgo, is

> a mixture of utopian, Marxist, pre-Marxist or even anti-Marxist concepts whose origins and the ways in which they manifest themselves are highly varied and complex. "African Socialism" or — "African Socialisms" — would thus offer a middle way between capitalism and scientific (Marxist-Leninist) socialism at a historical juncture when the clear choice of capitalism would have been instinctively rejected by the poor who had recently emerged from the colonial system of monopoly capitalism.[3]

These unscientific concepts were accompanied by a justification of power — or ideology — which coincided with interests having very little to do with any political or economic breach with the capitalist system.

This form of socialism, which at times sought to remain equidistant from the East and the West, was more than anything a manifestation of nationalism. The ambivalent behavior of the petty bourgeoisie, the class which assumed power in almost all of these countries, was behind some of the vicissitudes experienced by this movement, which ended by taking refuge in its true dimension — populism.

When no clear structural and organizational base exists, and class alliances have no meaning, the course of populism is inevitable. It is accompanied by an ideological vagueness: an autocracy based on personal charisma as the only method of leadership and an infinite flexibility of concepts and actions. And as Entralgo notes, there is no inevitable correlation between populism and a progressive agenda, or populism and socialism. In addition, while populism may be left-wing, more frequently left-wing populism moves towards the right.

The limits of populism are clearly evident today, as the politics of exclusion inherent in the colonial situation does manifest itself in postcolonial Africa. Social inequality, economic exploitation, and political repression are not the exclusive monopoly of a colonial system, in which a dominant and basically alien minority oppresses a dominated nation. This explains why social claims by the latter are first expressed in nationalist terms, as well as the strength of the nationalist ideology. In this context, the anti-nationalism of Western progressives clashes with the nationalism of Third World progressives.

In postcolonial Africa, the social exclusion once associated with colonialism does not take long to rear its ugly head. Although the criterion of social exclusion is not applicable to the socialist ideal, rejecting other ideologies of nation-building on the grounds that they promote exclusion does not make someone a socialist. And the facts demonstrate that states which so proclaim themselves, do not necessarily believe they are socialist.[4]

Generally speaking, almost all the national liberation movements which engaged in armed struggle adopted as their own the Soviet theses of national liberation and the building of socialism. Almost all believed that the struggle for liberation would lead to social revolution, and saw these two aspects of building the body politic as concomitant and part of a chain reaction. All of them believed the assumption, very often without knowing that it originated with Vladimir Lenin, that socialism can be built in an economically backward country. Moreover, it must be recognized that the statements of fidelity to the principles of building socialism, perhaps with the exception of some elements of the intelligentsia, were just that: assumptions, principles, orders, and methods remote from Marxist theory. The collapse of this model was inevitable from 1986 onwards, and became much more pronounced with the introduction of structural adjustment programs which necessitated major shifts in the macroeconomic models.

The Portuguese-speaking African countries thus became part of an African wave, unstoppable and characterized by the models inspired in Western values. Owing to their proximity to South Africa, Angola and Mozambique were particularly severely punished for their ideological boldness. The regimes also lost their base of support as a result of the growing polarization of income distribution.

With failed ideas, and an international context in full transformation, nothing was left for the Portuguese-speaking African countries other than to recognize the end of the political legitimacy afforded by national liberation. The burial of nationalism coincided with a revival of internal struggles within the regimes as the foundations for their existence came to be questioned. The resounding electoral defeats sustained by the African Party for the Independence of Cape Verde (PAICV) and the Liberation Movement of Sao Tome and Principe (MLSTP), both ruling parties of the respective countries, were the first signs that the magnitude of the discontent had been underestimated. Difficult times followed for all of the Portuguese-speaking African countries. There was a reappraisal of the structural sphere of the state, increasingly dictated by the absence of an internal agenda rather than by external pressures.

Limits of Alternative Construction

According to Tom Jobim, the admired and recently deceased Brazilian poet and composer, "Between a rock and a hard place, it's the end of the road." Will he be proven right? For Africans, while the roads are certainly difficult, pessimism should not prevail.

The restructuring of the state must be carried out as soon as possible. In embarking on this task, the rationality of the state needs to be understood. Placing it in opposition to the market is certainly an error which many are beginning to recognize. The role of the state in development was crucial in the Western countries, just as it is today in the countries of the Pacific rim.[5] Unless other arguments are put forward, the topicality of this observation will continue to be an important element in charting less didactic courses.

The definition of the structural sphere of the state in the Portuguese-speaking countries, if clearly articulated, will also call into question a democratic model that appears to reduce these countries once again to the stage of imitation. If in the past they needed money to pay civil servants, they shall now be starting to ask for money to hold elections every four years.

As long as the debate about development does not dominate the African political scene, there will be reasons for continuing to be skeptical about the relationship between democracy and development. For the time being, the linkage appears to be determined by exogenous conditionalities. Domesticating this new discourse is all the more difficult in that the room to maneuver offered by the international context itself is limited. The optimists hope, nevertheless, that the day is not distant when an African democracy based on participation and the distribution of wealth, not simply on the model of normative representativeness, will not be far off.

Analytical Limits of the Problem

The debate about governability is central to a better understanding of the difficulties relating to the construction of alternative development scenarios. Partial answers to all of the questions discussed above are to be found in the debate on governability. This debate in turn is dominated by the policies proposed by structural adjustment programs.[6]

According to Yusuf Bangura and Peter Gibbon, two main approaches may be identified in the orthodox political science literature on adjustment policies today.[7] The first interprets political processes on the basis of the *theory of public choice,* which relates to the distribution of losses and benefits among competing social groups. Political dynamism would thus be ensured by a transition from the structure of incentives based on state intervention to another in which the market is seen as completely free and competitive. Leaving out of the analysis the institutional and political processes that link economic change to political behavior, this approach prefers a technocratic vision of politics.

The second approach deals with economic and political informalization, and the rise of civil society, as the two most important phenomena of social dynamics in contemporary Africa. An automatic linkage is established between adjustment and the emergence of social movements driven by the informal sector. Consequently, this interpretation ignores the political and social background needed to understand the ongoing changes.

Both approaches overlook the international dimension, seeking to focus on domestic relations. On the other hand, conventional theories of political science are so overpowered by the force of structural adjustment that they readily accept the transposition of categories from neoclassical economics to the political sphere. This results in the emergence of absurd dichotomies between the market and the state, the state and civil society, and the formal and informal sectors. The interrelationship of these categories is increasingly being neglected, and this limits understanding of the true crisis of governability in Africa.[8]

This reductionism leads to situations in which it is felt possible to resolve in the political sphere defects which economic adjustment is unable to resolve, and in many cases, as for example in Guinea-Bissau and Sao Tome and Principe, even aggravates. By extrapolation, it is also felt that representative democracy on the liberal model will resolve the contradictions that have been exacerbated through the destruction of economies by war, as in the case of Angola and Mozambique.

The truth is that, as Bangura and Gibbon tell us, the informalization of institutions and economic activities is not a linear, one-way isolated process. Democracy cannot in fact be understood as the natural expression of any social institution, process, or group. The conditions for the building of democracy can consist only of political, historical, and empirical conditions which cannot be integrated with poorly defined and speculative tendencies.[9]

In fact, what continues to prevail is the tendency to simplify the problem of Africa and the impression that the decision regarding the type of political system, authoritarian or democratic, can be taken from the top down, with some input from outside. But the reality is in fact deceptive, and the experiments with elections in the Portuguese-speaking African countries could be rapidly transformed into serious cases of ungovernability owing to the ignored complexity of the political realities.

Only when it is understood that adjustment did not succeed because it confined its analysis to the nature of modern economic phenomena (in addition, obviously, to applying an economic model that was full of false premises), reducing the problem to a question of will, can the lessons of alternative governability be drawn. In the specific case of Angola, this error, although not formally or officially committed, in that the World Bank and IMF are now only about to launch their programs, will occur. In the remaining countries, the reality has already caught up with the question discussed here, namely, a severe crisis of governability.

Notes

[1] This chapter is an expansion of a paper presented at the Twelfth International Lisbon Conference on "Democracy and Integration in the Portuguese-Speaking World: 1974-1994," organized by the Institute of Strategic and International Studies, Lisbon, in December 1994. The views expressed here are those of the author, who is currently a senior United Nations official, and do not necessarily represent those of the UN Organization.

[2] Australia is one of the exceptions. Over ninety-five years of compulsory voting has established two trends: most people vote (est. over 90%); and political parties do not pitch their agendas at a small section of the electorate. The agendas must appeal to the majority.

[3] Armando Entralgo, "De Berlin a las Independencias: Antecedentes, Desenvolvimento y Limites de lo Particular Africano," *Enfoques*, No. 9, CEAMO, 1986, p. 56.

[4] Taken from Carlos Lopes, *Para uma Leitura Sociologica da Guine-Bissau* (Bissau: INEP, 1988), pp. 198-200.

[5] A recent World Bank publication, *The East Asian Miracle* (New York: Oxford University Press, 1993), recognizes this role despite the recipes developed more recently by the same Bretton Woods organizations.

[6] See the argument that follows, developed in Peter Gibbon, Yusuf Bangura and Arne Ofstad (*eds.*), *Authoritarianism, Democracy and Adjustment* (Uppsala: SAIS, 1992).

[7] *Ibid.*, p. 9.

[8] *Ibid.*, p. 24.

[9] *Ibid.*, p. 25.

15
Democracy, Human Rights, and Peace in Africa

Horace Campbell

The end of the cold war opened new prospects for demilitarization and conversion of the military industrial complex of the advanced capitalist countries. Unfortunately, this opening did not materialize, because of the huge investment to build up this sector of the industrialized economies since World War II. Hence, though the "threat" of war with the Soviet Union receded, there were many wars in the South generated by local struggles and the fueling of military transfers by the leading arms merchants. The invasion of Kuwait by Iraq and the subsequent war against Iraq, exposed the fact that weapon producers wanted to test new weapons, such as cruise missiles, and were willing to invoke ideas of peacekeeping to wage war.

The circumstances of war and destruction in Bosnia, Afghanistan, Angola, Somalia, Liberia, and the Sudan, have energized the peacekeeping operations of the United Nations. Yet, in all such cases, the gulf between theory and practice of peacekeeping has been exposed. This has confirmed the position of the militarists in the United States who understand peacekeeping as an important component of low intensity warfare. This doublespeak of the arms manufacturers is evident in US Defense Department guidelines for low intensity conflict, of which peacekeeping is said to be a feature.[1] It has also been borne out by the way the Security Council of the United Nations has been mobilized to invoke Chapter VII in Kuwait, Somalia, and Rwanda to formalize the strategic goals of both the United States and France.

The UN was established as a peacekeeping institution in the aftermath of the depression and World War II. The major purpose of the UN is to maintain international peace and security. The Charter of the UN was written from April to June 1945 when conceptions of peace were being developed as a counterweight to the racist ideas of Nazism. The reality, however, was that the racism of Nazism was being practiced in colonial societies. All colonial societies were by definition undemocratic. In the fifty year existence of the UN, African and other Third World societies have identified colonization as a threat to peace.

The Universal Declaration of Human Rights (UDHR) was born after the war and at that time did not differentiate between political/civil and socio/economic rights. The UDHR did not contain the right to self-determination, which, at that historic moment, was the most important right for colonized Africans. Politically, the UN saw the right to self-determination in the limited context of the right to independence. It was the organized and spontaneous struggles of peoples in Southern Africa which forced the issue of racism as a central human rights issue. The struggles against racial superiority in Southern Africa demonstrated that imperialism and apartheid bred war, destabilization, and destruction. In most cases, the struggles against apartheid and regional destabilization were caught in the net of the cold war. The colonial powers branded all genuine freedom fighters as communists.[2]

The distortions generated by this position were nowhere more evident than in the Congo. For two decades, the murder of Patrice Lumumba and the rule of Mobutu Sese Seko represented the lesson of UN peacekeeping operations in Africa. Subsequently, the equivocation of the UN in Angola exposed to the African peoples that the political interests of the permanent members of the Security Council would bias the UN against genuine peacekeeping efforts.[3] The US led invasion of Somalia under the flag of the United Nations brought home the fact that the UN was being manipulated to serve the foreign policy interests of the US and her allies in the North Atlantic Treaty Organization (NATO). These episodes have led some social groups in Africa to call for the democratization of the Security Council.

This problem of the democratization of the agencies of the United Nations and the search for peace and human rights are now as important as they were in 1945. The declared determination "to save future generations from the scourge of war, to reaffirm faith in fundamental human rights, and to promote social progress and better standards of life in larger freedom," is just as relevant today as when the Charter was written in San Francisco. The major difference is that the contradictions between the imperatives of imperial domination and human rights for oppressed peoples are now more exposed. This exposure finds expression in the contentious terrain of the differences between those who point to the need for development and socioeconomic rights and those who see human rights simply in terms of the rule of law, constitutionalism, and multiparty democracy.[4]

Issa Shivji has pointed out that conceptions of human rights and peace, which dovetailed with the politics and diplomacy of the cold war, were at variance with the real issues of the struggle: the right to food, to be human, and to organize. This contradiction is most evident in Africa, where the rights of poor farmers, women, and children are abused daily. It is now more evident that exploitation and oppression generate wars of resistance. Indeed, it was the US founding fathers who affirmed the right to self-determination and the right to wage war for independence. Yet, in the context of the cold war, the US supported dictatorial regimes and apartheid as long as the dictators supported the struggles against communism.

The thrust for dignity and the battle against racism have challenged the conceptions of white supremacy and the institutionalized forms of domination which place Africans at the bottom of the international division of labor. Indeed, though the US in its constitution had enshrined important principles such as equality before the law, the philosophical basis of this equality did not include Africans who were not considered human beings. It required a civil war, the struggles of the working class, the suffragette movement, and the civil rights movement, to enrich the principles of democracy which were articulated in the context of the American Declaration of Independence. This declaration is still important for Africans because the most vigorous supporters of liberal democracy in Africa come from foundations and intellectual centers in the United States. In Africa, the decolonization process sought to bring sovereignty, but democracy was not viewed as a priority. Instead, theories of development, including modernization, were articulated as a means of placing the African political elite in the ranks of those fighting against socialism and a new international economic order.

Military assistance and training programs helped to shape a generation of leaders on the African continent who facilitated the exploitation of the labor power of the masses. By the end of the eighties, these leaders had been discredited and struggles for democratic change began to take root. The struggles were led by working people,

African women, progressive intellectuals, and those who wanted to remain part of the political and economic system. The present protracted struggle against dictatorships in Africa has opened up a new stage of the history of the continent. Within this vein, the partial victory of the peoples of South Africa was a step forward.

The struggle for peace and democracy is being carried out in a context where there is a major effort to create a culture of submission by African intellectuals. This submission is orchestrated by those agencies which seek to devalue the importance of African intellectuals. There is now a consensus that "complex and often compelling ideological, political, and economic factors have contributed to intellectual silence and forced some African scholars to follow the research agenda of donor agencies."[5] This has brought about a shift in the preoccupation of scholars. Structural adjustment, country policy studies, poverty alleviation strategies, and studies on ethnic conflict, have replaced studies on working people, exploitation, the cost of living index, and class struggles. The intervention of donors is most evident in the plethora of gender studies which seek to integrate gender with development. This has led to a new stratum of intellectuals called gender technicians.[6] There has been a mushrooming of these technicians who acquire the right discourse with little effort or encouragement to search for an understanding of the complexities and nuances of patriarchal domination and its intimate relations to other forms of domination.

It is becoming increasingly necessary to distinguish between these technicians and those African women who are struggling for the end of all forms of domination and the transformation of gender relations. These women and men who are committed to the transformation of social relations are now at the forefront of articulating demands for democracy, peace, and human rights. Women have suffered disproportionately from war and violence at the level of the state, the community, and the household. Their struggles have indicated that the concept of rights articulated in 1948 was too narrow to deal with the multiple forms of abuses and violations which are visited on women.

This chapter looks at the issues of democracy and human rights, particularly as they relate to current struggles for peace and the rights of women in Africa. It begins with a brief analysis of the question of democracy and democratization in Africa.

Liberal and Popular Democracy in Africa

The issues of democratic participation, peace, and human rights have emerged as fundamental aspects of African politics in the nineties. After the period of decolonization, when the class alliances of the struggle masked internal contradictions, the oppressive conditions in Africa generated undemocratic forms of governance. The view of peace activists, that war and militarism were an enemy of the poor, can be seen all over the African continent where force, the threat of force, and coercion remained the dominant form of alienating labor power. During this period, the continued production of raw materials for the industrialized world dictated that African people were at the bottom of the international division of labor.

It is this context of the international division of labor which must be the starting point for discussing democracy. According to Shivji, in a world divided hierarchically between powerful countries, nations, states, and classes, global discourses on democracy become ideological:

In a situation where rights, rule of law and democracy are presented as the ultimate good, a universal human value, a panacea for all our ills in Africa, it is important to remind ourselves that not only our sickness but the medicine on offer are historically and socially determined. Nature did not posit the civilised, developed rich and powerful North on the one hand, and the backward underdeveloped poor and powerless South on the other as an original condition. That condition was created historically through the application of "universal " violence. The violence, force and domination were in turn legitimised and rationalised through layers of historically and determined languages of religion, race, culture, ethnicity etc., all of which at one time or another claimed superiority and universality just as human rights ideology does today.[7]

The issue of the centrality of violence, force, and domination in social relations in Africa also must be at the fore of any discussion on democracy. Colonialism was based on force, cheap labor, and discrimination. The anti-democratic conditions ensured the export of surplus and the underdevelopment of the continent and its peoples.

In the first years of independence, in cases where the military seized power, there were scholars and consultants who justified support for military intervention in politics on the basis of the fact that the military were preserving "order."[8] Theoretical models which underscored the modernizing role of the military concentrated on institutional and organizational questions in analyzing African societies. The overt failure of the projects of nation building and modernization are now evident with the plethora of reports on the indebtedness and impoverishment of African workers and small farmers. Structural adjustment and devaluation of the returns for labor have compounded the colonial legacies to the point where many Africans are saying that the peoples of the continent are being recolonized.

The objective conditions of oppresion and the struggles for democracy have led to new forms of resistance to unjust governments at all levels of the political economy of Africa. This resistance against one-partyism and militarism took the form of armed confrontation, notably in Ethiopia, Eritrea, Uganda, and the Western Sahara. The success of guerrilla movements in societies such as Uganda and Ethiopia has shown that the elaboration of democratic practices involves more than the capture of political power. The Eritrean example stands out in the profound attempt to build new relations at all levels of the society and to reduce the size of the forces of coercion and administration.

Side by side with this upsurge of popular struggles for democracy has been the active participation of the working poor in demonstrations, strikes, boycotts, and other forms of direct action. Societies such as Nigeria, Tanzania, Tunisia, Algeria, Kenya, and Zaire have given rise to new organs which contest the power of the leaders who dominate the political structures. This new activity has already led to the creation of a new platform for political assembly, *the National Conference*. The national conference phenomenon arose in Francophone Africa as a transition mechanism or an instrument for regime change. Beginning with the Benin conference in 1990, there have been conferences in Congo (1991), Togo (1991), Mali (1991), Niger (1991), and Zaire (1991-92). There have been calls for national conferences in the Central African Republic, Cameroon, Madagascar, and Mauritania. The conferences unleashed a new wave of creativity, and even in societies such as Zaire, where the conference failed to remove the Mobutu regime, the experience of the deliberations of the conference exposed the potentialities of emancipative politics.[9]

The fact that there has been regime change in many parts of Africa raises three fundamental questions. Do the conditions exist for the establishment of democracy? Who or what are the social forces capable of establishing democracy? And what are the fundamental changes which would be required to maintain democratic relations in African societies? These questions can heighten the level of debate in Africa beyond the simple empirical and organizational question of the number of parties, the holding of elections, and other institutional approaches to politics. The intellectual limits of this institutional approach are already evident in countries such as Mali, Ghana, Zambia, Malawi, and Kenya, where the infrastructure of democracy did not seek to go beyond the concern with "free and fair elections."

The institutional approach to democracy is concerned with state positions and not with the reality of constitutional procedures and political organizations. Ernest Wamba-dia-Wamba has been critical of this institutional approach, which subordinates parties under state consensus, where parties are state organizations competing for the distribution of state positions and not for the people's reconstruction of the state.[10] In many ways, the Western concept of democracy based on multipartyism, the market, and simply electing a government every several years, can be seen as a silencing narrative to preempt more profound issues of democratization arising from people's initiatives.

Progressive African women are at the forefront of breaking the silencing narratives of democracy and human rights by raising new questions and creating new sites of politics. In this regard, it can be said that the women's movement has become the site of the most intense struggles for peace, democracy, and peoples' rights. There is a lively discussion between those who are simply gender technicians and those who want to challenge oppression of all forms. In this way, the women's movement has pointed out that it represents a major force in the democratization of social relations.

Numerous groups and organizations in Africa have raised questions about the true meaning of democracy, and in every African state there are routine meetings on democracy and democratization. Western aid agencies are intervening in this debate by sponsoring seminars and meetings which reinforce the preoccupation with the state and constitutional questions. Since for these donors, democracy is identified with the number of parties and free elections held, there are many cases where individuals create parties to gain access to "donor funds." One is even faced with the situation in Africa of political leaders who live outside their own country, but jet in to form parties at the time of elections.

There are scholars who are concerned with democracy in Africa, not only as process and structure, but in terms of its substance. Wamba-dia-Wamba, past President of the Council for the Development of Social Science Research in Africa (CODESRIA), has argued that

> Current African experiences of democratization are bringing to the fore the fact that "democracy" is a plurivocal term. "Democracy" may be an imperialist project made an integral part of the conditionality package of those who use even "humanitarian aid" as a way of dominating or subverting the weak. Democracy may be imposed from the top down as for example when the dictator Babangida claimed to build "democracy" single handedly in the same way as junta leaders, self proclaiming Marxist-Leninists, claimed to build socialism in the 1960s and 1970s. To bring democracy about, some leaders have demanded full powers and increased centralization of power in one person as a condition. Often,

unfortunately, democracy from below has been confused with anarchy ... Due to the above circumstances, I think that democracy must be conceptualized at the level of the whole planet earth. The thrust of democracy has been the necessity to handle contradictions which emerged with the social differentiation of the human community. In different circumstances, different types of society produced different social forms of handling their respective contradictions. This gave rise to different conceptions of democracy ranging from peoples relating to themselves, specific forms of state and civil society, direct or indirect people's sovereignty. Democracy is a process of struggles to win, defend and protect rights of people (producers, women, minorities), and individuals against one sidedness (for tolerance, respect of the absolutely other, for example) including the rights of self organization for autonomy and not necessarily the right of participation in the state process.[11]

This definition of democracy answers the first question, whether the conditions exist for its establishment. The concept of democracy is not new, and people have always developed means to handle contradictions in society. One of the most important criteria for democracy now exists in Southern Africa — the liberation of South Africa. Apartheid South Africa was a stumbling block, not only to democracy in that society, but to the entire region of Southern Africa as a result of destabilization by the apartheid war machine.

The experience with colonial and neocolonial economic relations suggests that the current model of ownership and control of productive resources cannot be the basis for democracy in Africa. The democratization of society requires the dismantling of the coercive structures which were implanted to alienate the labor power of Africans. Democratic participation in political parties on the eve of independence provided the conditions for self rule, but the coercive institutions of the colonial system which were in place meant that those who assumed political power reinforced them. Africanization of the administrative apparatus became the answer to the demand for real emancipation.

In Africa, capitalism was never able to disguise its dominance through ideas of equality and the market. Hence, the centrality of force and extra economic coercion in production. Militarism and force were used to partition and "pacify" the African continent. Force was used to alienate the land to settle white settlers. Taxation was used as a means to force Africans to grow cash crops. Forced labor on plantations and mines meant that industrial relations at the place of work followed the coercive relations of African states. State violence and coercion meant that in many cases Africans had to resort to armed confrontations to gain political independence. Commandism and force at the level of state operations led to the preeminence of the military in power, and to the militarization of the state and society. War and violence are the logical consequences of this process, and this makes the question of peace inseparable from the issue of transformation of the labor process.

The present conditions of the working people have exposed the reality that regime change can be positive but in no way minimizes the effects of extra economic coercion and force in production. African researchers have recently begun to address the military dimensions of the democratization process. Eboe Hutchful, in his research agenda on "Military Issues in the Democratic Transitions in Africa," has argued that, while subordinating the military to democratic control is crucial, it is by no means an isolated issue. "There appears to be a fundamental institutional crisis of the military in Africa, or perhaps to put it more accurately, a political, economic and military crisis of the colonial military model. Without solutions to these institutional issues, the transition to democracy may be shortlived."[12] The issues which are usually addressed in relation to the military are civilian control over the military, the relationship of the military to the political process, military privileges, and the role and mission of the military, including its functions relating to internal security. However, the Western research agenda with respect to the military and democratization uses the narrow definition of liberal democracy. Since independence, the use of the military against students, workers, and poor peasants has led to the centrality of the military in politics.

In many cases, the economic reforms of structural adjustment actually required more force and coercion leading to greater participation of the military in solving social issues. Wamba-dia-Wamba has argued that

> Supporters of many different forms of capitalism — including forms based on global international corporations and forms based on local nationalism — have reduced the notion of democratic transition to the following: emergence of a market economy, privatization of state enterprises, multipartyism, laissez-faire government and a democratic constitutional order. The structural adjustment programmes, sponsored by the IMF (International Monetary Fund), for example, give no historical references in which the process of transition viewed above has led to social and political self emancipation of the people. It is merely assumed that the process will lead to self emancipation. No satisfactory explanation has been given as to why multipartyism in the early sixties led to authoritarian regimes, rather than social and political emancipation of the people.[13]

The implicit point here is that the democratization process must involve the self organization and emancipation of the people. This position on democracy is a tremendous advance over the limited Western notions of monitoring elections, which is usually invoked in Africa as democracy. Indeed, this idea of choice is central to the classical definition of democracy, that, "Democracy is a system of government usually including freedom of the individual in various aspects of political life, equality among citizens, justice in relations between the people and the government and the participation of the people in choosing the government."[14]

Such a definition reduces democracy to decision-making and government, while ignoring economic relations in the community or in the family. Feminists have shown that the concept of citizenship did not include women when bourgeois democracy was being developed. In many African states, women are treated as minors and the basic right to participate in the life of the community is denied on the basis of customary and religious laws. "African women are denied access to land, property and other economic resources which should constitute a basic human right, and are treated as pawns or objects in marriage, divorce, inheritance, and citizenship." It is this condition which has led to the slogan by African feminists that, "Democracy without women's human rights is not democracy."[15] Women in Africa continue to be the objects of masculinist social control, not only through direct violence (murder, rape, battering, and incest), but also through ideological constructs such as "women's work" and the call of motherhood that justifies structural violence in inadequate health care, sexual harassment, and segregated wages.

One has to scrutinize the idea that democracy is based on multipartyism. It is necessary to distinguish between the struggles of the peoples for human rights and the visible operations of elections monitoring and the registration of parties. This is not to say that the development of the forms of Western democracy with respect to freedom of speech, freedom of worship, freedom of the press, freedom of movement, the institutionalization of electoral processes, and the separation of powers would not be an advance beyond the present authoritarian forms of governance. However, these forms of governance are impossible when economic relations are untransformed and basic human rights are violated. Despite this reality, organic intellectuals of the oppressed support liberal democracy in Africa and believe that the space and time created by liberal democratic openings should be seized to elaborate democratic practices in the community and at grassroots levels.

The operationalization of democratic practices in professional organizations is an important aspect of the democratic process in Africa. In the last forty years, the activities of the African middle class have shown that professional organs have been the breeding ground for authoritarian and arbitrary decision-making. In this sense, the African Association of Political Science (AAPS) has to be self critical in examining whether in its operation it has advanced the cause of democracy or encouraged manipulation and petty conflicts. Groups such as AAPS must make it clear how their conception of democracy is linked to the struggles at all levels of society. The basic experience of anti-democratic practices at the level of the school, the religious institution, and the family is fed into the practice of undemocratic governance.

The one-party model and military rule have been discredited, and now the very external forces which supported anti-democratic elements want to manage the transition to democracy in such a way that political change does not challenge economic exploitation, cultural repression, and gender inequality. Democracy, peace, and human rights cannot be achieved without real economic transformation and fundamental changes in the relationship between Africa and the international monetary system.

Peace and Human Rights in Africa

There has been considerable debate and discussion within UN agencies as to the real content of peace. One author notes that, "by peace we mean the absence of violence in any given society, both internal and external, direct and indirect. We further mean the nonviolent results of the equality of rights, by which every member of the society, through nonviolent means, participates equally in decisional power which regulates it, and the distribution of resources which sustains it."[16]

Nearly every year since the United Nations designated 1986 as the International Year of Peace, the United Nations Educational, Scientific, and Cultural Organization (UNESCO) has mounted conferences to refine the concept of peace. UNESCO took the lead from the UN General Assembly by declaring that "every nation and every human being, regardless of race, conscience, language or sex has the inherent right to live in peace." Since 1982, UNESCO has adopted a position that peace is indistinguishable from fundamental human rights and is therefore incompatible with extreme poverty, malnutrition and the refusal of the right of self-determination.

Africans will not experience peace unless fundamental changes occur in the international system with respect to disarmament and demilitarization.[17] Peace scholars now abound, and the principal nations which produce weapons are the most strident in the production of information on peace. For many conflict resolution consultants of the

North, wars and conflict are necessary for them to make a living. This has created a spate of publications by war makers who now serve in "Institutions of Peace" and write about how to build peace.

For the peoples of Southern Africa, the most blatant work of this genre is by Chester Crocker, the former US Assistant Secretary of State for African Affairs. After spending eight years in a position where support for apartheid was justified under the banner of "Constructive Engagement," Crocker produced a book entitled *High Noon in Southern Africa: Making Peace in A Rough Neighborhood.* With individuals such as Crocker at the forefront of organizations such as the United States Institute of Peace, serious peace activists in the Third World have pointed out that the language of the culture of peace becomes a silencing narrative to direct the discussion away from those who feel the full impact of war.

Concerned scholars, like Jacques Depelchin, have brought to the fore the ways in which paradigmatic silences have been created with respect to African history. "Relative and absolute silences on certain aspects of African history is the result of a long agony of low intensity genocide, the victims of which have found themselves caught in the dilemma of rape victims: either remain silent or recount the trauma within the parameters most acceptable to the perpetrator of the crime." Depelchin and others have warned that among certain international agencies, issues of war and peace have become commodities which can be dispensed at a price in the global market (or in the Security Council of the UN). Depelchin asks: "How do those who long for peace, but reap war conceptualize such destructive experiences when the most accessible modes of expression and communication are imposed by the very forces which are directly or indirectly responsible for such a situation?"[18]

The war in Angola demonstrated more than anywhere else that the interests of the Western powers were more important than peace and democracy. After years of supporting the National Union for the Total Independence of Angola (UNITA) as a pawn of the cold war, the US brokered a peace accord in Portugal in 1991. This accord laid the foundation for a ceasefire, demobilization of soldiers, elections, and the drafting of a new constitution. Yet, when the elections were held in 1992, Jonas Savimbi and his party lost. Savimbi and UNITA went back to war and brought untold destruction and misery to the society. Despite the rejection by UNITA of the election results, Savimbi was still able to obtain military, political, and financial support from certain permanent members of the UN Security Council. The ensuing war in Angola led to the death of even more civilians than during 1975-1991. In the disinformation campaign of the Western media, the war was referred to as a civil war as a way of delegitimizing the long struggle for self-determination by the Angolan people.[19]

Since African problems are often depicted in "tribal" terms, militarism and armed conflicts are interpreted as if Africans have a natural proclivity to war. Nowhere was this tribal narrative employed with such negative consequences as in the 1992 US military intervention in Somalia. The crisis in Somalia, which precipitated the "humanitarian intervention" of the UN, exposed how the United States was willing to manipulate public opinion to achieve "strategic goals." The diplomatic attempts by Mohamed Sahnoun (the UN envoy) to reach a peaceful solution to the real humanitarian tragedy were never given a chance. After intervening, the US retreated under conditions where African fighters showed that they were not intimidated by the military might of the Americans. The peacekeeping efforts of the UN in Somalia left an even greater problem than prior to the intervention.

The experience of misguided "humanitarian intervention" in Somalia crippled the UN to the point where it evacuated its personnel from Rwanda at precisely the moment when UN peacekeepers were most needed in April 1994. For two months, the UN equivocated over the issue of deploying peacekeepers after an estimated one million people had been killed. Salim Ahmed Salim, the Secretary General of the Organization of African Unity (OAU), was critical of the decision and said:

> The decision to pull out troops from Rwanda is a sign of lack of concern for Africa when the world body was increasingly involved elsewhere. This is particularly so when account is taken of the fact that the United Nations is increasingly involved in situations affecting peace and security in other regions.[20]

The deployment of peacekeepers by the UN in the past ten years has been at the behest of the major powers. In reality, the deployment of peacekeepers must go through the long bureaucratic channels of the UN Department of Peacekeeping. When France or the US want to deploy troops under the banner of the UN, however, they can do so in a matter of days. But the whole logistical requirements of mobilizing the support and funds for peacekeeping ensure that the UN will be paralyzed when real peacekeepers are needed.[21] This is the concrete lesson of the genocide in Rwanda.

The presentation of the carnage in Rwanda as ethnic strife has not only diverted attention from the ways in which Western countries armed and supported those who were carrying out genocide, but more importantly, how the IMF-World Bank policies helped to create the social and economic conditions for the Rwandan holocaust. In a penetrating analysis, one scholar noted that "to lay the blame solely on deep-seated tribal hatred not only exonerates the great powers, and the donors, it also distorts an exceedingly complex process of economic, social and political disintegration affecting an entire nation of more than seven million people."[22] The quest for peace in Africa involves the democratization of information to break the silences with respect to the last centuries of violence, conquest, wars of resistance, and economic warfare.

The Contradictions of Human Rights in Africa

The recent experience of genocide in Rwanda and the initial resistance of the UN Security Council in labeling the massacres genocide, exposed the hollowness of the human rights campaigns which originate in the West. The decades of hypocrisy of those who exploited colonies, yet shout about human rights, has been documented by African jurists and political activists. In particular, scholars such as Willy Mutunga, Shivji, and Shadrack Gutto have been unequivocal in spelling out the imperial motives of a certain brand of human rights ideology. In the study by Shivji on human rights in Africa, he emphasized that "human rights talk has been one of the central planks in the foreign and domestic ideologies of the United States."[23]

There is a very highly developed critique of Western initiatives with respect to human rights in Africa. From this critique three points are critical: the idea of human rights emanated from the Western concept of who is human and what is a right; human rights became a major aspect of the foreign policy of particular states; and the African Charter on Human Rights was written to rescue the image of the OAU and to legitimize the existing state structures.

It is out of the scope of this study to revisit the debate by leading African scholars on these three points, since there is a developed body of literature on the state centered human rights debate. In this study, the points which are being made are to centralize the ways in which African men and women are attempting to expand the frontiers of the human rights discourse. Church groups, local human rights organizations, legal aid clinics, and the women's movement, have all contributed to the changing of the political landscape by holding African governments accountable for their actions. In some societies, human rights activists are more progressive than opposition parties, who often champion human rights and democracy to gain access to governmental positions. The former have, in many cases, inspired international campaigns in situations where the pressures of the cold war had induced Western governments to cover up human rights violations. [24]

The human rights lobby of Kenya stands out in this regard in the impressive work undertaken to expose the gross violations of human rights. The campaign was so successful that the world was exposed to the fact that Kenya is not a stable success story of capitalist development. Through the Law Society of Kenya, books, pamphlets, and clinics were opened to educate the working people's as to their rights.[25]

The radical intellectual tradition of East Africa has made this area one of the places in Africa where the local discourse on human rights is most developed. Here, the focus has been on human rights for the most oppressed in the society. One of the scholars from this region has developed a working definition of the oppressed as follows:

> a social group or groups who find themselves, or may be objectively determined
> to be, disadvantaged or accorded unequal, differential treatment, either because
> of deliberate policies or structural arrangements in (a) the family, community,
> country, region or world they live in, and or (b) the position they occupy in the
> prevailing relations of production or arrangements and, as a consequence,
> become especially exposed to human rights denials and abuses.[26]

From this definition, one can make an objective categorization of principal oppressed social groups and the oppressors. In differentiating the oppressors from the oppressed, leading African scholars want to be able to distinguish the human rights discourse of the oppressed as distinct from the discourse of the oppressors. In this sense, African critics of internationally sponsored human rights initiatives stress self-determination as a collective right. Shivji identifies the rights of peoples to self-determination as follows: equality of all peoples and nations; the right of colonized people to independence and formation of their own sovereign states; the right of oppressed nations to self-determination up to and including the right to secession; the right of all peoples, nations, nationalities, national groups, and minorities to freely pursue and develop their culture, traditions, religion, and language; freedom of all peoples from alien subjugation, domination and exploitation; and the right of all peoples to determine democratically their own socioeconomic and political system of governance and government.[27]

Given the ways the African continent was carved up in the 19th century, the question of the right to self-determination can be seen at two levels: in the first instance, the right to be free from foreign domination, and, the rights of minorities to freely pursue and develop their culture, traditions, religion and language. These basic rights are compromised by the African Charter, which stipulates the right of the individual in the specific duties to the state, the most important of which are "not to compromise the security of the state whose national resident he is; to preserve and strengthen social and national integrity, particularly when the latter is threatened and to preserve and strengthen national independence and territorial integrity of his country and to contribute to the defence in accordance with the law."

These elements of the African Charter on Human and Peoples' Rights were adopted by the OAU Summit at its meeting in Nairobi in 1981 and bore the stamp of the authoritarian leadership in Africa. The African Charter came into force on October 21, 1986, and more than forty countries promised to respect the limited rights contained in this charter. It was significant that the states of Africa did not support the struggles of the Eritrean people, for the principle of non-interference in the internal affairs of member states undermined one of the central rights in Africa — the right of minorities to freely pursue and develop their culture, religion and language. The experience of the Eritrean people is being replicated all over Africa, where there is a conspiracy of silence on the issue of the self-determination of oppressed groups.

The issue of the nation and nationalities in Africa has been manipulated in the context of multiparty politics, so that in many countries, the democratization process has reinforced the concepts of ethnic conflict in Africa. Shivji, in his critique of the African Charter, noted that, "taking into account the notorious authoritarian practices of African states, it is clear that what is demanded of the African people in this catalogue of duties is absolute allegiance to the existing state and the family — both of which represent, politically and historically, retrogression. This retrogression is most evident in the absence of the rights of African workers to organise independently of the state and state supported trade union centers."[28]

The right to organize, or the freedom of association, is one of the most important contentions of international human rights statutes. Even in the Western industrialized countries, the right of workers to organize continues to be the site of the most intense social struggles. It was the struggles of the workers in the Western industrialized countries which cemented the principal rights of trade unions, which were incorporated in the International Labour Organization (ILO) Convention on the *Freedom of Association and the Right to Organize.*

Such rights, which were promulgated with respect to trade unions, were articulated in 1948 when most of Africa was under colonial rule. Colonialism did not support the right of African workers and peasants to organize. One of the primary impetuses behind the independence struggle in Africa was the democratic right of African workers to organize in trade unions to demand better working conditions.

Thirty years after independence, the standards of the ILO with respect to the rights of trade unions, are hardly met in Africa. Even in the countries which reinforce multiparty democracy, the rights of workers are being daily eroded by structural adjustment programs. Up to the present, one of the basic rights which is being demanded by African workers is the freedom to form and join trade unions. The African Charter does not provide for this right. In essence, by arguing for individual rights, the African charter is weak on the question of collective rights for workers, women, and minorities.

African human rights activists and progressive church groups have been able to organize local groups to expose the limitations of the African Charter, while enriching the spirit of the international human rights conventions. Because the African continent until recently was the scene of the struggle against apartheid, African activists are sensitive to the question of the rights to self-determination. It is therefore, not surprising that Africans, at their meetings, continue to raise the issue of colonial domination where people are oppressed in Puerto Rico, the Western Sahara, Martinique, Guadeloupe, and Cayenne, as well as those societies where France and the US use confusing concepts such as "departments" or "commonwealth status" to conceal the colonial reality of their possessions at the end of the twentieth century.[29]

African Women and Human Rights

As in the case of the silence in Africa with respect to the ILO conventions for workers' rights, there is an even greater silence on the provisions of the ILO conventions and recommendations concerning women workers. These conventions include the right to paid work; equal training and career opportunities; equal pay; equal treatment; the right to share work and family responsibilities; the right to maternity protection; and minimum wages.[30] One of the greatest abuses experienced by women is sexual harassment.[31] In every African language, there is the code on how working women are coerced to provide sexual favors for employers.

In the present economic crisis, women are more vulnerable to exploitation, and the pressures to survive force many into what is called the "informal sector." Those who make their living in this sector have none of the basic rights accorded to workers in settled occupations. In many parts of Africa, informal sector work and self employment are the only employment opportunities available. Although women usually bear the costs of setting up their informal activity, they often do not control the benefits, which may be entirely taken by male relatives or patrons. Women and men in the informal sector do not have the basic protection accorded to workers, and they work under unhygienic conditions without the usual health and safety considerations which are implemented by governments.

This stress on the rights of working women is outside the agenda of the "women in development" (WID) industry. African feminists have drawn attention to this phase of foreign domination which is predicated on drawing African women deeper into the process of commodity production. Under colonialism, the state (especially working through missionaries) developed many schemes to modernize African women, who were seen to be backward. Education for women was to save their souls and this salvation required the civilizing influence of hard work, discipline, and obedience to authority.[32] The modern variant of expanding economic activities of women (in most cases women working under conditions of extreme exploitation), is to develop piecemeal programs which do not question the vestiges of the colonial political economy. The thrust is to get women into the labor market, into wage employment, without serious questions being raised about their basic rights. The salvation of souls has been replaced by the salvation of the market. Yet, in the real marketplace where African women dominate, they do not have access to credit, training facilities, technical support, and management services, although they dominate the sector.

Between 1985 and 1995, the WID ideology was "translated into an entire industry of research, publications, college courses, and development projects administered by universities in donor and government agencies."[33] Projects to empower women through employment were being conceptualized, while the same agencies were the most vigorous in promoting structural adjustment, which reduced the government expenditure on water, health, and education. Side by side with this WID ideology has been the maturation of the gender technicians and gender trainers whose vision is limited to the relevant discourse to satisfy donors. There is a major concern among progressive

African women that not all gender training is geared at developing critical consciousness. Some of this training serves the status quo.

The issue of the contradictions between WID ideologues and serious fighters for peace comes out in major meetings when governmental representatives cite relevant passages of the UN Convention on the Elimination of Discrimination Against Women, yet support economic policies which oppress women, workers, and children. However, one of the positive by-products of this international discourse has been the growth of a strong women's movement in Africa. The struggles are taking place at different levels, with the two most important being (1) the level of equality with men and the transformation of discriminatory legal systems relating to inheritance, property ownership, and women in politics; and (2) the more profound questions relating to the rights of women and the transformation of social relations to break all forms of sexual violence and oppression.

On the African continent, the limitations of flag independence have become more pronounced with the strictures of externally imposed structural adjustment programs. African women bear the brunt of the adjustment programs, and the call for human and people's rights have now included the rights for health care, child care, and for an end to all forms of violence against women. Indeed, this position was reinforced at the World Conference on Human Rights held in Vienna, Austria in June 1993. The Vienna Declaration consisted of 139 paragraphs, thirteen of which were specifically concerned with the rights of women and girls.

The Vienna Declaration of 1993 represents a major step forward beyond the individual rights which were being championed by the 1948 Declaration on Human Rights. Although the OAU drafted an African Charter on Human and Peoples' Rights, the reality has been that violations of basic rights are compounded by exploitation, war, violence, and authoritarianism. In this new situation, the African poor, especially poor women, are confronted with a new wave of religious fundamentalism which seeks to exploit the spiritual aspirations of the people to entrench oppressive conditions. The call for reproductive rights as a basic right comes as a necessary antidote to this new wave of fundamentalism. Moreover, some of the agencies of the United Nations speak of peace and human rights when other agencies promote policies of population control and forms of family planning which are inimical to the rights of women, especially African and Third World women.[34]

The struggles of women against domestic violence and economic marginalization have also sharpened the concept of peace in Africa. Africans are fighting wars on many different fronts. They are fighting a war against racism and combating psychological warfare, biological and chemical warfare, and economic warfare. These wars are not as well known as the military confrontations which take place with soldiers. In this sense the struggles for peace in Africa are bound up with the global struggles for disarmament and the destruction of weapons of mass destruction. The changed conditions of struggle dictate that those who seek to carry forward the traditions of the African Revolution do so with the shift in emphasis from seeking to integrate into capitalist structures to an emphasis on emancipative politics which seeks to transform the relationships between human beings, in other words a revolutionary break with the traditions of exploitation and racism.[35]

Reproductive Rights and Human Rights

"The human rights of women and the girl child are an inalienable, integral and indivisible part of universal human rights." This declaration by the World Human

Rights Conference in 1993 has brought out in the open the question of rights which hitherto have been violated under the guise of "custom, tradition and culture." This meeting deepened the key Convention of the United Nations *On the Elimination of all Forms of Discrimination Against Women.* Though this convention was ratified by member states in 1979, its elements are hardly known in Africa.

In his book *Human and Peoples' Rights for the Oppressed,* Gutto analyzes in great detail the contradictory position of women and human rights in Africa.[36] Gutto has joined the ranks of African feminists who have pointed out that violence against women is a persistent and growing form of human rights violation. Feminist scholars have challenged the principal patriarchal formulations which have been justified in the name of tradition, to put to the fore the issues of social violence.[37] Women continue to be the ones who bear the brunt of military violence with the rape and abduction of women and girls (most recently in Rwanda and Angola).[38] Military violence in times of war may be exceptional, but women also face violence economically and in the household.

Patricia McFadden, one of the important spokespersons on the rights of African women, has elaborated in many articles and speeches on how reproductive rights intersect with the questions of race, class, and unequal economic relations between the South and the North.[39] She has argued that the women's movement is increasingly distancing itself from state supported policies of fertility control, while engaging in a redefinition of the issues by introducing the concepts of rights and choices. The issues of democracy and human rights now include the question of the democratic choice of women over who should have control over the uterus.

The 1994 UN International Conference on Population and Development in Cairo demonstrated that there are many forces fighting for the right to make decisions with respect to the uterus — the state, the church, family units, and women themselves. At this conference, the real questions of reproductive rights and democracy came to the fore. An alliance developed between the most conservative forces, who hid behind the guise of religion to mobilize opinion against human rights for women. The battles over abortion have brought the question of reproductive rights into the open and made it clear that issues of democracy and human rights cannot be separated from the question of health. This is even more so in Africa where health care is being reduced under the burden of economic reforms.

Religious fundamentalism, whether Christian, Islamic or Hindu, has now emerged as a major negative force in the struggle for human rights. Feminists all over the world have recognized this fact. The Declaration of the Reproductive Health and Justice Conference in Rio de Janeiro, Brazil, in January 1994 was most explicit on this issue. The Declaration asserted that:

> The discussion of fundamentalism brought strong agreement that, whatever its origins or religious claims, its aim is political. Central to fundamentalist attempts to gain political power is the control of women's lives and in particular female sexuality, including the right to self determination and reproductive decisions. There was criticism of the role of major northern countries in supporting fundamentalist groups for their own political ends. Fundamentalists use religion, culture and ethnicity in their pursuit of power; such movements represent a new form of war against women and an aggressive attempt to mutilate their human rights. A major site of the fundamentalist war against women is over the meaning of families.[40]

This issue of the family and "family values" has become the banner for those who want to preserve tradition. In Africa, the deformities of the "nuclear family" and the forms of inheritance central to private property, have led to a distortion of extended family relations and obligations which existed in ancient Africa. Despite the fact that the conditions of capitalism have eroded the relations of the past, conservative African scholars and leaders call on African women to remember traditions. The traditions which are usually referred to are those of the harmonious family unit where authority rests with the father or the husband. In this narrative, ideas of gender equality and rights for women are identified with the disintegration of the family and the loss of male privilege.

Increasingly, ideas relating to marriage, divorce, birth control, inheritance, property rights, freedom of movement, and other behaviors, are encoded in legal statutes and enforced by state authorities. "The essence of patriarchy is that girls and women have little control over the circumstances under which they work, the returns for their labour, their sexuality, and the timing and number of their children."[41]

African Women and the Question of Population Control

Under structural adjustment, the little expenditures which had been allocated for social services have been drastically reduced. This reduction comes at precisely the moment when the need is greatest, especially with respect to the prevention and treatment of HIV-AIDS. Women all over the world, especially African women, are demanding, as a right, reproductive health services, which include pre-natal, childbirth and postpartum care; nutritional and lactation programs; safe contraception and safe non-compulsory abortion; and the prevention, early diagnosis and treatment of sexually transmitted diseases, as well as cancers (e.g., breast, cervical).[42]

Progressive human beings all over the world support the demand for reproductive rights and more democracy with respect to experiments with contraceptive technology. In the past thirty years, there has been an explicit attempt to develop population policies which target certain racial groups. African women, inside and outside the continent, have become guinea-pigs for the testing of contraceptives. In Africa, women, without their consent, are innoculated to make them infertile. International agencies, such as the World Bank, have made a correlation between economic growth and population growth, and, in the process, have seduced some African governments to undertake sterilization without the consent of the population. Long term and permanent methods of contraception are being encouraged because Africa is supposed to be overpopulated.

The massive international lobby which promotes birth control in Africa, Latin America, and Asia, suggests that issues of population control have a different meaning in the advanced capitalist countries. In Africa, especially Southern Africa, population control systems which were established in the colonial period are now being cemented with the assistance of agencies such as the World Bank, the United States Agency for International Development (USAID), and the United Nations Fund for Population Activities (UNFPA). There is in this case an explicit racial agenda. When feminists from the advanced capitalist countries support the racial agenda of the international population control lobby, they reinforce the ideas of white superiority. At the same time, these feminists provide ammunition for those who declare that feminism in Africa is donor driven.

In the past one hundred years, the African continent has been devastated by wars, epidemics, and hunger. This devastation has been compounded by the absence of control over the environment. In many parts of the continent, people are losing skills acquired over the centuries. This loss of skills is not matched by the learning of new ones. In fact, as the technological gap widens, African societies are becoming more marginalized.

The Seventh Pan African Conference, held in Kampala in April 1994, made the issue of the resistance to recolonization a key element of the forthcoming democratic struggles. With emphasis on the creation of a popular grassroots movement, the congress gave birth to the Pan African Women's Liberation Organization. The Kampala Declaration noted that:

> A central component of the struggle is to oppose all forms of oppression and exploitation of women both in the public and private domain. The democratisation process includes the transformation of gender relations on the continent and in the Diaspora.[43]

Conclusion

In the short run, the transition to democratic forms in Africa will not be easy since cultural and political repression emanates directly from the economic dependence in which Africa is presently entrenched. There is still room for the politicization of region, religion, and ethnicity. The Angolan, Burundi, Liberian, and Rwandan experiences demonstrated that the international community and African demagogues do not respect human life in Africa. Human rights in Africa must depart from the eighteenth century concepts of natural law and recognize that Africans are human beings. This is a fundamental challenge to racist doctrines. A challenge to these doctrines has already shaken the foundations of undemocratic rule in Southern Africa.

The massive uprisings which are taking place in Africa expose the fact that the continent is in ferment. This ferment recently pointed to new democratic questions for the people of South Africa away from racial identity politics. Elsewhere in Africa, the creation of the national conference has demonstrated that there are new forms of democratic expression and participation which will be thrown up by the concrete struggles of the peoples of Africa. The creativity of the working poor is producing a new political situation, and this has been most manifest in the struggles of African women. The issues of human rights and the rights of women have been exposed so that the questions of rape, domestic violence, defilement of young girls, incest, and genital mutilation are now contested issues. In this contestation, the questions are now taken from the realm of the private domain of the household to the public arena.

The gap between the rhetoric of governments with respect to the elimination of all forms of discrimination against women and concrete reality has become clearer with the absence of real machinery to uphold international human rights conventions. This has placed the initiative for the struggle for rights in the hands of those who are the most oppressed. In the cases where governments are influenced by religious fundamentalism, conservative ideas of the male headed family are reproduced in order to support male domination. African feminists, though representing a small minority, are at the cutting edge of the African revolution, since the question of human rights and peace requires nothing less than the transformation of social relations.

The African revolution invariably brings out a violent reaction against it from local and foreign sources. Consequently, those who dominate the multilateral agencies of the United Nations hope to steal the initiative from the women's movement in placing resources in the hands of women who support oppressive governments. The retrogression of this state centered form of organization was manifest in Dakar, Senegal, where African delegates to an international conference allowed the Senegalese government to expel freedom fighters from the Polisario movement. This demonstrated the political retreat of the state centered organs which yesterday supported the basic right of self-determination for all peoples, one of the basic tenets of international human rights conventions.

This period of African independence can open up real prospects for an anti-capitalist alliance internationally. Real struggles for democracy and peace in Africa demand that the anti-racist movement in Europe develop a new basis for internationalism, one which is rooted in basic respect for the democratic rights of all human beings. It is important that there is the democratization of education on Africa so that the citizens of Europe do not continue to support authoritarian forces in Africa or humanitarian invasions which strengthen the strategic designs of militarists. At present, detailed knowledge about Africa is in the hands of a minority in Europe and America, while there is widespread ignorance on the part of the rest of the population. This is compatible with public policy, as governments which support killers can do so under the guise of humanitarian aid, as the French did with their so called *Opération Turquoise* in Rwanda.

There is a new generation of Africans who are not mesmerized by the wealth of Europe. This generation is prepared to challenge the Western culture of commodity fetishism. In the short run, and in the absence of clear ideology, this resistance is manifest in terms of religious expression. The tragedy is that this very same form of religious identification sharpens the war against women. The Cairo meeting brought out the battle lines very clearly. Those who support democracy, peace, and human rights are being challenged to reassess the political forms which guided the decolonization process. The new stage of the political struggle is a battle for the self organization and self emancipation of the producers.

Notes

[1] For details on the peacekeeping ideas of low intensity warfare in the Pentagon report, see Michael Klare and Peter Kornblu (*eds.*), *Low Intensity Warfare: Counterinsurgency, Proinsurgency and Antiterrorism in the Eighties* (New York: Pantheon Books, 1987), p. 53.

[2] P. Johnson and D. Martin, *Frontline Southern Africa: Destructive Engagement* (New York: Four Walls Eight Windows, 1988).

[3] Horace Campbell, "The United Nations and Angola," *Southern African Political and Economic Monthly,* November, 1993.

[4] Issa Shivji, "Human Rights and Development: A Fragmented Discourse," Paper presented at the Workshop on Fundamental Rights and Freedoms in Tanzania, Dar es Salaam, April 1995.

[5] Report of CODESRIA 8th General Assembly, in *CODESRIA Bulletin,* No. 4, 1995, p. 13.

[6] Bunie M. Sexwale, "The Politics of Gender Training," *Agenda: A Journal of Women and Gender,* No. 23, 1994, pp. 57-63.

[7] Shivji, 1995, p. 2.

[8] Samuel P. Huntington, *Political Order in Changing Societies* (Yale: Yale University Press, 1968).

[9] Wamba-dia-Wamba, "Democracy, Multipartyism and Emancipative Politics in Africa: The Case of Zaire," *Africa Development,* Vol. 18, No. 4, 1993, pp. 95 -110.

[10] Wamba-dia-Wamba, "Beyond Elite Politics of Democracy in Africa," *Quest,* Vol. 4, No. 1, 1992, p. 30.

[11] Wamba-dia-Wamba, "Democracy in Africa and Democracy for Africa," *CODESRIA Bulletin,* No. 2, 1994. See also, *Ibid.*

[12] Eboe Hutchful, "Military Issues in the Democratic Transitions in Africa," Paper Presented at the CODESRIA Seminar on the Military and Militarism in Africa, Accra, Ghana, April 1993.

[13] Wamba-dia-Wamba, 1992.

[14] O. Nnoli, *Introduction to Politics* (Lagos: Longmans, 1986), p. 117.

[15] Editorial, *African Woman,* Special Issue on African Women and Human Rights, No. 8, December 1993, p. 1.

[16] Birgit Brock-Utne, *Educating For Peace* (New York: Pergamon Press, 1985).

[17] Seymour Melman, *The Demilitarized Society* (Montreal: Harvest House, 1988).

[18] Jacques Depelchin, "War and Peace in Southern Africa (1880-1993): Between Popular and Institutional/Memories/Histories/Silences," unpublished paper, 1993.

[19] Horace Campbell, "The Delegitimisation of the Liberation Struggles in Africa: The Experience of Angola," *Southern African Political and Economic Monthly,* November 1993.

[20] Quoted in Horace Campbell, "The United Nations and the Genocide in Rwanda," in Napoleon Abdulai (*ed.*), *Genocide in Rwanda* (London: Africa Research and Information Center, 1994).

[21] "United Nations Peacekeeping," *The Economist,* January 25, 1994, p. 19.

[22] Michael Chossudovsky, "The IMF-World Bank Policies and the Rwandan Holocaust," *Third World Resurgence,* No. 52, 1994.

[23] Issa Shivji, *The Concept of Human Rights in Africa* (Dakar: CODESRIA Books, 1989).

[24] Amnesty International, *Kenya: Torture, Political Detention and Unfair Trial* (London: Amnesty International, 1987).

[25] Willy Mutunga, *The Rights of the Arrested and Accused Person* (Nairobi: Oxford University Press, 1990).

[26] S. B. O. Gutto, *Human and Peoples' Rights for the Oppressed* (Lund, Sweden: Lund University, 1993), p. 31.

[27] Shivji, 1989, p. 80.

[28] *Ibid.*

[29] See the *Declaration of the 7th Pan African Congress,* Kampala, Uganda, 1994.

[30] International Labour Organization, *ABC of Women Workers' Rights, A Practical Guide* (Geneva: International Labour Office, 1993).

[31] Jill Taylor and Sheelagh Stewart, *Sexual and Domestic Violence: Help, Recovery and Action in Zimbabwe* (Harare: Women in Law in Southern Africa, 1991).

[32] For a critique of the missionary education for women and girls in Africa, see E. Schmidt, *Peasants, Traders and Wives: Shona Women in the History of Zimbabwe 1870-1939* (Harare: Baobab Books, 1992).

[33] For a critique of the women in development ideology in Africa, see Marjorie Mbilinyi, "Research Methodologies in Gender Issues," in Ruth Meena (ed.), *Gender in Southern Africa: Conceptual and Theoretical Issues* (Harare: SAPES Books, 1992).

[34] Patricia McFadden, "The Population Issue Reconceptualized in Africa," in *Success and Failures in Population Policies and Programmes* (Oslo: Norwegian Forum for Environment and Development, 1994).

[35] Manning Marable, "Beyond Racial Identity Politics: Towards a Liberation Theory for Multicultural Democracy," *Race and Class,* July-September 1993.

[36] Gutto.

[37] Political leaders of all ideological stripes have used this language of the family and tradition to support patriarchal structures. For the most recent of these ideas see Kempton Makamure, *Sunday Gazette* (Harare), February 5, 1995.

[38] Africa Rights, *Rwanda: Death, Despair and Defiance* (London: Africa Rights, 1994), Chapter 10.

[39] McFadden.

[40] Women, Population and Development, Special Report on the Declaration on "Reproductive Health and Justice," International Women's Health Conference, Cairo 1994. *Women's Health Journal,* Latin America and Caribbean Women's Health Network, 1994.

[41] Ruth Dixon-Mueller, *Population Policy and Women's Rights: Transforming Reproductive Choice* (London: Praeger, 1993).

[42] *Women's Health Journal,* pp. 48.

[43] *Declaration of the Delegates and Participants at the 7th Pan African Congress.*

16

Ombudsman Institutions and Democracy in Africa: A Gender Perspective

Victor O. Ayeni

The ombudsman is today widely accepted as a standard part of democratic development. In Africa, early adoptors of the ombudsman concept include Tanzania, Zambia, Mauritius, Ghana, Uganda, Nigeria, and Zimbabwe. Most recently, countries like South Africa, Lesotho, Malawi, Senegal, Namibia, Botswana, and Ethiopia have established ombudsman institutions. In addition, the majority of Francophone African countries, the scene of many recent pro-democracy struggles, have embarked on measures to establish and reorganize existing human rights institutions to undertake various ombudsman like activities. The ombudsman's institution is, indeed, an ineluctable part of contemporary democratization in Africa.[1]

However, there is a curious paradox to this development. Read literally, the word "ombuds-man" is sexist. It seems surprising that this seemingly sexist concept has become so widely identified with an idea of democracy whichs is strongly critical of any semblance of bias against particular social groups, notably women. For sure, prevailing democratization is not just an expression of a sentiment. On the contrary, it is sustained by concrete experiences of history, the persistent failure of development in most parts of the world, and the actual situation of women and other disadvantaged groups. The commitment of the ombudsman to this phenomenon of democratization is not, judging by its name, self-evident.

Notwithstanding the above, the suffix "man" in Swedish, from which the title ombudsman originates, has no sexist connotation (it means person), and most standard English dictionaries endorse this position. Still, the literal meaning of the word has proven to be offensive enough for some scholars. Thus, in spite of her professional commitment to the concept, Linda Reif, the editor of the International Ombudsman Institute, prefers to use the female pronoun to describe the office. Similarly, Brenda Danet has suggested that, "as women begin to take on this role, we shall have to speak of 'ombudswomen' and perhaps of 'ombudsperson'." Recent developments in many places, particularly the United States, vindicate this assessment.[2]

It has also been suggested that the reasons why the new democratic constitution of South Africa opted for the title "Public Protector" in place of ombudsman, used by the country's offices hitherto, was the need to: (1) disabuse the public of any gender bias; (2) provide assurance on the constitution's fundamental commitment to a non-sexist society; and (3) de-link the new regime from the oppression and wanton disregard of women's rights that the apartheid system was associated with. Where the word "Public Protector" is not used in government policy documents in South Africa, the alternative word found is "ombuds" — never ombudsman.

It is certain that the prevailing show of faith in the ombudsman will, as the years go by, metamorphose into increased pressure for concrete proof. Evidence of sensitivity to gender concerns will almost certainly be an important component of this shift. As noted by some participants at a gender conference held preparatory to the new democratic regime in South Africa, "women bodies need to be a focal point in the office of the ombudsman."[3] In the same vein, some recent constitutions in Africa expressly commit their political processes to the "principle of a non-sexist society" (e.g., South Africa, Malawi, and Namibia). The ombudsman institution cannot escape the implications of this development.

This chapter will examine the current role of the ombudsman in Africa to determine if such a role makes any difference to the situation of women.

Orientation and Setting

The ombudsman is essentially a complaint handling institution, and to this extent represents an essential feature of social coexistence. It derives its significance from the unique way it assists the aggrieved to take-on the huge and enormously powerful bureaucracies of modern society. It receives complaints from aggrieved persons or acts on its own motion, and has powers to investigate, recommend corrective actions, and issue reports. In this way, the ombudsman can operate speedily, cheaply, and informally. This also makes it particularly inclined to the plight of people who have to interact with bureaucrats regularly and/or who are powerless, deprived, and in need. Needless to say, such people often constitute the majority of society. The desire of the ombudsman to empower the people makes him/her an instrument for the promotion of democracy. However, the ombudsman's office does not have the authority to enforce its decisions.

Since the beginning of the 1980s, the state system all over the world has been subjected to downsizing. A principal reason for this is the understanding that reducing the size of the state and reversing most of its erstwhile activities to the private sector, is ultimately the most potent mechanism of maintaining control and promoting productivity. "Government is being reinvented," David Osborne and Ted Gaebler claim in a recent publication.[4] Interestingly, rather than being a casualty, and in spite of its previous close association with government bureaucracy, the ombudsman concept is enjoying a renewed popularity.

So, the ombudsman is perceived in the light of attempts to establish viable democracies, and thereby ensure that the ordinary citizen is heard and his/her rights and interests protected. In the same vein, there is a general agreement that the ombudsman is easily reconcilable with prevailing governmental concern about administrative reform, productivity, and value for money. In redressing individual grievances for example, the institution also provides some form of feedback mechanism for service providers and consequently helps eliminate potential constraints to efficient and effective administration.

A brief portrait of the situation of women in Africa would seem appropriate as a background to the work of the ombudsman. It is useful to recall that the importance now commonly attached to improving the status of women is indicative of the fact that African women not only suffer from simply being women, but also because the continent itself remains the most underdeveloped in the world. This situation justifies a need for a special place for women in contemporary ombudsmanship. After all, how else can democracy benefit women other than in creating a society which strives to enhance their overall well-being? As the fifth African Regional Conference on Women held in Dakar, Senegal in November 1994 concluded, "equality is not only the absence of discrimination but also the equal enjoyment of rights, responsibilities and opportunities by women and men."

The list of international initiatives on improving the status of women is long, and, as the Dakar Conference noted, much progress has been made in the last decade-and-a-half. Nevertheless, the overall situation remains strikingly appalling. Women are directly at the receiving end of Africa's miseries, instability, and pervert policy measures. They are the most severe victims of on-going structural adjustment programs, and are neglected, disregarded, deprived, oppressed, and underrated. Women make-up over half the population of Africa, but constitute the bulk of the nearly 250 million people that are in abject poverty. Similarly, women, together with children, constitute 80 percent of Africa's refugee population. It is also estimated that the proportion of female-headed households now stands at around 35 percent continent-wide. In spite of this, and the fact that women generally have limited access to ownership and co-ownership of land and housing, they provide 60 to 80 percent of the continent's food supply. What some scholars have characterized as the feminization of poverty is an obvious African reality.

If the plight of women in the rural and informal sector is so depressing, the situation in the urban and formal sectors is barely better. Girls are disadvantaged in terms of the quality, relevance, and appropriateness of the education and training they receive. Women's access to education is concentrated at the lowest level. About 23 percent of primary school graduates enter secondary institutions, while less than 3 percent of graduates at that level are admitted into tertiary education. It is said that Africa's female adult literacy of less than 50 percent is the lowest in the world. The implications of these statistics reverberate in other sectors, including employment, health, and human rights. In any event, the fact that most of Africa is under some form of IMF/World Bank initiated economic structural adjustment means that the situation of women is systematically deteriorating. The Dakar Conference on Women succinctly sums up the situation thus:

> Structural adjustment packages also have gender implications, since their impact on women is characteristically more severe than on men in a variety of ways. If women's contributions have been neglected in the past, current policies may overestimate the ability of women to take up the slack, compensating for low wages and rising prices by new income generating activities. Indeed the former underestimation, and accompanying assumption that women have time and energy to spare, are directly implicated in current misconceptions ... Women are increasingly having to work harder, as prices rise with the removal of subsidies, price controls and as payment is increasingly required for services formerly provided free by the state.

The work of the ombudsman is set against the sharp differences this survey implies between women and their male counterparts. Arguably, it is easy to sensitize any institution to these differences when the target audience can be readily disaggregated into the two sexes. In contrast, the issue is much more difficult when services are loosely meant for so-called disadvantaged people or the poor, or when the servicing institution chooses to define recipients in such terms as clients, citizens, or the needy. The problem with this perspective is that the concepts used already define a situation of deprivation which, presumably, impact on male and female sexes in the same way.

Women as a special group of deprived people, requiring special attention, somehow lose out in such situations, as do other groups like children, the aged, prisoners, minorities, people with disabilities, refugees, and others. As one African woman politician has brilliantly articulated it, "these categories of people deserve special attention when considering human rights because they are all, one way or another, disadvantaged and vulnerable. They are people who, even under normal situations find themselves incapable of enjoying the rights accorded to them simply because of the status they have in society."[5] Suffice it to say, a lot of purpose could be served by a specialized complaint office able to address the problems of the relevant group with depth and expertise.

Incidentally, African countries have generally established their governmental ombudsman institutions as general-purpose offices. This means that each office handles a wide variety of complaints covering practically all of the national administrative system. In this way, the concern of the office is not specialized or restricted to any group of persons. Rather, its clientele is defined as members of the public and any one who feels aggrieved is free to approach the ombudsman. This may be defined as a philosophical bias in favor of equality rather than equity. The implication of this characterization for the actual work of the African ombudsman is self-evident.

Reference was made earlier to the conceptual link between the ombudsman and administrative organizations. Unfortunately, very little has been done on the relationship between women and the administration in Africa. Still, it is difficult to argue that the problems women face with modern bureaucracies are necessarily more problematic to resolve that those of men. However, in the absence of a specialized interest in women matters, a complaint handling institution needs to make itself highly attractive to enable African women to resort to it for help. This is more so when we consider that women form the bulk of the illiterate, the poor, and the rural population in Africa. Their position in the economy is largely one of subordination and subservience bolstered by a tradition of antipathy to the resistance against male domination and exploitation. So even if the situation of women vis-a-vis the state appears susceptible to the generation of grievances, most women may lack the necessary incentives to take the required actions.

Ease of access by the public to the ombudsman office, and eagerness to use it, are inherent in its overall institutional logic. But not all African ombudsman offices fully appreciate this, and in turn translate it into concrete operational strategies. Reference should again be made to the issue of the name of the institution. Notwithstanding the Swedish history of the word "ombudsman," it is impossible to ignore the influence its literal meaning could have on the ordinary public, particularly with the profile of the average woman presented above. Surely, it is unlikely that most members of the public know that "man" in Swedish is not gender specific. In fact, we see similar confusion in the history of the human rights movement before 1945, when the phrase "the rights of man" was in vogue. Clearly, in the absence of proper and sustained education, the title "ombudsman" could be misconstrued.

Partly because of this problem, but more because of a deeper desire to indigenize imported concepts, earlier African ombudsman offices adopted alternative names such as Permanent Commission of Inquiry (in Tanzania); Investigator-General (in Zambia); Public Complaints Commission (in Nigeria); and Inspector-General (in Uganda). These titles do help ameliorate the misconception alluded to. However, there have been some unattractive fall-outs from them too.

The most important point is that such alternative names also tend to cloud the essential ombudsman character of the institutions concerned and, by implication, their affinity with the international movement. In fact, all the offices named above were not recognized for a long time as genuine ombudsman institutions. With the recent enhancement of the international prestige of the concept, especially in the context of contemporary democratization, the name "ombudsman" has once again become popular. Thus, most of Africa's post-1990 adoptions, and several of those in the preceding five years, use this name. Of course, what this means is that the gender issue alluded to from the title "ombudsman" remains problematic.

Whatever concerns are raised about the name, they are compounded by the fact that none of the continent's offices has any policy on attracting female clients. Their periodic reports corroborate this point, in that they are usually very sketchy on female complainants. It is not uncommon to find reports that do not include any sample cases of women related matters. The initial two reports of the Namibian office illustrate this problem.

As previously mentioned, the most obvious requirement of accessibility is that the ombudsman can be consulted with ease and at little or no cost. Generally, African ombudsman offices are easily accessible and have not adopted the much criticized "MP-filter" used in Britain to control the load of the ombudsman office and to reconcile it with the parliamentary system. Similarly, those African offices, such as the initial state versions in Nigeria which adopted the erstwhile practice in New Zealand to charge a fee for the use of the offices, have since been abolished. Also, some offices accept complaints sent in by an agent or anyone on behalf of the aggrieved. The defunct 1980 Ghanaian Act, on the other hand, required that the complaint be "made in writing and duly signed by the complainant or his agent." Botswana's 1995 legislation has an identical provision. This is an unnecessary burden for illiterate clients as well as a restriction on the use of more speedy means of contact with the office, such as the telephone. As experience elsewhere proves, ombudsmen do not need a provision requiring written complaints to be circumspect about taking up cases.

Accessibility can also be constrained by the geographic location of the office. Because the ombudsman is a government agent, African offices are logically located in the seat of government. In a way this coincides with the fact that African governments are highly centralized and tend to have most of their bureaucracies in the same location. But the office of the ombudsman can be inconspicuously placed, even in the capital. This can be said, for example, of offices in Lesotho, Nigeria, South Africa, and Ghana. Location of the office in the capital can isolate the ombudsman from complainants living elsewhere. The majority of Africans live outside the seat of government, and they often have the greatest difficulty when dealing with public agencies. Yet, it is within this categorization that most women fall.

Studies of the Nigerian plan, for example, confirm that the highest yearly rates of complaints are recorded in high urban conurbations of Kano, Sokoto, Edo, Delta, Lagos, Ondo, and Ogun States. This means that even when the ombudsman makes an effort to extend his or her activities outside the capital, the concrete results are barely felt beyond urban places. Indeed, when we disaggregate the Nigerian data, this conclusion is brought out sharper. On the average, each state capital, normally the most urbanized center, accounts for not less than 30 percent of the total yearly load. The figure is as high as 40 to 50 percent in places like Edo, Delta, and Ondo. The available figures from former Bophuthatswana are consistent with these. The Molopo area, where the state capital was located, accounted for about 55 to 57 percent of the annual case load.

Furthermore, most African offices do not as yet have any program to decentralize their operations beyond the center or regional government (as in the case of federal states). Nigeria is probably an exception to this rule. Bophuthatswana, before it was abolished, also operated a fairly elaborate decentralized system. The above figures suggest that even in these cases, such decentralization efforts are at best a qualified success. Anyway, African administrations in general have had limited success with decentralization arrangements.

Women-related Activities

African ombudsman offices do not generally involve themselves in informal person-to-person civil matters, nor with complaints arising out of private sector activities. Therefore, restricting offices from reviewing the private sector should not harm women peculiarly. We may indeed argue that special group interests are ultimately better served if a general purpose complaint office is not overwhelmed with grievances — which is bound to be the case with a free excursion into the private sector. In any event, the logic of the ombudsman institution requires that it operates within certain specified parameters. It is fair, therefore, to limit one's assessment of what the institution does within its defined boundaries.[6]

Some statistics on women-initiated complaints were randomly pieced together from selected African reports. The conclusion that such complaints constitute a significantly small percentage of total work and caseload is self evident. In Nigeria, just about 7.8 percent of complainants were women. Of the 45 sample complaints analyzed in Mauritius, only 3, or 6.7 percent, were received from women. An average of 16 percent of complaints in the former Bophuthatswana directly related to, or emanated from, women. In Zambia and Tanzania, the figures derived were 12.5 percent and 5.3 percent, respectively. The former Transkei in South Africa generated the highest frequency of complaints from women, with 27 percent of cases received in 1991. Taken together, the survey reported gives a mean figure of approximately 13 percent.

These figures are difficult to justify. Clearly, they do not reflect the population of women. Neither do they agree with the percentage of women in formal employment, put at a regional average of about 30 percent, in a continent in which the state is the largest employer. In any event, about 40 to 45 percent of ombudsman complaints, going by the figures from Nigeria, Namibia, former Bophuthatswana, and Zambia, are employment-related. This means substantial figures arise in other areas, including among the rural population, from social services administrations, and from clients of bureaucratic institutions in general. So, regardless of the economic status of women in African society, there are several non-employment issues that necessarily affect them. But this is not discernible in the small proportion of complaints from women outlined above.

Of course, like their male counterparts, women sometimes team up with others, even marriage partners, to present joint complaints. What is called group complaints here invariably account for a negligible proportion of the ombudsman's work-load in Africa. In Nigeria, for example, these amount to about 8.8 percent of the national total. If the sample of cases presented in other ombudsman offices' annual report is anything to go by, this figure probably represents a continent-wide pattern. The point then is that so-called group complaints do not remarkably change the above assessment of the volume of cases that come from women.

Do the above figures suggest that African women are unwilling to approach the ombudsman with their problems? Or, do the figures suggest they have fewer grievances against the system because they are better served than men? Without any doubt, the answer to both questions must be negative. Surely, the situation of African women cannot by any imagination be taken as indicative of any proper treatment by the state machinery. Be that as it may, women have a real cause to approach the ombudsman.

One could argue that because African ombudsman's complainants are predominantly people of some minimal level of literacy, and in view of the institution's bureaucratic location, women would naturally be disadvantaged. In Nigeria, about which some fairly definitive figures have been calculated, close to 75 percent of complainants are able to read and write either in English (the official language), or an appropriate vernacular. Set against the relatively smaller proportion of women within Africa's literate population, women's complaint-generating capacity is naturally restricted. In fact, as the said study concluded, "female complainants better represent the urban and educated women population than their male counterparts do of the population of educated and urbanised men."[7]

But while the level of literacy seems an influential factor, it certainly does not provide all the explanation simply because the population of literate women vis-a-vis their male counterparts is incongruous with the relative distribution of male and female complainants. Moreover, as noted above, one of the main attractions of the ombudsman is its lack of strict formalization of the grievance-handling process as a result of which the office is able to initiate its own complaints as well as attend to matters transferred to it from elsewhere, in and outside the governmental system. In other words, even if women are unwilling or constrained for some reason, these other sources of complaints can be improved.

Let us now attempt a review of the issues women generally complain about. Some feminist writers have suggested that women's concerns are essentially different from those of men, in that they tend to reflect some of the former's natural commitment to, for instance, "children and the family." It is largely because of this that a number of commentators also insist that institutions that claim to target women but leave out this important dimension are invariably inadequate. Incidentally, the fact that African ombudsmen are often excluded from person-to-person private disagreement limits what can be done regarding some of the matters. All the same, a number of women's complaints directly or indirectly relate to their position in the family situation, and include cases relating to matrimony and maintenance, claims of employment benefits of deceased partners, and children's education.

In the main, however, complaints brought to ombudsman offices from and concerning women are similar to those of men. And there is no evidence that more women's cases as against men's are turned down by ombudsmen. So, even if we accept that the lack of jurisdiction over person-to-person private issues may somewhat disadvantage women, female clients are often not mistaken about this or about what the ombudsman can do, and in fact does. About 65 percent of cases declined in Nigeria, for example, are on grounds other than the ombudsman's lack of jurisdiction, the category to which the problem portrayed here would fall. In short, the more frequent use of the institution by men has very little to do with any natural inclinations on the part of women, or men, to certain grievance-types.

With reference to the distinction between employment-related and non-employment-related complaints, women cases arising from work-place situations raise the same common issues that ombudsmen are faced with in matters of unfair dismissals or termination, benefit claims, victimization, harassment, etc. It is also useful to note that the ombudsman's approach to these, particularly in terms of interpretation, investigative strategy, and recommendation is, from all available evidence, regardless of sex differences.

As in the above illustrations, the work of African ombudsmen in so-called non-employment-related areas are difficult to tie-down to any particular gender-oriented patterns. Complaints in this category would include those about non-issuance of certificates and credentials; breach of contract; provision of social services; administrative decisions; abuse of office; and consumer-oriented matters. The general impression arising from this is that complaints are more commonly motivated by a desire to redress personal injustice, as against social or communal, and to satisfy some pecuniary interests. This fact also applies to men as much as to women complaints.

We may now conclude this section by reviewing the extent to which the internal organization and administration of the ombudsman is sensitive to gender differences. Complaint handling is inseparable from the administrative system put in place for the purpose. Indeed, an important principle of democratic administration is that the more diverse and representative institutions are of their target population, the more responsive they tend to be. This argument is central to the various efforts to expand the opportunities open to women in top governmental positions. The same is valid for the ombudsman office, more so that its name, as earlier shown, is prone to being misconstrued. Putting women in conspicuous positions in the ombudsman office, it may be argued, could help correct any misconception, and thus enhance the office's attraction to the female population.

There is no evidence indicating that the filling of posts in the ombudsman office is deliberately biased by any misreading of its name. There is also no known record of any policies or official statements suggestive of this. In fact, except for the recent constitutional reforms in South Africa, wherein gender representation is obliged in all public appointments, there are no deliberately set out guidelines on how the ombudsman office should be composed. The impression is that issues of representation are unnecessary concerns in the ombudsman context — the ombudsman is a good person, hence his/her office would rise above such mundane distractions. This is obviously naive. In fact, African ombudsman institutions generally display the male bias found in the larger administrative system toward gender concerns. The situation is, however, not unique to Africa.

Of the 177 names listed in a 1991 survey of ombudsman institutions compiled by the International Ombudsman Institute in Alberta, only 29, or 16 percent, are women. The figure would have been even smaller if women listed as associate and assistant ombudspersons were excluded. Remarkably, too, women, more than men, are associated with specialized social service oriented offices operating at sub-national levels, that is provincial and municipal governments. This is indicative of how directly people-oriented women's high-profile roles in the institution are. However, one may also deduce from this the embarrassing conclusion that women tend to be relegated even in the ombudsman system to so-called traditional female portfolios in social service administration.

If this worldwide pattern appears disappointing, the African situation is certainly depressing. As of December 1995, there were only two serving female ombudspersons on the continent, in Zambia and Zimbabwe. Tanzania and Zambia have over the years often reserved one position in their ombudsman college for a woman. Of the two countries, only Zambia has had a female chairperson. In addition, the Nigerian Public Complaints Commission, which presently consist of thirty-one commissioners, has not had a female ombudsperson since its establishment in 1974. This is in spite of the commitment successive military and civilian governments have expressed in favor of appointing women to top public offices. South Africa's multiple ombudsman system in the apartheid regime was equally male dominated. However, as already indicated, prevailing constitutional requirements are likely to compel the appointment of one or more women in the system in the on-going exercise to constitute the national and provincial offices.

The composition of the ombudsman support staff, and the offices' overall personnel policies, mirror the situation portrayed above. Although several ombudsman offices operate as autonomous parastatal institutions, there is nevertheless a common tendency in all to set personnel policies along the lines of their respective national civil services. The following characterization of the situation of women in the Zambian civil service also readily fits the situation of the ombudsman office in general. According to Thomas Turner and Pat O'Connor:

> Although women are disproportionately employed in the civil service as compared with other areas of the formal economy, evidence from other developing countries would lead one to expect that they would not be found at the higher technical and managerial levels, but rather that the same principles of horizontal and vertical segregation that have emerged in developing countries would exist in Zambia as in other Third World countries, i.e. that women would be crowded into a small range of occupations and that they would not move to the top of the hierarchy even in such occupations (i.e. that the "glass ceiling" phenomenon would exist) ...[8]

What makes the situation of the ombudsman especially disappointing is that the institution does not require rare expertise in which women are scarcely trained in. On the contrary, there has been a phenomenal expansion in the African population of females in professions such as law, administration, and communication, that ombudsman offices often need. It is evident that the African ombudsman movement does not give priority to personnel representative of women.

Incidentally, some offices identify all their staff by name in annual reports. On the basis of a survey of such lists from Zambia, Nigeria and the former Bophuthatswana, it was found that the ombudsman staff was, on the average, 40 percent female. Of this, as much as 75 percent are junior to lower middle secretariat personnel. In fact, in some of the lists reviewed, all typists and stenographers were women.

Conclusion

In conclusion, the situation of the African ombudsman largely reproduces the indifference with which women are regarded in the larger administrative system. This is curious given that the institution essentially exists to correct situations of discrimination and inequality. This, of course, is not to say that the ombudsman does not entirely serve the female population. On the contrary, this study has drawn attention to several ways in which women can and do benefit from the existence of the institution. One would also be over stretching the point to suggest that the situation of disappointment portrayed here is a deliberate creation to relegate women to secondary attention.

The African ombudsman is a product of the continent's sociopolitical and economic circumstances. What has diminished its usefulness, is the fact that the institution is founded on a number of essential characteristics that take women for granted. Among other things, this fundamental defect needs to be corrected by reviewing particular features of the institution and by complementing its work with bodies such as the Commission on Human Rights and Gender Equality (as in South Africa) that is better adapted to tackle wider issues of human rights violations.

Notes

[1] For an update insight into the popularity of the ombudsman see, among others, S. Anderson, "Ombud Research — A Bibliographical Essay," *The Ombudsman Journal*, No. 2, September 1982, pp. 32-84; L. Reif, M. Marshall and C. Ferris (*eds.*), *The Ombudsman — Diversity and Development* (Alberta: International Ombudsman Institute, 1993); *The Ombudsman Journal*, No. 12, 1994; and G. E. Caiden (*ed.*), *International Handbook of the Ombudsman*, Vol. I and II (Westport, Connecticut: Greenwood Press, 1983).

[2] See Reif *et al*; B. Danet, "Towards a Method to Evaluate the Ombudsman Role," *Administration and Society*, Vol. 10, No. 3, November 1978.

[3] Commonwealth Secretariat, *South Africa — Report of the Commonwealth Advisory Mission on National Machinery on Advancing Gender Equality* (London, 1995), p. 24.

[4] David Osborne and Ted Gaeber, *Reinventing Government: How the Entrepreneurial Spirit is Transforming the Public Sector* (New York: Plume and Penguin, 1993).

[5] M. R. K. Matembe, "Human Rights of the Disadvantaged Under the Ombudsman," *The Ombudsman Journal*, No. 10, 1992, p. 139.

[6] Unfortunately, there is as of now no book-length study on the African ombudsman experience. However, several short articles have been done and these are well-documented by the International Ombudsman Institute in Alberta. See the Institute's publication, *The Ombudsman Journal*, especially the editions since 1984/85, for useful references to some of the issues raised below. Also, see Anderson.

[7] V. Ayeni, "The Public Complaints Commission and Bureaucracy in Nigeria," Unpublished Ph.D. thesis, University of Ife, Nigeria, 1994, especially Chapter 6.

[8] T. Turner and P. O'Connor, "Women in the Zambian Civil Service: A Case of Equal Opportunities?" *Public Administration and Development*, Vol. 14, No. 1, February 1994, pp. 79-81.

Select Bibliography

Adam, Heribert and Kogila Moodley. *The Negotiated Revolution: Society and Politics in Post-Apartheid South Africa*. Johannesburg: Jonathan Ball Publishers, 1993.

Adejumobi, Said and Abubakar Momoh (*eds.*). *The Political Economy of Nigeria under Military Rule*. Harare: SAPES Books, 1995.

African Rights. *Rwanda: Death, Despair and Defiance*. London: African Rights, 1994.

Agbango, George A. (*ed.*). *Issues and Trends in Contemporary African Politics: Stability, Development and Democratization*. New York: Peter Lang Publishers, 1997.

Ake, Claude. *Democracy and Development in Africa*. Washington, DC: Brookings Institution, 1996.

Akindés, Francis. *Les mirages de la démocratie en Afrique subsaharienne francophone*. Dakar: CODESRIA, 1996.

Anyang' Nyongo', Pete *ed.*). *Popular Struggles for Democracy in Africa*. London: UNU and Zed Books, 1987. French translation: *Afrique: la longue marche vers la démocratie*. Paris: UNU et Publisud, 1988.

Badie, Bertrand. *L'Etat importé: Essai sur l'occidentalisation de l'ordre politique*. Paris: Fayard, 1992.

Bangura, Yusuf. *Authoritarian Rule and Democracy in Africa: A Theoretical Discourse*. Discussion paper 18, United Nations Research Institute for Social Development, Geneva, 1991.

_____. "The Crisis of Underdevelopment and the Transition to Civil Rule: Conceptualizing the Question of Democracy in Nigeria." *Africa Development*, Vol. 13, No. 1 (1988).

Bayart, Jean-François. *L'Etat en Afrique, la politique du ventre*. Paris: Fayart, 1989. English translation: *The State in Africa: The Politics of the Belly*. London: Longman, 1993.

_____, Comi Toulabor et Achille Mbembe. *La politique par le bas en Afrique noire: Contribution à une problématique de la démocratie*. Paris: Karthala, 1992.

Buijtenhuijs, Rob and Elly Rijnierse. *Democratization in Sub-Saharan Africa (1989-1992): An Overview of the Literature*. Leiden: African Studies Centre, 1993.

Caron, B., A. Gboyega and E. Osaghae (*eds.*). *Democratic Transition in Africa*. Ibadan: CREDU, 1992.

Clapham, Christopher. *Africa and the International System: The Politics of State Survival*. Cambridge: Cambridge University Press, 1996.

Conac, G. (sous la direction de). *L'Afrique en transition vers le pluralisme politique*. Paris: Economica, 1993.

Drah, F.K. and Kwame Ninsin (*eds.*). *Ghana's Transition to Constitutional Rule*. Accra: Ghana Universities Press, 1991.

Dunn, J. *Democracy: The Unfinished Journey, 508 BC to AD 1993*. Oxford: Oxford University Press, 1992.

Eboussi Boulaga, Fabien. *Les conférences nationales en Afrique noire*. Paris: Karthala, 1993.

Eshetu Chole et Jibrin Ibrahim (sous la direction de). *Processus de démocratisation en Afrique: Problèmes et perspectives*. Dakar: CODESRIA, 1995.

Esman, M. *Ethnic Politics*. Ithaca: Cornell University Press, 1994.

Gibbon, Peter, Yusuf Bangura and Arve Ofstad (*eds.*). *Authoritarianism, Democracy and Adjustment: The Politics of Economic Reform in Africa*. Uppsala: Scandinavian Institute of African Studies, 1992.

Guichaoua, André (sous la direction de). *Les crises politiques au Burundi et au Rwanda (1993-1994)*. Lille: Université de Lille 1, 1995.

Gutto, S.B.O. *Human and Peoples' Rights for the Oppressed*. Lund: Lund University Press, 1993.

Harbeson, John W., Donald Rothchild and Gnome Casein (*eds.*). *Civil Society and The State in Africa*. Boulder: Lynne Rienner Publishers, 1994.

Himmelstrand, Ulf, Kabiru Kinyanjui and Edward Mburugu (*eds.*). *African Perspectives on Development*. New York: St. Martin's Press; Harare: Baobab Books, 1994.

Holm, J. and P. Molutsi (*eds.*). *Democracy in Botswana. Gaborone:* Macmillan Botswana, 1989.

Ishemo, Shubi. "Historical Dispossession and the Crisis of the Nation-State." *Review of African Political Economy*, Vol. 22, No. 65 (1995), pp. 359-365.

Kankwenda Mbaya (sous la direction de). *Le Zaïre: Vers quelles destinées?* Dakar: CODESRIA, 1992. English Translation: *Zaire: What Destiny?* Dakar: CODESRIA, 1993.

Kpundeh, Sahr John (*ed.*). *Democratization in Africa: African Views, African Voices*. Washington, DC: National Research Council, 1992.

Jega, Attahiru M. *Nigerian Academics under Military Rule*. Stockholm: University of Stockholm, Department of Political Science, 1994.

Lemarchand, René. *Burundi: Ethnic Conflict and Genocide*. New York: Woodrow Wilson Center Press and Cambridge University Press, 1995.

Mamdani, Mahmood. *Citizen and Subject: Contemporary Africa and the Legacy of Late Colonialism*. Princeton: Princeton University Press, 1996.

_____ and Ernest Wamba-dia-Wamba (*eds.*). *African Studies in Social Movements and Democracy*. Dakar: CODESRIA, 1995.

Mbembe, Achille. "Traditions de l'autoritarisme et problèmes du gouvernement en Afrique". *Afrique et Développement*, Vol. 17, No. 1 (1992), pp. 37-64.

Médard, Jean-François (sous la direction de). *Etats d'Afrique noire: Formation, mécanismes, crises*. Paris: Karthala, 1991.

Minc, Alain. *L'ivresse démocratique*. Paris: Gallimard, 1995.

Mukandala, Rwekaza S. and Haroub Othman (*eds.*). *Liberalization and Politics: The 1990 Election in Tanzania*. Dar es Salaam: Dar es Salaam University Press, 1994.

Murray, Martin J. *The Revolution Deferred: The Painful Birth of Post-Apartheid South Africa*. London and New York: Verso, 1994.

Nnoli, Okwudiba. "Ethnicity," *Oxford Companion to Politics of the World*. New York: Oxford University Press, 1993, pp. 280-284.

Nzongola-Ntalaja, Georges. *Nation-Building and State Building in Africa*. Harare:

SAPES Books, Occasional Paper Series No. 3, 1993.

O'Donnell, G.A., P.C. Schmitter and L. Whitehead. *Transitions from Authoritarian Rule: Prospects for Democracy*. Baltimore: Johns Hopkins University Press, 1986.

Olagunju, Tunji, Adele Jinadu and Sam Oyovbaire. *Transition to Democracy in Nigeria (1985-1993)*. Ibadan: Safari Books, 1993.

Olowu, Dele. *African Local Governments as Instruments of Economic and Social Development*. The Hague: International Union of Local Authorities, 1988.

Olukoshi, Adebayo O. and Liisa Laakso (*eds.*). *Challenges to the Nation-State in Africa*. Uppsala: Nordic Africa Institute, 1996.

Parkinson, C. Northcote. *The Evolution of Political Thought*. Boston: Houghton-Mifflin, 1958.

Phillips, A. *Engendering Democracy*. Cambridge: Polity Press, 1991.

Prunier, Gérard. "Violence et histoire en Afrique". *Politique Africaine*, No. 42 (1991), pp. 9-14.

Pye, Lucian W. "Political Science and the Crisis of Authoritarianism," *American Political Science Review*, Vol. 84, No. 1 (1990).

Ramonet, Ignacio. "La pensée unique". *Le Monde Diplomatique*, janvier 1995.

Rudebeck, Lars (*eds.*). *When Democracy Makes Sense: Studies in the Democratic Potential of Third World Popular Movements*. Uppsala: AKUT, 1992.

Sachikonye, Lloyd (*ed.*). *Democracy, Civil Society and the State: Social Movements in Southern Africa*. Harare: SAPES Books, 1995.

Sebudandi, Gaëtan et Pierre-Olivier Richard. *Le drame burundais: Hantise du pouvoir ou tentation suicidaire*. Paris: Karthala, 1996.

Sichone, Owen and Bornwell C. Chikulo (*eds.*). *Democracy in Zambia: Challenges for the Third Republic*. Harare: SAPES Books, 1996.

Sindjoun, Luc. "La Cour Suprême, la compétition électorale et la continuité politique au Cameroun: la construction de la démocratie passive". *Afrique et Développement*, Vol. 19, No. 2 (1994).

Shivji, Issa. *The Concept of Human Rights in Africa*. Dakar: CODESRIA, 1989.

Sparks, Allister. *Tomorrow is Another Country: The Inside Story of South Africa's Negotiated Revolution*. Wynberg, Sandton: Struik Publishing Co., 1994.

Tshiyembe Mwayila. *L'Etat post-colonial, facteur d'insécurite en Afrique*. Paris: Présence Africaine, 1990.

UNRISD. *Etat de désarroi: Les répercussions sociales de la mondialisation*. English version: *States of Disarray: Global Effects of Globalization*. Geneva: United Nations Research Institute on Social Development, 1995.

Wamba-dia-Wamba, Ernest. "Democracy, Multipartyism and Emancipative Politics in Africa: The Case of Zaire." *Africa Development*, Vol. 18, No. 4 (1993), pp. 95-110.

_____. "Zaire: From the National Conference to the Federal Republic of the Congo?" *Development Dialogue*, No. 2 (1995), pp. 125-146.

Willame, Jean-Claude. *L'Automne d'un despotisme: pouvoir, argent et obéissance dans le Zaïre des années quatre-vingt*. Paris: Karthala 1992.

Wunsch, J.S. and D. Olowu (*eds.*). *The Failure of the Centralized State: Institutions and Self-governance in Africa*. Boulder: Westview, 1990.

Zartman, I. William (*ed.*). *Collapsed States: The Disintegration and Restoration of Legitimate Authority*. Boulder: Lynne Rienner, 1996.

Notes on the Contributors

Said Adejumobi is a lecturer in political science at Lagos State University, Lagos, Nigeria.

Amos Anyimadu is a lecturer in political science at the University of Ghana, Legon, Ghana.

Victor O. Ayeni, formerly head of public administration at the University of the North in Sovenga, South Africa, is currently with the Commonwealth Secretariat in London.

Horace Campbell is professor of African and African American Studies at Syracuse University, Syracuse, NY, USA.

Cheryl Hendricks is a lecturer in political science at the University of the Western Cape, Bellville, South Africa.

Jibrim Ibrahim, a Nigerian political scientist, is currently building a policy research center in Kano, Nigeria.

Kalele-ka-Bila is professor of sociology at the University of Kinshasa, and the National Organization Secretary of the Union for Democracy and Social Progress (UDPS), a leading party of the democracy movement in Zaire.

Margaret C. Lee, a US political scientist, is currently an independent consultant and the representative of the African diaspora in North America on the AAPS Executive Committee.

Carlos Lopes, a sociologist from Guinea-Bissau, is currently the Resident Representative of the United Nations Development Programme, and the Resident Coordinator of the United Nations, in Harare, Zimbabwe.

Abubakar Momoh is a lecturer in political science at Lagos State University, Lagos, Nigeria.

Akiiki B. Mujaju is professor of political science at Makerere University, Kampala, Uganda.

Mulambu Mvuluya is professor of political science at the University of Kinshasa, and Secretary General of the AAPS National Chapter in Zaire.

Georges Nzongola-Ntalaja is professor of African Studies at Howard University, Washington, DC, USA, and the current President (1995-97) of AAPS.

Dele Olowu is on leave as professor of political science at the Obafemi Awolowo University, Ile-Ife, Nigeria, to serve as Public Administration Officer at the United Nations Economic Commission for Africa in Addis Ababa, Ethiopia.

Onalenna Doo Selolwane is senior lecturer at the Centre for Continuing Education, University of Botswana, Gaborone, Botswana.

Geoffrey Wood is senior lecturer in sociology at Rhodes University, Grahamstown, South Africa.